Designing the 21st Century

Design des 21. Jahrhunderts Le design du 21ᵉ siècle

Right page/rechte Seite/page de droite:
Shin + Tomoko Azumi, **Wireframe** chair and stool/
Stuhl und Hocker/chaise et tabouret (self-production), 1998

© 2001 TASCHEN GmbH
Hohenzollernring 53, 50672 Köln
www.taschen.com

© 2001 for the works by Martin Szekely, Arnout Visser,
Pia Wallén: VG Bild-Kunst, Bonn

Editorial coordination: Susanne Husemann, Cologne
Collaboration: Michael Cramm, Cologne
Design: UNA (London) designers
Production: Martina Ciborowius, Cologne
German translation: Karin Haag, Vienna
French translation: Philippe Safavi, Paris

Printed in Italy
ISBN 3–8228–5883–8

Designing the 21st Century

Design des 21. Jahrhunderts   Le design du 21ᵉ siècle

Edited by Charlotte and Peter Fiell

TASCHEN

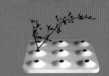

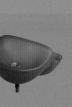

Dumoffice, Whoosh lamp (prototype)/
Lampe (Prototyp)/lampe (prototype), 2000

Introduction
Designing the 21st Century

Einleitung
Design im 21. Jahrhundert

Introduction
Le design du 21ᵉ siècle

With the unrelenting globalization of the free-market economy, so design has become a truly global phenomenon. Throughout the industrialized world, manufacturers of all types are increasingly recognizing and implementing design as an essential means of reaching new international audiences and of gaining competitive advantage. More than ever before, the products of design are shaping a worldwide material culture and impacting on the quality of our environment and daily lives. The importance of design, therefore, cannot be understated. For not only has design come to encompass an extraordinary range of functions, techniques, attitudes, ideas and values, all of them influencing our experience and perception of the world around us, but the choices we make today about the future direction of design will have a significant and possibly enduring effect on the quality of our lives and the environment in the years to come.

This book is first and foremost about the future of design. It focuses on those individuals who generally have the greatest input in the conception and planning of new products – designers. These are the creative thinkers able to identify and respond to the real needs and concerns of society, and whose decision-making can have a critical influence upon the nature and success of new products, manufacturing strategies and trends in the marketplace. What they think about the future really matters – thus *Designing the 21st Century* features the future vision statements and latest, most progressive work of 100 contemporary designers and design

Mit der fortschreitenden Globalisierung der freien Marktwirtschaft ist auch Design zu einem wahrhaft globalen Phänomen geworden. Überall in den Industriestaaten wird Design von den Produzenten sämtlicher Fertigungsbereiche zunehmend als ein wesentliches Instrument erkannt und eingesetzt, um neue, internationale Käuferschichten zu erreichen und um Wettbewerbsvorteile zu erlangen. Mehr als je zuvor prägen Designprodukte heute weltweit unsere Konsumkultur und beeinflussen die Qualität unserer Umwelt und unseres Alltagslebens. Die Bedeutung von Design darf daher nicht unterschätzt werden. Design umfasst inzwischen eine enorme Bandbreite an Funktionen, Techniken, Einstellungen, Ideen und Werten, die alle unser Erleben und unsere Wahrnehmung der Welt beeinflussen, und unsere jetzigen Entscheidungen im Bereich des Designs werden sich in den kommenden Jahren tiefgreifend auf unsere Lebensqualität und unsere Umwelt auswirken.

In diesem Buch geht es in erster Linie um die Zukunft des Designs. Dabei stehen diejenigen im Mittelpunkt, die im allgemeinen den größten Anteil an der Konzeption und Planung neuer Produkte haben – die Designer.

Als kreative Denker erkennen sie die wirklichen Bedürfnisse der Gesellschaft und gehen auf deren Anliegen ein. Ihre Entscheidungen können für Entwicklung und Erfolg neuer Produkte, Herstellungsstrategien und Markttendenzen ausschlaggebend sein. Weil es deshalb von großer Bedeutung ist, was Designer über die Zukunft denken, präsentiert *Design im 21. Jahrhundert* die Zukunftsvisionen

Avec la mondialisation acharnée de l'économie de libre marché, le design est véritablement devenu un phénomène planétaire. Partout dans le monde industrialisé, de plus en plus de fabricants de tout poil reconnaissent sa valeur. Ils s'en servent comme d'un outil primordial pour toucher un nouveau public international et se démarquer de la concurrence. Plus que jamais, les produits du design façonnent une culture matérielle à l'échelle mondiale et influent sur notre milieu ambiant et notre quotidien. L'importance du design ne doit donc pas être sous-estimée. Non seulement il concerne désormais une extraordinaire variété de fonctions, techniques, attitudes, idées et valeurs, toutes influençant notre expérience et notre perception du monde autour de nous, mais les décisions que nous prenons aujourd'hui sur la future orientation du design auront un effet significatif et sans doute durable sur la qualité de nos vies et de notre environnement dans les années à venir.

Ce livre traite avant tout de l'avenir du design. Il est centré sur ces individus qui jouent généralement le premier rôle dans la conception et la planification de nouveaux produits, à savoir les designers.

Ces penseurs et créateurs sont souvent les mieux à même d'identifier et de répondre aux vrais besoins et préoccupations de la société. Leurs choix peuvent avoir une influence déterminante sur la nature et le succès de nouveaux produits, sur les stratégies de fabrication et les tendances du marché.

La manière dont ils envisagent l'avenir est donc particulièrement pertinente.

groups, drawn from a wide range of disciplines – product design, transportation, furniture, ceramics, glassware and textiles – and many different parts of the world, from Europe to America, Australia, Brazil and Japan. Well-known figures such as Philippe Starck, Ron Arad, Ross Lovegrove and Marc Newson are joined by other, less familiar names who represent the equally important up-and-coming generation of designers. Also included are in-house designers who work for large corporations such as Apple Computer, Audi, Ford and Sony, and who often have a tremendous understanding of brand issues and the commercial imperatives of design. *Designing the 21st Century* is thereby not intended as a "chart-topping one hundred". Rather, the aim has been to bring together a highly representative cross-section of the international contemporary design community, so as

Emmanuel Dietrich, **Nutcracker** (prototype)/
Nussknacker (Prototyp)/casse-noisettes (prototype)
for Carl Mertens, 1998

und aktuellen Arbeiten von 100 zeitgenössischen Designern und Designgruppen aus unterschiedlichsten Tätigkeitsfeldern – Produktdesign, Fahrzeugdesign, Möbel, Keramik, Glaswaren und Textilien – und verschiedensten Teilen der Erde von Europa bis Amerika, Australien, Brasilien und Japan. Berühmten Gestaltern wie Philippe Starck, Ron Arad, Ross Lovegrove und Marc Newson sind bislang noch weniger bekannte Namen zur Seite gestellt, welche die gleichermaßen bedeutende aufstrebende Generation junger Designer repräsentieren. Berücksichtigt werden darüber hinaus Designer, die bei großen Unternehmen wie Apple Computer, Audi, Ford und Sony arbeiten und häufig über außerordentliche Kenntnisse im Hinblick auf vermarktungstechnische Fragen und kommerzielle Notwendigkeiten von Design verfügen.
Design im 21. Jahrhundert ist folglich nicht als eine »Hitliste der hundert Besten« gedacht, sondern bietet einen repräsentativen Querschnitt der international aktuellen Designszene und damit eine detaillierte, aussagekräftige und zum Nachdenken anregende Sammlung von Statements zu jenen Kernfragen, die das Design und dessen mögliche Entwicklung in näherer Zukunft bestimmen werden.

Aus den Aussagen der in diesem Buch vorgestellten Designer lässt sich folgern, dass praktisch alle das Hauptziel von Design darin sehen, das Leben der Menschen zu verbessern. Es scheint ein allgemeiner Konsens darin zu bestehen, dass Designprojekte auf technische, funktionale und kulturelle Bedürfnisse reagieren und weiterhin innovative Lösungen schaffen sollten, die Sinn und Gefühl vermitteln und im Idealfall über die Grenzen ihrer jeweiligen Form, Konstruktion und Herstellungsweise hinausgehen. Abgesehen von dieser Gemeinsamkeit sind die auf den folgenden Seiten wiedergegebenen Antworten der Designer auf die Frage »Was ist Ihre Vision vom Design der Zukunft?« jedoch ausgesprochen vielfältig. Unter den vielen verschiedenen Anliegen,

C'est pourquoi *Le Design du 21ᵉ siècle* présente la vision du futur ainsi que les travaux les plus récents et innovateurs de 100 designers et groupes de design contemporains venant des horizons les plus variés – conception de produits, transport, mobilier, céramique, verrerie et textile – et travaillant aux quatre coins du monde, de l'Europe aux Etats-Unis en passant par l'Australie, le Brésil et le Japon. Aux grands maîtres du design tels que Philippe Starck, Ron Arad, Ross Lovegrove et Marc Newson se joignent des noms moins familiers qui représentent la nouvelle génération montante. Les créateurs indépendants sont associés à des designers travaillant au sein de grandes entreprises telles que Apple Computer, Audi, Ford et Sony et qui ont souvent une profonde compréhension des problèmes liés aux marques et des impératifs commerciaux du design.
Le Design du 21ᵉ siècle n'est donc pas un annuaire des « cent meilleurs » mais vise plutôt à réunir un échantillon très représentatif de la communauté internationale des designers afin d'offrir un ensemble de prévisions approfondies, pertinentes et inspirantes sur les questions clefs qui affecteront le design et sa trajectoire éventuelle dans un avenir prévisible.

Sam Hecht, NTT Docomo phone/Telefon/
téléphone for Electrotextiles, 2000

to present an in-depth, relevant and thought-provoking collection of projections on the key issues that will affect design and its possible course for the foreseeable future.

Of the designers included in this survey, it can be reasonably deduced that virtually all believe the primary goal of design is to make peoples' lives better. Design practice should respond – it seems to be agreed – to technical, functional and cultural needs and go on to create innovative solutions which communicate meaning and emotion and which ideally transcend their appropriate form, structure and manufacture. Given this commonality of purpose, however, when posed the question "What is your vision for the future of design?", their responses – outlined on the following pages – are remarkably varied. Among the many different concerns, issues and predictions which are articulated, however, several recurring themes come to the fore: the potential offered by new materials; the effect of new technology (computing, communications and industrial processes); the need for simplification; emotionalism (the psychological aspects of design); and the tendency towards either individualistic or universal solutions.

The increasing availability of new synthetic materials is broadly identified as one of the key motivational forces behind the emergence of new products – a trend that is forecast to continue well into the future. The culture of continuous development within the field of material science has led to a plethora of advanced materials that challenge our preconceived notions of how plastics, metals, glass and ceramics should behave under accustomed conditions. With the recent introduction of flexible ceramics, foamed metals, conductive light-emitting plastics and shape-memory alloys, for example, the most basic properties of materials are being turned on their head.
In parallel with this, there is also a distinct trend towards the development

Problemen und Zukunftsvorstellungen, die geäußert wurden, kristallisieren sich aber mehrere Themenschwerpunkte heraus: das in neu entwickelten Materialien enthaltene Potential, die Auswirkungen neuer Technologien (Datentechnik, Kommunikationswesen und industrielle Produktionsabläufe), das Bedürfnis nach Vereinfachung, Emotionalität (die psychologischen Aspekte von Design) sowie die Tendenz zu entweder individualistischen oder universellen Lösungen.

Die zunehmende Verfügbarkeit neuer synthetischer Werkstoffe wird allgemein als eine der Hauptantriebskräfte hinter der Einführung neuer Produkte identifiziert – ein Trend, der sich voraussichtlich bis weit in die Zukunft fortsetzen wird. Die kontinuierliche Weiterentwicklung auf dem Gebiet der Werkstoffkunde hat zu einer Fülle von verbesserten Materialien geführt, die unsere Vorstellungen davon, wie sich Kunststoff, Metall, Glas und Keramik - unter üblichen Bedingungen verhalten sollten, infrage stellen. So werden beispielsweise mit der jüngsten Einführung von flexibler Keramik, Schaummetall, leitfähigen lichtemittierenden Kunststoffen und formstabilen Legierungen die grundlegendsten Materialeigenschaften auf den Kopf gestellt. Parallel dazu lässt sich außerdem ein eindeutiger Trend zur Entwicklung

On peut raisonnablement supposer que les designers inclus dans ce panorama sont pratiquement tous convaincus que l'objectif premier du design est d'améliorer la vie des gens. Sa pratique devrait d'abord répondre à des besoins techniques, fonctionnels et culturels (tout le monde semble être d'accord sur ce point). Ensuite, il devrait proposer des solutions innovantes qui communiquent un sens et une émotion et qui, idéalement, transcendent leurs formes, leur structure et leur mode de fabrication. Toutefois, en dépit de cet objectif commun, lorsqu'on pose la question « Quelle est votre vision de l'avenir du design », les réponses – brièvement synthétisées plus loin – sont remarquablement variées. Parmi les nombreuses préoccupations, questions et prédictions avancées, on observe néanmoins plusieurs thèmes récurrents : le potentiel offert par les nouveaux matériaux; l'effet des nouvelles technologies (l'informatisation, les outils de communication et les procédés industriels) ; le besoin de simplification ; l'émotivité (les aspects psychologiques du design) ; et l'opposition entre les solutions tendant vers l'individualisme ou l'universalité.

La disponibilité croissante de nouvelles matières synthétiques est généralement interprétée comme l'une des principales forces de motivation derrière l'émergence de nouveaux produits, une tendance dont on prévoit qu'elle perdurera. La culture du développement perpétuel au sein du domaine de la science matérielle a donné le jour à une myriade de matériaux très sophistiqués qui remettent en question nos idées préconçues sur la manière dont les matières plastiques, les métaux et les céramiques devraient se comporter dans des conditions habituelles. Avec l'introduction récente des céramiques flexibles, des mousses métalliques, des plastiques conducteurs et émetteurs de lumière ou des alliages capables de mémoriser des formes, entre autres, les propriétés les plus élémentaires des

Philippe Starck, TeddyBearBand toy/Kuscheltier/
nounours (Catalogue GOOD GOODS–La Redoute)
for Moulin Roty, 1998

and application of lightweight yet high tensile strength materials – from carbon-fibre to "floating" concrete – which are predicted to lead to either more expressive or essentialist forms. Synthetic polymers, which are increasingly able to mimic the properties of natural materials while also often possessing remarkable tactile qualities, have been shown in particular to be radically altering the formal potential of new products. Many of the designers included in this book are pioneering remarkable applications for materials such as these, as the product designs illustrated here demonstrate. But while most designers predict, like Jane Atfield, that "the integration of highly technological materials and processes will widen and become more accessible", others such as Emmanuel Dietrich have voiced concern that synthetics can sometimes be difficult to work with and are not always developed for their capacity to wear well.

New technologies – computers, communications and industrial processes – have in the last five years assisted enormously in the research and implementation of design, and are widely predicted to lead to increasingly miniaturized, multifunctional and better-performing products. More sophisticated CAD/CAM (computer-aided design/computer-aided manufacture) systems, RP (rapid prototyping) and aligned processes such as 3D stereolithography have considerably expedited the manufacture of smaller runs of products which are tailored more to meet individual needs. At the same time, these types of technologies are helping to streamline the design process from initial concept to working prototype.
Today, computer-generated designs can be sent via ISDN lines directly to RP facilities and to manufacturers at the touch of a button. By ultimately accelerating the design process, these technologies are not only reducing front-end costs for manufacturers but are also providing designers with greater freedom for experimentation. CAD/CAM and its related technologies have already had

und Anwendung leichtgewichtiger und dennoch hoch-elastischer Materialien ausmachen – von Kohlenstoff-Fasern (C-Fasern) bis zu »schwimmendem« Beton –, was in Zukunft entweder zu expressiveren oder essentielleren Formen führen wird. Insbesondere synthetische Polymerstoffe, die in immer stärkerem Maß die Eigenschaften natürlicher Materialien nachahmen können und häufig auch beachtliche taktile Qualitäten besitzen, haben das Potential neuer Produkte radikal verändert. Wie die in diesem Buch gezeigten Beispiele für Produktdesign verdeutlichen, haben viele der vorgestellten Designer bahnbrechende Arbeit in der Anwendung solcher Materialien geleistet. Aber während die meisten Designer wie Jane Atfield prognostizieren, dass »sich die Einbeziehung hochtechnischer Materialien und Fertigungsprozesse ausweiten und leichter zugänglicher werden wird«, äußern andere, wie etwa Emmanuel Dietrich, ihre Bedenken, dass synthetische Stoffe schwierig in der Verarbeitung sein können und nicht immer im Hinblick auf bessere Nutzbarkeit entwickelt werden.

In den letzten fünf Jahren haben neue Technologien auf den Gebieten Computertechnik, Kommunikationswesen und Produktionsprozesse die Entwicklung und Umsetzung von Design enorm gefördert, was laut Aussage vieler Gestalter zu einer wachsenden Zahl miniaturisierter, multifunktionaler und leistungsstarker Produkte führen wird. Ausgefeilte CAD/CAM-Systeme (computergestütztes Design/computergestützte Fertigung), RP (Rapid Prototyping) und damit zusammenhängende Prozesse wie etwa die 3D-Stereo-Lithographie haben die Herstellung kleinerer Mengen von Produkten begünstigt, die stärker auf individuelle Bedürfnisse zugeschnitten sind. Gleichzeitig tragen diese Technologien dazu bei, den gesamten Gestaltungsprozess von der Konzeption bis zur Ausarbeitung von Prototypen zu rationalisieren.
Heutzutage können computergenerierte Entwürfe per Knopfdruck über ISDN-

matériaux ont été complètement chamboulées.
Parallèlement, on observe une tendance distincte vers le développement et l'application de matériaux ultralégers mais néanmoins très résistants et extensibles – des fibres de carbone au béton « flottant » – qui, selon les prévisions, devraient conduire à des formes plus expressives ou essentialistes. Les polymères synthétiques, qui sont de plus en plus capables d'imiter les propriétés des matières naturelles tout en possédant souvent également de remarquables propriétés tactiles, ont démontré qu'ils pouvaient modifier radicalement le potentiel formel de nouveaux produits. Un grand nombre de designers présentés dans ce livre ont mis au point de remarquables applications pour ce genre de matériaux. Mais, si la plupart d'entre eux prédisent, à l'instar de Jane Atfield, que « L'intégration de matériaux et de processus de pointe se répandra et ils deviendront plus accessibles », d'autres, dont Emmanuel Dietrich, s'inquiètent du fait que les matières synthétiques soient parfois difficiles à travailler et pas toujours développées pour résister à l'épreuve du temps.

Au cours des cinq dernières années, les nouvelles technologies – les ordinateurs, les outils de communication et les procédés industriels – ont énormément aidé la recherche et la mise en application du design. La plupart s'accordent à dire qu'elles mènent vers des produits de plus en plus miniaturisés, polyvalents et performants. La sophistication croissante des systèmes de CAD/CAM (Design et fabrication assistés par ordinateur), de PR (Prototypage rapide) et de procédés apparentés tels que la lithographie stéréo en 3D a considérablement facilité la fabrication de gammes plus petites de produits conçus pour satisfaire des besoins individuels. Parallèlement, ces types de technologie contribuent à affiner le processus du design, du concept initial au prototype de travail.
Aujourd'hui, d'un simple clic, des projets entièrement réalisés sur ordinateur peu-

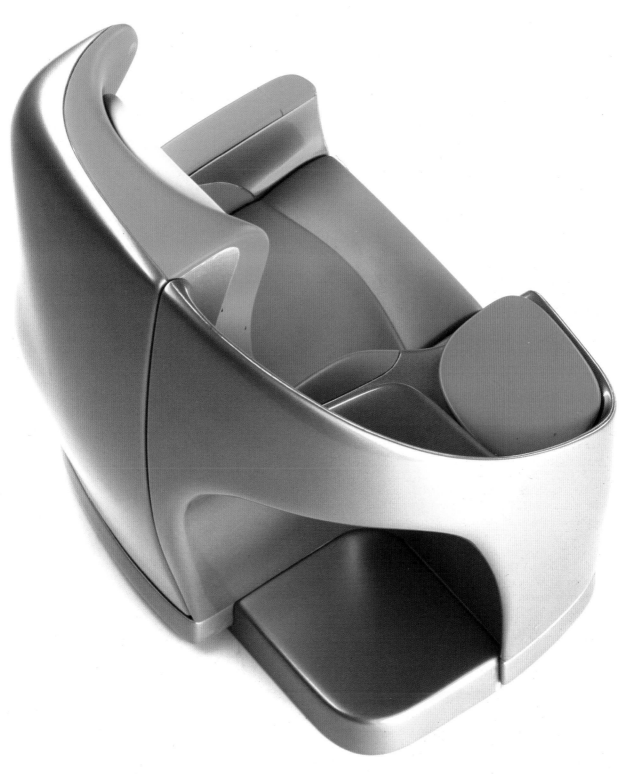

Ross Lovegrove, **First class seating**/Flugzeugsitz/
siège d'avion for Japan Airlines, 2000

a profound effect on product development, offering the designer the scope and flexibility to evolve exceptionally complex forms and to modify and customize products. Given the increasing potential for spawning a multiplicity of product variations, however, many of the featured designers agree with Jonathan Ive when he states that "our real challenge is to make relevant and extend technological capability."

Within the last five years, the Internet too has had a remarkable impact on the design process and has triggered, according to Lunar Design, "the move from mass production to mass customization". The freedom and ease of such communication technologies have also led to an ever-increasing transfer of design ideas and the cross-pollination of disciplines. This tendency towards integration is a result, too, of the increasing miniaturization of technology, which will undoubtedly continue unabated for the foreseeable future. Nano-technology has already led to the development of atomic-level mechanical components and will certainly play a significant role in the design of multi-functional "smart" products in the near to medium-term future. As the 21st century progresses, information technologies are widely expected to be incorporated into the design of products to such an extent that they will eventually be regarded as just another type of material – akin to glass or plastics – with which to develop innovative and better-performing solutions. Countering this vision of a brave new world of all-pervasive advanced technology, however, a few designers, such as Michael Marriott, are promoting the use of low-tech processes that not only have a minimal impact on the natural environment, but also reject the insatiable demand for ever more product variety and volume.

In response to the current and predicted technological complexity of the 21st century, simplification has clearly become a key objective in design. Many of the designers included here concur

Verbindungen an RP-Einrichtungen und Hersteller geschickt werden. Durch den beschleunigten Gestaltungsprozess stellen solche Technologien nicht nur eine Kostenersparnis für die Hersteller dar, sondern sie verhelfen auch den Designern zu einer größeren Freiheit beim Experimentieren. CAD/CAM und deren verwandte Technologien haben die Produktentwicklung bereits stark beeinflusst, indem sie den Designern den Spielraum und die Flexibilität bieten, um außergewöhnlich komplexe Formen zu entwickeln und Produkte an den speziellen Kundenbedarf anzupassen. Angesichts des stetig wachsenden Potentials für eine Vielzahl von Produktvariationen stimmen jedoch viele der hier vorgestellten Designer Jonathan Ives These zu, dass »unsere wahre Herausforderung darin liegt, die technologischen Kapazitäten leichter anwendbar und zugänglich zu machen«.

Auch das Internet hatte während der letzten fünf Jahre deutliche Auswirkungen auf den Gestaltungsprozess und war, wie Lunar Design feststellt, der Auslöser für »den Aufbruch von der Massenproduktion zur Anpassung an Kundenwünsche«. Die Freiheit und Leichtigkeit in der Anwendung dieser Kommunikationstechniken haben außerdem einen stetig wachsenden Transfer von Designideen und eine gegenseitige Befruchtung unterschiedlicher Disziplinen mit sich gebracht. Diese Tendenz zur Integration ist auch ein Resultat der zunehmenden Miniaturisierung von Technologie, welche in absehbarerer Zukunft unvermindert anhalten wird. Die Nano-Technologie hat bereits zur Entwicklung mechanischer Bauteile in atomarer Größenordnung geführt und wird in naher bis mittlerer Zukunft mit Sicherheit eine bedeutende Rolle bei der Gestaltung multifunktionaler »intelligenter« Produkte spielen. Es wird erwartet, dass die Informationstechnologien in einem solchen Maß in die Produktgestaltung mit einbezogen werden, dass sie schließlich nur noch als ein weiterer Werkstoff betrachtet werden – so wie Glas oder Kunststoff –, mit dem

vent être envoyés par les lignes ISDN aux centres de PR et aux fabricants. En accélérant ces différentes étapes, ces technologies réduisent les frais initiaux des fabricants mais offrent également aux designers une plus grande liberté pour expérimenter. Les CAD/CAM et leurs technologies apparentées ont déjà profondément changé le développement des produits, apportant aux créateurs la portée et la souplesse nécessaires pour élaborer des formes d'une complexité exceptionnelle, ainsi que pour modifier et personnaliser leurs produits. Cependant, compte tenu du nombre croissant de possibilités pour générer une multitude de variantes d'un même produit, un grand nombre des designers présentés dans ce livre conviennent avec Jonathan Ive que « leur vraie mission est d'étendre les capacités technologiques et de les rendre pertinentes ».

Au cours des cinq dernières années, Internet a également eu un impact considérable sur le processus du design et a déclenché, selon Lunar Design, « la transition de la " production de masse " au " sur mesure de masse " ». La liberté et la facilité d'utilisation de ces technologies de la communication ont également entraîné un transfert toujours plus important d'idées de design et la pollinisation croisée des disciplines. Cette tendance à l'intégration est également le résultat de la miniaturisation croissante de la technologie, qui se poursuivra certainement à un rythme soutenu dans les années à venir. Les nano-technologies ont déjà entraîné le développement de composants mécaniques à l'échelle atomique et joueront certainement un rôle crucial dans le design de produits « intelligents » et polyvalents dans un futur proche et à moyen terme. Beaucoup s'attendent à ce que, au fil du 21e siècle, les technologies de l'information soient incorporées dans le design des produits au point qu'elles finiront par être considérées comme un matériau comme un autre – à l'instar du verre ou du plastique – avec lequel élaborer des solutions plus innovatrices et performantes.

strongly with the words of Alberto Meda: "Technology must be tamed in order to realize things that have the simplest possible relation with man – we must reject technologically driven industrial goods that have no regard for human needs and no communicative rationality." There can be little doubt that the future onus on designers will be to devise products that can be easily understood and used in an intuitive way. Similarly, the simplification of structural form – essentialism – will not only provide the means by which designers can gain the most from the least, but will also assist in the realization of forms that possess an inherent emotional purity. Simplification in design will thus both reduce the white noise of contemporary living and provide one of the best ways of enhancing the quality of products and, thereby, their durability.

The psychological aspects of design are also extensively addressed and given prominence as never before. There is a general consensus that products need to go beyond considerations of form and function if they are to become "objects of desire" in an increasingly competitive marketplace. To achieve

Alberto Meda, Meda conference chair/Konferenzstuhl/ fauteuil de conférence for Vitra, 1996

sich innovative und funktional bessere Lösungen entwickeln lassen.
Im Gegensatz zu dieser Vision einer schönen neuen Welt, in der hochentwickelte Technologie allgegenwärtig ist, plädieren einige wenige Designer, wie etwa Michael Marriott, für den Einsatz von Low-tech-Verfahren, die nicht nur sehr viel weniger schädlich für die Umwelt sind, sondern die sich auch dem unersättlichen Verlangen nach immer größeren Produktmengen und -varianten widersetzen.

In Reaktion auf die bestehende und die prognostizierte technologische Komplexität des 21. Jahrhunderts ist Vereinfachung eindeutig zu einem der Hauptziele im Design geworden. Viele der hier vorgestellten Designer stimmen mit den Worten von Alberto Meda überein: »Die Technik muss gezähmt werden, damit man Objekte realisieren kann, die eine möglichst einfache Beziehung zum Menschen haben. Abzulehnen sind rein technisch orientierte Industrieerzeugnisse, die keine Rücksicht auf menschliche Bedürfnisse nehmen und keiner kommunikativen Logik folgen.« Deshalb liegt die zukünftige Verpflichtung für Designer darin, Produkte zu entwerfen, die leicht verständlich sind und auf intuitive Weise verwendet werden können. Gleichermaßen wird eine Vereinfachung der Konstruktionsform – Essentialismus – sich nicht nur als Instrument für Designer anbieten, um aus einem Minimum ein Maximum herausholen zu können, sondern sie wird auch zur Realisierung von Formen verhelfen, die eine emotionale Reinheit besitzen. Folglich wird sich Einfachheit im Design bereichernd und stabilisierend auf unser modernes Alltagsleben auswirken und einer der besten Wege sein, um die Qualität von Produkten und dadurch deren Lebensdauer zu verbessern.

Auch die psychologischen Aspekte des Designs werden ausführlich angesprochen, wobei ihre Bedeutung stärker in der Vordergrund gerückt wird als je zuvor. Wie übereinstimmend festgestellt wird, müssen Produkte über die Erwä-

Néanmoins, prenant à contre-pied cette vision idéalisée d'une haute technologie omniprésente, quelques designers tels que Michael Marriott défendent l'utilisation de processus plus naturels qui, outre le fait de ne pas nuire à l'environnement, rejettent la demande insatiable pour des produits toujours plus variés et nombreux.

En réaction à la complexité technologique actuelle et annoncée pour le 21e siècle, la simplification est clairement devenue un objectif clef du design. Un grand nombre de designers présents dans cet ouvrage conviennent avec Alberto Meda quand il dit : « La technologie doit être apprivoisée afin de réaliser des objets qui aient avec l'homme la relation la plus simple possible. Nous devons rejeter les produits industriels qui ne prennent pas en compte les besoins humains, qui n'ont aucune rationalité communicative ». Il ne fait aucun doute que les créateurs auront à l'avenir l'obligation de concevoir des produits faciles à comprendre et utilisables de manière intuitive. De même, la simplification de la forme structurelle – l'essentialisme – fournira les moyens par lesquels les designers obtiendront le plus par le moins, mais favorisera également la réalisation de formes pourvues d'une pureté émotionnelle inhérente. La simplification du design réduira donc à la fois le brouhaha du monde contemporain tout en fournissant l'un des meilleurs moyens de mettre en valeur la qualité des produits et, donc, leur durabilité.

Les aspects psychologiques du design sont également très souvent mentionnés et on leur accorde une importance plus grande que jamais. Le consensus général veut que, pour devenir des « objets de désir » sur un marché de plus en plus compétitif, les produits aient besoin d'aller au-delà des considérations sur la forme et la fonction. Pour atteindre cet objectif, ils doivent établir avec leurs utilisateurs des liens émotionnels associés au plaisir par la joie qu'ils auront à les manipuler ou la

this, products must make pleasurable emotional connections with their end-users through the joy of their use and/or the beauty of their form. Emotionalism is considered by many of the designers included here not only as a powerful and essential way of facilitating better and more meaningful connections between products and their users, but as an effective means of differentiating their solutions from those of their competitors. To this end, many designers, such as Ross Lovegrove, promote the use of soft, sensual, organic forms in an effort to provide their products with an emotionally seductive appeal. The innate tactility of such forms is deeply persuasive, even at a subconscious level. Cognitive of the fact that the emotional content of a design can determine its ultimate success, the general view among the majority of participating designers is that it is now as important to fulfil the consumer's desire for tools for loving as that for tools for living.

Of all the themes to emerge from the vision statements gathered here, the tendency towards either individualistic or universal solutions potentially holds the farthest-reaching consequences for the future direction of design. While some designers promote individualism in design as a channel for personal creative expression or to cater to consumer demand for individualistic products, others advocate universal solutions, which are generally more environmentally sound and whose emphasis upon greater functional and aesthetic durability offers better value for money. Individualism in design can be regarded as a reaction against the uniformity of mass production and, ultimately, the increasing homogenization of global culture. But with the objective of providing more expressive content, individualistic design solutions can often lead to higher costs and accelerated stylistic obsolescence. Given this, it is not surprising that, as an approach to design, individualism has hitherto generally remained in the realms of one-off and batch-manu-

gungen von Form und Funktion hinausgehen, wenn sie in der zunehmend schärfer werdenden Marktkonkurrenz zu einem »Objekt der Begierde« werden sollen. Aus diesem Grund sollten Produkte durch die Freude bei ihrem Gebrauch und/oder die Schönheit ihrer Form eine positive emotionale Verbindung zu ihren Benutzern herstellen. Emotionalität wird von vielen der hier zu Wort kommenden Designer nicht nur als ein wirksames und wichtiges Instrument angesehen, um Produkte und deren Käufer stärker aneinander zu binden, sondern sie betrachten Emotionalität auch als ein erfolgreiches Mittel, um ihre eigenen Entwürfe von denen ihrer Konkurrenten abzuheben. Zu diesem Zweck propagieren etliche Designer, wie etwa Ross Lovegrove, den Einsatz weicher, sinnlicher, organischer Formen mit dem Ziel, ihren Produkten eine emotional verführerische Ausstrahlung zu verleihen. Formen, die in solchem Maße zum Berühren einladen, wirken unbewusst zutiefst überzeugend. Da der emotionale Gehalt eines Designs letztendlich für dessen Erfolg ausschlaggebend sein kann, verfolgt die Mehrzahl der beteiligten Designer die Absicht, die emotionalen und funktionalen Bedürfnisse der Konsumenten zu erfüllen.

Zwei entgegengesetzte Trends werden an den hier zusammengetragenen Zukunftsvisionen deutlich: Während einige Designer gestalterischen Individualismus propagieren, sei es, um darüber den persönlich-kreativen Ausdruck zu transportieren, oder um das Verlangen der Konsumenten nach individualistischen Produkten zu bedienen, empfehlen andere universelle Lösungen, die im allgemeinen ökologisch verträglicher sind und funktional sowie ästhetisch einen höheren Gebrauchswert bieten.
Die Individualisierungstendenzen im Design lassen sich als Reaktion auf die Uniformität der Massenproduktion und auf die wachsende Homogenisierung der globalen Kultur verstehen. Individuelle, eigenwillige Designlösungen führen jedoch oftmals zu höheren Produktionskosten und veralten (stilistisch) schnel-

beauté de leur forme. L'émotivité est considérée par un grand nombre de designers comme un outil puissant et essentiel pour faciliter des relations meilleures et plus significatives entre les produits et leurs utilisateurs, mais également un moyen efficace de différencier leurs solutions de celle de leurs concurrents. A cette fin, de nombreux créateurs, tels que Ross Lovegrove, défendent le recours à des formes douces, sensuelles et organiques afin de donner aux produits un attrait séduisant et émouvant. Le caractère tactile inné de ces formes est profondément convaincant, même à un niveau subconscient. Sachant que le contenu émotionnel d'un design peut déterminer sa réussite sur le marché, la majorité des designers présentés dans cet ouvrage considèrent qu'il est désormais aussi important de satisfaire le désir du consommateur d'outils à aimer que d'outils pour vivre.

De tous les thèmes qui émergent des visions du futur exprimées dans ce livre, la tendance vers des solutions tantôt individualistes tantôt universelles est celle qui pourrait avoir les conséquences les plus considérables sur l'orientation future du design. Si certains défendent l'individualisme comme vecteur de la créativité personnelle ou pour satisfaire la demande du consommateur pour des produits individualistes, d'autres prônent la recherche de solutions universelles, qui sont généralement plus écologiquement saines et dont l'accent sur une durabilité fonctionnelle et esthétique plus grande permet une meilleure rentabilité.
En design, l'individualisme peut être considéré comme une réaction contre l'uniformité de la production de masse et, au bout du compte, de l'homogénéisation croissante de la culture planétaire. Mais, en cherchant à apporter un contenu plus expressif, les solutions individualistes se traduisent souvent par des coûts plus élevés et une obsolescence stylistique accélérée. Il n'est donc pas étonnant que, en tant que démarche de design, l'individualisme soit jusqu'à présent resté cantonné au do-

factured products, rather than making serious in-roads into large-scale industrial production. Although the individualism versus universality debate has raged since the earliest beginnings of Modern design practice, a fundamental paradox remains: while the nature of universal design solutions can sometimes be alienating, individualistic design solutions often remain the preserve of the wealthy élite. As has been discussed, however, new technologies are becoming widely available that would appear to be offering the means by which these two camps can be finally reconciled. The future of design may thus lie in the creation of universal solutions that can be efficiently adapted to meet individualistic needs.

The deliberation among the included designers on the appropriateness of individualistic versus universal solutions may well account for the relative absence of hypotheses on a unifying theory or new moral-philosophic basis of design. While many discuss the desirability of catering to the perceived need for greater individualism in design, for example, few comment on the future sustainability of such an approach, with

ler. Insofern blieb ein individuelleres Gestaltungsprinzip bislang hauptsächlich auf solche Produkte beschränkt, die in Einzelfertigung oder in kleinen Mengen produziert wurden, in der industriellen Großproduktion spielte es dagegen keine Rolle. Obwohl die Debatte um Individualismus kontra Universalität seit den frühen Anfängen des modernen Designs anhält, bleibt es bei einem grundlegenden Widerspruch: Während die Wirklichkeit universeller Designkonzepte manchmal entfremdend sein kann, bleiben individualistische Designlösungen häufig einer wohlhabenden Elite vorbehalten. Mit der beschriebenen Verbreitung neuer Technologien scheint sich aber eine Möglichkeit anzudeuten, die beiden Lager endlich miteinander zu versöhnen. Die Zukunft des Designs könnte deshalb in der Gestaltung universeller Lösungen liegen, die in ihrer Anwendung individuellen Bedürfnissen angepasst sind.

Ob sie eher individualistische oder universelle Lösungskonzepte bevorzugen, darüber äußern sich die beteiligten Designer sehr zurückhaltend, ebenso bleiben Aussagen über eine einheitliche Theorie oder eine neue moralisch-philo-

maine de l'exemplaire unique et des produits fabriqués par lots, et qu'il n'ait pas encore fait d'incursions sérieuses dans le secteur de la production industrielle à grande échelle. Bien que le débat entre individualisme et universalisme fasse rage depuis les début du design moderniste, un paradoxe fondamental demeure: si la nature des solutions de design universel peuvent parfois être aliénantes, les solutions de design individualiste restent souvent l'apanage d'une élite fortunée. Néanmoins, comme on l'a vu plus haut, les nouvelles technologies devenant de plus en plus accessibles, elles offriront peut-être le moyen de réconcilier enfin ces deux camps. L'avenir du design réside donc peut-être dans la création de solutions universelles qui puissent être adaptées avec efficacité pour répondre à des besoins individualistes.
Le débat des designers sur l'à-propos de l'opposition entre solutions individualistes et universalistes explique peut-être l'absence relative d'hypothèses sur une théorie unificatrice ou sur une nouvelle base philosophique et morale du design. Si beaucoup discutent de l'attrait qu'il pourrait y avoir à satisfaire le besoin d'un plus grand indi-

J Mays, **24.7 PickUp** concept vehicle/Konzept-Fahrzeug/ concept de véhicule for Ford Motor Company, 2000

its implications for increased waste production. Some designers, however, take an holistic view of current and longer-term concerns, and are in accord with Stephen Peart when he states: "By creating something, you are personally approving its existence and directing the fate of many resources."
Certainly, there is a growing need for designers to view themselves as stakeholders in their product solutions and to develop them within an understanding of the environmental impact of every aspect of their manufacture, use and eventual disposal – from cradle to grave. But there is also a pressing requirement to connect consumers in more meaningful ways with technologically increasingly complicated products. To this end, it would seem that a more

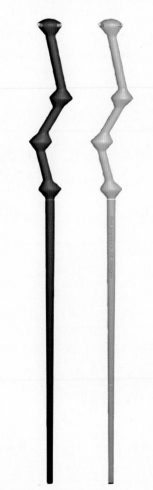

Björn Dahlström, Joystick walking stick/Spazierstock/ canne for Magis, 2000

sophische Basis für Design weitgehend aus. Während es viele von ihnen zwar für wünschenswert halten, das von den Konsumenten wahrgenommene Bedürfnis nach einem größeren Maß an Individualität zu befriedigen, äußern sich nur wenige über die zukünftigen Auswirkungen eines solchen Ansatzes und die damit verbundene wachsende Abfallproduktion. Allerdings betrachten einige Designer diese aktuellen und längerfristigen Fragen aus einer ganzheitlichen Perspektive. So äußert sich Stephen Peart zum Beispiel: »Indem wir etwas herstellen, billigen wir persönlich dessen Existenz und beeinflussen das Schicksal zahlreicher Ressourcen.«
Es lässt sich eindeutig feststellen, dass es für Designer eine wachsende Notwendigkeit gibt, sich als die Verantwortlichen für ihre Produktentwicklungen zu sehen. Das bedeutet, dass sie von Anfang bis Ende des gestalterischen Prozesses die Umwelteinflüsse zu jedem Aspekt der Produktion, Anwendung und schließlich Entsorgung ihrer Produkte mitbedenken müssen. Gleichzeitig aber ist es notwendig, die Konsumenten auf sinnvollere Weise mit technisch immer komplexer werdenden Produkten zusammenzubringen. Deshalb scheint ein Ansatz, der den Menschen noch bewusster als das Zentrum von Design auffasst, die beste Methode zu bieten, um gleichermaßen funktionale wie psychologische Bedürfnisse zu befriedigen.

Designer spielen eine entscheidende Rolle im Hinblick auf die Erwartungen und das Kaufverhalten der Konsumenten. Infolgedessen stellt sich ihnen immer wieder die Aufgabe, neue Wege im Bereich des Designs und der Produktentwicklung zu beschreiten, und zwar Wege, die zu dauerhaften Lösungen führen und nachhaltig den Anforderungen des Alltags entsprechen.
Indem sich Designer moderne Materialien und neue Technologien zunutze machen und Lösungen finden, die für Konsumenten verständlich und emotional leicht zugänglich sind, schaffen sie jene ethischen und sinnvollen Produkte, die zukünftig in hohem Maße benötigt wer-

vidualisme en design, par exemple, peu commentent la viabilité future d'une telle approche, avec ses implications quant à l'augmentation de la production de déchets. Toutefois, certains créateurs adoptent une vision holistique des préoccupations actuelles ou à plus long termes, approuvent Stephen Peart quand il déclare : « En créant quelque chose, on approuve son existence et on influe sur le sort de nombreuses ressources ».
En effet, les designers éprouvent un besoin croissant de se sentir impliqués dans leurs solutions de produits et de les développer en connaissant à l'avance l'impact écologique de tous les aspects de leur fabrication, de leur utilisation et, enfin, de leur élimination, autrement dit du berceau à la tombe. Mais il est également urgent de rapprocher de manière plus sensée les consommateurs des produits qui reposent sur une technologie de plus en plus complexe. A cette fin, il semblerait qu'une démarche réfléchie et davantage centrée sur l'homme offrirait le meilleur moyen de satisfaire à la fois des besoins fonctionnels et psychologiques.

Les créateurs jouant clairement un rôle déterminant dans le choix de la nature des produits manufacturés, il ne fait aucun doute qu'ils peuvent exercer une influence exceptionnelle sur les attentes et les habitudes d'achat des consommateurs. Par conséquent, il leur incombe moralement d'élaborer une nouvelle et meilleure orientation pour le design, une qui soit centrée sur le développement de solutions humanistes, viables et basées sur de vrais besoins.
En exploitant les matériaux et les technologies de pointe identifiés ici tout en s'efforçant d'apporter des solutions de design simplifiées avec des liens émotionnels plus aisés pour le consommateur, ils devraient être capables de créer les types de produits éthiques et pertinents dont nous aurons besoin à l'avenir. La qualité de notre culture matérielle planétaire de demain sera déterminée par les actes et les choix que nous faisons aujourd'hui. Il est donc

considered human-centric approach to design would provide the best means of satisfying both functional and psychological needs.

As designers clearly play a key role in determining the nature of manufactured products, there is little doubt that they can have an exceptional influence on the expectations and buying habits of consumers. There is consequently a growing moral imperative for them to chart a new and better direction in design, namely one which focuses on the development of real-need based, humanistic and sustainable solutions. By harnessing the advanced materials and technologies identified here while striving to provide simplified design solutions with an easier emotional connection for the consumer, designers should be able to create the types of ethical and relevant products that are needed for the future. The quality of our global material culture is being determined by the actions and choices we take now, and so it must be right that every individual – creator, maker and consumer – should acknowledge the need for a responsibility-based culture and should share in the collective goal of forging a better tomorrow.

CHARLOTTE AND PETER FIELL

Editors' note: We would like to express our immense gratitude to all those designers and design groups who have contributed to the successful realization of this unique project.

den. Da die Qualität der Kultur und des Lebens von unseren Handlungen und Entscheidungen geprägt wird, sollte jede und jeder Einzelne – sei es als Gestalter, Hersteller oder Konsument – die Notwendigkeit einer auf Verantwortlichkeit beruhenden Gesellschaft anerkennen und zu dem kollektiven Ziel beitragen, ein besseres Morgen zu gestalten.

CHARLOTTE UND PETER FIELL

Anmerkung der Herausgeber: Wir möchten uns ganz besonders bei allen in diesem Buch vorgestellten Designern und Designergruppen bedanken, die zum erfolgreichen Abschluss dieses Projektes beigetragen haben.

Sydney 612, LightBox lamp/Lampe/lampe (self-production), 2000, design: Tonka Andjelkovic and Tina Gounios

juste que chaque individu – créateur, fabricant, consommateur – reconnaisse le besoin d'une culture basée sur la responsabilité et participe à l'objectif collectif de forger un avenir meilleur.

CHARLOTTE ET PETER FIELL

Note des auteurs: Nous aimerions exprimer notre immense gratitude à tous les designers et groupes de design qui ont contribué à la réalisation de ce projet exceptionnel.

büro für form., Liquid Light
lamps/Lampen/lampes (self-production), 2000

"Exciting, visionary and innovative
design has always been the product
of new materials and technology."

Werner Aisslinger

Werner Aisslinger, Studio Aisslinger, Oranienplatz 4, 10 999 Berlin, Germany
T +49 30 31 505 400 F +49 30 31 505 401 aisslinger@snafu.de www.aisslinger.de

»Aufregendes, visionäres und innovatives
Design war immer schon das Produkt
neuer Materialien und Technologien.«

« Le design innovateur, excitant et
visionnaire a toujours été amené par de
nouvelles technologies et matières. »

1. **Plus Unit** trolley/Rollwagen/chariot for Magis, 2000
2. ↓ **Juli** chair/Stuhl/chaise for Cappellini, 1998-2000

« Au début du 21ᵉ siècle, le design surmontera le minimalisme branché de la décennie précédente dont la nouveauté résidait essentiellement dans les formes. Nous reviendrons aux paramètres qui ont toujours constitué la base des nouvelles époques et dimensions : une utilisation sophistiquée des technologies et des matériaux nouveaux. Les créations visionnaires et avant-gardistes qui ont marqué leur temps ont toujours reposé sur la transformation de matériaux et de technologies replacés dans un nouveau contexte. Aujourd'hui, des progrès technologiques fulgurants ont entraîné l'apparition de fibres de verre, de gels, de mousse d'aluminium, de textiles et de Néoprène tridimensionnels avec lesquels ont peut créer des produits radicalement différents. Sur le plan esthétique, leurs lignes seront utilitaires, organiques, réduites, douces, épurées, modulaires et nomades. Les produits du futur associeront des aspects pratiques à des fonctions intégrées. Au bout du compte, le contact quotidien avec ces produits dépassera toutes considération technique et fonctionnelle, si bien que les designers devront être plus réceptifs que jamais au dialogue entre les émotions et la technologie. Le système de distribution sera lui aussi radicalement modifié, chaque objet étant équipé d'une petite puce qui permettra de le commander directement. Dans ce scénario futuriste, la pureté du design sera un facteur primordial de décision pour les consommateurs du commerce électronique. »
WERNER AISSLINGER

3. ← **Juli** chairs/Stühle/chaises for Cappellini, 1998-2000 (permanent collection MoMA, New York, and Vitra Design Museum, Weil am Rhein)
4. **Linn** tables/Tische for Jonas & Jonas, 2000

"Design at the beginning of the 21st century will overcome the stylish minimalism of the last decade, with its innovation based purely on shape. Instead, there will be a return to parameters that have always been the basis of new epochs and dimensions in design: the sophisticated use of new materials and technologies. Historically, exciting, visionary and pioneering designs have always rested on the transformation of materials and technology into a new context. Today's lightning-speed technological advancements have led to the appearance of three-dimensional fibreglass, gels, aluminium foam, three-dimensional textiles and neoprenes from which entirely new products can be created. Aesthetically, the design of these future products will be utilitarian, organic, reduced, soft, puristic, poetic, modular and nomadic. The products of the future will combine functional aspects with certain built-in event facilities. Eventually the act of experiencing products will become more important than functional or technical considerations and designers will have to be ever more sensitive to the dialogue between emotions and technology. The distribution of products will also alter radically, with every object possessing a small chip that will allow you to order it directly. In this kind of future scenario, pure design quality will be a major decision factor for e-commerce consumers." WERNER AISSLINGER

»Design am Beginn des 21. Jahrhunderts wird den modischen Minimalismus der letzten Dekade mit seinen ausschließlich auf Form basierenden Innovationen überwinden. Stattdessen wird es eine Rückkehr zu Parametern geben, welche immer schon die Basis neuer Epochen und Dimensionen im Design waren: die intelligente Nutzung neuer Materialien und Technologien. Historisch gesehen beruhte aufregendes, visionäres und bahnbrechendes Design stets auf der Übertragung von Werkstoffen und Technologien in einen neuen Kontext. Der rasante technische Fortschritt von heute hat zur Erfindung von Glasfasern, Gels, Aluminiumschaum, von dreidimensionalen Textilien und Neopren geführt – Materialien, aus denen vollkommen neue Produkte kreiert werden können. In ästhetischer Hinsicht wird das Design dieser zukünftigen Produkte utilitaristisch, organisch, reduziert, weich, puristisch, poetisch, modulierbar und nomadisch sein. Die Produkte der Zukunft werden praktische Aspekte mit integrierten situationsspezifischen Funktionen verbinden. Letztendlich wird der Erlebnischarakter der Produkte wichtiger sein als funktionale oder technische Überlegungen, und die Designer müssen stets sensibel sein für den Dialog zwischen Emotionen und Technologie. Auch der Vertrieb der Produkte wird sich radikal verändern, wobei jedes Objekt einen kleinen Chip enthalten wird, der dem Käufer ermöglicht, es direkt zu bestellen. In dieser Art von Zukunftsszenario wird die makellose Qualität des Designs zu einem wichtigen Entscheidungsfaktor für die Konsumenten im elektronischen Handel.«
WERNER AISSLINGER

5
6
7

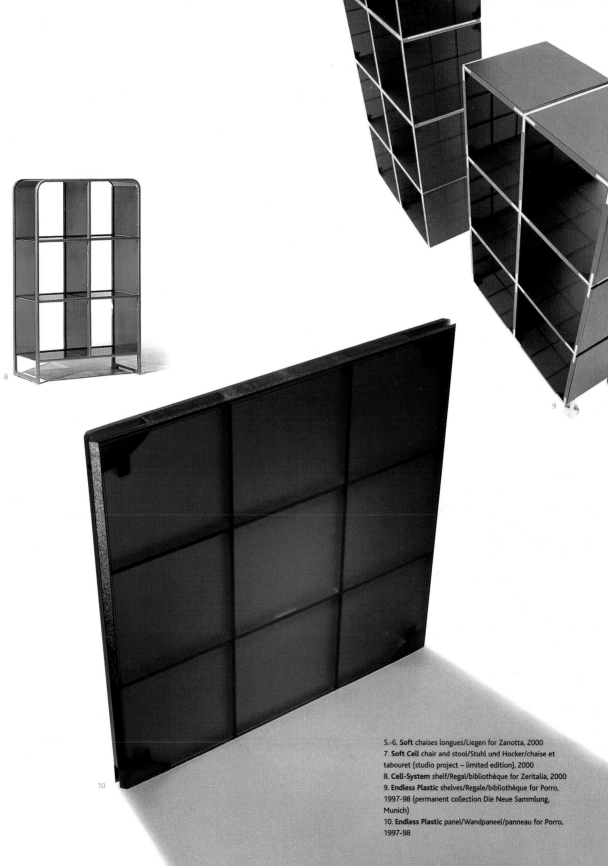

8

9

10

5.-6. **Soft** chaises longues/Liegen for Zanotta, 2000
7. **Soft Cell** chair and stool/Stuhl und Hocker/chaise et
tabouret (studio project – limited edition), 2000
8. **Cell-System** shelf/Regal/bibliothèque for Zeritalia, 2000
9. **Endless Plastic** shelves/Regale/bibliothèque for Porro,
1997-98 (permanent collection Die Neue Sammlung,
Munich)
10. **Endless Plastic** panel/Wandpaneel/panneau for Porro,
1997-98

WERNER AISSLINGER		CLIENTS
BORN	1964 Nördlingen, Germany	Arflex
STUDIED	1986 History of Art and Communication Sciences at Munich University	Bertelsmann
	1987-91 diploma in design at Hochschule der Künste, Berlin	Cappellini
PRACTICE	1989-92 design offices of Jasper Morrison, Ron Arad, London and Michele de Lucchi, Milan	DaimlerChrysler
	1993 founded Aisslinger Corporate Design	E-Plus
	1993- teacher at Hochschule der Künste, Berlin and the Lahti Design Institute, Finland	Interlübke
	1998- professor of product design, Hochschule für Gestaltung, Karlsruhe	Lufthansa
AWARDS	1992 Design Plus Award, Frankfurt/Main	Magis
	1994 Wogg Design Award, Zurich; Design Selection Award, Design Zentrum Nordrhein-Westfalen, Essen	Porro
		Rolf Benz
	1995 Compasso d'Oro selection, Milan	Stilwerk
	1996 Bundespreis Produktdesign, Frankfurt/Main	Zanotta
	2000 Design Selection Award, Design Zentrum Nordrhein-Westfalen, Essen	Zeritalia
EXHIBITIONS	1994 Design Innovationen, Design Zentrum Nordrhein-Westfalen, Essen	ZDF
	1995 *Die Kunst und das schöne Ding*, Neues Museum Weserburg, Bremen; Compasso d'Oro exhibition, Milan	
	1996 Bundespreis Produktdesign, Frankfurt/Main	
	1998 Design Yearbook collection, Museum für Angewandte Kunst, Cologne; BIO 16 Biennial of Industrial Design, Ljubljana; *bewußt, einfach*, Vitra Design Museum, Weil am Rhein	
	1999 *Identity Crisis – The 90s Defined*, The Lighthouse, Glasgow	
	2000 *soft cell-down light*, Galerie Fiedler, Cologne; *vetro*, Museo Correr, Venice	

11

12

13

14

11. **Plateau-System** trolley/Rollwagen/chariot (studio project), 1997
12. **Juli** table/Tisch for Cappellini, 2000
13. **Global Board** cupboard & shelf system/Schrank & Regalsystem/bibliothèque avec placard (studio project – limited edition), 1997
14. ↑ **Linn** table/Tisch for Jonas & Jonas, 2000

"Boredom is the mother of creativity."

Ron Arad

Ron Arad, Ron Arad Associates, 62, Chalk Farm Road, London NW1 8AN, England
T +44 20 7284 4963 F +44 20 7379 0499 info@ronarad.com www.ronarad.com

»Langeweile ist die Mutter der Kreativität.«

« L'ennui engendre la créativité. »

1. **RTW** shelves/Regale/bibliothèque
by Ron Arad Associates, 1996
2. ↓ **BOOP** coffee table/Couchtisch/table basse by
Ron Arad Associates for Gallery Mourmans, 1998

« Lors d'un communiqué de presse légèrement ironique pour " Non fabriqué à la main, non fabriqué en Chine ", une exposition d'objets réalisés par stéréo-lithographie et découpage sélectif au laser (Milan 2000), j'ai déclaré que, jusqu'à récemment, il n'y avait eu que quatre moyens de faire les choses. Tout processus de fabrication peut être décomposé en une ou plusieurs des étapes suivantes : ELIMINER (tailler, graver, tourner, moudre, buriner – soit enlever la matière en excès) ; MOULER (mouler par injection, par rotation, couler dans un moule, extruder – soit verser un matériau liquide qui, en durcissant, prend la forme de son contenant) ; MODELER (courber, presser, marteler, plier, façonner sous vide – soit donner une forme à une feuille de matériau) ; ASSEMBLER (visser, coller, riveter, clouer, souder, soit joindre des parties par un moyen ou un autre). Puis j'ajoutai qu'il existait désormais un quatrième moyen : DEVELOPPER, un objet peut croître dans un bac, couche après couche, à l'aide de rayons laser contrôlés par ordinateur.

Tout ceci peut encore être réduit : un objet peut-être fabriqué par ADDITION ou SOUS-TRACTION. Les ordinateurs, avec leur ZEROS et leurs UNS, adorent ça. Avec le CNC (Contrôle numérique informatisé), le RP (Prototypage rapide), les matériaux GM et un petit ↓

"In a slightly tongue-in-cheek press release for 'Not Made By Hand, Not Made in China', an exhibition of objects made by stereolithography and selective laser sintering (Milan 2000), I claimed that until recently there had been only four ways of making things. The process of making any object could be broken down into one or more of the following steps: WASTE (chip, carve, turn, mill, chisel – i. e. removal of excess material), MOULD (injection moulding, casting, rotation moulding, extruding etc. – i. e. pouring liquid material to take the form of its vessel when hardened); FORM (bending, pressing, hammering, folding, vacuum forming etc. – i. e. forcing sheet material into a shape), ASSEMBLE (bolting, gluing, riveting, soldering, welding etc. – i. e. joining parts together by any means), and, I went on to claim, there is now a fifth way – GROW, an object can be grown in a tank, layer by layer, by computer controlled laser beams. Now I think all this can be reduced further – an object can be made by either ADDING or SUBTRACTING. Computers, with their ZEROS & ONES, love it. With CNC (Computer Numeric Control), RP (Rapid Prototyping), GM materials, and a little help from robotic friends, virtual can easily become actual; an image on screen rapidly transforms to a ↓

»In einer leicht ironischen Pressemitteilung für ›Not Made By Hand, Not Made in China‹, eine Ausstellung von Objekten, die durch Stereolithographie und selektive Laser-Sinterung hergestellt wurden (Mailand 2000), habe ich behauptet, dass es bis vor kurzem nur vier Arten gegeben habe, Dinge anzufertigen. Jeder Produktionsprozess lasse sich nämlich einem oder mehreren der folgenden Verarbeitungsschritte zuordnen: ENTFERNEN (abraspeln, schnitzen, drehen, fräsen, meißeln – d. h. Entfernen von überflüssigem Material), MODELLIEREN (Spritzgießen, in Formen gießen, Rotationsschmelzen, Strangpressen etc. – d. h. flüssiges Material in eine Form gießen), FORMEN (biegen, pressen, hämmern, falten, Vakuumformen – d. h. einer Materialplatte eine Form geben), ZUSAMMENSETZEN (schrauben, kleben, nieten, löten, falzen – d. h. einzelne Teile zusammenfügen). Dann fuhr ich fort, dass es nun eine fünfte Art gebe: ZÜCHTEN – d. h. man kann ein Objekt Schicht um Schicht durch computergesteuerte Laserstrahlen in einem Tank wachsen lassen.

Inzwischen glaube ich, dass man das Ganze noch weiter reduzieren kann: Objekte lassen sich entweder durch HINZUFÜGEN oder ENTFERNEN produzieren. Computer mit ihren NULLEN & EINSEN lieben das. Mittels CNC (Computer Numeric Control), RP (Rapid Prototyping), GM-Materialien und ein wenig Hilfe von unseren Roboter-Freunden kann das Virtuelle leicht zum Reellen werden. Ein Bild auf ↓

coup de main de la part de nos amis de la robotique, le virtuel peut facilement devenir réel : une image sur un écran peut rapidement se transformer en une masse solide. Tout peut être dessiné, modelé et fabriqué. (Qui sont ces gens qui créent les logiciels capables de satisfaire nos moindres caprices ? Comment ont-ils pu prévoir, depuis leur vallée, qu'un designer de Chalk Farm (à Londres) voudrait construire, par exemple, une balle en spirale au diamètre toujours changeant, la faire rebondir, enregistrer avec précision ses distorsions en une série de modèles puis les développer en objets solides dans un réservoir de résine époxy ?) Il n'y a virtuellement plus de limites. Les matières intelligentes, les outils de pointe, une production digne de la science-fiction, tout est déjà là. Aujourd'hui. Le présent est trop fascinant pour s'appesantir trop longuement sur le futur. En examinant attentivement le présent, on peut y lire l'avenir. » RON ARAD

5. **BOOP** small vases/kleine Vasen/petits vases by Ron Arad Associates for Gallery Mourmans, 1998
6.-8. **Ge-Off Sphere** lamp/Lampe/lampe, **Not Made by Hand, Not Made in China** series by/Serie von/séries de Ron Arad Associates for Gallery Mourmans, 2000

solid mass. Anything can be drawn, modelled and made. (Who are those people who write the software to cater for any eventual possible obscure whim we might come up with? How could they anticipate, from their valley, that some designer in Chalk Farm (London) would want to build, say, a spiral ball with an ever-changing section, to bounce it, accurately record the distortions in a series of virtual models and then grow them as solid objects in a tank of epoxy resin?). There are virtually no limits. Smart materials, sharp tools, sci-fi production, it's all here. Now. The present is too fascinating to stop and worry too much about the future. If you look at the present deeply enough, the future will become discernible." RON ARAD

dem Monitor lässt sich dann rasch in eine feste Masse transformieren. Alles Erdenkliche kann gezeichnet, modelliert und angefertigt werden. (Wer sind eigentlich diese Leute, die eine Software entwickeln, mit der sich jeder obskure Einfall, der uns vielleicht mal durch den Kopf geht, verwirklichen lässt? Wie können sie von Silicon Valley aus vorhersehen, dass irgendein Designer in Chalk Farm, London, beispielsweise einen spiralförmigen Ball mit einem flexiblen Teil basteln möchte, der die Verformungen, die entstehen, wenn man den Ball aufspringen lässt, in einer Serie virtueller Modelle genauestens festhält und diese dann als feste Objekte in einem mit Epoxidharz gefüllten Tank entwickelt?) Es gibt praktisch keine Grenzen mehr. Intelligente Materialien und Werkzeuge, Produktionsmethoden wie aus der Sciencefiction-Welt – es ist alles da. Jetzt. Die Gegenwart ist viel zu faszinierend, um innezuhalten und sich allzu viele Gedanken über die Zukunft zu machen. Wenn man die Gegenwart aufmerksam genug betrachtet, wird darin die Zukunft erkennbar.« RON ARAD

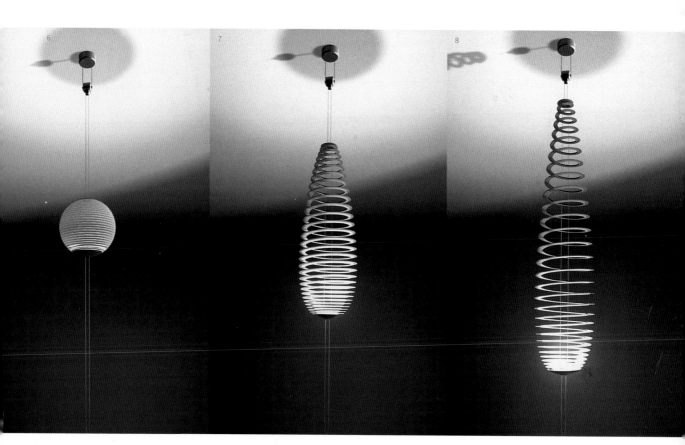

9. **Victoria & Albert** armchair/Sessel/fauteuil for Moroso, 2000
10. ↓ **Victoria & Albert** chaise longue/Liege for Moroso, 2000

11. **Victoria & Albert** chairs/Stühle/
chaises for Moroso, 2000
12. ↓ **Victoria & Albert** sofa/Sofa for Moroso, 2000

"I am interested in the familiar elemental forms found in archetypes leading to simple and functional objects that evoke strong associations and narratives, often addressing environmental issues."

Jane Atfield

Jane Atfield, 244, Grays Inn Road, London WC1X 8JR, England
T +44 20 7278 6971 F +44 20 7833 0018 janeatfield@btinternet.com

»Mein Interesse gilt den vertrauten Elementarformen in Archetypen, die zu einfachen und funktionalen Objekten führen. Sie evozieren lebhafte Assoziationen und Geschichten, die häufig mit ökologischen Fragen zu tun haben.«

« Je m'intéresse aux formes élémentaires et familières des archétypes qui conduisent à des objets simples et fonctionnels, évoquant des associations et des histoires puissantes, traitant souvent de questions écologiques. »

1. **Felt Divan**/Diwan/divan (self-production), 1992
2. **Strawbale outdoor nursery seating**/Sitzbank/
siège, **Hanging Things and Stuffing Things Series**
(self-production), 2000

« Les gens rejetteront l'empire du consumé-risme et seront déçus par les marques et le matérialisme. Du coup, le shopping cessera d'être amusant et sera remplacé par l'Internet. La demande réduite pour le choix et les biens matériels cédera la place à un engouement pour les expériences sociales, ainsi que pour des systèmes et des communications mieux conçus.

Les designers seront davantage motivés par des besoins réels et chercheront à résoudre des problèmes liés aux enfants, aux personnes âgées, aux handicapés, aux célibataires et aux familles en difficulté. Un processus d'interac-tion se développera, les designers cherchant à rendre possible et à faciliter les idées et les exigences propres à chaque groupe. Des fac-teurs moraux et politiques interviendront dans le choix de ce qui sera développé , les solutions localisées et les ressources dépen-dant peu de la technologie prenant de l'im-portance. Les préoccupations écologiques primeront sur les marges de profit avec, par exemple, le recyclage régulier de matériaux, de bâtiments et d'objets. L'intégration de ma-tériaux et de processus de pointe se répandra et ils deviendront plus accessibles, contrôlant et régulant notre environnement de manière toujours plus sophistiquée. » JANE ATFIELD

3. ← **T-towels**/Handtücher/torchons, **Washing Up Series 1** for Up fabric, 2000 – Sink, Bottles, Drainer & U-bend/ Motive: Spüle, Flaschen, Abtropfgestell und U-Bogen/ évier, bouteilles, égouttoir, courbure en U (designed in collaboration with Robert Shepherd)
4. **Soft Shelves**/Gestell/casiers (self-production), 1995

"People will reject the dominance of consumerism and grow disillusioned with branding and materialism. As a result, shopping will lose its leisure and entertainment status and will be replaced by the Internet. The reduced demand for choice and pos-sessions will be replaced with an emphasis on social experiences and better designed systems and com-munications.

Product designers will increasingly be motivated by meeting real needs and solving problems connected with children, older people, the dis-abled, single people and complicat-ed families. An interactive process will develop with the designers act-ing as enablers and facilitators for the various groups' own ideas and requirements.

Moral and political factors will be important in determining what is developed and where, with localised solutions and low-tech resources becoming more important. Environ-mental concerns will increase in value over profit margins with, for example, materials, buildings and objects being routinely recycled. The integration of highly techno-logical materials and processes will widen and become more accessible, controlling and regulating our environment to increasingly sophisticated levels." JANE ATFIELD

»Die Leute werden die Dominanz des Kon-sumdenkens ablehnen und von Markenpro-duktion und Materialismus zunehmend des-illusioniert sein. Als Folge davon wird das Einkaufen seinen Status als Freizeitvergnügen und Unterhaltung verlieren und durch das Internet ersetzt werden. Der verminderte Be-darf an Auswahl und Besitz wird durch eine Betonung sozialer Erfahrungen und besser erdachter Systeme und Kommunikations-mittel abgelöst.

Produktdesigner werden ihre Motivation zunehmend daraus beziehen, dass sie reale Bedürfnisse befriedigen und Problemlösun-gen für den Alltag von Kindern, älteren, be-hinderten, alleinstehenden Menschen und Problemfamilien anbieten. Es wird sich ein interaktiver Prozess entwickeln, in dem Designer die Rolle von Vermittlern und För-derern der Ideen und Bedürfnisse verschiede-ner Gruppen übernehmen. Moralische und politische Faktoren werden für die Entschei-dung, was wo entwickelt wird, ausschlag-gebend sein, und örtlich begrenzte Lösungen und Ressourcen an Bedeutung gewinnen. Ökologische Belange werden einen höheren Stellenwert erhalten als Gewinnspannen, wo-bei zum Beispiel die Wiederverwertung von Werkstoffen, Gebäuden und Produkten zur Regel wird. Hochtechnische Materialien und Herstellungsprozesse werden breitere Ver-wendung finden und leichter verfügbar sein, wodurch sich unsere Umwelt auf immer dif-ferenziertere Weise kontrollieren und regu-lieren lassen wird.« JANE ATFIELD

JANE ATFIELD	CLIENTS

JANE ATFIELD

			CLIENTS
BORN	1964	London, England	Beams
STUDIED	1983-87	BA (Hons) Arch, Polytechnic of Central London (School of Architecture)	Björl
	1988-89	Diploma in Furniture Design and Production, London College of Furniture	Body Shop
	1990-92	MA Furniture Design, Royal College of Art, London	Conran Shop
PRACTICE	1987-88	assistant architect Biscoe & Stanton Architects, London	Formica
	1989-90	assistant architect Devereux & Partners, London and Bowerbank, Brett & Lacey, London	Habitat
	1992	freelance furniture designer	IKEA
	1993	visiting tutor to numerous institutions. Began researching and developing post-consumer recycled plastics	Katherine Hamnett
	1994	founded Made of Waste	Oreka
	2000	co-founded UP fabric with Robert Shepherd	also self-production
AWARDS	1992	Gunton Award, The Worshipful Company of Furniture Makers, London; *Elle Decoration*/Habitat Furniture for the 90s Award	
	1999	Commendation Ergonom Awards; finalist *Blueprint*/100% Design Award, London	
EXHIBITIONS	1994	*Eco Design*, Brussels; *Every Angle*, London; *Green Seating Tour*, St Louis, Chicago	
	1995	*Not So Simple*, Barcelona, Cologne	
	1996	*Deja Vu*, Galerie Andrea Leenarts, Cologne; *Design im Wandel*, Übersee-Museum, Bremen; *Domestic Plastics*, Salon du Meuble, Paris; *Design of the Times*, Royal College of Art, London	
	1997	*Six Designers for Loft Living*, Berlin; *Design mit Zukunft*, Focke Museum, Bremen	
	1998	Designers Block, London, Flexible Furniture, Crafts Council, London	
	1999	*Identity Crisis – The 90s Defined*, The Lighthouse, Glasgow; *Jerwood Applied Arts Exhibition*, Crafts Council, London	
	2000	*Home Sweet Home, Cause and Effect*, touring exhibition, British Council; Transformations, Pitt Rivers Museum, Oxford	

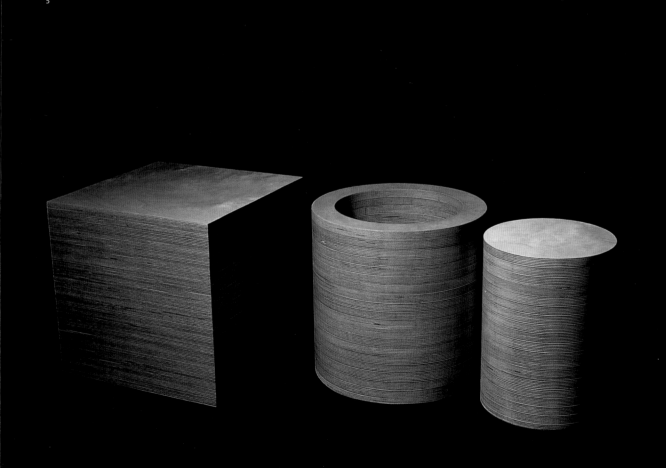

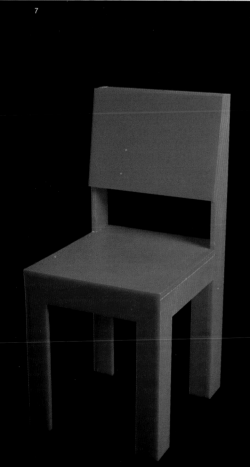

5. **Insert tables**/Tische (self-production), 1999
6. **Pillows Lounger**/Kissenliege/lit de repos from **Hanging Things and Stuffing Things Series** (self-production), 2000
7. **RCP2** chair/Stuhl/chaise for Made of Waste, 1993 – reissued in monochrome recycled plastic derived from chopping boards/neuaufgelegt in einfarbigem aus Hackbrettern recyceltem Kunststoff/rééditée en plastique monochrome recyclé à partir de planches à découper, 1998
8. **Amaretti** children's play trolley/Kinder-Rollwagen/chariot d'enfant from **Biscuit Collection** for Oreka Kids, 2000

"Simplicity and surprise, materiality and immateriality, from object to space."

Shin + Tomoko Azumi

Shin + Tomoko Azumi, 953, Finchley Road, London NW117PE, England
T +44 20 8731 9057 F +44 20 8731 7496 azumi@uk2.so-net.com www.azumi.co.uk

»Schlichtheit und Verblüffung, Materialität und Immaterialität, vom Objekt zum Raum.«

« Simplicité et surprise, matérialité et immatérialité, de l'objet à l'espace ».

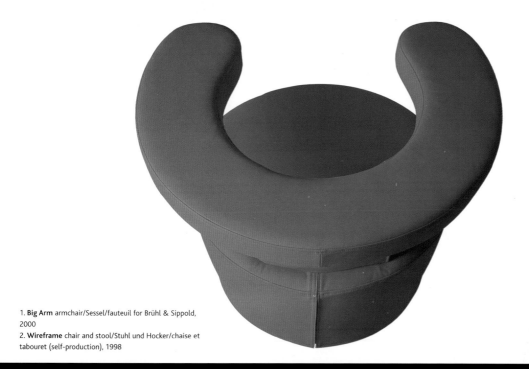

1. **Big Arm** armchair/Sessel/fauteuil for Brühl & Sippold, 2000
2. **Wireframe** chair and stool/Stuhl und Hocker/chaise et tabouret (self-production), 1998

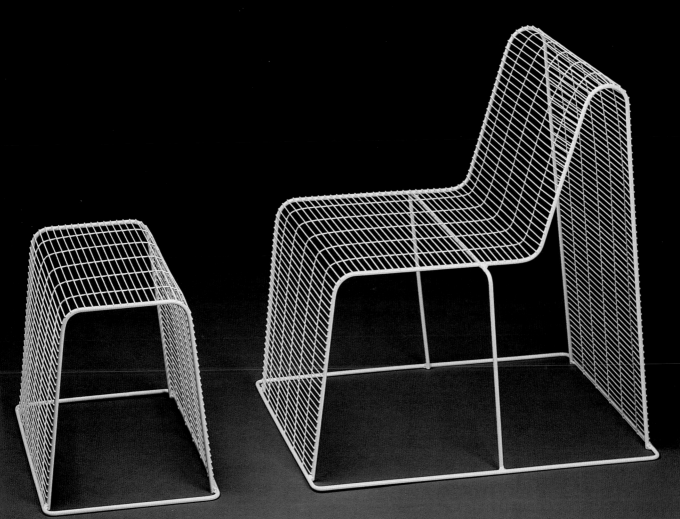

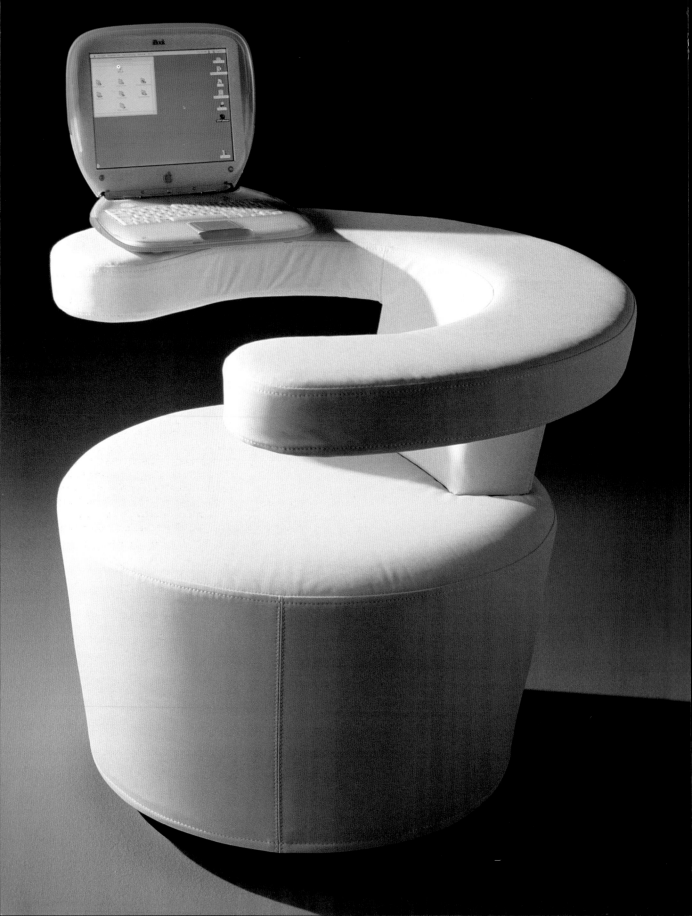

"In the future we hope that design will help us achieve a 'better life' rather than just 'better sales'. Between the 80's and early 90's, design became a tool for commercial marketing. That was not altogether a bad thing, but now we think it should be used to create a desirable environment and that greater emphasis should be placed on 'individuality' in the future. People will have more choice as quick communication and fast transportation make a wider range of designs from across the world accessible to them. In that situation, personal attachment will become a more important factor in design. Finally, for us, the future of design is an extended horizon of where we are and what we feel at the moment. It is not an entity in itself." SHIN + TOMOKO AZUMI

« Pour l'avenir, nous souhaitons un design au service d'une "meilleure vie" plutôt que de "meilleures ventes". Des années 80 au début des années 90, il a servi d'outil de marketing. Ce n'était pas forcément un mal, mais nous préférerions qu'il serve à créer un environnement désirable et que l'accent soit mis davantage sur les besoins "individuels". Les moyens de communication et les transports devenant toujours plus rapides et accessibles, l'offre de produits provenant des quatre coins du monde ne cessera de s'élargir. Dans ce contexte, le goût et les affinités de chacun deviendront un facteur important de la création. Enfin, l'avenir du design dépend de l'horizon élargi de ce que nous sommes et de ce que nous ressentons dans l'instant. Il n'existe pas en lui-même. » SHIN + TOMOKO AZUMI

»Für die Zukunft erhoffen wir uns ein Design, das uns zu einem ›besseren Leben‹ statt bloß zu ›besseren Umsätzen‹ verhelfen wird. Das Design wurde während der achtziger und frühen neunziger Jahre zu einem Marketinginstrument. Das war nicht durchwegs schlecht, wir finden jedoch, dass Design nun dazu dienen sollte, eine erstrebenswerte Umwelt zu gestalten. Außerdem sollte in Zukunft mehr Nachdruck auf ›Individualität‹ gelegt werden. Die Menschen werden mehr Wahlmöglichkeiten haben, da ihnen durch schnellere Kommunikations- und Transportmittel eine größere Bandbreite an Designprodukten aus der ganzen Welt zugänglich gemacht wird. In diesem Zusammenhang wird der persönliche Bezug zu einem wichtigen Faktor für die Gestaltung von Design. Und schließlich sehen wir das Design der Zukunft als einen erweiterten Horizont dessen, was wir im Moment sind und fühlen. Es ist keine feste Größe an sich.«
SHIN + TOMOKO AZUMI

3. ← **Big Arm** armchair/Sessel/fauteuil for Brühl & Sippold, 2000
4. **Snowman** salt and pepper shakers/Salz- und Pfefferstreuer/salière et poivrière for Authentics, 1999
5. **Upright** salt and pepper shakers/Salz- und Pfefferstreuer/salière et poivrière by Azumi, 1998

6. **Cross** tables/Tische for Trunk/Sumitomo Bakelite, 1999
7.-9. **Table=Chest**/Tisch=Truhe/table = coffre (self-production), 1995
10. **Keen Stand**/Ausstellungsstand/présentoir at *100%* *Design* exhibition, London 2000 (with animation by Yuko Hirosawa)
11. **Music Tube**/Musik-Röhre/tube musical at Resitr, Kobe 2000 (in collaboration with Noriyuki Ohtsuka)
12. **Stacking Chair**/Stapelstuhl/chaise encastrable by Azumi for Kettle's Yard Gallery, 1998
13.-14. **H3** speaker/Lautsprecher/haut-parleur and **HB-1** sub woofer/unterer Basstonlautsprecher/amplificateur de graves for TOA, 2000

9

12

13

14

SHIN + TOMOKO AZUMI

FOUNDED	1995	Azumi Design Studio, London by Shin (b. 1965 Kobe, Japan) and
		Tomoko Azumi (b. 1966 Hiroshima, Japan)
STUDIED		SHIN AZUMI
	1989	BA Product Design, Kyoto City University of Art, Japan
	1994	MA Industrial Design, Royal College of Art, London
		TOMOKO AZUMI
	1989	BA Environmental Design, Kyoto City University of Art, Japan
	1995	MA Furniture Design, Royal College of Art, London
PRACTICE		SHIN AZUMI
	1989-92	NEC Design Centre Co., Tokyo (Personal Computer Dept)
		TOMOKO AZUMI
	1989-90	Kazuhiro Ishii Architect & Associates, Japan
	1990-92	Toda Construction Corporation, Japan (Design Office)
AWARDS		SHIN AZUMI
	1989	Grand Prize, Seki Cutlery Design Competition, Japan
	1991	G-Mark/Good Design Award, JIDPO, Tokyo
	1992	G-Mark/Good Design Award, JIDPO, Tokyo
		TOMOKO AZUMI
	1989	Misawa Student Housing Design Award, Japan
	1993	ABSA/Arthur Andersen Trophy Design Award, London
	1995	FX-HNB Furniture Award, New Designers Exhibition, London
		JOINT
	1998 & 99	finalist *Blueprint*/100 % Design Award, London; Peugeot Design Award, London
	2000	Product of the Year Award, FX International Interior Design Awards, London
EXHIBITIONS	1996	*Design of the Times – 100 Years of the Royal College of Art*, London
	1997	*Flexible Furniture*, Crafts Council, London
	1998	*Objects of Our Time*, American Craft Museum, New York
	1999	*Lost and Found*, Museum für Kunsthandwerk, Frankfurt/Main
	2000	room installation *Misty Lounge* in *Tectonic*, Crafts Council, London
	2001	*Home Sweet Home*, Kulturhuset, Stockholm

CLIENTS

Authentics
Brühl & Sippold
E&Y
Guzzini
Habitat
Hitch Mylis
Lapalma
TOA
Wire Works
also self-production

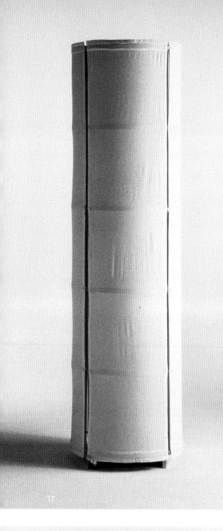

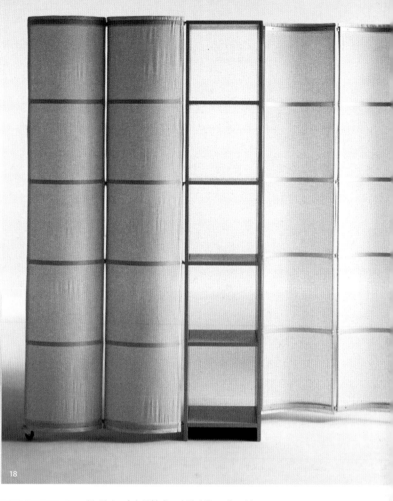

14.-16. **Armchair=Table**/Sessel=Tisch/fauteuil = table (self-production), 1998

17.-18. **Overture & Cabinet with Screens**/Overture & Kabinettschrank mit Wandschirmtüren/ouverture & cabinet avec paravent for Lapalma, 1998

19. **LEM** high stool/Barhocker/tabouret de bar for Lapalma, 2000

"Simple forms, sensitive, tactile materials, products made to stand the test of time."

Babylon Design

Babylon Design, 301, Fulham Road, London SW10 9QH, England
T +44 20 7376 7233 F +44 20 7376 7244 info@babylondesign.demon.co.uk www.babylonlondon.com

»Schlichte Formen, sensible, greifbare Materialien, Produkte, die vor der Zeit bestehen.«

« Des formes simples, des matières sensitives et tactiles, des produits conçus pour résister à l'épreuve du temps. »

1. **Geo** bowls/Schalen/bols for Babylon Design,
1999 – designer: Peter Wylly
2. ↓ **DNA** lamp/Lampe/lampe for Babylon Design,
1998 – designer: Peter Wylly

»In Zukunft wird es eine eklektischere Mischung von Stilen und Materialien geben. Heutzutage ändern sich die Trends sehr schnell, und den Konsumenten stehen bereits viele verschiedene Wahlmöglichkeiten zur Verfügung. Wir glauben, dass sich die Leute in Zukunft nicht scheuen werden, verschiedene Stile zu mischen – man wird Altes mit Neuem und Teures mit Billigem kombinieren. Unser Zuhause wird in zunehmenden Maß die eigene Persönlichkeit widerspiegeln. Jeder ist anders.« BABYLON DESIGN

"In the future there will be a more eclectic mix of styles and materials. Trends are changing very fast now with so many different choices already available to consumers. We believe that in the future people will not be afraid to combine various styles – old will be mixed with new and expensive with cheap. Peoples' homes will increasingly reflect their personality. Everyone is different." BABYLON DESIGN

« L'avenir sera marqué par un mélange plus éclectique de styles et de matériaux. Aujourd'hui, les tendances se succèdent très rapidement et les consommateurs bénéficient déjà d'une offre très variée. Nous pensons qu'à l'avenir les gens ne craindront plus de marier différents styles, le nouveau avec l'ancien, le cher avec le bon marché. Les intérieurs refléteront toujours plus la personnalité de leurs occupants. Nous sommes tous différents. » BABYLON DESIGN

3. **Stork** desk lamp/Schreibtischlampe/lampe de bureau for Babylon Design, 1999 – designers: Birgit & Christoph Israel
4. **The Lightwood Family** floor lamps/Stehlampen/lampadaires for Babylon Design, 1999 – designers: Vogt & Weizenegger
5. **Oxo** lights/Leuchten/luminaires for Babylon, 1998 – designer: Peter Wylly
6. **Eclipse 5** lamp/Lampe/lampe for Babylon Design, 1997 – designer: Peter Wylly

BABYLON DESIGN		CLIENTS
FOUNDED	1997	London, England by Peter Wylly (b. 1963 Leicester, England) and Birgit Israel (b. 1967 Lüneburg, Germany)	Arcade
			Blindenanstalt Berlin
STUDIED		PETER WYLLY	Body Shop
	1989	BA (Hons) Fashion Design, Middlesex University	Conran Shop
		BIRGIT ISRAEL	Habitat
	1989-97	international freelance stylist	also self-production
AWARDS	2000	two Design Plus Awards, Frankfurt/Main	

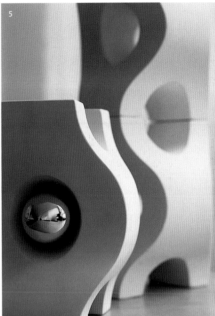

"We like to design friendly, non-obtrusive products, which you feel might always have been where you place them."

Bartoli Design

Bartoli Design, Via Grigna 2, 20052 Monza, (MI), Italy
T +39 039 387 225 F +39 039 386 698 pbartoli@iname.com

»Wir gestalten gern freundliche, unaufdringliche Produkte, die den Eindruck erwecken, als seien sie immer schon dort gewesen, wo man sie hingestellt hat.«

« Nous aimons concevoir des produits sympathiques et discrets qui, une fois qu'on les a placés chez soi, semblent avoir toujours été là. »

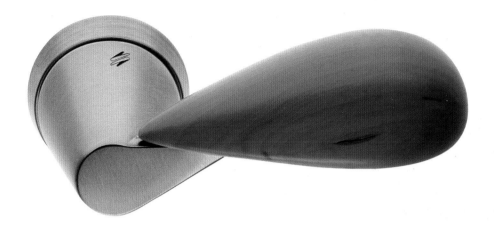

1. **Tacta** doorhandle/Türgriff/poignée de porte for
Colombo Design, 1992 – design: Carlo Bartoli
2. ↓ **Cloud** armchairs/Sessel/fauteuils for Segis, 1999 –
design: Carlo Bartoli

3. **Sha** sofas and ottomans/Sofas und Fußhocker/canapés
et repose-pieds for Rossi di Albizzate, 2000

»Ich weiß nicht, wie die Zukunft des Designs tatsächlich aussehen wird, aber ich weiß, wie sie aussehen sollte: Gebrauchsgüter sollten stets ein selbstverständlicher Teil der alltäglichen Umgebung des Benutzers sein. Aus diesem Grund sollte die Designsprache möglichst ungezwungen und normal sein. Das heißt nicht, dass Design banal, sondern mehr auf eine ausgewogene Balance ausgerichtet sein sollte. Und es sollte die in unserer Kultur geachteten Werte auf das Produkt übertragen – mit Respekt vor der menschlichen Würde von Tradition.« CARLO BARTOLI FÜR BARTOLI DESIGN

"I don't know what the future of design will be but I know what it should be: I think objects for widespread use should always become part of the user's daily landscape in a non-prevaricating way. For that reason the project language should be 'non-emerging', not far from normality. This does not mean banal, but rather oriented to a proper balance, transferring what is valued in culture to the product, with respect for the human dignity of tradition." CARLO BARTOLI FOR BARTOLI DESIGN

« J'ignore ce que nous réserve l'avenir du design mais je sais ce qu'il devrait être : les objets usuels devraient toujours s'intégrer au paysage quotidien de leurs utilisateurs sans se faire remarquer. Pour cette raison le projet de langage devrait être " non émergeant ", proche de la normalité. Cela ne signifie pas " banal " mais plutôt orienté vers un juste équilibre, transférant au produit ce qui est précieux dans la culture, en respectant la dignité humaine de la tradition. » CARLO BARTOLI POUR BARTOLI DESIGN

4. **Temper** heater/Heizung/radiateur for Deltacalor, 1998
5. **Maxima** cupboard/Anrichte/buffet for Laurameroni Design Collection, 2000
6. **Gallery** chair/Stuhl/fauteuil for Segis, 2000

		BARTOLI DESIGN	**CLIENTS**
FOUNDED	1963	by Carlo Bartoli	Arclinea
	1999	name adopted by a studio in Monza, Italy by Albertina Amadeo (b. 1932 Cadorago), Anna Bartoli (b. 1963 Milan), Carlo Bartoli (b. 1931 Milan), Paolo Bartoli (b. 1968 Milan), Paolo Cresenti (b. 1966 Rome) and Giulio Ripamonti (b. 1952 Lecco)	Arflex
			Colombo Design
			Confalonieri
STUDIED		ANNA BARTOLI	Delight
	1988	Architecture degree, Politecnico di Milano	Deltacalor
		CARLO BARTOLI	Kartell
	1957	Architecture degree, Politecnico di Milano	Kristalla
		PAOLO BARTOLI	Laurameroni Design Collection
	1994	Architecture degree, Politecnico di Milano	Matteograssi
		PAOLO CRESCENTI	Multipla 2000
	1990	Industrial Design degree ISIA (Istituto Superiore per le Industrie Artistiche), Rome	Rossi di Albizzate
		GIULIO RIPAMONTI	Segis
	1976	Architecture degree, Politecnico di Milano	Tisettanta
AWARDS		CARLO BARTOLI	Varenna-Poliform
	1991	Compasso d'Oro selection, Milan	Ycami
	1996	*I. D. Magazine Annual Design Review* Award, New York; Roter Punkt Award, Design Zentrum Nordrhein-Westfalen, Essen; IIDA Apex Product Design Award; iF Design Award, Hanover	
	1998	iF Design Award, Hanover	
EXHIBITIONS		CARLO BARTOLI	
	1968	*Plastics as Plastics*, Museum of Contemporary Crafts, New York	
	1970	*Modern Chairs 1918-1970*, Whitechapel Art Gallery, London	
	1972	*Design and Plastic*, Museum of Decorative Arts, Prague	
	1975	*The Plastic Chair*, Centrokappa, Noviglio (Milan)	
	1979	*Design & Design*, Milan; *Italian Office Design*, Milan; *Italian Design*, Hong Kong	
	1980	*Italian Design*, Athens	
	1981	*Italienisches Möbeldesign 1950-1980*, Museum für Angewandte Kunst, Cologne	
	1983	*From the Spoon to the City – Paths of 100 Designers*, Milan	
	1988	*Kitchens in the Shop Window*, Milan	
	1992	Biennial of Industrial Design, Ljubliana	
	1998	*Due Generazioni di Designer*, Udine	

5

6

"I am happy with a design when it
makes people smile."

Sebastian Bergne

Sebastian Bergne, 2, Ingate Place, London SW8 3NS, England
T +44 20 7622 3333 F +44 20 7622 3336 mail@sebastianbergne.com
also Via Bellombra 10, 40136 Bologna, Italy T/F +39 051 3395 609

»Ich bin zufrieden mit einem Design,
wenn es die Leute zum Lächeln bringt.«

« Je suis satisfait d'une création quand
elle fait sourire les gens. »

1. **Kult** egg cup/Eierbecher/coquetier for WMF, 1999
2. ↓ **Torso** lamp/Lampe/lampe for Authentics, 1996

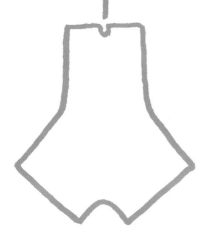

"There are many ways an object can make someone smile: familiarity, surprise, beauty, satisfaction, pride, simplicity, humour or wonder. If an object can stimulate this reaction whilst performing the function for which it was created, then it is well designed. It has in some way improved our lives. Design is the process by which these objects are created; it is not the object itself.

The future of design is the future of a way of thinking, a complex process of creativity that ultimately relies on the humanity of its audience to validate its existence. Designers always have and always will create for people's known or unknown needs and offer their solutions to new or age-old problems. Changes in society, technologies and materials alter the palette available to the designer to solve problems, but the process of creativity remains constant in its variety and unpredictability. In the end, however, the future of design is not in the hands of designers but rests on our ability to smile." SEBASTIAN BERGNE

»Ein Objekt kann die Leute auf vielerlei Arten zum Lächeln bringen: durch seine Vertrautheit, einen Überraschungseffekt, seine Schönheit, seine Schlichtheit, seinen Humor oder durch die Befriedigung, den Stolz und das Erstaunen, die es hervorruft. Wenn ein Objekt solche Reaktionen bewirkt, während es gleichzeitig die Funktion ausübt, für die es entworfen wurde, dann handelt es sich um gelungenes Design, das auf gewisse Weise unser Leben bereichert. Design ist der Prozess, durch den solche Objekte geschaffen werden und nicht das Objekt selbst.

Die Zukunft des Designs ist die Zukunft einer bestimmten Denkweise, eines komplexen kreativen Vorgangs, der existentiell von der Humanität derer abhängt, an die er sich wendet. Designer haben immer für die bewussten oder unbewussten Bedürfnisse der Menschen gearbeitet und ihre Lösungen für neue oder uralte Probleme angeboten. Und das werden sie auch weiterhin tun. Die Veränderungen in Gesellschaft, Technologien und Materialien modifizieren die Palette an Möglichkeiten, die dem Designer für die Lösung von Problemen zur Verfügung steht. Aber der kreative Prozess selbst bleibt konstant in seiner Vielfalt und Unvorhersehbarkeit. Letzten Endes liegt die Zukunft des Designs jedoch nicht in den Händen der Designer, sondern sie beruht auf unserer Fähigkeit zu lächeln.« SEBASTIAN BERGNE

« Un objet peut faire sourire de multiples manières : par sa familiarité, par l'effet de surprise, par sa beauté, par la satisfaction qu'il apporte, par sa fierté, sa simplicité, son humour ou par l'émerveillement qu'il suscite. Si un objet déclenche cette réaction tout en répondant à la fonction pour laquelle il a été créé, c'est qu'il a été bien conçu. D'une certaine manière, il a amélioré notre vie. Le design est le processus par lequel ces objets sont créés, ce n'est pas l'objet en lui-même. L'avenir du design est celui d'une façon de penser, d'un processus créatif complexe qui, pour justifier son existence, dépend totalement de l'humanité de ceux auxquels il s'adresse.

Les designers ont toujours créé et créeront toujours pour satisfaire les besoins – connus ou inconnus – des hommes et offrir des solutions à leurs problèmes nouveaux ou ancestraux. Les changements sociaux, les innovations technologiques et les nouveaux matériaux modifient la palette dont ils disposent pour résoudre ces problèmes, mais le processus créatif reste toujours aussi varié et imprévisible. Toutefois, au bout du compte, l'avenir du design ne dépend pas des designers mais de notre capacité à sourire. »
SEBASTIAN BERGNE

3. ← Leg Over stool/Hocker/tabouret for Authentics, 1997
4. Torso lamp (drawings)/Lampe (Zeichnungen)/lampe (dessins), 1996

5

6

7

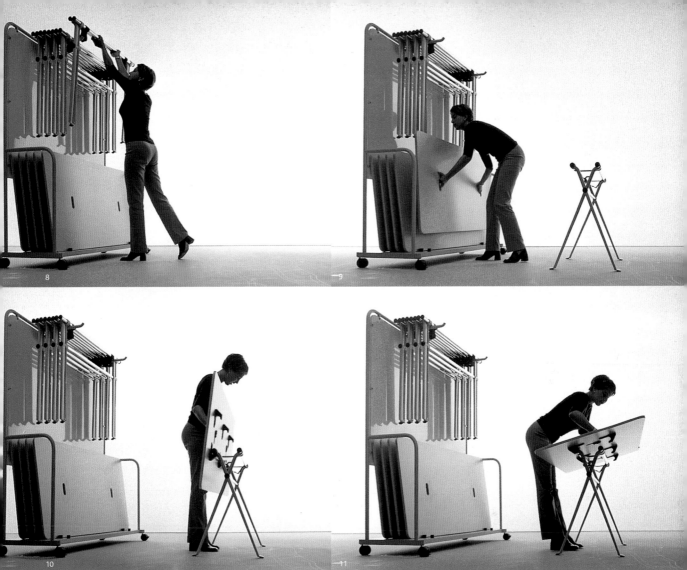

5. **Dr Spock** lamp (detail-prototype)/Lampe (Detail-Proto-typ)/lampe (détail-prototype) for O-Luce, 1999
6. **Dr Spock** table lamp (prototype)/Tischlampe (Proto-typ)/lampe (prototype)
for O-Luce, 1999
7. **Lid** pendant lamp/Hängelampe/plafonnier for O-Luce, 1997
8.-11. **IXIX** all-purpose table/Allzwecktisch/table polyvalente for Vitra, 1997
12. **Candloop** candlestick clip/Kerzenhalter/bougeoir-clip for Wireworks UK, 1998

SEBASTIAN BERGNE			CLIENTS
BORN	1966	Teheran, Iran (British)	Authentics
STUDIED	1985-88	BA (Hons) Industrial Design, Central St Martin's College of Art and Design, London	Driade
	1988-90	MA (Distinction) Industrial Design, Royal College of Art, London	Lexon
PRACTICE	1990	established Bergne: Design for Manufacture, London	O Luce
AWARDS	1993	Design Plus Award, Frankfurt/Main	Oreka Kids
	1998	International Design Prize, Nordrhein Westfalen; Design Plus Award, Frankfurt/Main	Procter & Gamble
	1999	2 Design Plus Awards, Frankfurt/Main; Roter Punkt Award, Design Zentrum Nordrhein-Westfalen, Essen; if Design Award, Hanover	Vitra
			Wireworks
	2000	Design Plus Award, Frankfurt/Main	WMF
	2001	Design Plus Award, Frankfurt/Main	
EXHIBITIONS	1992	*The Inventive Spirit*, Brussels	
	1993	*West*, Tokyo	
	1995	*Mutant Materials in Contemporary Design*, Museum of Modern Art, New York	
	1999	*Zuppa Inglese* touring exhibition, starting Milan	
	2000	*Freeze – Frame*, Design Museum, Lisbon	

13

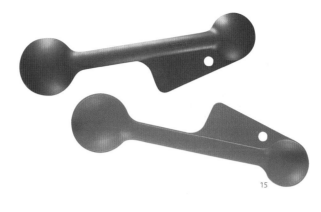

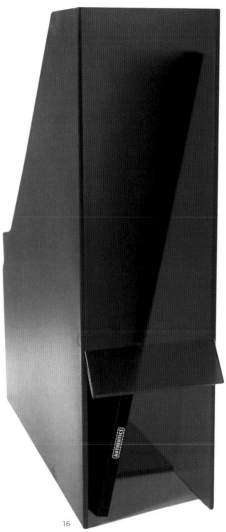

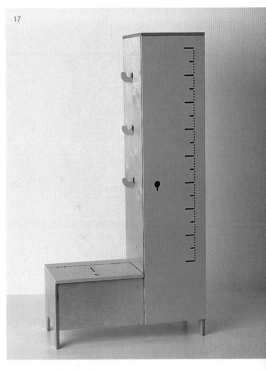

13. **Slot** chair/Stuhl/chaise for View, 2000
14. **Dovetail** bookends/Bücherstützen/serre-livres
for Authentics, 1997
15. **Sip** tasting spoons/Probierlöffel/cuillères de
dégustation for Authentics, 1997
16. **Index** standing file/Ablage/dossier for Authentics, 1996
17. **Flapjack** children's wardrobe/Kleiderschrank für
Kinder/garde-robe pour enfants for Oreka Kids, 2000

"Within our designs we try to juggle humour, technology and materials."

Bibi Gutjahr

Sven-Anwar Bibi, Alteburger Strasse 36, 50678 Cologne, Germany
T/F +49 221 310 1794 sven@bibi-gutjahr.de www.bibi-gutjahr.de
Mark Gutjahr, Metzer Strasse 24, 50677 Cologne, Germany
T +49 221 310 1717 F +49 221 310 1719 mark@bibi-gutjahr.de www.bibi-gutjahr.de

»In unseren Designentwürfen versuchen wir, mit Humor, Technologie und Material zu jonglieren.«

« Dans nos créations, nous tentons de conjuguer humour, technologie et matériaux. »

1. **Vetter Hans** chair/Stuhl/chaise from
the heimweh-Collection for Edra by Bibi/
Gutjahr/Zimmermann, 1999
2. ↓ **Missy** chair/Stuhl/chaise for Hidden
by Gutjahr/Rombinat, 2000

»Das Design der Zukunft wird eine Mischung aus high-tech Materialien und schönen Geschichten sein. Nachdem wir unsere eigene Designgeschichte neu entworfen haben, wird die Verschmelzung verschiedener Aspekte des Gestaltungsprozesses (formale, wirtschaftliche und ökologische) immer wichtiger für uns werden. Neue Medien und Technologien werden die Welt des Produktdesigns beeinflussen, ebenso wie es Kunst und Musik in früheren Generationen getan haben.
Computer sind zu einem Teil des Alltagslebens geworden – die virtuelle Realität ist nicht mehr bedrohlich. Das Instrumentarium hat sich verändert, die Mittel bleiben jedoch die selben. Design ist weder die endgültige Antwort auf alle Lebensfragen, noch kann es sämtliche Menschheitsprobleme lösen. Aber Design kann ein Lächeln hervorzuzaubern und uns helfen, bequem zu sitzen, gut zu schlafen und das Leben zu genießen. Vielleicht wird man den Designobjekten die zukünftigen Veränderungen nicht sofort ansehen, aber wenn man sie benutzt, wird man einen Unterschied feststellen.
Unsere Entwürfe sind sich der bevorstehenden Veränderungen bewusst – manchmal verarbeiten sie sie und manchmal ignorieren sie sie. In unseren Entwürfen versuchen wir, funktionalen Emotionalismus zu beschreiben – auf kurviger Graden der vollgestopften Warenwelt entgegen – immer wieder auf die Vergangenheit und die Zukunft blickend.« BIBI GUTJAHR

"The design of the future will be a mixture between high-tech materials and nice stories being told. After redesigning our own design history, the merging of different aspects of the design process (formal, economical and ecological) will become more and more important to us. New media and technologies will influence the world of product design just as much as art and music have done in previous generations. Computers have become an everyday experience to us – virtual reality is no longer shocking. The tools have changed but the means remain the same. Design is not the ultimate solution to life nor is it able to solve all of mankind's problems. But design can evoke a smile and enable comfortable sitting, good sleep and the enjoyment of life in a very pleasant way. Within design the changes of the future might not be visible at first glance, but while using designed objects, people will experience a difference. Our designs are aware of the changes ahead – sometimes they work with these changes and sometimes they ignore them. They try to depict functional emotionalism, a curved right angle approach towards the crowded world of products – always peeping back and forth in time."
BIBI GUTJAHR

« Le design du futur sera un mélange de matériaux high-tech et de belles histoires. Après avoir revu et corrigé notre propre histoire du design, la fusion des différents aspects de la création (formels, économiques, et écologiques) nous apparaîtra encore plus importante. Les nouveaux médias et la technologie influenceront le monde du design tout autant que l'art et la musique l'ont fait au cours des générations précédentes.
Les ordinateurs font désormais partie de notre vie quotidienne. La réalité virtuelle n'est plus choquante. Les outils ont changé mais les moyens restent les mêmes. S'il ne résout pas tous les problèmes de la vie et de l'humanité, le design peut faire naître un sourire. Il nous permet d'être assis confortablement, de bien dormir et de mieux apprécier la vie. Les transformations futures ne seront peut-être pas visibles tout de suite mais, en manipulant les objets, on sentira une différence. Nos créations tiennent compte des changements à venir. Parfois elles les exploitent, parfois pas. Elles cherchent à décrire une émotivité fonctionnelle, une approche indirecte du monde saturé des produits, lançant toujours un coup d'œil vers le passé et un autre vers l'avenir. »
BIBI GUTJAHR

3. **Marlene** leaning shelf/Lehnregal/casiers muraux for Hidden by Bibi/Rombinat, 2000
4. **High in the Sky** shelves/Regalsystem/bibliothèque for Hidden by Bibi/Rombinat, 2000
5. **Zebra** seat & lamp/Sitz & Lampe/banquette & lampe for Hidden by Rombinat, 2000

BIBI GUTJAHR		CLIENTS
FOUNDED	2000	Cologne by Sven-Anwar Bibi (b. 1971 Herford, Germany) and Mark Gutjahr (b. 1973 Kirchheim/Teck, Germany)	Edra Hidden
STUDIED		SVEN-ANWAR BIBI	Osram
	1993-96	cabinet-making apprenticeship, Herford, Germany	SDB
	1996-2001	Fachhochschule Köln, Fachbereich Design, Cologne	
		MARK GUTJAHR	
	1995-96	P.ART art school, Stuttgart	
	1996-2001	Fachhochschule Köln, Fachbereich Design, Cologne	
PRACTICE		SVEN-ANWAR BIBI	
	1998-2000	on editorial team of *about* magazine; co-founded kombinat design group with Mark Gutjahr and Jörg Zimmermann	
		MARK GUTJAHR	
	1997	internship TBWA, Munich	
	1998-2000	co-founded kombinat design group with Sven-Anwar Bibi and Jörg Zimmermann	
AWARDS	2000	*Architektur & Wohnen* Design Award; honorable mentioning at the Design for Europe Competition, Kortrijk	
EXHIBITIONS	1999	Designers Block, London; *heimweh*, Cologne	
	2000	Biennale, Turin; *Europalette*, Milan; *Design 4:3 – Fünfzig Jahre italienisches und deutsches Design*, Kunst- und Ausstellungshalle der Bundesrepublik Deutschland, Bonn; *waschtag*, an european design project, Cologne	
	2001	*drive in*, an international design project, Cologne	

4

5

"As far as I am presently concerned
(I do not know about the future), design
is what joins our senses to the soul,
thereby providing the only union that
produces happiness."

Riccardo Blumer

Riccardo Blumer, Via Scalette 1/B, 21 020 Casciago (Varese), Italy
T +39 0332 229 056   F +39 0332 822 840   architettoblumer@tin.it

»Soweit es mich gegenwärtig betrifft
(ich weiß nicht, wie es in der Zukunft
sein wird), ist Design das, was unsere
Sinne mit der Seele verbindet, und damit
ist es die einzige Vereinigung, die glücklich macht.«

« Au point où j'en suis aujourd'hui
(je ne sais pas si ce sera le cas dans
le futur), le design est ce qui lie nos
sens à l'âme, offrant la seule union
qui apporte le bonheur. »

1. **Laleggera** stool/Hocker/tabouret for Alias, 1999-2000
2. ↓ **LightGlass** table/Tisch for Alias, 1998

»Es ist faszinierend, sich Design als ein Feld wissenschaftlicher Forschung über die Zukunft der Menschheit vorzustellen. Nach vorne zu sehen in dem Versuch, die funktionalen Probleme der Menschen zu behandeln, bedeutet nicht nur, besser sitzen, besser beleuchten oder das Verhältnis zwischen Notwendigkeit und Praxis optimieren zu können. Es führt auch dazu, dass man die der Gegenwart zugrundeliegenden Gefühlsregungen entdeckt. Funktionalität ist nicht länger bloß eine Vereinfachung des Gebrauchs, sondern impliziert ebenso all die Pläne, die wir für unser Leben machen, und das in erster Linie auf spiritueller Ebene. Deshalb können wir heute frei über die Funktionalität des Geistes reden. Die Schönheit des Objekts ruft ein Gefühl hervor, das unser Leben formt. Dieses Gefühl ist Schönheit. In meiner Arbeitsweise entsteht die Beziehung zwischen äußerer Gestalt und innerem Gehalt im Design zwangsläufig aus dem Gefüge seiner Konstruktion. Die Aneignung dieser Methode führt uns immer näher an die Wahrheit heran, während sich alles andere im Laufe der Jahre einfach ›in Luft auflöst‹.«
RICCARDO BLUMER

"It is fascinating to think of design as a field of advanced research on the future of man. Looking ahead in an attempt to address man's functional problems means not only being able to sit down better, illuminate better, or optimize the relationship between necessity and practice, but also discovering the underlying sentiments of the present time. Functionality is no longer merely the simplification of use, but also implies all the plans we make in life, first and foremost on the spiritual level. This is why we can now speak freely about the functionality of the spirit. The beauty of the object provokes a feeling that constructs our life. This feeling is beauty. In the way I work, the relationship between image and substance in design inevitably arises from its constructive structure. The adoption of this method takes one closer and closer to the truth, while everything else easily 'evaporates' over the years."
RICCARDO BLUMER

« Il est fascinant de considérer le design comme un champ de recherche avancé sur l'avenir de l'homme. Se projeter en avant pour tenter de traiter les problèmes fonctionnels de l'homme signifie non seulement être mieux assis, mieux éclairé ou optimiser la relation entre la nécessité et la pratique, mais également découvrir les sentiments sousjacents du temps présent. La fonctionnalité n'est plus simplement la simplification de l'emploi, elle englobe aussi tous les projets que nous faisons dans la vie, surtout sur le plan spirituel. C'est pourquoi nous pouvons désormais parler librement de la fonctionnalité de l'esprit. La beauté de l'objet provoque un sentiment qui construit notre vie. Ce sentiment *est* beauté. Dans ma manière de travailler, la relation entre l'image et la substance découle inévitablement de la structure constructive du design. Adopter cette méthode nous rapproche de plus en plus de la vérité, alors que tout le reste " s'évapore " facilement au fil des ans. » RICCARDO BLUMER

3. **Mandraki** desk light/Schreibtischlampe/lampe de bureau
for Artemide, 1996
4. **Laleggera** chair/Stuhl/chaise for Alias, 1996
5. **Ilvolo** table/Tisch for Alias, 1999-2000
6. **LightGlass** table (detail)/Tisch (Detail)/table (détail)
for Alias, 1998

		RICCARDO BLUMER	CLIENTS
BORN	1959	Bergamo, Italy	Agea
STUDIED	1972-77	Art diploma Liceo Sperimentale Unificato, Milan	Alias
	1977-82	architecture, Politecnico di Milano	Artemide
	1982	Laurea degree (Urban Design), Politecnico di Milano	Cassina
PRACTICE	1983-89	worked in Mario Botta's architectural practice in Lugano	Danese
	1989	established own architectural/design office	Lumina Italia
	1990-	commercial, residential office projects and buildings; interior and industrial design	Nemo
	1993-96	member of the building commission for the provinces of Milan and Varese	Promelit
	1996	participated in the formation of the Accademia di Architettura della Svizzera Italiana	
AWARDS	1997	Design-Preis Schweiz (First Prize), Switzerland	
	1998	Compasso d'Oro, Milan; Catas Prize, Udine	
	2000	Observeur du Design prize A. P. C. I., Paris	
EXHIBITIONS	1991	*Halogen – 20 Jahre neues Licht*, Museum für Angewandte Kunst, Cologne, Museum für Kunsthandwerk, Frankfurt/Main	
	1995	*Aperto Architettura '95*, Flash Art Museum, Trevi	
	1996	*Riccardo Blumer, architetture, design, Il progetto Laleggera, un libro*, Paris; *Riccardo Blumer Architekt Designer*, Basle	
	1999	*Riccardo Blumer – Intersezioni*, Milan; *Deconstructing Design*, Milan	
	2000	*Riccardo Blumer – Ultime realizzazioni: sperimentazione e professione*, Bergamo; *Riccardo Blumer – Intersezioni*, Padua	

4

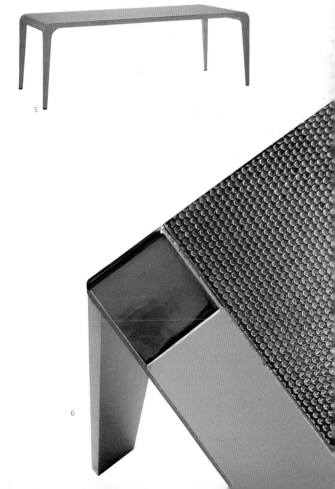

5

6

"Life meets death in objects
as in the theatre of life."

Jonas Bohlin

Jonas Bohlin, Jonas Bohlin Design AB, Södermalmstorg 4, 11645 Stockholm, Sweden
T +46 8 615 2389 F +46 8 615 2398 info@jonasbohlindesign.se
www.scandinaviandesign.com/jonasbohlin

»Das Leben trifft mit dem Tod zusammen, in Objekten ebenso wie im Theater
des Lebens.«

« La vie rencontre la mort dans des
objets comme dans le théâtre de la
vie. »

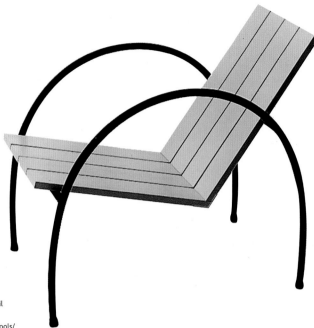

1. **Liv-Collection** easy-chair/Stuhl/fauteuil
(self-production), 1997
2. ↓ **Liv-Collection** pendant lamps and stools/
Hängelampen und Hocker/lustres et tabourets
(self-production), 1997

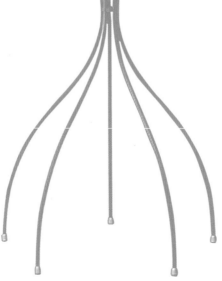

»Zur Zeit arbeite ich an einem Objekt mit dem Titel ›Theater‹. Dabei handelt es sich um einen bettähnlichen Tisch aus schwarz gestrichenem Stahl und weiß gestrichenem Holz mit einem handgemalten Kissen, einem ledernen Polster und einem aus seiner Rinde geschälten Zweig. Es wird ein Objekt sein, mit dem man leben und interagieren kann. Ich will, dass meine Möbel berühren und erfreuen, dass sie mit Zeit und Raum kommunizieren, mit der Hand und dem Herzen gemacht und achtsam gegenüber Mensch und Natur sind. Möbel sind zum Gebrauch bestimmt, können jedoch auch Stärke und Seelenruhe vermitteln. In ihnen trifft das Funktionale mit dem Dekorativen zusammen, das Kommerzielle mit dem Künstlerischen und das Unendliche mit dem Endlichen.«
JONAS BOHLIN

"Right now I am working on a piece entitled 'Theatre'. The idea is to create a bed-like table of black painted steel and white painted wood with a hand-painted pillow, a leather-upholstered cushion and a branch stripped of its bark. It will be a piece to live with and to interact with. I want my furniture to touch and please, to communicate with time and space, to be made by hand and heart, and to be considerate of mankind and nature. Furniture is meant to be used yet it can also provide strength and peace. Functional meets decorative. Commercial meets artistic. Infinite meets finite." JONAS BOHLIN

« En ce moment, je travaille sur une pièce intitulée " Théâtre ". C'est une table qui rappelle un lit, en acier noir et en bois blanc, avec un oreiller peint à la main, un coussin en cuir et une branche écorcée. Ce sera une pièce avec laquelle vivre et interagir. Je voudrais que mes meubles émeuvent et plaisent, qu'ils communiquent avec le temps et l'espace, qu'ils soient faits à la main et avec le cœur, et qu'ils respectent l'homme et la nature. Les meubles sont faits pour être utilisés mais cela ne doit pas les empêcher de conférer un sentiment de force et de paix, d'être fonctionnels *et* décoratifs, commerciaux *et* artistiques, infinis *et finis.* » JONAS BOHLIN

3. **Spira** coat-stand/Kleiderständer/portemanteau (self-production), 1999
4. **Formula 2000** sofa/Sofa (self-production), 1999
5. **Liv-Collection** table/Tisch (self-production), 1997
6. **Liv-Collection** chair/Stuhl/chaise (self-production), 1999

JONAS BOHLIN		CLIENTS
BORN	1953	Stockholm, Sweden	Asplund
STUDIED	1976-81	Interior Architecture, Konstfackskolan (National College of Arts, Crafts and Design), Stockholm	Jonas Bohlin Design
PRACTICE	1983	established own architectural office	Källemo
	1985-87	founded "Stockholm Mobile" art/design gallery, Stockholm	Kasthall
	1988-	professor, Beckman's School of Design, Stockholm	Lammhults
	1991-93	Chairman of SIR (The National Association of Swedish Interior Architects)	Reimyre
	1998	established Bohlin Design in Stockholm	Rörstrand
AWARDS	1981	Konstfackskolan scholarship, National College of Arts, Crafts and Design, Stockholm	
	1981	Svensk Form scholarship, Swedish Society of Crafts and Design, Stockholm	
	1983 & 92	honorary mention, Excellent Swedish Design Award, Stockholm	
	1984	Swedish State Cultural Grant	
	1985	Grant, Estrid Ericson Foundation	
	1986	Grant, Swedish Board of Fine Arts	
	1988	The Georg Jensen Prize, Copenhagen	
	1989	Best Interior of the Year, *Forum* magazine	
	1994	Project grant, Swedish State Fund for the Arts	
	1997	Major grant, Swedish State Fund for the Arts	
EXHIBITIONS	1985	*Art & Craft 100 Years*, National Art Gallery, Stockholm	
	1986	*Nordic Furniture Design*, Design Center, Malmö	
	1987	*A Way of Life*, touring exhibition, Japan	
	1988	*Excellent Swedish Design*, touring exhibition, USA	
	1991-92	*Swedish Design*, touring exhibition, India	
	1993	*Four Furniture Designers: Mathsson/Chambert/Kandell/Bohlin*, National Art Gallery, Stockholm	
	1994	*Nordic Profiles*, National Art Gallery, touring exhibition, Stockholm & Scandinavia	
	1997	*Nordic Touch*, Kalmar Art Museum, Kalmar	
	1998	*Sven Lundh's Eye*, Färgfabriken gallery, Stockholm	
	1999	*Sweden Builds*, Museum of Architecture, Stockholm	
	2000	*Angles Suedois*, European travelling exhibition; *Designers for Their Time*, Rörstrand	

4

5

6

"Our work finds its characteristic in a diversity of approaches, from industry to craft, from the micro to the macro."

R. & E. Bouroullec

Ronan & Erwan Bouroullec, 51 Rue des Ursulines, 93200 Saint Denis, France
T/F +33 1 4820 3660 bouroullec@wanadoo.fr

»Unsere Arbeit ist gekennzeichnet durch eine Mannigfaltigkeit der Herangehensweisen: von der Industrie zum Handwerk, vom Mikro- zum Makro-Bereich.«

« Notre travail se caractérise par la diversité des approches, de l'industrie à l'artisanat, du micro au macro. »

1. **Square** vase/Vase for Cappellini, 1999
2. ↓ **Lis Clos** bed/Bett/lit for Cappellini, 2000

« Le futur du design tend pour nous vers un déplacement des domaines d'interventions, moins lié a la seule question de l'objet ou de la propriété, il repose sur une harmonie des situations, un écosystème personnel équilibré. La production s'établira, dans le futur, autour des propriétés/capacités qu'auront les objets/les hommes/le savoir, à reguler les tensions engendrées par une vie en mouvement. Se dégageant ainsi d'une notion d'objet, le design alors engendré par un système complexe, sera une intelligence des situations, une liberté permanente de mouvement. Des objets/matériaux/ustensiles sensibles (thermorégulation, du léger au lourd, etc.) pourront déjà accompagner le corps de l'homme d'une manière réactive, mais, par-delà la notion de sensations/facilités/conforts, la question sera surtout celle d'une intelligence des dialogues entre l'objet, les différentes dimensions de sa production et celui qui en jouit; où les efforts consentis par chacun concrétisent cet écosystème serein et conscient de son développement/histoire. » RONAN & ERWAN BOUROULLEC

3. ← **Torique** ceramic collection/Keramikwaren/ligne de céramiques for Vallauris (limited edition), 1999
4. **Torique** ceramic stools/Keramikstühle/tabourets en céramique for Vallauris (limited edition), 1999

"We believe the future of design will tend towards a displacement of the fields of intervention. It will no longer rest solely on the question of the object or property, but rather on a harmony of situations, on a balanced personal ecosystem. In the future, production will be established around the properties/capacities of objects/people/the management of the tensions generated by a constant movement in life.
Liberated from the concept of the object, design will be generated by a more complex system which will involve an understanding of situations and a permanent freedom of movement. Objects/materials/sensitive devices (thermoregulated, lighter instead of heavier, etc.) are already able to accompany the human body in a responsive way. But, beyond the concept of emotions/ease of operation/comfort, it will be a question above all of a knowledge of the dialogues between an object, the various dimensions of its production and the user; where the individual efforts that have gone into its realization reflect a well-balanced ecosystem and an awareness of its development/history."
RONAN & ERWAN BOUROULLEC

»Wir glauben, dass die Zukunft des Designs zu einer Verlagerung der Interventionsebenen tendieren wird. Es wird nicht länger ausschließlich um die Frage von Objekt oder Besitz gehen, sondern mehr um eine Harmonie der Situationen, um ein ausgeglichenes persönliches Ökosystem. In Zukunft wird sich die Produktion von Design ansiedeln um Eigenschaften/Fähigkeiten von Objekten/Menschen/Wissen, wie sich die von einem sich kontinuierlich verändernden Leben erzeugten Spannungen in Grenzen halten lassen. Befreit vom Konzept des Objekts wird Design durch ein komplexeres System hervorgebracht werden und ein Verständnis für Situationen sowie eine dauerhafte Bewegungsfreiheit umfassen. Objekte/Materialien/sensitive Vorrichtungen (wärmereguliert, leichter statt schwerer etc.) sind bereits heute imstande, den menschlichen Körper auf stabilisierende Weise zu begleiten. Über das Konzept der Gefühle/des Bedienungskomforts hinaus aber geht es besonders um eine Kenntnis der kommunikativen Verbindungen zwischen einem Objekt, den verschiedenen Dimensionen seiner Fertigung und dem Anwender. An diesem Punkt reflektieren die individuellen Bemühungen, die in die Realisierung des Objekts eingeflossen sind, ein wohl ausbalanciertes Ökosystem und ein Bewusstsein seiner Entwicklung/Geschichte.« RONAN & ERWAN BOUROULLEC

	RONAN & ERWAN BOUROULLEC		CLIENTS

RONAN & ERWAN BOUROULLEC

CLIENTS

Ardi
Authentics
Boffi
Cappellini
Domeau & Perès
Evans and Wong
Habitat
littala
Issey Miyake
La Monnaie de Paris
Ligne Roset
Magis
Ricard
Rosenthal
Smack Iceland
Sommer
Units

BORN — RONAN BOUROULLEC
1971 Quimper, France

ERWAN BOUROULLEC
1976 Quimper, France

STUDIED — RONAN BOUROULLEC
1991 Industrial Design diploma, École Nationale Supérieure des Arts Appliqués et des Métiers d'Arts, Paris
1995 post-graduate diploma, École Nationale Supérieure des Arts Décoratifs, Paris

ERWAN BOUROULLEC
1999 diploma, École Nationale d'Arts, Cergy

PRACTICE — RONAN BOUROULLEC
1995 began work as freelance designer
1997 taught at the École Nationale des Beaux Arts, Nancy
1998 taught at the École Nationale des Beaux Arts, Saint-Étienne
1999 established partnership with his brother Erwan
2000 taught at the École Cantonale d'Art, Lausanne, and at the École Nissim de Camondo, Paris

ERWAN BOUROULLEC
1998 began assisting his brother Ronan on numerous projects
1999 established partnership with Ronan

AWARDS — RONAN BOUROULLEC
1998 First Prize, Biennale du Design, Saint-Étienne; grand prize Salon du Meuble, Paris
1999 New Designer Award, International Contemporary Furniture Fair, New York

EXHIBITIONS
1997 *Homo Domus*, French Cultural Centre, Milan; *Made in France*, Centre Georges Pompidou, Paris
1998 *La vie en Rose*, Fondation Cartier, Paris
1999-2000 *A Grand Design*, Victoria & Albert Museum, London; *Joint-Venture*, Neuilly
2000 solo exhibition, Galerie Peyroulet & Cie, Paris; *Byob*, Galerie Néotu, Paris

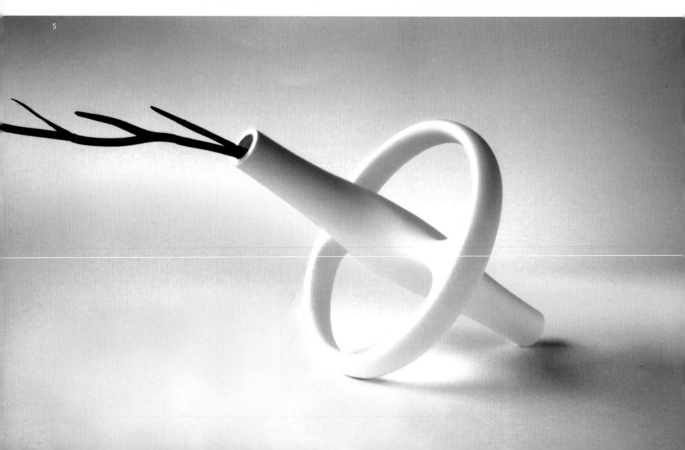

5

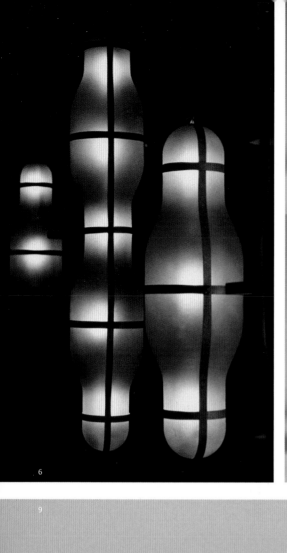

6

7

5. **Sans Titre** vase/Vase for Cappellini, 1998
6. **Hole** lamps/Lampen/lampes for Cappellini, 1999
7. **Vases Combinatoires Collection** polyurethane vase/
Vase aus Polyurethan/vase polyuréthane for Galerie
Néotu, 1997
8. **Vases Combinatoires Collection**/Vasen/vases for
Galerie Néotu, 1997
9. **Safe Rest** day-bed/Liege/lit de repos for Domeau &
Pérès, 1999

8

9

"The difference between good design and bad design is like the difference between a good story and a bad joke: one is worth hearing again and again; the other, preferably not!"

Julian Brown

Julian Brown, StudioBrown, 6, Princes Buildings, George Street, Bath BA1 2ED, England
T +44 1225 481 735 F +44 1225 481 737 Julian@studiobrown.com

»Der Unterschied zwischen gutem und schlechtem Design ist wie der Unterschied zwischen einer guten Geschichte und einem schlechten Witz: erstere kann man sich wieder und wieder anhören, den zweiten besser nicht!«

« La différence entre un bon et un mauvais design est comme celle entre une bonne histoire et une mauvaise blague : on ne se lasse pas d'entendre la première alors que la seconde, une fois c'est déjà de trop ! »

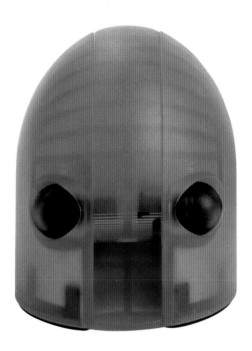

1.-2. **Hannibal** tape dispenser/Klebebandspender/
distributeur de ruban adhésif for Rexite, 1998

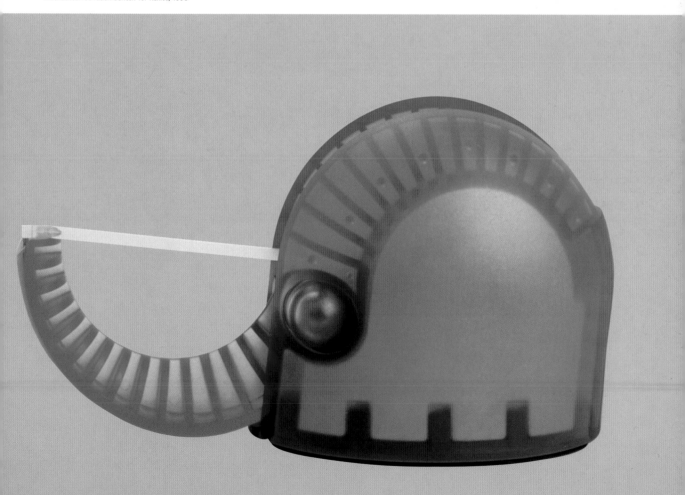

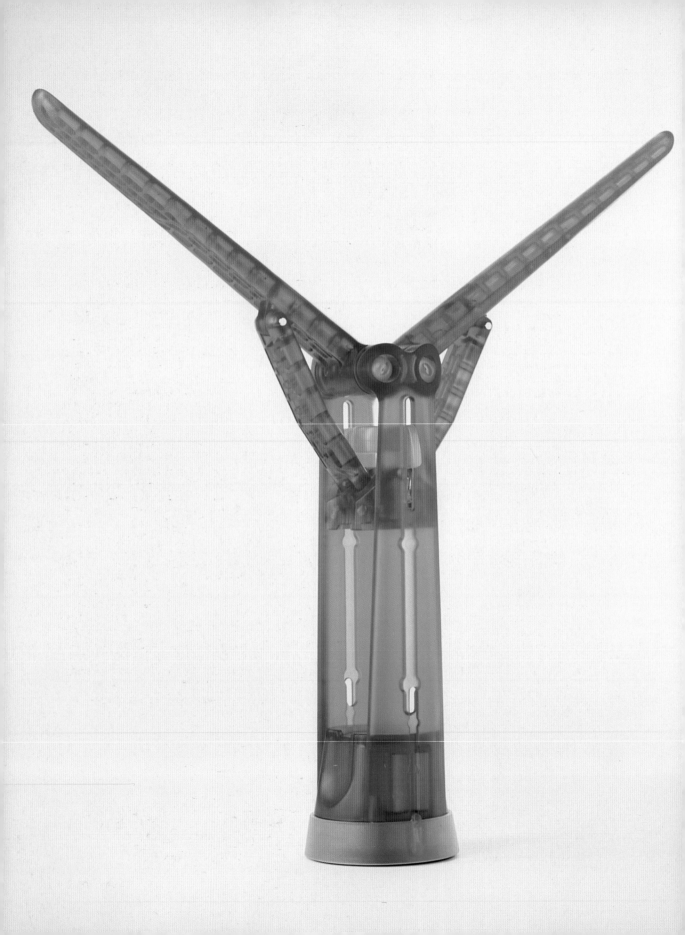

« Comme l'expérience et la culture, le design reflète son époque et les technologies de son temps. Il répond à un objectif commun : servir et aider l'homme en lui permettant d'être efficace (sur le plan physique et émotionnel) dans les environnements qu'il s'est choisis. Cela ne devrait pas changer et ne changera probablement jamais. Le processus de la création non plus n'a pas besoin de changer. En effet, les racines intellectuelles et " artisanales " du design sont toujours aussi solides. On ne peut nier que la technologie, les ordinateurs et le web contribuent énormément à la recherche et à l'implantation de nouveaux designs, mais rien ne pourra jamais remplacer les mains, le cerveau et la sensibilité de l'homme. De fait, je suis convaincu que, plus la technologie nous soutiendra et progressera, plus nous verrons clairement ce dont nous avons besoin et envie, et plus nous trouverons des moyens créatifs d'arriver à nos fins. Les ordinateurs et les machines (les outils) ne sont que des aides. Les designers les plus influents seront ceux qui n'ont jamais rejeté ces racines et ont l'individualité, le souffle et la souplesse de pratiquer leur " artisanat " au sein de différentes cultures d'entreprise. A la longue, cela favorisera le retour du " conseiller " ou " designer " individuel et expert, comme ce fut le cas de Charles Eames, de Herman Miller ou d'Eliot Noyes chez IBM. En conclusion, le " design " devrait surfer sur la vague de la technologie (en tant que maître, pas maîtresse) tandis que les philosophies originales et individuelles seront de plus en plus recherchées et appréciées. » JULIAN BROWN

3. ← **Attila** beverage can compactor/Pressgerät für Getränkedosen/compacteur de canettes for Rexite, 1996
4. **X-Act** wineglasses/Weingläser/verres à vin for FX Nachtmann, 2000

"Like experience and culture, design reflects the times and technologies of today, but at its centre is a common purpose, namely to serve and assist man and to enable him to perform (physically and emotionally) within any of his chosen environments. This should not and probably never will change. Neither does the design process itself need to change; indeed, the intellectual and 'craft' roots of design remain as sound today as they ever were. It is undeniable that technology, computers and the web assist enormously in the research and implementation of new designs, but the brain, hands and feel of man will never be substituted. Indeed, I am confident that the more advanced our supportive technology becomes, the freer we will become to see clearly what we need or want to do and to find imaginative ways of getting there. Computers or machines (tools) will simply aid us. The designers who will contribute the most will be those who have never discarded these roots and who have the individuality, breadth and flexibility to practice their 'craft' within different enterprise cultures. Historically, this too will turn the tide in favour of the single or expert 'advisor' or 'designer', as was the case with Charles Eames and Herman Miller or Eliot Noyes at IBM. To conclude, while 'design' should ride the waves of technology (as master not mistress), unique and individual philosophies will become increasingly sought after and valued." JULIAN BROWN

»Ebenso wie unsere Lebenspraxis und Kultur spiegelt Design die Verhältnisse und Technologien unserer Zeit wider. Das Wesentliche am Design ist jedoch ein allgemeiner Zweck, nämlich den Menschen zu dienen und ihnen zu helfen, die an sie in ihren individuell gewählten Lebenswelten gestellten physischen und emotionalen Anforderungen zu erfüllen. Das sollte sich nicht und wird sich wahrscheinlich auch nie ändern. Auch der Gestaltungsprozess selbst muss sich nicht verändern, denn tatsächlich sind die intellektuellen und ›handwerklichen‹ Wurzeln des Designs heute so intakt wie eh und je. Unbestreitbar bedeuten Technik, Computer und World Wide Web eine enorme Erleichterung bei der Entwicklung und Ausführung neuer Designprodukte, aber nichts wird jemals Verstand, Hände und Gefühl des Menschen ersetzen können. Ich bin sogar zuversichtlich, dass wir, je ausgefeilter unsere technischen Hilfsmittel werden, desto klarer erkennen können, was wir brauchen oder wollen, und phantasievolle Wege finden werden, unsere Ziele zu erreichen. Computer oder Maschinen sind lediglich Werkzeuge, die uns dabei helfen. Die einflussreichsten Designer werden jene sein, die diese Wurzeln nie aufgegeben haben und die über die Individualität, den Weitblick und die Flexibilität verfügen, um ihr ›Handwerk‹ in unterschiedlichen Unternehmenskulturen auszuüben. Im Hinblick auf die Vergangenheit lässt sich voraussagen, dass diese Entwicklung einen Umschwung zugunsten des einzelnen, erfahrenen Beraters oder Designers einleiten wird, wie es auch bei Charles Eames und Herman Miller oder Eliot Noyes bei IBM der Fall war. Abschließend gesagt: Während ›das Design‹ auf der Technologiewelle reiten sollte (als Gebieter, nicht als Geliebter), werden ungewöhnliche und individuelle Denkmodelle zunehmend gefragt sein und geschätzt werden.« JULIAN BROWN

JULIAN BROWN

BORN	1955	Northampton, England
STUDIED	1978	BA (Hons) Industrial Design, Leicester Polytechnic
	1981-83	MA Industrial Design, Royal College of Art, London
PRACTICE	1979-80	David Carter Associates, England
	1983-86	Porsche Design Studio, Zell am See, Austria
	1986	co-founded Lovegrove Brown design studio with Ross Lovegrove, London
	1990	founded StudioBrown, Bath
	1992	guest professor Hochschule der Künste, Berlin
AWARDS	1996	Good Design Award, Chicago Athenaeum
	1998	Best of Category, *I. D. Magazine Annual Design Review* Award, New York; Elected RDI (Royal Designer for Industry) by the Royal Society of Arts, London
	1999	Best New Product, Stationery Fair, New York; two Good Design Awards, Chicago Athenaeum; iF Product Design Award, Hanover

CLIENTS

Acco
Alfi Zitzmann
Bauknecht
Boker
Curver
Frighetto
FX Nachtmann
Johnson & Johnson
NEC
Piz Buin
Rexite
Sony
WMF

5

6

7

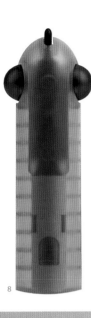

5. **Pump and Go** pump flask/Pumpflasche/bouteille avec siphon for Alfi Zitzmann, 1999

6. **La Ola** vacuum flask/Isolierflasche/bouteille Thermos for Alfi Zitzmann, 1997

7. **Active Use Binder 1.5** file/Ablage/classeur for Acco Brands Inc, 1999

8.-9. **Isis** stapler/Hefter/agrafeuse for Rexite, 1999

10. **Titanum** cooking knives/Küchenmesser/couteaux de cuisine for Boker, 2000

11. **CD.2** cd storage system/CD-Aufbewahrungssystem/ système de rangement pour cd for Rexite, 2000

10

8

9

11

"Communication not decoration."

Debbie Jane Buchan

Debbie Jane Buchan, 3, Hutchison Avenue, Edinburgh EH14 1QE, Scotland
T +44 131 539 9036

»Kommunikation statt Dekoration.«

« La communication, pas la décoration. »

1. **Wee Flowers** surface design (prototype)/
Oberflächendesign (Prototyp)/design de surface
(prototype), 1999
2. ↓ **Red Optic 3 Seps** surface design (prototype)/
Oberflächendesign (Prototyp)/design de surface
(prototype), 1998

»Mich hat immer schon die Frage beschäftigt, was Design eigentlich ist, und welche Bedeutung es in der heutigen Gesellschaft hat. Jean Nouvel hat einmal gesagt: ›Design wird weitgehend zu Stil‹. Viele Leute würden sich dem anschließen und behaupten, Design werde bedeutungslos. Ich bin zwar nicht der Ansicht, Design an sich sei bedeutungslos, aber ich denke, der Begriff ›Design‹ wird an Bedeutung verlieren, und insofern wird Design tatsächlich weitgehend zu Stil.
Außerdem glaube ich, dass Designer, die ihren Arbeiten einen bestimmten ›-ismus‹ umhängen, das pluralistische Wesen der Kultur leugnen. Wenn Design ein Ausdruck seiner Zeit sein soll, muss es jedoch die Komplexität dieser Zeit ausdrücken, dabei eng mit den Sinnen zusammenarbeiten und diese zutiefst respektieren. Möglicherweise ist das eine künstlerische und romantische Vorstellung, aber was ist das Leben anderes als eine Sache des Gefühls und des Ausdrucks? Wir können ein neues Verständnis nicht nur von der Welt, sondern vor allem von uns selbst vermitteln, wenn wir nach Kommunikation statt nach Dekoration suchen.
Die Erscheinungsform ist wichtig, aber sie sollte nicht alles andere dominieren. Die Entwicklung des Designs sollte vielmehr durch die Eigenart des Denkens und der Philosophie bestimmt werden. Für mich sind die Schlüsselwörter für das Design der Zukunft: Expressivität, Freiheit, Erforschung, Kommunikation und Kreativität.
Wir sollten den Kommerzial-ismus vergessen und zu vermeiden suchen, dass wir in den kommenden Jahren zu Opfern der Mode werden.« DEBBIE JANE BUCHAN

"It has always been a preoccupation of mine to understand what design actually is and what it means in today's society. Many people would agree with Jean Nouvel's statement that 'Design is becoming largely style' and say that design is becoming meaningless. While I do not believe that design is meaningless, I do tend to think that the word is becoming so and that design is largely becoming style.
I also believe that to design with any singular 'ism' denies the pluralistic nature of culture. But for a design to be an expression of its time, it must be an expression of its complexity, where it works in close proximity to and has a deep consideration of the senses. Possibly this is an artistic and romantic notion, but what is life if not emotive and expressive? We can relate a new understanding not only of the world but more importantly of ourselves if we explore communication rather than decoration. Image is important but should not be dominant. It is the nature of thought and philosophy that should dictate design development. For me, the key words for design in the future are 'expression', 'freedom', 'exploration', 'communication' and 'creativity'. Forget the commercialism and let's try and avoid becoming victims of fashion in the years ahead." DEBBIE JANE BUCHAN

« J'ai toujours cherché à comprendre ce qu'était le design et ce qu'il signifiait dans la société d'aujourd'hui. Beaucoup de gens conviendraient avec Jean Nouvel que "le design est en train de devenir un style au sens large " et diraient qu'il perd son sens. Si je ne suis pas d'accord avec cette dernière affirmation, j'admets que le terme lui-même ne veut plus dire grand chose et que le design est effectivement en passe de devenir style.
Je pense aussi que créer un design en lui attachant un "isme", c'est nier la pluralité de la culture. Toutefois, pour qu'une création soit l'expression de son époque, elle doit exprimer sa complexité, fonctionner en étroite collaboration avec les sens et respecter ces derniers. C'est sans doute là une notion artistique et romantique, mais la vie n'est-elle pas une question d'émotion et d'expression ? Nous acquerrons une meilleure compréhension du monde et, plus important, de nous-mêmes, en explorant la communication plutôt que la décoration. L'image est importante mais ne devrait pas primer. C'est l'essence de la pensée et de la philosophie qui devrait dicter l'évolution du design. Pour moi, les mots clefs de l'avenir sont "expression", "liberté", "exploration", "communication" et "créativité". Oublions le commercial-isme et évitons d'être victimes de la mode dans les années à venir. » DEBBIE JANE BUCHAN

3. **Daisy** textile/Stoff (self-production, limited-edition), 1999
4. **DJB-Blue** computer-generated surface design (prototype)/computergeneriertes Oberflächendesign (Prototyp)/design de surface généré par ordinateur (prototype), 1998
5. **Hidden Rectangles** silk-screen textile (prototype)/Siebdruckgewebe (Prototyp)/textile en sérigraphie, 1998
6. **Contemporary Florals-Blue** computer generated surface design (prototype)/computergeneriertes Oberflächendesign (Prototyp)/design de surface généré par ordinateur (prototype), 2000

DEBBIE JANE BUCHAN

BORN	1973	Edinburgh, Scotland
STUDIED	1991-95	BA(Hons) Textiles and Surface Decoration, Gray's School of Art, Robert Gordon University, Aberdeen
	1995-96	MA Art & Design Gray's School of Art, Robert Gordon University, Aberdeen
PRACTICE	1996-98	in-house design for Slumberdown Enterprises Ltd.
	1998-	instructor in AVA CAD/CAM technology, Macclesfield
AWARDS	1994	Commendation RSA (Royal Society of Arts) Design Awards
	1995	Abertay Paper Sacks Colour Award
	1997	Grampian Arts Trust Window Design
EXHIBITIONS	1989	Haymarket, Edinburgh
	1995	Nagoya University of Arts, Japan; *New Designers*, London

CLIENTS

Abertay Paper Sacks
Brit Bit Limited
First Bus
Slumberdown Enterprises
Snugfit International

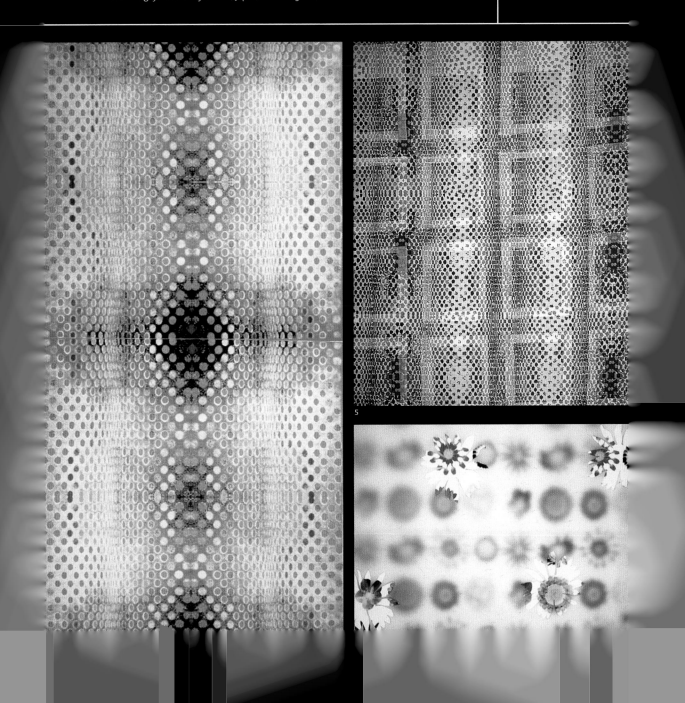

5

"Products need more than perfect
function and ergonomics, they need
some poetry."

 büro für form.

Benjamin Hopf & Constantin Wortmann, Büro für Form, Hans-Sachs-Str. 12, 80 469 Munich, Germany
T +49 89 26 949 000 F +49 89 26 949 002 buerofuerform@metronet.de www.buerofuerform.de

»Produkte brauchen mehr als perfekte
Funktion und Ergonomie, sie brauchen
Poesie.«

« Il faut aux produits plus qu'une fonctionnalité et une ergonomie parfaites,
ils ont besoin de poésie. »

1. **Tria** modular hanging lamp/Hängelampe/
lustre for Habitat, 2000
2. ↓ **Eat & Lounge** chaise longue & thronelike chair
(prototype)/Liege & thronartiger Stuhl (Prototyp), 1999

»Unser Zeitalter der rapiden technologischen Veränderung und des wachsenden Konsums hat das Design verändert: Jedes Jahr werden noch mehr neue Produkte mit noch kürzerer Lebensdauer entwickelt. Während hierbei die Faktoren Zeit, Kosten, Daten und Funktion bestimmend sind, stellen sie gleichzeitig Gebote dar, die wiederum ein Bedürfnis nach Träumen und Gefühlen erzeugen. Die Qualität der Dinge, mit denen wir uns umgeben, können bei der Erfüllung dieses Bedürfnisses eine wichtige Rolle spielen. Bei Design geht es um mehr als nur um das Objekt selbst. Und es geht auch nicht bloß darum, ein Produkt durch einen neuen Stil aufzupolieren. Produkte korrespondieren mit unseren Bedürfnissen und Wünschen und haben einen direkten Einfluss auf unsere Lebensqualität. Je besser ein Produkt ist, desto länger wird man es behalten. Das ist gut für die Umwelt. Das Design der Zukunft wird diesen ökologischen Aspekt berücksichtigen müssen, während es gleichzeitig auf neue und sinnvolle Art eine Verbindung zwischen Funktionalität und Emotionalität – also zwischen der physischen und der psychologischen Verwendung eines Produkts – herstellt.« BÜRO FÜR FORM.

"Our age of rapid technological change and increasing consumption has changed design – each year even more new products are developed with an even shorter lifespan. While time, costs, facts and function are the determining factors in this, they are dictates that create the need for dreams and emotion. The quality of the things with which we surround ourselves can play an important part in fulfilling this need. Design is about more than just the object. Nor is it simply about revamping a product in a new style. Products correspond with our needs and desires and impact directly on the quality of our lives. The better a product is the longer it will be kept. This is good for the environment. Design in the future will have to take this into consideration while combining functionality and emotion – the physical and psychological use of a product – in new and more meaningful ways." BÜRO FÜR FORM.

« Notre époque de transformations technologiques rapides et de consommation accrue a modifié le design : chaque année, on développe toujours plus de produits à la durée de vie réduite. Si le temps, le coût, les faits et la fonction sont des facteurs déterminants dans ce phénomène, ce sont autant de diktats qui créent un besoin de rêves et d'émotions. La qualité des objets dont nous nous entourons peut jouer un rôle important dans la satisfaction de ce besoin. Le design, c'est plus que l'objet lui-même. Il ne s'agit pas uniquement de re-dessiner un produit pour l'adapter à un nouveau style. Celui-ci doit correspondre à nos besoins et à nos désirs et influencer directement notre qualité de vie. Mieux un produit est conçu, plus on le gardera longtemps. C'est bon pour l'environnement. A l'avenir, le design devra en tenir compte tout en conjuguant fonctionnalité et émotion – l'utilisation physique et psychologique d'un produit – de manières nouvelles et plus censées. » BÜRO FÜR FORM.

3. **Fingermax** paint brush/Malerpinsel/pinceau for Fingermax GBR, 1998-99
4. **Flat** chair/Stuhl/chaise for Habitat, 2000
5. **Dio** modular hanging lamp/Hängelampe/lustre for Habitat, 2000
6. **Il Crollo** chair/Stuhl/chaise for Kundalini, 2000

		BÜRO FÜR FORM.	CLIENTS

FOUNDED	1998	Munich, Germany by Benjamin Hopf (b. 1971 Hamburg) and Constantin Wortmann (b. 1970 Munich)	Fingermax
STUDIED		BENJAMIN HOPF	Habitat
	1998	MA Industrial Design, University of Design, Munich	Kundalini
		CONSTANTIN WORTMANN	Next
	1998	MA Industrial Design, University of Design, Munich	
AWARDS	1997	Hewi Innovation Award (special award); Hoesch Design Award (special award)	
	1998	Nachlux (special award); Designale Third Prize	
	1999	Bonaldo Design Contest (Third Prize); Design Award Neunkirchen (Second Prize)	
	2000	Best of Category, iF Design Award, Hanover; Design for Europe, Kortrijk	
EXHIBITIONS	1999	*Light & Lounge*, Büro für Form, Munich	
	2000	*Light & Lounge*, International Furniture Fair, Cologne; *Urban Gravity*, International Furniture Fair, Milan; *Liquid Light*, Munich; *Form 2000*, International Furniture Fair, Cologne	
	2001	*Charlie's Angels*, International Furniture Fair, Milan	

"We subvert the utility of materials
so as to create in our objects a restless
world of experimentation, creativity
and innovation."

F. & H. Campana

Fernando & Humberto Campana, R. Barão de Tatuí 219, São Paulo SP, 01 226-030 Brazil
T +55 11 366 64152   F +55 11 382 53408   campanad@uol.com.br

*»Wir hinterfragen die Nützlichkeit von
Materialien, um mit unseren Objekten
eine rastlose Welt der Experimente, Kreativität und Innovation zu erschaffen.«*

« Nous détournons l'utilité des matériaux afin de créer dans nos objets un
monde toujours changeant d'expérimentation, de créativité et d'innovation. »

1. **Xingu** fruitbowl/Obstschale/coupe à fruits
(self-production), 1998
2. ↓ **Tattoo** table/Tisch for Fontana Arte, 2000

« En expérimentant de nouveaux matériaux, le design du futur pourra revisiter des objets existants et détourner leurs fonctions vers de nouvelles "destinations". Parfois, une technique de fabrication établie peut favoriser le développement de nouvelles technologies pour de nouveaux projets et de nouvelles méthodes de recyclage. Aujourd'hui, de nombreux designers travaillent seuls dans de petits ateliers, détournant la fonction de produits afin d'obtenir de nouveaux résultats. Ils réorganisent les parties ou les composants d'un objet existant de sorte à lui donner une nouvelle fonction, ou ils "répètent" le même objet afin de produire de nouvelles textures. A notre avis, c'est dans ce sens que le design continuera à se développer de manière créative et qu'il participera à la transformation et à l'extension de notre mode de vie. Le designer du futur devrait faire des références à ses propres origines culturelles, à ses traditions, ses couleurs, son histoire, afin que ses produits aient une authenticité et une originalité qui ne soient pas régies par la mode ou les tendances générales. Ces références de l'âme aideront les produits à communiquer plus directement. L'avenir du design dépendra peut-être de sa capacité à permettre à des projets très originaux et personnels de jouer un rôle sur la scène industrielle afin de rendre la vie plus créative et agréable : meubles "en conserve" pouvant prendre n'importe quelle forme ; maisons pliées dans des enveloppes pouvant être déployées n'importe quand et n'importe où ; lampes portables alimentées par leur propre source d'énergie à l'intérieur de boules de cristal. »

FERNANDO & HUMBERTO CAMPANA

3. ← **Jenette** chair/Stuhl/chaise for Cappellini, 2000
4. **Batuque** vases/Vasen (self-production), 2000

"By experimenting with new materials, design in the future will be able to re-visit existent objects and subvert their functions into new 'destinations'. Sometimes, an established manufacturing technique can assist the development of new technologies for new projects as well as methods of recycling. Nowadays, we see a number of designers working individually in small studios, subverting the function of products to create new results. They may assemble parts or components of an existing object in such a way as to give it a new function or they may 'repeat' the same object in order to produce new textures. This is how we believe design will continue to grow creatively and take part in changing and extending our ways of living in this world.
The designer of the future should use references from his cultural background – traditions, colours, history – so that his products have an authenticity and originality that is not governed by fashion or global trends. These 'soul' references will help products communicate more directly. The future of design might be about allowing very imaginative projects with their own unique characteristics to play a part in the industrial scene so as to make life more creative and enjoyable – from 'canned-gassy' furniture that can be shaped into any form to folded houses inside envelopes that can be folded and unfolded any time any place to portable lamps that are powered by their own energy source inside crystal balls."

FERNANDO & HUMBERTO CAMPANA

»Durch das Experimentieren mit neuen Materialien wird das Design der Zukunft bestehende Objekte neu entdecken und deren Funktionen zu neuen Bestimmungen umwandeln können. Manchmal kann eine etablierte Fertigungstechnik helfen, sowohl neue Technologien für neue Projekte als auch Recycling-Methoden für bereits existierende zu entwickeln. Gegenwärtig sind viele einzelne Designer in kleinen Ateliers damit beschäftigt, die Funktion von Produkten zu verwerfen, um neue Ergebnisse zu erzielen. Sie setzen Teile oder Komponenten eines bestehenden Objekts so zusammen, dass sie ihm damit eine neue Funktion verleihen, oder sie ›wiederholen‹ das gleiche Objekt, um neue Oberflächen anzufertigen. So wird sich Design unserer Vorstellung nach kreativ fortentwickeln und dazu beitragen, unser Leben in dieser Welt zu verändern und zu verlängern.
Die Designer der Zukunft sollten Bezüge aus ihrem jeweiligen kulturellen Hintergrund in ihre Entwürfe einbringen – dessen Traditionen, Farben, Geschichte – und damit ihren Produkten eine Authentizität und Originalität verleihen, die nicht von Mode oder globalen Trends bestimmt ist. Diese ›seelischen‹ Bezugspunkte werden den Produkten helfen, auf direkterem Weg zu kommunizieren. In Zukunft kommt es beim Design möglicherweise auf die Fähigkeit an, zuzulassen, dass gerade außerordentlich phantasievolle Projekte mit ihren eigenen unverwechselbaren Merkmalen im industriellen Sektor zum Zug kommen – um unser Alltagsleben kreativer und angenehmer zu machen. Dabei könnte die Produktpalette von Möbeln ›aus der Konserve‹, die jede beliebige Form annehmen können, über faltbare Häuser, die sich jederzeit und an jedem Ort zusammen- und auseinander falten lassen, bis zu tragbaren Lampen reichen, die von ihrer eigenen, in Kristallkugeln enthaltenen Energiequelle gespeist werden.« FERNANDO & HUMBERTO CAMPANA

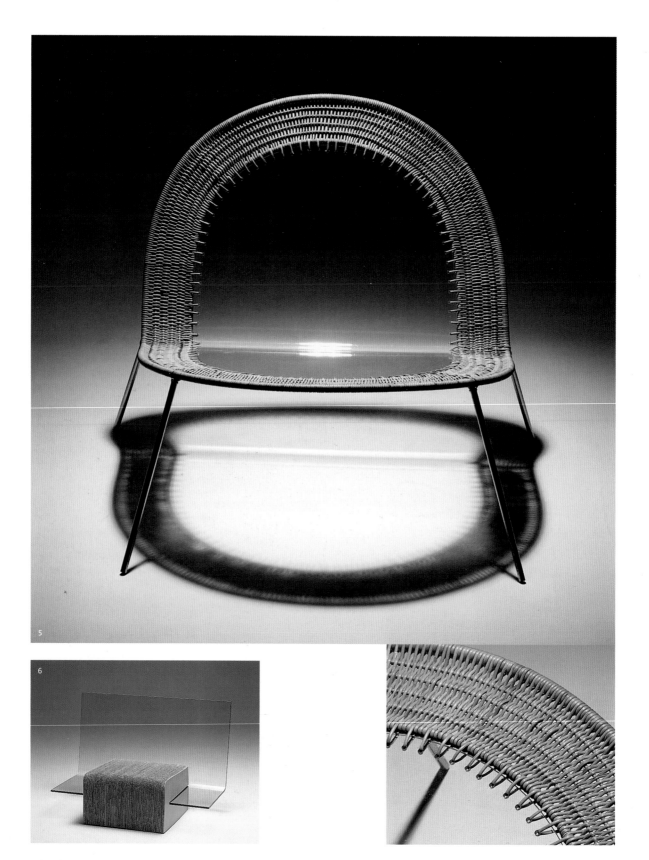

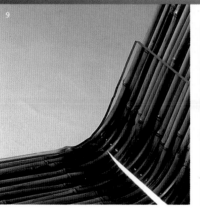

5. **Mixed Series – Rush & Acrylic** chair/Stuhl/fauteuil (self-production), 2000
6. **Mixed Series – Cardboard & Polycarbonate** chair/Stuhl/fauteuil for Hidden, 2000
7. **Mixed Series – Rush & Acrylic** chair (detail)/Stuhl (Detail)/fauteuil (détail) (self-production), 2000
8. **Mixed Series – Bamboo & Acrylic** chair/Stuhl/fauteuil (self-production), 2000
9. **Mixed Series – Bamboo & Acrylic** chair (detail)/Stuhl (Detail)/fauteuil (détail) (self-production), 2000
10. **Mixed Series – Bamboo & Metal** chair/Stuhl/chaise for Hidden, 2000

FERNANDO & HUMBERTO CAMPANA

BORN		FERNANDO CAMPANA
	1961	São Paulo, Brazil
		HUMBERTO CAMPANA
	1953	São Paulo, Brazil
STUDIED		FERNANDO CAMPANA
	1979-84	BA Architecture, Faculdade de Belas Arts de São Paulo
		HUMBERTO CAMPANA
	1972-77	BA Law, University of São Paulo
PRACTICE		FERNANDO CAMPANA
	1998	taught Industrial Design, Fundação Armando Alvares Penteado, São Paulo
	1999-2000	taught at the Museu Brasileiro de Escultura (Brazilian Museum of Sculpture)
		HUMBERTO CAMPANA
	1998	taught Industrial Design, Fundação Armando Alvares Penteado, São Paulo
	1999-2000	taught at the Museu Brasileiro de Escultura (Brazilian Museum of Sculpture)
AWARDS	1992	Prêmio Aquisição, Museu de Arte Brasileiro (FAAP), São Paulo
	1996	First Prize – Design Category, Salão de Arte de Ribeirão
	1997	First Prize – Domestic Furniture ABIMÓVEL; Second Prize – Domestic Furniture Museu da Casa Brasileira, São Paulo
EXHIBITIONS	1989	*From Modernism to Modernity*, New York
	1990	*Desconfortáveis*, São Paulo; *Orgânicos*, São Paulo; *Brasilian Design*, San Francisco
	1991	*Esculturas*, Pinacoteca do Estado de São Paulo
	1993	*Edição 93 Nucleon 8*, São Paulo
	1994	*Travels in Italy*, Verona
	1995	*Il Brasile fá Anche Design*, Milan
	1996	*O Brasil faz Design*, Palazzo Reale, Milan
	1997	*WWEIRREDD – Young Design in Milan*, Milan; *Design mit Zukunft*, Focke Museum, Bremen
	1998	*Brasilian Design*, Miami; *Project 66 – Campana/Ingo Maurer*, Museum of Modern Art, New York
	1999	*Retrospectiva Campana*, Casa França Brasil, Rio de Janeiro; *Numeros*, Museu Brasileiro de Escultura, São Paulo
	2000	*Entre o Design e a Arte*, Museu de Arte Moderna de São Paulo

CLIENTS

ACME
Cappellini
Edra
Fontana Arte
Forma
Hidden
HStern
MoMA
O Luce
also self-production

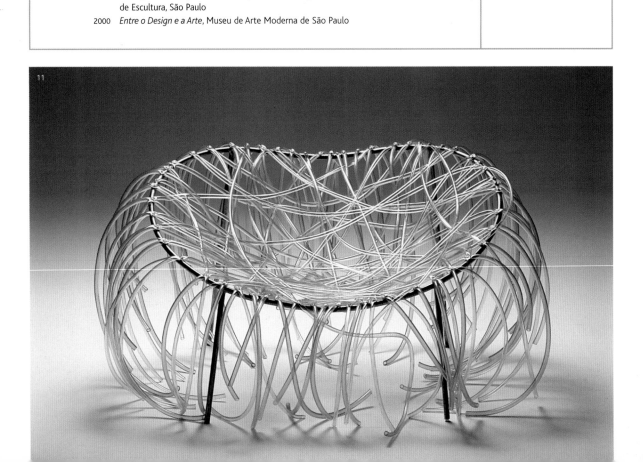

11

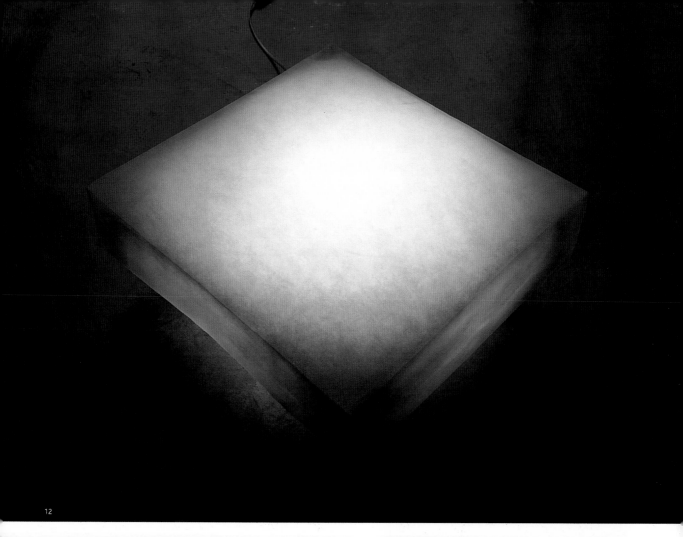

12

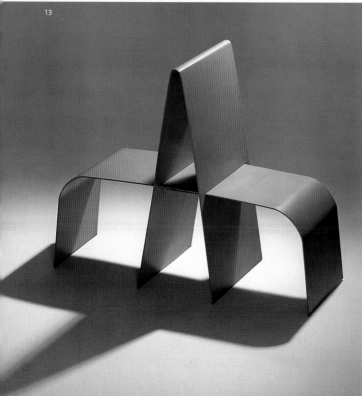

13

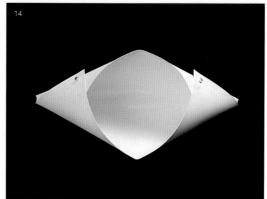

14

11. **Anemona** chair/Sessel/fauteuil for Edra, 2001
12. **Pillow** lamp/Lampe/lampe (self-production), 1998
13. **Gangorra** bench/Sitzbank/banc (self-production), 1998
14. **Nova** fruitbowl/Obstschale/coupe à fruits
(self-production), 2000

"It is the relationship between the object and its use, together with a capacity for ageing while increasing in value, that will deem an object classical."

Antonio Citterio

Antonio Citterio, Antonio Citterio & Partners, Via Cerva 4, 20 122 Milan, Italy
T +39 02 763 8801 F +39 02 763 88080 citterio@mdsnet.it

»Was ein Objekt zu einem Klassiker macht, ist der Bezug zu seiner Verwendung zusammen mit seiner Fähigkeit, zu altern und dabei an Wert zu gewinnen.«

« Ce qui fait d'un objet un classique, c'est sa relation avec son utilisation ainsi que sa capacité à vieillir tout en prenant de la valeur. »

1. **Citterio 2000** cutlery/Besteck/couverts for Hackman, 2000
2. ↓ **Web** armchairs/Sessel/fauteuils for B&B Italia, 1998

« Je n'emploie jamais le mot "moderne". Le concept de modernité implique de comprendre ce qui est ancien. Cela peut paraître paradoxal mais c'est ainsi. Pour décrire la recherche de "l'esprit du temps" qui sous-tend mon travail, je préfère le terme "contemporain". La contemporanéité d'un projet de design inclut et nourrit un profond désir d'anticipation. L'interaction constante entre l'anticipation du projet et la contemporanéité du produit fini constitue l'essence même de ma démarche. J'essaie toujours de concevoir des objets qui soient absolument contemporains, précisément parce qu'ils coïncident parfaitement avec leur temps. Ces dernières années, l'évolution sociale qui a accompagné l'émergence de nouvelles technologies et de nouveaux codes de communication a incité de nombreux designers à intégrer ces éléments dans leur propres conceptions, d'une manière directe mais inexpliquée, au sein des paramètres proposés par l'informatisation du design. Toutefois, je ne pense pas que ce genre de design, qui ne nécessite pas un effort formel pur, puisse aboutir à des résultats substantiels. Pour moi, la pertinence du sujet (sans réveiller le vieux débat sur la forme et la fonction) dépend avant tout de la capacité à créer des objets clairs et compréhensibles, puis de celle à susciter le plaisir et le désir de les posséder. Je travaille comme un connaisseur hypothétique du design. Je cherche moins à être surpris ou amusé par un objet qu'à travailler sur sa précision, résultat d'une ↓

3. **Freetime** sofa/Sofa/canapé for B&B Italia, 1999
4. **Freetime** chaise longue & sofa/Liege & Sofa/chaise longue & canapé for B&B Italia, 1999
5. **Beam** lighting system/Beleuchtungssystem/système d'éclairage for Flos, 2000

"I never use the word 'modern'. The concept of modernity implies an understanding of ancient things. I know this sounds like a paradox, but so it is. When expressing the tension found in my work, which is about the search for the 'spirit of the time', I use the word 'contemporary'. The contemporaneity of a design project includes and feeds the deep desire of anticipation. There is a perpetual shift between the anticipation of the project and the contemporaneity of the final product, which is the essence of my approach to design. I always try to design objects that are absolutely contemporary, exactly because they coincide perfectly with their time. The past years have seen a social evolution with the emergence of new technologies and new codes of communication, which have driven many designers to combine these elements in their own design, in a direct but unexplained way, within the stylistic parameters suggested by the computerization of design. I do not think, however, that this kind of design, which involves no pure formal effort, can lead to any substantial result. For me, the pertinence of the subject (without raising old questions of form and function) relies firstly on the ability to create clear and understandable objects and secondly on the ability to excite pleasure and the desire for ownership. I work like a hypothetical connoisseur of design, a man not so much interested in being surprised and deriving fun from an object but pursuing an interest in the precision of an object that is the result of an appropriate use of construction and detailing. I am fascinated by the intrinsic qualities of materials and the way in which ↓

»Ich verwende niemals das Wort ›modern‹. Das Konzept von Modernität impliziert ein Verständnis für alte Dinge. Ich weiß, das klingt paradox, aber es ist so. Wenn ich die in meiner Arbeit enthaltene Spannung, bei der es um die Suche nach dem ›Zeitgeist‹ geht, beschreiben soll, verwende ich das Wort ›zeitgemäß‹. Die Aktualität eines Designprojekts beinhaltet und nährt den tiefen Wunsch nach gedanklicher Vorwegnahme. Der fortwährende Wechsel zwischen der Antizipation des Projekts und der Aktualität des Endprodukts ist die Essenz meiner Herangehensweise. Ich bin immer bestrebt, Objekte zu entwerfen, die absolut zeitgemäß sind, gerade weil sie sich in vollkommener Übereinstimmung mit ihrer Zeit befinden. Während der vergangenen Jahre fand eine soziale Evolution statt, die mit dem Aufkommen neuer Technologien und Kommunikationssysteme einherging. Viele Designer reagierten auf diese Entwicklung, indem sie die neuen Techniken mittels stilistischer Parameter, die sich durch die Computerisierung des Designs ergeben, auf direkte, aber unausgesprochene Weise in ihre Entwürfe einbezogen. Ich glaube jedoch nicht, dass diese Art von Design, die kein rein formales Bemühen erfordert, zu irgendwelchen nennenswerten Ergebnissen führen wird. Für mich beruht die Relevanz von Design (ohne die alte Debatte über Form und Funktion wieder aufwärmen zu wollen) auf der Fähigkeit, Objekte zu entwerfen, die erstens leicht verständlich sind und zweitens Freude hervorrufen, sowie den Wunsch, das Objekt zu besitzen. Ich arbeite wie ein hypothetischer Connaisseur von Design. Mir liegt weniger an der Verblüffung durch ein Objekt und dem Spaß daran, als an der Präzision eines Objekts, welche das Resultat eines ausgewogenen Verhältnisses zwischen Gestaltung und Ausführung ist. Ich bin fasziniert von den inneren Eigenschaften der unterschiedlichen Materialien und von der Art, wie sie ein Projekt durchdringen. Meiner Meinung nach erlaubt nur eine profunde Kenntnis von Werkstoffen und Techniken, dass ein Projekt glatt und ohne allzu große Abweichung vom ursprünglichen Konzept verläuft. Abgesehen von meinen Prinzipien ↓

ANTONIO CITTERIO		CLIENTS
BORN	1950 Meda, Italy	Ansorg
STUDIED	1972 graduated in architecture at the Milan Polytechnic	Arclinea
PRACTICE	1973-81 partnership with Paolo Nava	B&B Italia
	1987-96 partnership with Terry Dwan	Boffi Cucine
	1999 founded Antonio Citterio and Partners with Patricia Viel	Flexform
AWARDS	1987 Compasso d'Oro, Milan	Flos
	1995 Compasso d'Oro, Milan	Fusital
EXHIBITIONS	1988 *I segni dell'Habitat*, Paris	Hackman
	1992 *Objets et Projets* (concept and layout), Paris	Hansgrohe
	1994 *Antonio Citterio & Terry Dwan* (design), AXIS Gallery, Tokyo	Inda
	1999 *Antonio Citterio and Partners. Progetti di architettura 4 case e 4 uffici* (concept and layout), Galleria Aam, Milan	JCDecaux
		Kartell
	2000 *Design 4:3 – Fünfzig Jahre italienisches und deutsches Design*, Kunst- und Ausstellungshalle der Bundesrepublik Deutschland, Bonn; *Esercizi di Stile*, Ace Gallery, New York – ICE	MaxData
		Pozzi & Ginori
		Tisettanta
		Vitra

6

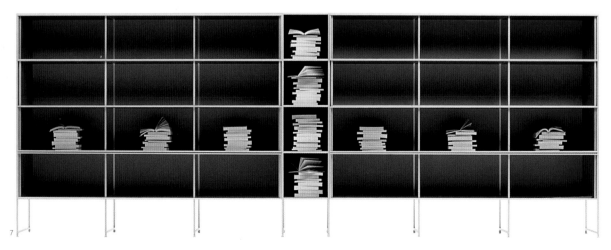

7

utilisation adéquate de la construction et du détail. Je suis fasciné par les qualités intrinsèques des matériaux et par la manière dont elles influent sur un projet. A mon avis, seule une profonde connaissance des matières et des techniques peut permettre à un projet d'aboutir sans trop dévier de son concept initial. Outre mes principes sur " la pertinence du sujet " et la " précision ", je crois aussi que le design devrait s'appuyer sur une éthique qui ne s'aventure pas dans d'improbables transformations technologiques mais, plutôt, recherche un résultat univoque basé sur la relation entre les techniques de production, la forme et la fonctionnalité. » ANTONIO CITTERIO

they inform a project. In my opinion, only a profound understanding of materials and techniques will allow a project to run smoothly without deviating too far from the initial concept. Apart from my principles regarding 'the pertinence of the subject' and 'precision', I also believe that design should rely on a kind of 'ethic' that does not venture into improbable technological transformations but instead searches for an unequivocal result based on the relationship between production techniques, form and functionality." ANTONIO CITTERIO

bezüglich ›Relevanz‹ und ›Präzision‹ bin ich der Ansicht, dass sich Design auf eine Art ›Ethik‹ stützen sollte, die sich nicht in abgehobenen technologischen Transformationen erschöpft, sondern nach dem bestmöglichen Ergebnis sucht, das auf einem ausgeglichen Verhältnis zwischen Fertigungstechniken, Form und Funktionalität beruht.« ANTONIO CITTERIO

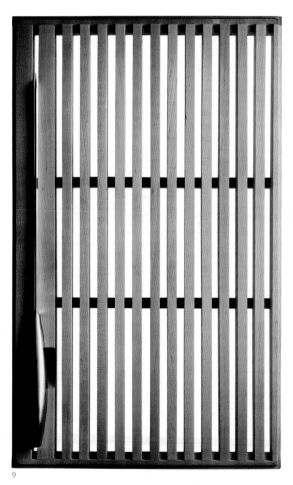

6. **Dado** sofa/Sofa/canapé for B&B Italia, 2000
7. **Cross** shelving/Regale/bibliothèque for B&B Italia, 1999
8. **H-Beam** lighting/Beleuchtungskörper/plafonnier for Flos, 2000
9. **Citterio Collective Tools 2000** bread knife and cutting board/Brotmesser und Schneidebrett/couteau à pain et planche à découper for Hackman, 2000

9

"For me, design is ultimately about communicating ideas."

Björn Dahlström

Björn Dahlström, Dahlström Design, Frejgatan 20, 11349 Stockholm, Sweden
T +46 8 673 4200   F +46 8 673 4201   dahlstrom@dahlstromdesign.se

»Für mich ist Design in erster Linie der Austausch von Ideen.«

« Pour moi, créer c'est avant tout communiquer des idées. »

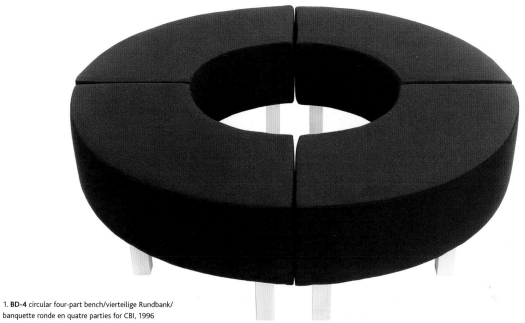

1. **BD-4** circular four-part bench/vierteilige Rundbank/
banquette ronde en quatre parties for CBI, 1996
2. ↓ **Camper 3** tent/Zelt/tente for Fjällräven, 2000

3

4

« Aujourd'hui, on a tendance à travailler chacun dans son coin, le designer d'un côté, le commanditaire de l'autre. On ferait mieux de baser nos systèmes sur la pensée intégrée. Le designer doit participer au processus industriel, assumer le rôle catalyseur de libre penseur. En tant que designer, passer d'un aspect de l'industrie à l'autre m'inspire énormément. Le design devrait influer davantage sur le côté ingénierie du processus de développement. L'histoire nous montre que les techniques et les matériaux nouveaux influencent directement l'évolution du design. J'aime à penser qu'à l'avenir, le designer intégrera une équipe de chercheurs essayant de repousser les frontières toujours plus loin : trouver des moyens techniques pour aider les produits et les compagnies à mieux servir les gens, créer des environnements plus accueillants, une ergonomie plus sophistiquée, adapter les matériaux existants et en développer de nouveaux. Le design est avant tout une manière de communiquer des idées. Pour qu'il évolue, les designers doivent donc occuper un rôle plus central dans l'élaboration du contexte dans lequel les produits sont utilisés. » BJÖRN DAHLSTRÖHM

3. **BD-1** easy chair/Sessel/fauteuil for cbi, 1994
4. **Toycar** child's toy/Kinderspielzeug/jouet à roulettes pour enfant for Playsam, 1996
5. **Skeppshult-Z** bicycle/Fahrrad/bicyclette for Skeppshult, 1999

"Today we tend to work in separate cells, the designer on one side and the client on the other. Instead, we should build our systems on integrated thinking. The designer needs to be part of the industrial process, adopting the role of free-thinking catalyst. As a designer, I get a lot of inspiration moving from one type of the industry to another. I think design should have more influence on the engineering side of the development process. History shows that new materials and techniques have a direct effect on the evolution of design. I like to think that the designer in the future will be part of a research team trying to push frontiers forward: finding ways to help products and companies serve people better, creating more environmental friendliness, fine-tuning ergonomics, adapting existing materials and helping to develop new ones. Design is ultimately about communicating ideas. So if design in itself is going to evolve, designers will have to play a more central role in moulding the context in which the products are used." BJÖRN DAHLSTRÖM

»Wir tendieren heute dazu, in getrennten Sphären zu arbeiten – die Designer auf der einen und die Kunden oder Auftraggeber auf der anderen Seite. Stattdessen sollten wir unsere Arbeitssysteme auf einem ganzheitlichen Denken aufbauen. Der Designer sollte Teil des Herstellungsprozesses sein, indem er die Rolle eines frei denkenden Katalysators annimmt. Als Designer beziehe ich eine Menge Inspiration daraus, dass ich mich von einem industriellen Bereich zum anderen bewege. Ich finde, das Design sollte einen größeren Einfluss auf die technische Seite der Produktentwicklung haben. Die Geschichte zeigt, dass neue Materialien und Technologien immer direkte Auswirkungen auf die Entwicklung von Design haben. Ich wünsche mir, dass die Designer der Zukunft Teil eines Teams von Forschern sein werden, die beständig versuchen, Grenzen zu erweitern: durch das Ausklügeln neuer Methoden zur Herstellung von Produkten, die menschenfreundlicher, umweltfreundlicher und ergonomischer sind, wobei bestehende Materialien adaptiert und neue entwickelt werden. Für mich ist Design in erster Linie der Austausch von Ideen. Soll sich also das Design als solches weiterentwickeln, so müssen Designer stärker an der Gestaltung des Kontextes beteiligt werden, in dem die Produkte verwendet werden.« BJÖRN DAHLSTRÖM

BJÖRN DAHLSTRÖM

BORN	1957	Stockholm, Sweden
STUDIED		Self-taught
PRACTICE	1978-	art director and graphic designer for advertising agencies
	1982	established Dahlström Design
	1999-2001	professor of furniture design, Konstfackskolan (National College of Arts, Crafts and Design), Stockholm
AWARDS	1991-95	Excellent Swedish Design Awards, Stockholm
	1996	Design Plus Award, Frankfurt/Main
	1999	Design Plus Award, Frankfurt/Main
	2000	Special Prize – Excellent Swedish Design Award, Stockholm

CLIENTS

Atlas Copco
Aqua Play
cbi
Gewa
Hackman
Magis
Plank
Playsam
Primus
Schopenhauer-Fontana Arte
Skeppshult
Zoltan

6

7

8

6. **Atlas-Copco Cobra** Motor breaker/Pressluftbohrer/ coque de moteur for Atlas-Copco, 1997
7. **Hackman Tools** saucepan/Kasserolle/casserole for Hackman, 1998
8. **Bank** bench/Sitzbank/banquette for Zoltan, 1996
9. **Joystick** walking stick/Spazierstock/canne for Magis, 2000
10. **BD Relax** chaise longue/Liege for CBI, 2000
11. **BD3** candlestick/Kerzenständer/bougeoir for CBI, 1995
12. **Primus Powerjet** soldering torch/Lötkolben/fer à souder for Primus, 1996

"Design always springs from an idea,
it is the form given to an idea."

Emmanuel Dietrich

Dietrich design, 20 bis Rue de Beauregard, 78 490 Les Mesnuls, France
T +33 1 34 86 95 01 F +33 1 34 86 84 30 e-mail: atelier@dietrich-design.com
www.dietrich-design.com

*»Design entspringt immer einer Idee.
Es ist die Form, die man dieser Idee
gegeben hat.«*

« Le design naît toujours d'une idée.
Il est la forme donnée à cette idée. »

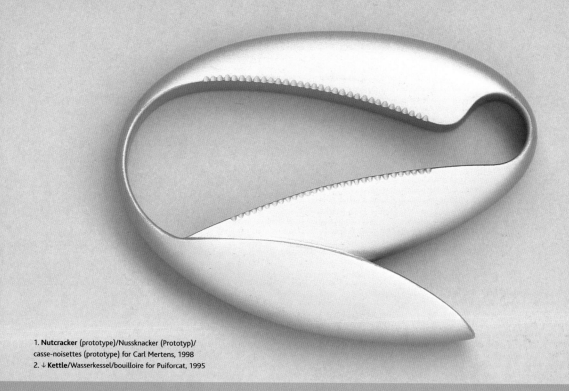

1. **Nutcracker** (prototype)/Nussknacker (Prototyp)/
casse-noisettes (prototype) for Carl Mertens, 1998
2. ↓ **Kettle**/Wasserkessel/bouilloire for Puiforcat, 1995

« Les idées sont éphémères. Pour qu'elles nous soient utiles, il faut leur donner une forme physique. Un bon design est celui qui incarne parfaitement l'idée qui l'a inspiré. Chaque créateur interprétant une idée à sa manière, le produit fini, qu'il soit pittoresque, sobre, criard ou baroque, reflète la personnalité de celui qui l'a conçu. Ensuite, il y a des considérations pratiques, des limites techniques et des contraintes commerciales. Mais, en dépit de ces aspects matériels, il existe une infinité d'approches créatives possibles. L'élaboration d'un design soulève des questions auxquelles les commanditaires doivent être préparés, car chaque projet devrait ouvrir une nouvelle voie.

Je suis fasciné par les défis techniques imposés par le design : les relations spatiales entre les différentes parties, leur interdépendance et l'équilibre général. Je travaille et retravaille sans cesse ces aspects, les peaufinant jusqu'à en être satisfait.

J'aime les possibilités inhérentes à chaque matériau. Les matières naturelles, notamment, sont une incroyable source d'inspiration. Les matières artificielles n'ont jamais tout à fait le même potentiel que les organiques, mais les nouveaux matériaux sont de plus en plus proches de la nature et, parfois, conjuguent plusieurs de leurs qualités en une. Ces matières synthétiques ne sont pas toujours faciles à travailler, ayant généralement été développées plus pour leurs performances que pour leur aspect, leur texture ou leur capacité à bien se patiner avec le temps. Mais on ne cesse de les améliorer, ouvrant de nouvelles possibilités. » EMMANUEL DIETRICH

3. ← **Doumbia** stacking fruit boards/stapelbare Fruchtschalen/plateaux à fruits empilables for Meta Concept, 1999
4. **Pocket Knives**/Taschenmesser/canifs for Hermès, 1997

"Ideas are transient and to be useful to us we have to give them physical form. A successful design is one that perfectly encapsulates the idea that inspired it. Each designer will interpret an idea in a different way, so that a finished design — whether colourful, sober, loud or baroque — reflects the character of the person who created it. Then there are practical considerations, technical limitations and commercial constraints. But despite these practicalities, there is always room for an infinite number of creative approaches. The process of design raises questions, and clients must be prepared for this, because each project should lead somewhere new.

I am fascinated by the technical challenges posed by design. The spatial relationships between different parts, their interdependence and the overall balance — I work and rework these aspects of a design, refining them until I am satisfied.

I love the possibilities inherent in different materials — natural materials, above all, are incredibly inspiring. Man-made materials never have quite the potential of organic ones, but new materials are coming closer to natural ones all the time and sometimes combine several of their qualities at once. These synthetics are not always easy to work with — they are usually developed for performance rather than appearance, texture or capacity to wear well — but they are constantly being improved, leading to new opportunities." EMMANUEL DIETRICH

»Ideen sind flüchtig, und damit sie uns nützen, müssen wir ihnen eine sinnlich wahrnehmbare Form geben. Ein gelungenes Design ist eines, das die Idee, von der es inspiriert wurde, vollkommen verkörpert. Jeder Designer wird eine Idee auf unterschiedliche Weise interpretieren, und deshalb spiegelt ein fertiges Designobjekt – sei es bunt, nüchtern, grell oder verschnörkelt – den Charakter der Person wider, die es entworfen hat. Außerdem gilt es praktische Überlegungen, technische Grenzen und kommerzielle Zwänge zu berücksichtigen. Aber trotz dieser Zweckmäßigkeiten gibt es immer Raum für eine unbegrenzte Zahl an kreativen Herangehensweisen. Der Entstehungsprozess von Design wirft Fragen auf, worauf die Käufer vorbereitet sein müssen, denn jedes Projekt sollte in eine neue Richtung führen.

Ich bin fasziniert von den technischen Herausforderungen, die mit dem Design verbunden sind. Die räumlichen Beziehungen zwischen verschiedenen Teilen, ihre gegenseitige Abhängigkeit und die Balance des Ganzen – das sind Aspekte, die ich immer wieder überarbeite und so lange verfeinere, bis ich mit einem Design zufrieden bin.

Ich liebe die den unterschiedlichen Materialien innewohnenden Möglichkeiten – vor allem natürliche Materialien sind unglaublich inspirierend. Künstliche Werkstoffe haben zwar nie das volle Potential von organischen, aber die neuen Materialien kommen immer näher an die natürlichen heran und vereinigen manchmal mehrere ihrer Eigenschaften in sich. Die Verarbeitung dieser synthetischen Stoffe ist nicht immer einfach, denn sie wurden meistens mehr im Hinblick auf Gebrauchsfähigkeit als auf Aussehen, Oberflächenbeschaffenheit oder Tragekomfort entwickelt. Sie werden jedoch fortwährend verbessert, was wiederum zu neuen Verarbeitungsmöglichkeiten führt.« EMMANUEL DIETRICH

EMMANUEL DIETRICH

BORN   1969   Besançon, France
STUDIED   1986   B. T. Agencement LTE Jules Haag, Besançon
          1989   B. T. S. Interior Design, Ecole Boulle, Paris
PRACTICE 1989-90   Agence Isabelle Hebey
          1990   Agence Martine Dufour
          1990-91   Agence C. R. I. C. Design
          1991-93   collaborated with Michel Lefranc
          1993-   freelance designer

CLIENTS

Ardi
Artelano
Carl Mertens
Designware
Diamed
Ebel
Facom
Hermès
Läsko
Ligne Roset
Magis
Stamp
Zenith

5

6

5. **Baby sampler** blood analysis machine/Mini-Blut-
analysegerät/appareil pour analyser le sang for Diamed,
2000
6. **Watch**/Armbanduhr/montre for Hermès, 1997
7. **Highlight** stacking candleholder/stapelbare Kerzen-
halter/bougeoirs empilables for Ardi, 1999

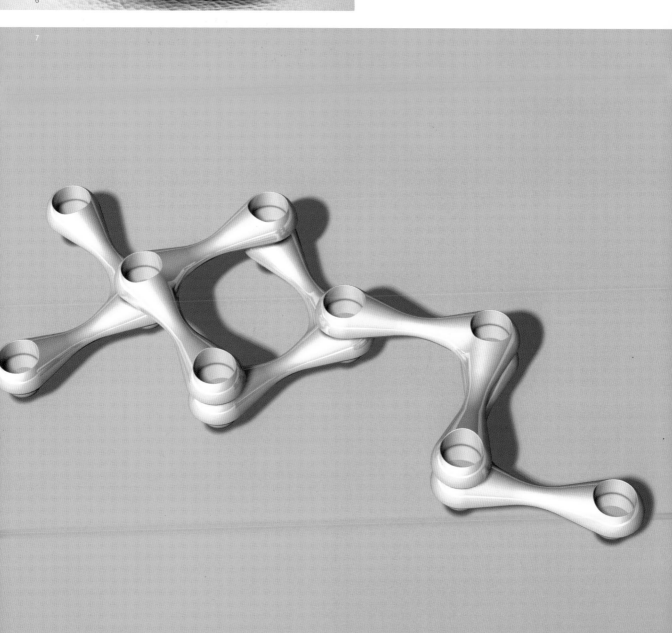

7

"Besides the intellect of high design,
we like a bit of nasty tuning."

Dumoffice

Dumoffice, Tollensstraat 60, 1053 RW Amsterdam, The Netherlands
T +31 20 489 0104 F +31 20 489 0601 dumoffice@planet.nl www.dumoffice.com

»Neben der Intelligenz von hochwerti-
gem Design haben wir gern einen etwas
frechen ›Dreh‹.«

« Outre l'aspect intellectuel du grand
design, nous aimons bien les dérapages
contrôlés. »

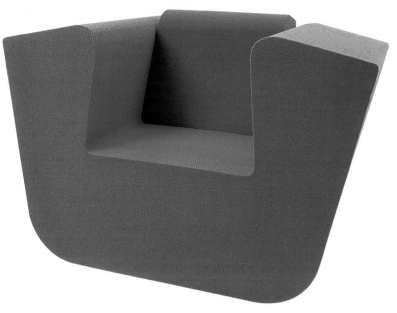

1. **Unkle** chair/Stuhl/chaise (self-production), 2000
2. ↓ **Surve** light/Leuchte/luminaire for Belux, 1996

« En dehors de nos travaux de commande, nous lançons également nos propres projets d'intérieur. Chaque nouvel objet nécessite une approche raisonnée et spécifique de sa forme et de sa fonction. C'est pourquoi nous ne sommes pas attachés à un style ou à un dogme particulier. Nous adoptons plusieurs caractéristiques formelles à la fois, si bien que notre définition du style est un mélange décontracté et anticonformiste de matériaux, de techniques de production et de références, allant du sportswear et de la mode en général à l'art et à l'architecture. Nous aimons échantillonner des images et des matières à partir de sources autres que domestiques et les intégrer à nos propres " designs d'intérieur ". » DUMOFFICE

"Besides working under assignment, we also initiate new interior objects ourselves. Every new assignment requires an intelligent and unique approach towards form and function. That is why we are not tied to any one style or dogma. Adopting more than a few form-characteristics, our definition of style is a crossover of cool non-conformist materials, production techniques, and references extending from sportswear and fashion to art and architecture. We like to sample images and materials from sources other than the home environment and incorporate them into our own 'homewear' designs." DUMOFFICE

»Neben unseren Auftragsarbeiten entwerfen wir auch Einrichtungsgegenstände in Eigenregie. Jedes neue Projekt erfordert eine intelligente und unverwechselbare Herangehensweise an Form und Funktion. Das ist der Grund, warum wir nicht an einen bestimmten Stil oder ein Lehrsystem gebunden sind. Indem wir eine ganze Bandbreite charakteristischer Formgestaltungen adaptieren, besteht unsere Definition von Stil aus einer Kreuzung ›cooler‹ nonkonformistischer Materialien, Produktionstechniken und Bezüge, die von Sportbekleidung und Mode bis zu Kunst und Architektur reichen. Wir mixen gerne Bilder und Materialien aus anderen Quellen als der häuslichen Umgebung und beziehen sie in unsere ›Homewear‹-Einrichtungsentwürfe ein.« DUMOFFICE

3. ← **Photek** hanging lamp/Hängelampe/plafonnier (self-production, limited edition), 1999
4. **Whoosh** lamp (prototype)/Lampe (Prototyp)/ lampe (prototype), 2000

DUMOFFICE	CLIENTS

		DUMOFFICE	CLIENTS
FOUNDED	1997	Amsterdam by Wiebe Boonstra (b. 1968 Drachten), Martijn Hoogendijk (b. 1970 Bergam-bacht) and Marc van Nederpelt (b. 1965 Zwolle) – all graduated in 1994 from the Design Academy, Eindhoven	Belux
AWARDS	1999	Nominated Rotterdam Design Award	De Bijenkorf
	2000	Roter Punkt Award, Design Zentrum Nordrhein-Westfalen, Essen; nominated for *Design Report* Award, Hamburg	DRK-architects
EXHIBITIONS	1998	Salone del Mobile, Milan; Designers Block, London; Interieur 98, Kortrijk	Hidden
	2000	Salone del Mobile, Milan; *Waschtag*, Cologne	maxwan-architects

Clients list:
- Belux
- De Bijenkorf
- DRK-architects
- Hidden
- maxwan-architects
- Nike
- Rijkswaterstaat
- also self-production

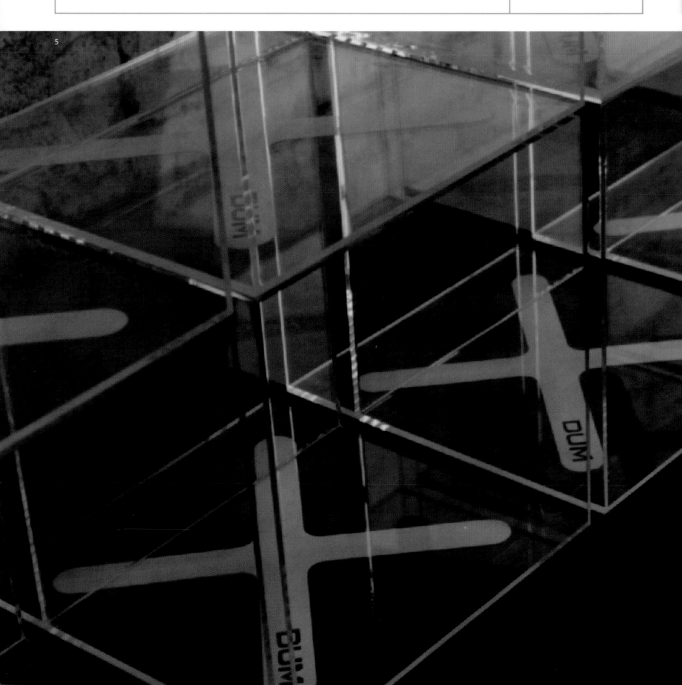

5

6

7

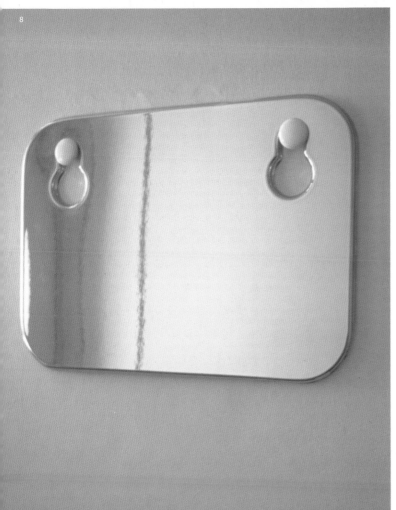

8

9

5. **Stacker** shelving system (prototype)/Regalsystem
(Prototyp)/bibliothèque (prototype), 2000
6. **Slide** wall-mounted cabinet/Wandschrank/meuble de
rangement à accrocher au mur (self-production), 1997
7. **Slide** wall-mounted cabinet (detail)/Wandschrank
(Detail)/meuble de rangement à accrocher au mur (détail)
(self-production), 1997
8. **Silverscreen** mirror (prototype)/Spiegel (Prototyp)/
miroir (prototype), 1996
9. **KS** chairs designed site-specific for a Protestant church
in Amsterdam/speziell für eine protestantische Kirche in
Amsterdam entworfene Stühle/chaises conçues spéciale-
ment pour un temple protestant d'Amsterdam, 1998

"Design is about how something works, not how it looks. It's what's inside that counts. The best designs are the result of someone's questioning everything around them."

 # James Dyson

James Dyson, Dyson Appliances Ltd., Tetbury Hill, Malmesbury, Wiltshire SN16 0RP, England
T +44 1666 827 200   F +44 1666 827 299   dyson.@dyson.com   www.dyson.com

»Beim Design kommt es darauf an, wie etwas funktioniert und nicht, wie es aussieht. Was zählt, ist der Inhalt. Die besten Entwürfe entstehen, wenn jemand alles in Frage stellt.«

« Ce qui compte en design, c'est la manière dont un objet fonctionne, pas son aspect. L'important, c'est ce qui est à l'intérieur. Les meilleurs créations sont conçues par des designers qui remettent tout en question. »

1. **DC05** dual cyclone cleaner/Dual-Zyklon-Bodenstaub-
sauger/nettoyeur double cyclone for Dyson,1998
2. ↓ **DC06** dual cyclone robotic cleaner/Dual-Roboter-
Zyklon-Bodenstaubsauger/robot nettoyeur double cyclone
for Dyson, 1999

« Autrefois, on pensait qu'au 21ᵉ siècle l'homme aurait davantage de temps libre alors qu'en fait, il travaille de plus en plus. Dans les foyers, je pense qu'on utilisera de plus en plus de nouvelles technologies recourant à l'intelligence artificielle, libérant hommes et femmes des corvées domestiques. Quand j'étais petit, on lavait le linge avec une essoreuse à rouleaux. Aujourd'hui, 93 % des foyers sont équipés de machines à laver. Cela laisse plus de temps pour les loisirs. On peut lire un livre ou regarder un film pendant que des machines font le ménage. D'un autre côté, la nouvelle technologie risque de devenir de plus en plus compliquée et je crois que le rôle du design sera de la rendre plus simple à utiliser, notamment grâce à la reconnaissance vocale, surtout pour des systèmes tels le chauffage central. Pour le moment, ils sont assez difficiles à programmer à cause du jargon absurde des modes d'emploi. A mon avis, les innovations futures et le bon design rendront la technologie moderne plus accessible à tous. L'avenir du design et de l'industrie dépend des jeunes qu'on forme actuellement dans les écoles, les collèges et les universités. Nous devons nous assurer que ce secteur d'activité reste créatif, passionné par les produits qu'il fabrique et les gens qui les utilisent. Pour ça, il faut s'y intéresser dès son plus ↓

3. ← **CR01** Contrarotator two-drum washing machine/ Waschmaschine mit Doppeltragwalze/machine à laver à double tambour for Dyson, 1996-2000
4. **DC04** Absolute dual cyclone cleaner/Absolut-Dual-Zyklon-Bürststaubsauger/nettoyeur double cyclone for Dyson, 1999

"We once thought that the 21st century would mean increased leisure time for all, but in fact more people are working, and working longer hours. I believe that in the home we will increasingly see new technology using artificial intelligence, liberating men and women from household chores. When I was born we washed our clothes using a mangle, now 93 % of homes have automatic washing machines. It allows more time for leisure; we can read a book or watch a film while machines help with the housework. Yet new technology is in danger of becoming increasingly complicated, and I think it is the role of design to make it simpler to use, for example through voice recognition, especially for things such as central heating systems. At the moment these are rather difficult to program because of the ridiculous vernacular used in instruction manuals. I think that in the future innovation and good design will make complex modern technology more available and accessible to everyone. The future of design and the manufacturing industry ultimately rests with the young people being educated in schools, colleges and universities today. We need to make sure that it is a creative industry ↓

»Wir dachten einmal, das 21. Jahrhundert würde mehr Freizeit für alle bedeuten. Aber faktisch arbeiten mehr Menschen, und sie arbeiten immer länger. Ich glaube, dass neue Technologien auf der Basis von künstlicher Intelligenz verstärkt Einzug in unser Zuhause halten werden, was Männer und Frauen im Haushalt entlasten wird. Als ich geboren wurde, haben wir unsere Wäsche noch mit der Hand gewaschen, heute besitzen 93 Prozent der Haushalte eine Waschmaschine. Das verschafft uns mehr Freizeit. Wir können ein Buch lesen oder uns einen Film ansehen, während die Maschinen bei der Hausarbeit helfen. Es besteht jedoch die Gefahr, dass die neuen Technologien immer komplizierter werden. Deshalb sehe ich die Aufgabe von Design darin, Gebrauchsgegenstände in der Anwendung einfacher zu machen, beispielsweise durch Spracherkennung. Das gilt besonders für Dinge wie Zentralheizungsanlagen, die gegenwärtig wegen der unverständlichen Ausdrucksweise in den Bedienungsanleitungen schwierig zu programmieren sind. Ich denke, dass die komplexen modernen Technologien in Zukunft durch Innovation und gutes Design für jeden einzelnen leichter verfügbar und nutzbar gemacht werden können.
Die Zukunft des Designs und der weiterverarbeitenden Industrie liegt letzten Endes bei den jungen Menschen, die heute in Schulen, Akademien und Universitäten ausgebildet werden. Wir müssen dafür Sorge tragen, dass sie Design als ein kreatives Gewerbe erlernen, das den Produkten, die es hervorbringt und den Menschen, die sie benutzen, leidenschaftlich zugetan ist. Und das muss meiner Meinung nach bereits in einem frühen Alter einsetzen. Der Akt des kreativen Gebrauchs der ↓

JAMES DYSON			CLIENTS
BORN	1947	Norfolk, England	Self-production
STUDIED	1965-66	Byam Shaw School, London	
	1966-70	MA furniture and interior design, Royal College of Art, London	
PRACTICE	1970-74	Rotork, Bath	
	1974-79	developed *Ballbarrow*	
	1979-84	developed *Dual Cyclone* vacuum cleaner	
	1993	established Dyson Appliances, Chippenham, Wiltshire	
AWARDS	1975	Duke of Edinburgh's special prize, England	
	1977	Building Design Innovation Award, England	
	1991	International Design Fair Prize, Japan	
	1995	elected Fellow of the Chartered Society of Engineers	
	1996	Gerald Frewer Memorial Trophy, Institute of Engineering Design, England; Grand Prix Trophy and Consumer Product Design Award, UK Design Council and Design in Business Awards (DBA)	
	1997	Honorary Doctor of Science, Brookes University, Oxford; Honorary Doctor of Science, Huddersfield University Business School; Prince Philip Designers Prize	
	1998	Honorary Doctor of Science, Bradford University	
	1999	Honorary Doctor of Engineering, West of England University; Internationaler Designpreis Baden-Württemburg, Design Center Stuttgart; G-Mark/Good Design Award, JIDPO, Tokyo	
	2000	Etoiles de l'Observeur du Design, Paris	
EXHIBITIONS	1989	*British Design – New Traditions*, Rotterdam	
	1996	Glasgow International Festival of Design; *Doing a Dyson*, Design Museum, London	
	1997	Sonsbeek Design and Art Museum, Arnhem	
	1999	*Designing in the Digital Age*, Victoria & Albert Museum, London	

5

6

jeune âge. Apprendre à utiliser ses mains et son cerveau de manière créative représente un aspect vital de l'éducation et un défi immense. C'est une activité socialement inclusive et cohésive, dont tous les étudiants peuvent bénéficier quelles que soient leurs capacités académiques. Connaître et comprendre le processus du design ne peut qu'être utile à tous les adolescents. Pour que le design ait un avenir, nous devons tous comprendre la valeur de la créativité, de la technologie et de la fabrication. Ceci dit, au bout du compte, quels que soient les obstacles rencontrés, on continuera à inventer et à fabriquer de nouveaux produits: il est dans la nature humaine de créer, d'améliorer ses conditions de vie. » JAMES DYSON

5. **DC03 Clear** dual cyclone cleaner/Dual-Zyklon-Bürst-staubsauger/nettoyeur double cyclone for Dyson, 1998
6. **DC02** dual cyclone cleaner/Dual-Zyklón-Bodenstaub-sauger/nettoyeur double cyclone for Dyson, 1995
7. **CR01** washing machine, two-drum contrarotator/Waschmaschine mit Doppeltragwalze/machine à laver, double tambour for Dyson, 1996-2000

that cares passionately about the products it makes and the people who use them. I believe this needs to start at an early age. The act of creatively using your hands together with your brain is a vital part of education and an immensely challenging one. It is a socially inclusive and cohesive activity, which benefits all students whatever their academic abilities. It is helpful for everyone to grow up knowing and understanding the design process. People need to understand the value of creativity, technology and manufacturing for the future of design. In the end though, whatever obstacles are thrown in their way, people will continue to invent and make new products: it is part of the human drive to create, to improve our lot." JAMES DYSON

Hände zusammen mit dem Verstand ist ein wichtiger – und zudem ungeheuer herausfordernder – Bestandteil von Erziehung. Von dieser sozial integrativen und bindenden Aktivität profitieren alle Schüler, unabhängig von ihren akademischen Fähigkeiten. Es ist für jeden Heranwachsenden von Nutzen, den Prozess des Gestaltens zu kennen und zu verstehen. Damit das Design eine Zukunft hat, müssen die Menschen den Wert von Kreativität, Technologie und Produktion begreifen. Im Grunde werden die Menschen jedoch ständig neue Produkte erfinden und herstellen, gleichgültig welche Hindernisse ihnen dabei in den Weg gelegt werden, denn es gehört einfach zur menschlichen Natur, schöpferisch tätig zu sein und danach zu streben, unsere Lebenswelt zu verbessern.« JAMES DYSON

7

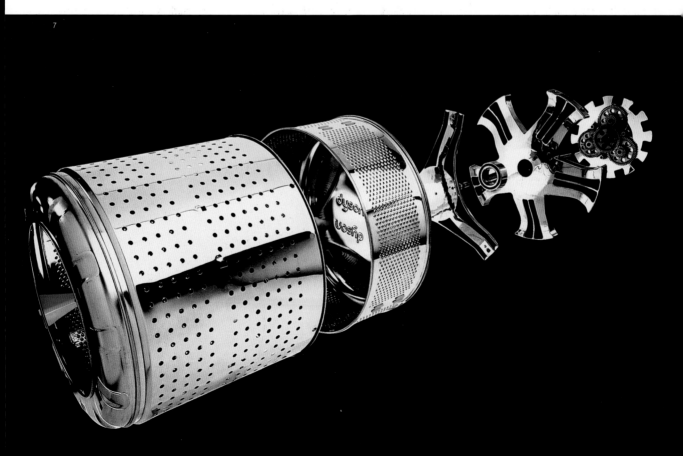

"More technology is not the right answer, but the right technology can help us find new answers."

ECCO Design

Eric Chan, ECCO Design, 16, West 19th Street, New York, NY 10011, USA
T +212 989 7373 F: +212 989 7381 info@eccoid.com www.eccoid.com

»Mehr Technologie ist nicht die richtige Antwort, aber die richtige Technologie kann uns helfen, neue Antworten zu finden.«

« Il ne s'agit pas de rechercher la technologie à tout prix mais une technologie pertinente qui nous aide à trouver de nouvelles solutions. »

1. **Beepwear** watch & pager/Armbanduhr & Pager/
montre et pager for Motorola/Timex, 1999
2. ↓ **For Women Only** hairbrushes/Haarbürsten/
brosses à cheveux for Goody, 1997

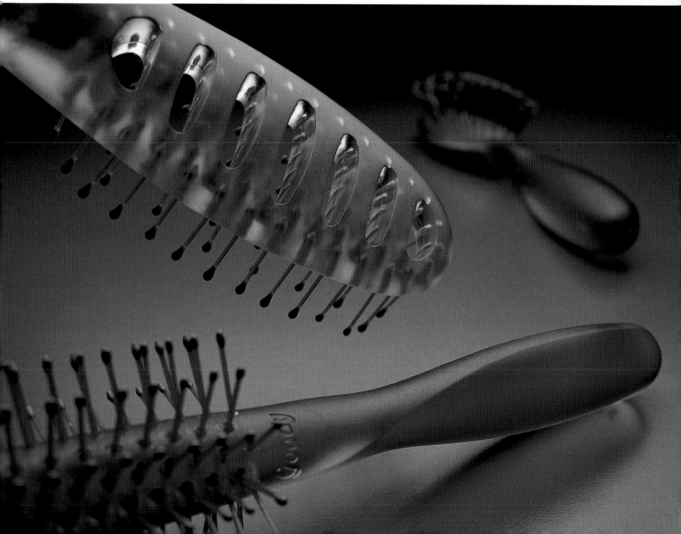

»Unsere einst vertraute Umgebung wurde von der digitalen Informationsflut weggerissen. Die westliche Welt hat sich faktisch über Nacht von einer Fertigungswirtschaft zu einer wissensbasierten Ökonomie entwickelt. Und das ist noch nicht alles: In Zukunft werden Massenkonsumartikel unglaublich schnell zu entwickeln, billig herzustellen und sofort in Umlauf zu bringen sein. Designprodukte werden zu Gebrauchsgegenständen, die Märkte werden enger, und unsere Kinder werden noch abhängiger von zweischneidigen Technologien sein.

Wie können wir als Designer sicherstellen, dass wir das Instrumentarium und das Wissen besitzen, um mit dieser Veränderung Schritt zu halten und die positiven Möglichkeiten zu nutzen, die sie bietet? Wenn wir es schaffen, erfolgreich die gegenläufigen Strömungen von Kultur, Technologie und menschlichen Gefühlen zu nutzen und unser Wissen dazu verwenden, Produkte zu gestalten, die unsere Gefühle wirklich bereichern, dann können wir diesen Objekten eine Bedeutung verleihen, die sowohl ihre Benutzer wie auch ihre Hersteller zufrieden stellt. Unabhängig davon, ob die Verheißungen der auf World Wide Web und Internet basierenden Einrichtungen zur dominierenden Lebensart werden oder nicht, müssen wir uns einen Sinn für Visionen und Werte bewahren. In der Vergangenheit waren unsere Werte auf rationaler Gewissheit gegründet. In Zukunft wird Erfolg von unserer Fähigkeit abhängen, Vieldeutigkeit zuzulassen, und – wie eh und je – von unseren imaginativen, kreativen und intuitiven Kräften.« ERIC CHAN

"Our once familiar landscape has been swept away by the digital information flood. Overnight and virtually, the developed world has moved from a manufacturing to a knowledge-based economy. And there's more to come: Mass-produced consumer goods will become incredibly fast to develop, cheap to make and quick to cycle. Products will turn into commodities, markets will become narrow and our children will become even more dependent on double-edged technologies.

As designers, how can we ensure we have the tools and knowledge to keep pace with this change and build on the opportunities it offers? If we can successfully navigate the crosscurrents of culture, technology and human emotion, and use our knowledge to create products that truly enhance our feelings, then we can build intrinsic meaning into them for users and producers. Whether or not the promise of web-connected appliances becomes a way of life, we must retain a sense of vision and of value. Yesterday our values were founded on rational certainty. Success tomorrow will depend on our ability to tolerate ambiguity and as always, upon our powers of imagination, creativity and intuition." ERIC CHAN

« Le paysage qui nous était familier a été balayé par le déluge de l'information numérique. Du jour au lendemain, le monde développé est passé virtuellement d'une économie basée sur la fabrication à une économie basée sur la connaissance. Ce n'est qu'un prélude : bientôt, les produits de consommation de masse pourront être développés à une vitesse hallucinante, ils seront bon marché à fabriquer et se recycleront rapidement. Ces produits deviendront des matières premières, les marchés se rétréciront et nos enfants dépendront de plus en plus de technologies à double tranchant.

En tant que designers, comment nous assurer que nous avons les bons outils et la connaissance adéquate pour ne pas être dépassés par ce changement et pour pouvoir bâtir sur les débouchés qu'il offre ? Si nous parvenons à naviguer sur les courants croisés de la culture, de la technologie et des émotions, et à utiliser notre connaissance pour créer des produits qui mettent réellement en valeur nos sentiments, alors nous pourrons leur infuser un sens qui satisfera à la fois leurs utilisateurs et leurs producteurs. Que notre futur mode de vie soit connecté à l'Internet ou pas, nous devons conserver une vision et des valeurs. Hier, celles-ci étaient fondées sur la certitude rationnelle. Demain, notre réussite dépendra de notre capacité à tolérer l'ambiguïté et, comme toujours, de notre imagination, notre créativité et notre intuition. » ERIC CHAN

3. **Grip'Ems** toothbrushes/Zahnbürsten/brosses à dents for Colgate, 1998
4. **Kiva Soft** screen/Wandschirm/écran for Herman Miller, 1999
5. **Executive** stapler/Hefter/agrafeuse for Hunt, 2000
6. **Dentsply SPS Scaler, Dualselect Dispenser**/Zahnreinigungsset/détartreur dentaire à ultrasons et jet double vitesse for Cavitron, 1997
7. **Kiva Wing** table/Tisch for Herman Miller, 1999

ERIC CHAN		CLIENTS
BORN	1952 Canton, China	Apple Computer
STUDIED	1980 MA Industrial Design, Cranbrook Academy of Arts, Bloomfield Hills, Michigan, USA	Bausch & Lomb
PRACTICE	1989 founded Ecco Design, New York	Colgate
AWARDS	1989 Best Product Design, *Business Week*	Corning
	1990 Best Product of 1990, *Design News*; Winner of Forma Finlandia 2 International Design Competition; Design-Innovationen 90, Highest Award, Industrieforum Essen; First Prize Design Plus Award, Frankfurt/Main	Cuisinart
		Goody
		Herman Miller
	1994-98 seven Good Design Awards, Chicago Athenaeum	LG Electronics
	1998 Best Overall Design, *Appliance Manufacturer Magazine*	Motorola
	1999 Comfia 99 Premier Award, Australia Furniture Exposition	Nissan
	1988-2001 twelve *I. D. Magazine Annual Design Review* Awards, New York	Sharp
	1989-2001 ten IDEA Awards, Industrial Designers Society of America	Timex
	2000 Neocon Design Excellence Award; Adex Design Journal Gold Award	
EXHIBITIONS	1994 *Design in America*, Frankfurt/Main	
	2000 *National Design Triennial – Design Culture Now*, Cooper-Hewitt National Design Museum, New York	
	2001 *Workspheres*, Museum of Modern Art, New York	

4

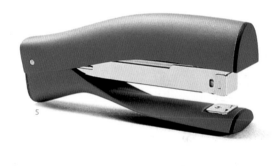

5

6

7

"Minimal Maximum – our work feeds on bread, cheese, coffee, the borough, the cinema, on smells, on comics, on a song, on sounds and noises, on colours ... on the world that surrounds us."

El Ultimo Grito

El Ultimo Grito, Studio 8, 23-28, Penn Street, London N15DL, England
T +44 20 7703 9939 F +22 20 7739 2009 grito@btinternet.com

»Minimales Maximum – unsere Arbeit nährt sich von Brot, Käse, Kaffee, der Stadt, dem Kino, von Gerüchen, Comics, von einem Lied, von Klängen und Geräuschen, von Farben ... von der Welt, die uns umgibt.«

« Maximum minimal – notre travail se nourrit de pain, de fromage, de café, du voisinage, de cinéma, d'odeurs, de bandes dessinées, d'une chanson, de sons ou de bruits, de couleurs ... du monde qui nous entoure. »

1. **Brain storming?** Magazine & toilet roll holder/
Zeitschriften- & Toilettenpapierhalter/porte magazines
& rouleau de papier hygiénique (self-production), 1998
2. ↓ **Don't run we are your friends!** pendant light/
Hängelampe/plafonnier (self-production), 1997

»Für uns besteht der kreative Prozess in der Beobachtung. Beobachtung der Welt, die uns umgibt und der Welt, mit der wir uns umgeben. Deshalb beziehen wir unsere Inspiration ebenso sehr daraus, beim Lebensmittelhändler in der Nachbarschaft ein Käsesandwich zu essen, wie aus dem Experimentieren mit neuen Materialien. Wir betrachten Design als eine Möglichkeit, Geschichten zu erzählen: Geschichten, die unser Alltagsleben kommentieren und ein Gefühl von ›Leichtigkeit‹ vermitteln, was als Einladung an alle gemeint ist, weniger zu konsumieren und mehr zu gestalten.« EL ULTIMO GRITO

"For us the creative process is one of observation. Observation of the world that surrounds us and the one with which we surround ourselves. That is why we draw our inspiration as much from eating a cheese sandwich in the local deli as from researching and playing with materials. We see design as a way of telling stories: stories that comment on our daily lives and put across a sense of 'easiness' as an open invitation to consume less and design more." EL ULTIMO GRITO

« Pour nous, la créativité est une question d'observation : l'observation du monde qui nous entoure et de celui dont nous nous entourons. C'est pourquoi manger un sandwich au fromage dans le bistrot du coin nous inspire autant que rechercher des matières et jouer avec. Créer des objets est une manière de raconter des histoires : des histoires qui commentent nos vies quotidiennes et mettent en avant une sensation " d'aisance " qui est une invitation ouverte à consommer moins et à créer davantage. » EL ULTIMO GRITO

3.-4. **What goes down ... must come up** laundry bin/ Wäschekorb/panier à linge sale for Hidden, 2000
5. **Miss Ramirez** chair/Sessel/fauteuil (limited edition) (self-production), 1997
6. **Good Morning Moneypenny** coat rack/Kleiderständer/ portemanteau (self-production), 1999
7. **Mind the Gap** magazine rack & coffee table/Couchtisch & Zeitschriftenhalter/table basse & porte-magazines for Punt Mobles, 1998
8. **La Lú** table lamp/Tischlampe/lampe for BD Spain, 1998

		EL ULTIMO GRITO	**CLIENTS**
FOUNDED	1997	in London by Roberto Feo (b. 1965, London), Rosario Hurtado (b. 1966, Madrid) & Francisco Santos (b. 1966, Seville)	BD (Spain) Punt Mobles also self-production
STUDIED		ROBERTO FEO	
	1995	HND Furniture Design, London Guildhall University	
	1997	MA Industrial Design, Royal College of Art, London	
		ROSARIO HURTADO	
	1996	HND Furniture Design, London Guildhall University	
	1998	BA Industrial Design, Kingston University	
		FRANCISCO SANTOS	
	1991-93	Cabinet Making, London Guildhall University	
	1992-94	HND Furniture Design, London Guildhall University	
EXHIBITIONS	1997	100 % Design, London, *Design Resolutions*, London	
	1998	*El Ultimo Grito*, Cologne; *Form and Function*, New York, *El Ultimo Grito*; Tokyo, *Design 4 Living*, Barnsley	
	1999	*Premillennium Tension*, Cologne; *Lost and Found*, touring exhibition, British Council	
	1999-2000	*A Grand Design*, Victoria & Albert Museum, London; *Material World*, London	
	2000	*Creative Britain*, Stilwerk, Berlin, *Six Moments*, London, *Happening*, Tokyo	
AWARDS	1997	*Blueprint/*100 % Design Award, London	
	1998	*Blueprint/*100 % Design Award, London; Mencion de Honor, International Design Competition, Valencia Furniture Fair	
	1999	Peugeot Design Award, London; *Blueprint/*100 % Design Award, London	
	2000	Peugeot Design Award, London	

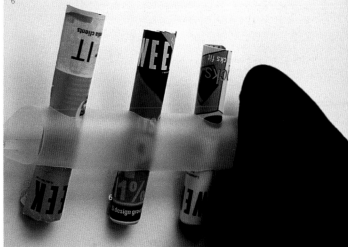

"Designing free of the constraints of mass production."

Elephant Design

Elephant Design, Nikko Akasaka Building 6F, 2-9-11 Akasaka Minato-ku, Tokyo 107-0052, Japan
T +81 3 5545 3061 F +81 3 5545 3062 www.elephant-design.com

»Ein Design, das frei ist von den Zwängen der Massenproduktion.«

« Créer, libéré des contraintes de la production de masse. »

1. **Nuigurumi-kun** remote control/Fernbedienung/
télécommande (self-production), 1999
2. ↓ **Washing machine**/Waschmaschine/machine à
laver (concept study, designed by Klein Dytham
architecture), 1999

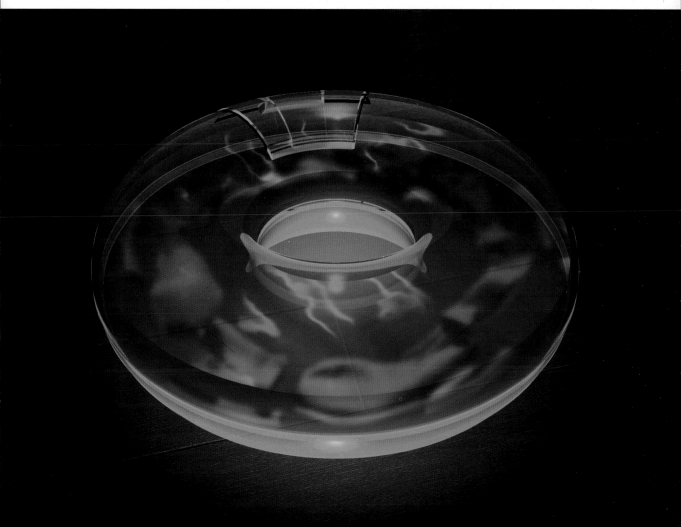

« Ce qui manque au design industriel aujourd'hui ? Il a perdu son rôle de symbole du futur. Partout autour de nous, on ne voit qu'un design assujetti aux tendances arrêtées pour l'année en cours. On rencontre rarement des créations qui soient excitantes en soi, comme c'était souvent le cas dans les années 60. D'un autre côté, on sent une puissante créativité chez les architectes et les stylistes de mode. Pourquoi cette différence ? Probablement parce que ces derniers peuvent travailler sans être soumis aux contraintes de la production de masse.

En relevant le défi de ce paradigme, nous avons trouvé une solution – grâce à l'Internet – en rassemblant les idées de créateurs sur notre site web puis en les peaufinant à l'aide du feed-back des consommateurs qui visitent notre site. Nous réunissons les amateurs qui approuvent ces projets de design puis nous nous mettons en quête d'un fabricant capable de les produire. Une fois que le nombre de commandes atteint le minimum requis pour la fabrication d'un lot, le consommateur obtient ce qu'il " voulait vraiment ". Les créateurs peuvent ainsi offrir au public un design très original. L'avenir du design industriel peut être radieux, à condition de ne pas se sentir obligé d'obéir aux vieux diktats de la production de masse. » ELEPHANT DESIGN

3.-4. ← **Cigarro** personal computer/Personalcomputer/ ordinateur PC, (limited production of 100 units), 2000
5.-10. **Denki-Hataki** static electric duster/statischer Elektroentstauber/dépoussiéreur à électricité statique (self-production), 2000

"What is lacking in industrial design today? We could say it no longer provides a symbol of the future. Everywhere we look, we see designs that serve only to distinguish new models year by year. We rarely encounter a design that excites us just by looking at it, as was often the case in the sixties. On the other hand, the powerful imagination of architects and fashion designers is coming right across. What is the difference? The answer lies in whether or not one is allowed to design free of the constraints of mass production.

Taking up the challenge of this paradigm, we have found a solution in the Internet – gathering the ideas of artistic designers on our web site and then refining them through the opinion of consumers who visit the site. We bring people together who approve of certain design ideas and then begin looking for the right manufacturer. Once the number of orders reaches the volume required for a minimum lot, the consumer is then able to obtain what he or she 'really wanted'. In this way, artistic designers can present highly original designs to the public. The future could be bright for industrial design, as long as we don't feel the need to operate under the old dictates of mass production". ELEPHANT DESIGN

5

»Woran mangelt es dem heutigen Industriedesign? Man könnte sagen, es stellt kein in die Zukunft weisendes Symbol mehr dar. Überall um uns herum sehen wir eine Form von Design, die lediglich Jahr für Jahr die jeweils aktuellen Trends hervorhebt. Nur selten treffen wir auf ein Design, das uns durch seinen bloßen Anblick in Begeisterung versetzt, wie es in den 60er Jahren häufig der Fall war. Im Gegensatz dazu ist der Ideenreichtum heutiger Architekten und Modedesigner deutlich erkennbar. Was ist der Grund für diesen Unterschied? Das hängt davon ab, inwieweit es den Gestaltern erlaubt ist, frei von den Zwängen der Massenproduktion zu arbeiten. Wir haben die Herausforderung dieses Paradigmas angenommen und die Lösung im Internet gefunden: Auf unserer Website versammeln wir die Ideen von Gestaltern und überarbeiten diese dann in Absprache mit den Konsumenten, die unser Informationsangebot abrufen. Dadurch bringen wir Menschen zusammen, denen bestimmte Designideen gefallen, und suchen dann nach dem geeigneten Hersteller für die Objekte. Hat die Anzahl der Bestellungen die erforderliche Mindestabnahmesumme erreicht, kann der Kunde das Objekt kaufen, das er oder sie ›wirklich haben wollte‹. Auf diese Weise können Designkünstler höchst originelle Ideen in die Öffentlichkeit bringen. Das Industriedesign kann einer freundlichen Zukunft entgegensehen, sofern wir uns nicht dem alten Diktat der Massenproduktion unterwerfen.« ELEPHANT DESIGN

6-10

ELEPHANT DESIGN	CLIENTS
FOUNDED 1997 by Kohei Nishiyama (b. 1970 Hyogo, Japan) and Yosuke Masumoto (b. 1970 Okayama, Japan) STUDIED KOHEI NISHIYAMA 1991-93 Industrial Design, Kuwasawa Design School, Tokyo YOSUKE MASUMOTO 1991-93 Industrial Design, Kuwasawa AWARDS 2000 G-Mark/Good Design Award, JIDPO, Tokyo; Gold Prize, *Digital Design of the Year*, *Popeye* magazine EXHIBITIONS 1997 *Venture Fair Japan*, Tokyo 1999 first *cuusoo.kaden* (imaginary home electrical appliances) exhibition, AXIS Gallery, Tokyo 2000 First *cuusoo.com* exhibition, Daikanyama, Tokyo 2001 second *cuusoo.com* exhibiton, Living Design Center OZONE, Tokyo	Self-production

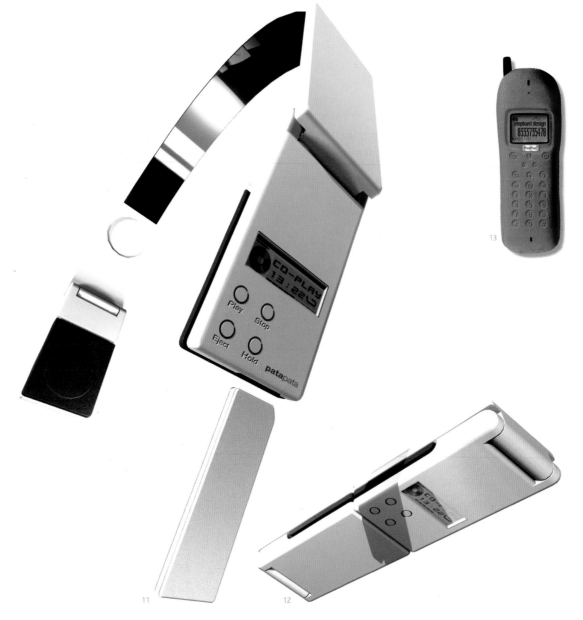

11

12

13

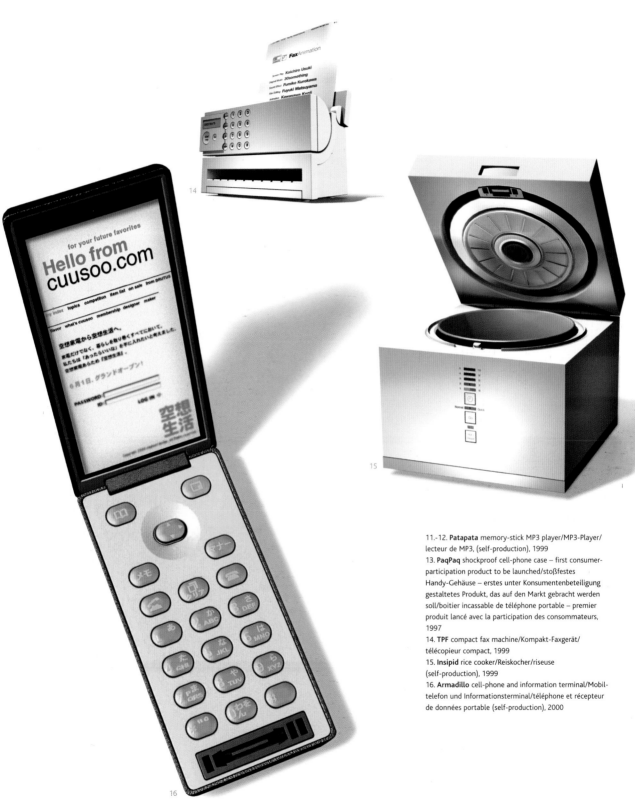

11.-12. **Patapata** memory-stick MP3 player/MP3-Player/
lecteur de MP3, (self-production), 1999
13. **PaqPaq** shockproof cell-phone case – first consumer-
participation product to be launched/stoßfestes
Handy-Gehäuse – erstes unter Konsumentenbeteiligung
gestaltetes Produkt, das auf den Markt gebracht werden
soll/boitier incassable de téléphone portable – premier
produit lancé avec la participation des consommateurs,
1997
14. **TPF** compact fax machine/Kompakt-Faxgerät/
télécopieur compact, 1999
15. **Insipid** rice cooker/Reiskocher/riseuse
(self-production), 1999
16. **Armadillo** cell-phone and information terminal/Mobil-
telefon und Informationsterminal/téléphone et récepteur
de données portable (self-production), 2000

"A design that is not intentional, that has the freedom to offer a variety of appeals, can be discovered over the course of time spent with the object."

Naoto Fukasawa

Naoto Fukasawa, c/o IDEO Japan, AXIS Bldg. 4F, 5-17-1 Roppongi, Minato-ku, Tokyo 106-0032, Japan
T +81 3 5 570 2664 F +81 3 5 570 2669 naoto@ideojapan.co.jp www.ideo.com

»Ein Design, das nicht zweckbestimmt ist, sondern auf vielfältige Weise Anreize gibt, kann im Laufe der Zeit entdeckt werden, die man mit dem Objekt verbringt.«

« Un design non intentionnel, assez libre pour présenter une variété d'attraits, se découvre au fil du temps que l'on passe avec l'objet. »

1. **Kinetic** watch/Armbanduhr/montre for Seiko, 1997
2. ↓ **Message Watch**/Nachrichten-Armbanduhr/montre
for Seiko, 1997

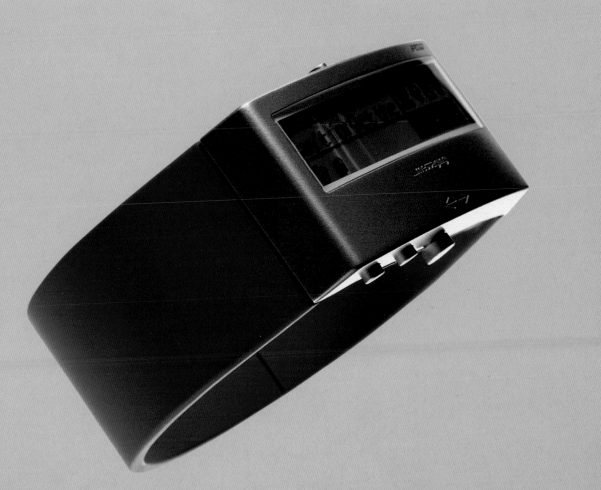

« L'environnement est un tout qui incarne le tout, mais il tend à être perçu comme existant à l'extérieur de soi. De même, on dessine parfois un objet en présumant qu'il ne sera vu que de face. On considère souvent un objet ou l'environnement comme ayant une fonction limitée, une seule raison d'être, mais ni l'environnement ni l'objet ne devraient jamais perdre leur immense potentiel de diversité. Se gratter le front avec son stylo ou empiler des documents sur une chaise sont également d'autres moyens d'utiliser ces objets. Le design peut être perçu comme un processus qui, non seulement répond à la fonction première de l'objet, mais facilite également ses fonctions alternatives que l'on découvre dans l'environnement actif de cet objet. »
NAOTO FUKASAWA

3. ← **Without Thought** cd player/CD-Player/lecteur de cd for DMN, as part of **Without Thought** project, 1990 manufactured and distributed by Muji
4. **Computer monitor**/Monitor/écran d'ordinateur for NEC, 1998

"Environment means the whole embodying the whole, but it tends to be perceived as if it exists outside of the self. Similarly, design is sometimes given an expression that assumes it will only be seen from the front. People often view an object or the environment as having a limited function, a single reason for being, but neither the environment nor the object should ever lose their immense potential for diversity. Scratching your forehead with a pencil or stacking documents on a chair are also ways of using these objects. Design can be seen as a process that not only accommodates the primary function of the object but also facilitates alternative functions that can be discovered within the object's active environment." NAOTO FUKASAWA

»Umwelt bedeutet die vollständige Verkörperung des Ganzen, aber sie wird meist als etwas wahrgenommen, das außerhalb des Selbst existiert. Auf ähnliche Weise wird Design manchmal als etwas dargestellt, vom dem man nur die Außenseite sieht. Die Leute betrachten ein Objekt oder ihre Umwelt häufig so, als hätten diese lediglich eine begrenzte Funktion, als gebe es nur einen einzigen Grund für ihre Existenz. Aber weder die Umwelt noch das Objekt sollten jemals ihr immenses Potential für Mannigfaltigkeit verlieren. Wenn man sich mit einem Bleistift am Kopf kratzt oder Schriftstücke auf einem Stuhl stapelt, sind auch das Möglichkeiten, diese Objekte zu benutzen. Design kann als ein Prozess betrachtet werden, der sich nicht nur in der primären Funktion des Objekts erfüllt, sondern darüber hinaus alternative Funktionen ermöglicht, die in der aktiven Umgebung des Objekts entdeckt werden können.« NAOTO FUKASAWA

off   on

5. **Visio** concept packaging/Verpackungskonzept/concept de packaging for Noevir, 1998
6. **Whitebox** central processing unit (CPU)/Zentralprozessor/unité centrale d'ordinateur for NEC, 1997
7.-8. **Tile** light/Lampe/luminaire for INAX, 1998
9. **Printables** printer/Drucker/imprimante for Epson, 1998
10. **New Domestic Cooking Tools** kettle/Kessel/bouilloire for Matsushita, 1998

"I try to break the usual codes in order to pursue new emotions."

Jean-Marc Gady

Jean-Marc Gady, 52 Rue des Abbesses, 75018 Paris, France
T/F +33 1 46 06 81 34   jmgady@club-internet.fr

»Ich versuche, die üblichen Regeln zu durchbrechen und dabei neue Emotionen zu entdecken.«

« Je tente de briser les codes habituels en quête de nouvelles émotions. »

1. **Moods** chaise longue/Liege for VIA project, 2000
2. ↓ **Air Cup** coffee cups/Kaffeebecher/tasses à café
for Ligne Roset, 2000

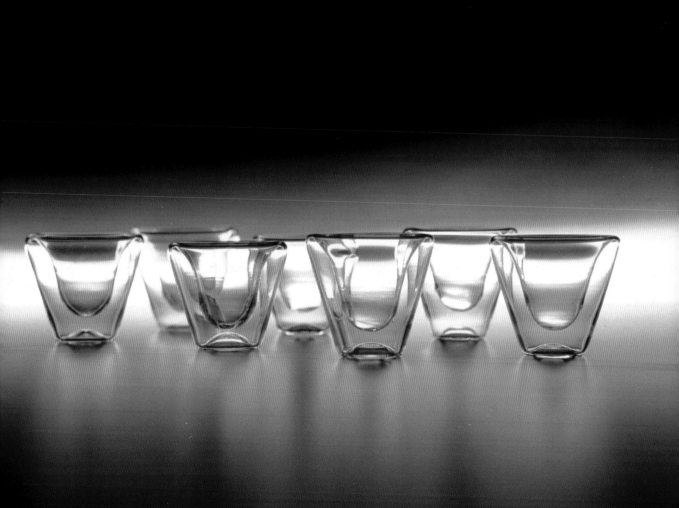

« En tant que dessinateur industriel et desi-gner de meubles, j'ai plusieurs " axes " de tra-vail : ma production est consacrée en grande partie à une recherche " typologique " et fonc-tionnelle. Quand je décide de m'attaquer à un projet (qu'il s'agisse d'un vase ou d'un aspira-teur), j'essaie d'oublier son passé esthétique et de l'aborder avec un regard " vierge ", d'ap-préhender l'objet par d'autres biais. L'interac-tion est également un thème récurrent de ma démarche. Ce qui compte pour moi, c'est que le produit fasse partie de l'évolution de son utilisateur sans créer de complications d'au-cune sorte. A mon avis, le designer d'aujour-d'hui doit être profondément imprégné de l'esprit de son temps, captant tous les signes dans l'air. Il doit être fin observateur afin d'accumuler assez de " matière " à marier à sa propre personnalité et anticiper ainsi les nouveaux schémas de consommation. Même ainsi, il n'y a pas de règles en design. »
JEAN-MARC GADY

3. ← **La Chose** ashtrays/Aschenbecher/cendriers for G2, 2000
4. **Cinémascope** lamp/Lampe/lampe for Project G2, 2000

"As an industrial and furniture designer, I have several work 'axes': for the most part my production is dedicated to 'typological' and functional research. According to my creative process, when I make up my mind to take on a project (whether a vase or a vacuum cleaner), I try to forget its aesthetic past and instead experiment using a 'virgin' eye so as to apprehend the object in other ways. Interaction is also a recurring theme in my approach to design. For me, it is im-portant that the product become part of the user's evolution without complications of any kind. I think that nowadays, a designer has to be deeply impregnated by his time, catching every sign floating around. The designer needs to be a sharp observer so that he can accumulate enough 'matter' to mix with his per-sonality so as to anticipate new patterns of consumption. Even so, there are no rules in design."
JEAN-MARC GADY

»In meiner Arbeit als Industrie- und Möbel-designer verfolge ich mehrere Interessen: Meine Produktion besteht zum größten Teil aus einer Auseinandersetzung mit den Themen ›Typologie‹ und ›Funktion‹. Wenn ich mich dazu entschließe, ein Designprojekt zu über-nehmen (sei es die Gestaltung einer Vase oder eines Staubsaugers), versuche ich zunächst, die ästhetische Vergangenheit des jeweiligen Objekts zu vergessen und es stattdessen mit ›jungfräulichen‹ Augen zu betrachten, um einen neuen Zugang zu ihm zu finden. Die Interaktion ist ebenfalls ein immer wieder-kehrendes Thema in meiner Art, an Design heranzugehen. Für mich ist es wichtig, dass das Produkt zu einem Teil der Entwicklung des Benutzers wird, und zwar ohne irgendwel-che Komplikationen. Ich finde, heutzutage müssen Designer ganz von ihrer Zeit durch-drungen sein und jedes noch so flüchtige Signal auffangen können. Designer müssen scharfe Beobachter sein, so dass sie imstande sind, genügend ›Material‹ zusammenzutragen, um es mit der eigenen Persönlichkeit zu ver-mischen und daraus neue Muster des Kon-sumverhaltens abzulesen. Aber dennoch: Im Design gibt es keine Regeln.« JEAN-MARC GADY

		JEAN-MARC GADY		CLIENTS
BORN	1971	Charenton, France		Aquamedic
STUDIED	1991	BTS Communication and Advertising Diploma		Cinna
	1993-96	Interior and Environmental Design Studies at l'Ecole Bleue		G2
PRACTICE	1992	artistic assistant at advertising agencies Publicis Etoile and Mac Caan Erickson		Ligne Roset
	2000-	design experiment teacher at l'Ecole Bleue		Liv'it
AWARDS	1997	Special Award at *Homo Domus* exhibition		Nestlé
EXHIBITIONS	1997	*Homo Domus*, Milan and Paris; *Escalator*, Paris; *Intramuros*, Milan, Paris		Pixelpark
	1998	*Material Connexion*, New York		VIA
	2000	Salon du Meuble, Paris		Wu' Gallery

5

6

7

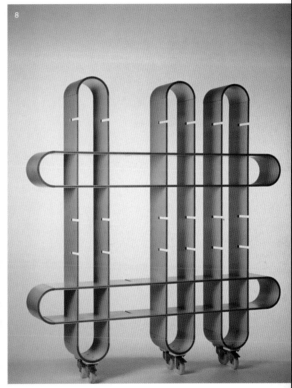

8

5. **Spirit** desk/Schreibtisch/bureau for VIA project and edited by Wu' Gallery, 1998

6. **Submarine** vase/Vase for Cinna, 2000

7. **Punch-Light**/Leuchte/luminaire for Project G2, 2000

8. **Isis** shelves/Regal/étagères for En Attendant Les Barbares project, 1997

"Moving to an emotional supermarket."

 # Stefano Giovannoni

Stefano Giovannoni, Giovannoni Design srl, Via Gulli 4, 20147 Milan, Italy
T +39 02 48703495 F +39 02 48701141 studio@stefanogiovannoni.com www.stefanogiovannoni.com

»Aufbruch zu einem emotionalen Super-
markt.«

« Vers un supermarché des émotions. »

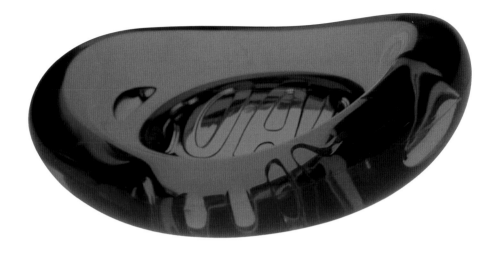

1. **Big Bubbles** soap dish/Seifenschale/porte-savon for
Alessi, 1999
2. ↓ **Big Switch** lamp/Lampe/lampe for Segno, 1996

« Les objets ne sont ni beaux ni laids, mais adaptés ou pas à leur époque. Par leur image et la technologie utilisée pour les produire, ils communiquent des valeurs particulières qui s'intègrent à notre culture. Communiquer à travers des objets signifie raconter une histoire qui parle de la vie au travers d'un attrait sensoriel et chaleureux lié à notre mémoire et à notre monde imaginaire.

Le designer est toujours plus impliqué dans la technologie et les concepts de marketing. Il ne se contente plus de concevoir des objets mais doit adapter ses objectifs à des stratégies de design. Son champ d'action n'est plus l'objet en soi mais une hypothèse de développement global pour un produit et/ou une marque. Cela signifie de placer au cœur de son travail des stratégies liées à la communication, au marketing et à la technologie. Les besoins et les désirs du public évoluant rapidement, il doit constamment tenir compte de ces transformations tout en exprimant haut et fort sa vision personnelle du monde.

Je me suis souvent demandé si nous avions vraiment besoin de nouveaux produits. Dans la société moderne, chacun possède des objets satisfaisant à tous ses besoins fonctionnels. Mais, pour créer la richesse, les compagnies doivent produire en quantités toujours plus grandes. D'un côté, nous n'avons pas besoin de nouveaux produits, de l'autre, nous devons développer un nouveau système virtuel afin d'anticiper l'architecture fictive et toujours plus sophistiquée de nos désirs. Les produits de cette nouvelle réalité virtuelle sont de plus en plus éloignés de toute véritable fonction. Notre réalité se construit étape par étape, en annexant de nouveaux paysages virtuels qui élargissent les frontières de notre pays des merveilles. »

STEFANO GIOVANNONI

3. ← **Magicbunny** toothpick holder/Zahnstocherhalter/ porte cure-dents for Alessi, 1998
4. **Molly** weighing scale/Küchenwaage/balance for Alessi, 1995
5. **Mago'** broom/Besen/balai for Magis, 1998
6. **Alibaba** vacuum jug/Thermoskanne/cruche Thermos for Alessi, 1998

4

"Objects are not beautiful or ugly but are either suited or not to their time. Through their image and the technology used to produce them they communicate particular values that become part of our culture. To communicate through objects means telling a story of something that relates to life through a warm sensorial appeal connected with our memory and imaginary world.

The designer is increasingly involved in marketing concepts and technology. He cannot simply 'design' objects but must now shift his goals towards design strategies. The field of action is no longer that of the object but a hypothesis of comprehensive development for the product/company. This means putting strategies linked to communication, marketing and technology at the core of one's work. The public's needs and desires evolve rapidly – so it is necessary to take in these transformations all the time, while delivering loud and clear your personal view of the world.

I have asked myself many times whether we really need new products. Everybody in a developed society is in possession of the objects that answer every functional need. But to create wealth, companies have to produce in larger and larger quantities – on the one hand we have no need for new products, but on the other hand we must develop a new virtual system in order to anticipate the new and increasingly sophisticated fictional architecture of our desires. Products belonging to this kind of virtual reality are further and further removed from real function. Our reality is built step by step by annexing new virtual landscapes which extend the borders of our wonderland."

STEFANO GIOVANNONI

5

6

»Die Frage ist nicht, ob Designobjekte schön oder hässlich sind, sondern ob sie zeitgemäß sind oder nicht. Durch ihr Image und durch die zu ihrer Herstellung eingesetzte Technik vermitteln sie bestimmte Werte, die zu einem Bestandteil unserer Kultur werden. Durch Objekte zu kommunizieren, bedeutet, eine Geschichte zu erzählen, die eine Beziehung zum Leben hat. Das gelingt mit Objekten, die eine warme, sinnliche Ausstrahlung haben, mit der sich unsere Erinnerungen und unsere Vorstellungswelt verbinden.

Designer sind zunehmend in die Bereiche Marketing und Technologie involviert. Sie können nicht mehr einfach nur Objekte gestalten, sondern müssen ihre Ziele nun darauf verlagern, Designstrategien zu entwerfen. Das Tätigkeitsfeld von Designern ist nicht länger auf das Objekt beschränkt, sondern es gehört jetzt auch eine Analyse der allgemeinen Entwicklung des Produkts oder des Unternehmens dazu. Das heißt, dass man die mit Kommunikation, Marketing und Technik verbundenen Strategien zum Kernpunkt seiner Arbeit macht. Da sich die in der Öffentlichkeit herrschenden Bedürfnisse und Wünsche mit großer Geschwindigkeit entwickeln, ist es notwendig, diese Wandlungen ständig zu reflektieren und gleichzeitig seine persönliche Weltsicht laut und deutlich kundzutun.

Ich habe mich schon oft gefragt, ob wir wirklich ständig neue Produkte brauchen. In unserer Industriegesellschaft besitzt jeder die Gebrauchsgegenstände, die zur Befriedigung sämtlicher funktionalen Bedürfnisse erforderlich sind. Um ihren Profit zu steigern, müssen die Unternehmen jedoch in immer größeren Mengen produzieren. Auf der einen Seite haben wir zwar keinen Bedarf an neuen Produkten, aber andererseits müssen wir ein virtuelles System entwickeln, um die neue und zunehmend differenzierte fiktive Struktur unserer Bedürfnisse vorauszusehen. Die Produkte dieser virtuellen Realität entfernen sich immer weiter von einer wirklichen Funktion. Unsere Realität entsteht Schritt für Schritt durch die Annexion neuer virtueller Landschaften, welche die Grenzen unserer Phantasiewelten ausdehnen.« STEFANO GIOVANNONI

7. **Bombo** chair/Stuhl/chaise for Magis, 1999

8. **Volcano** watch/Armbanduhr/montre for Alba-Seiko, 1998

STEFANO GIOVANNONI		CLIENTS
BORN	1954 La Spezia, Italy	Alessi
STUDIED	1978 graduated in Architecture, University of Florence	Asplund
	1979- teaching and research, Faculty of Architecture, University of Florence, Domus Academy, Milan and the Institute of Design, Reggio Emilia	Cappellini
		Flos
AWARDS	1980 First Prize, *Shinchenchiku Residential Design Competition*, Tokyo; First Prize, *Competition for a square at Santa Croce sull'Arno*, Florence	Kankyo
		Magis
	1985 Second Prize, *Shinchenchiku Residential Design Competition*, Tokyo	Pulsar
	1989 First Prize (with Andrea Branzi and Remo Buti), *Competition for the restructuring of the historical centre at Casteldisangro-Aquila*	Saab
		Seiko
	1994 Design Plus Award, Frankfurt/Main	
	1996 Design Plus Award, Frankfurt/Main	
	1999 if Design Award, Hanover	
EXHIBITIONS	1991 designed the Italian Pavilion at *Les Capitales Européennes du Nouveau Design*, Centre Georges Pompidou, Paris	

9

10

9. **Octopussy** watch/Armbanduhr/montre for Alba-Seiko, 1999

10. **Rimini** cutlery drainer/Abtropfgefäß für Besteck/ égouttoir à couverts for Alessi, 1998

11. **Rigatone** spaghetti storage jar/Spaghettiglas/ bocal à spaghettis for Alessi, 1998

12. **Bruce** table-lighter/Tischfeuerzeug/briquet de table for Alessi, 1999

13. **Big Clip** photo frame/Bilderrahmen/cadre de photo for Alessi, 1998

14. **Johnny the Diver** plunger/Tauchsieder/ventouse for Alessi, 2000

15. **Bombo** revolving stool/Drehhocker/tabouret pivotant for Magis, 1998

"When I design, I design for people,
not for an abstract entity, a market,
but for real people, people I know,
people I love."

Konstantin Grcic

Konstantin Grcic, Konstantin Grcic Industrial Design, Schillerstrasse 40, 80 336 Munich, Germany
T +49 89 550 79995 F +49 89 550 79996 mail@konstantin-grcic.com www.konstantin-grcic.com

*»Wenn ich entwerfe, entwerfe ich nicht
für ein abstraktes Gebilde oder einen
Markt, sondern für reale Menschen, die
ich kenne und liebe.«*

« Quand je crée un objet, je ne le
conçois pas pour une entité abstraite
ou pour un marché, mais pour des
gens bien réels, que je connais, que
j'aime. »

1. **Chef** microwave concept study/Entwurfsstudie für
eine Mikrowelle/étude conceptuelle de micro-ondes
for Whirlpool, 2000
2. ↓ **Belle & Bon** egg-cup and spoon/Eierbecher und
Löffel/coquetier et cuillère for Porzellan-Manufaktur
Nymphenburg, 1999

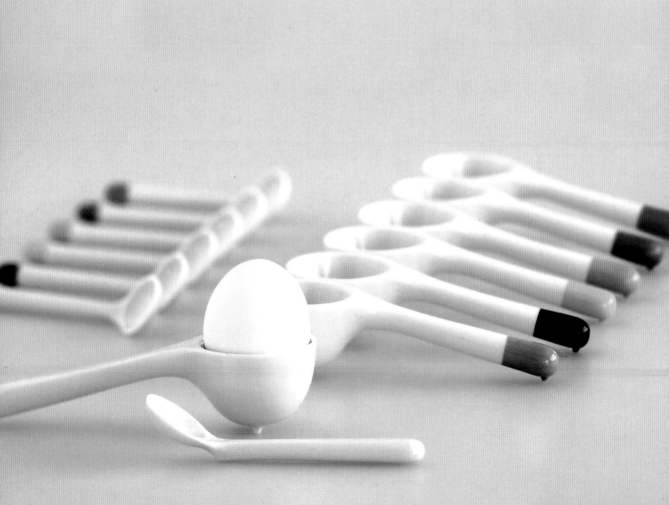

« De toute évidence, une des grandes expé-riences du passé déterminera le futur : l'évolution de la vie (et cela affecte le design) est conditionnée par la perte irrévocable d'une vérité absolue. Nous avons appris que la vie sur la planète n'est pas construite autour d'une seule explication mais permet de nombreuses interprétations différentes et simultanées. Deux systèmes prétendument contradictoires ne s'annulent pas nécessairement l'un l'autre. Par conséquent, l'avenir ne produira pas une formule universelle pour le design. Il n'y aura aucune mesure absolue de ce qui est un bon ou un mauvais produit. Ce qui, il n'y a pas longtemps, paraissait rassurant et clair peut soudain soulever des questions et des doutes. Ce qui était passé inaperçu peut soudain receler une beauté et un intérêt jusque là insoupçonnables. La fragilité inhérente de notre conception de l'ordre du monde sera une source d'inspiration permanente. »
KONSTANTIN GRCIC

3. ← **Chaos** chair/Sessel/chaise for ClassiCon, 2001
4. **Mayday** portable lamp/tragbare Lampe/lampe portable for Flos, 1998

"One principal experience from the past will clearly be determining our future: the evolution of life (and this affects design) is conditioned by the irrevocable loss of an absolute truth. We have had to learn that life on our planet is not built around a single interpretation but rather allows for many different interpretations simultaneously. Two supposedly contradictive systems do not necessarily have to cancel each other out. Future will therefore not produce one formula for design. There will be no truth about what is good and what is bad design. Something that a short time ago seemed reassuring and clear, might suddenly raise queries and doubt. Something that has been unnoticed, might suddenly bear an unexpected potential of beauty and interest. The fragility in our existing conception of the world order guarantees to be a permanent source of inspiration."
KONSTANTIN GRCIC

»Eine prinzipielle Erfahrung aus der Vergangenheit wird eindeutig unsere Zukunft bestimmen: Die Evolution des Lebens hat (und das betrifft auch das Design) den unwiderruflichen Verlust einer absoluten Wahrheit zur Bedingung. Wir mussten lernen, dass das Leben auf unserem Planeten nicht auf einer einzigen Interpretation gründet, sondern viele verschiedene Interpretationsmöglichkeiten gleichzeitig zulässt. Zwei einander scheinbar widersprechende Systeme müssen sich nicht unbedingt gegenseitig ausschließen. Daher wird die Zukunft keine allgemein gültige Formel für Design hervorbringen. Es wird keinen absoluten Maßstab dafür geben, was gutes und was schlechtes Design ist. Etwas, das vor kurzem noch sicher und klar zu sein schien, kann plötzlich Fragen und Zweifel aufwerfen. Und etwas, das unbemerkt geblieben war, kann auf einmal als etwas entdeckt werden, das unerwartete Tiefen an Schönheit und Bedeutung enthält. Die Fragilität, die unserer bestehenden Auffassung von der Weltordnung innewohnt, wird eine unerschöpfliche Inspirationsquelle **sein**.« KONSTANTIN GRCIC

KONSTANTIN GRCIC	CLIENTS

KONSTANTIN GRCIC

			CLIENTS
BORN	1965	Munich, Germany	Agape
STUDIED	1985-87	cabinetmaking, John Makepeace School for Craftsmen in Wood, Parnham College, Dorset	Authentics
	1988-90	MA in Industrial Design, Royal College of Art, London	Cappellini
PRACTICE	1990	worked in the design office of Jasper Morrison, London	ClassiCon
	1991	established own design practice, Konstanin Grcic Industrial Design, Munich	Driade
AWARDS	1997	Young Designer of the Year (sponsored by *Architektur & Wohnen*, Hamburg) nominated by Achille Castiglioni	Flos
			Iittala
	1999	Young Designer Award, Brooklyn Museum of Art-Modernism, New York	Montina
	2000	Guest of Honour, Interieur Biennial, Kortrijk	Moorman
EXHIBITIONS	1995	*13 Years after Memphis*, Museum für Kunsthandwerk, Frankfurt/Main	Porzellan-Manufaktur Nymphenburg
	1996	*Aspects of Design*, Louisiana Museum, Humlebæk; *Konstantin Grcic – Twinset*, solo exhibition, Binnen Gallery, Amsterdam	SCP
	2000	*Design 4:3 – Fifty Years of Italian and German Design*, Kunst-und Ausstellungshalle der Bundesrepublik Deutschland, Bonn; *Guest of Honour*, Interieur Biennial, Kortrijk	Whirlpool
			Wireworks
			WMF

5

6

7

5. **H2O** bucket with lid/Eimer mit Deckel/seau avec couvercle for Authentics, 1997
6. **Go** trolley/Rollwagen/chariot for Authentics, 1998
7. & 10. **Relations** glassware/Gläser/verres et plats en verre for Iittala, 1999
8. **Hertz** halogen light/Halogenstrahler/lampe halogène for Flos, 2000
9. **Scolaro** stool & table/Hocker & Ablage/tabouret & table for Montina, 2000

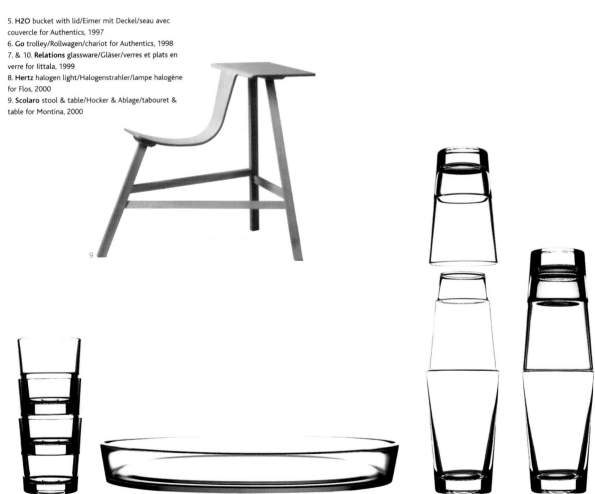

"The less you see the designer's effort in the work, the better – effort should not be a visual commodity; it's simply a means to an end."

Sam Hecht

Sam Hecht, c/o IDEO Europe, White Bear Yard, 144a, Clerkenwell Road, London EC1R 5DF, England
T +44 20 7713 2600 F +44 20 7713 2601 shecht@ideo.com www.ideo.com

»Je weniger man einem Objekt die Mühe des Designers ansieht, desto besser. Die Mühe sollte keine visuelle Ware werden; sie ist einfach Mittel zum Zweck.«

« Moins l'on perçoit l'effort du designer dans son travail, mieux c'est. L'effort ne devrait pas constituer un produit mais uniquement le moyen d'arriver à une fin. »

1. **Rice cooker**/Reiskocher/riseuse for Matsushita, 1997
2. ↓ **Water faucet** and control/Wasserhahn und Regler/
robinetterie for INAX, 1998

« Le design continue d'être confronté à un dilemme : déterminer quelle part du produit devrait être développée afin qu'il soit choisi en boutique et quelle part développer pour qu'il soit utilisable. Dans un modèle théorique, le design est conçu pour un usage spécifique et la popularité d'un produit se mesure à la réussite de cet objectif. Mais, dans la pratique, bien fonctionner ne suffit pas. Le produit doit être choisi et acheté sur un lieu de vente où il sera en concurrence avec de nombreux autres produits fonctionnant aussi bien. D'où une situation où les marchés saturés nécessitent que " l'attrait " prime sur la " fonction ". Les produits sont devenus l'incarnation de leur propre marque.

Si je veux créer un objet, dois-je renoncer à la fonction pour privilégier l'attrait ? Nous n'avons pas besoin de voir ce que nous faisons pour obtenir un résultat. La forme est un mécanisme plutôt qu'une esthétique (ou une surface sur laquelle intervient le choix). Elle doit être élaborée et non appliquée. La simplicité des outils illustre cette idée : leur simplification résulte d'une production culturelle complexe. La question " allons-nous concevoir un beau marteau ou un marteau tout court ? " n'a pas de sens. Pourquoi un ordinateur ou une télévision ne seraient-ils pas conçus de la même manière ? L'avenir deviendra simpliste. C'est indispensable si nous voulons consommer de la technologie. L'illustration de la complexité n'est pas importante, seul le résultat compte. La forme deviendra mécanique, puisant ses racines dans l'ordinaire. Les projets impliquant une complexité toujours croissante, la vérité doit être d'autant plus éclatante. » SAM HECHT

3. ← NTT Docomo phone/Telefon/téléphone for Electro-textiles, 2000
4. XY toaster/Toaster/grille-pain for Matsushita, 1999

"Design continues to face a dilemma when determining what portion of a product should be developed to be chosen in the shop, and what portion of it should be developed to be used. In an educational model, design is produced according to use, and a product's popularity is measured by how successfully it does its job. But in the shop model, working well is simply not enough. The product needs to be selected and purchased in an arena where many products, from different manufacturers, work just as well. This has led to a situation where saturated markets require the 'choosing' to be more important than the 'using'. Products have become their own embodiment of branding.

If I am to design, must I relinquish the using for the choosing? Like the phrase 'things become second nature', we do not need to see what we are doing to achieve a result. Form is a mechanism for use, rather than an aesthetic (or a surface upon which choice is played out). It is something that needs to be evolved and not applied. The simplicity of tools illustrates this idea: their simplification results from complex cultural production. The question 'shall we design a beautiful hammer or a plain hammer?' is absurd. And there is no reason why a computer or a television is not thought of in the same way. The future will become simplistic. It needs to be, if we are to consume technology, where the illustration of complexity is of no importance, but only the result. Form will become mechanical, with its roots in the ordinary. As projects involve an ever-greater complexity, the more resonant the truth needs to be." SAM HECHT

»Design steht weiterhin vor einem Dilemma, wenn es darum geht, zu entscheiden, welcher Aspekt eines Produkts für den Kaufanreiz und welcher für den Gebrauch entwickelt wird. Im theoretischen Modell wird Design im Hinblick auf seine Funktionalität produziert, und der Erfolg eines Produkts misst sich daran, wie gut es seine jeweilige Funktion erfüllt. In der Verkaufspraxis reicht es jedoch nicht, dass ein Produkt gut funktioniert. Denn es muss in einem Umfeld ausgewählt und gekauft werden, in dem es viele Produkte von anderen Herstellern gibt, die genauso gut funktionieren. Das hat zu einer Situation geführt, die gesättigte Märkte dazu zwingen, dem kommerziellen Aspekt Vorrang vor dem funktionalen Aspekt einzuräumen. Die Produkte sind damit zu ihrem eigenen Markenzeichen geworden. Muss ich als Designer zugunsten des Marktwerts auf den Gebrauchswert verzichten? Wie in dem Satz ›Dinge werden zur zweiten Natur‹ anklingt, brauchen wir nicht zu verstehen, was wir tun, um ein Ergebnis zu erzielen. Form ist mehr ein Mechanismus für den Gebrauch als ein ästhetisches Kriterium (oder eine Oberfläche, die den kommerziellen Aspekt ausspielt). Form ist etwas, das entwickelt und nicht angewendet werden muss. Diese Idee wird in der Einfachheit von Werkzeugen anschaulich, denn die Vereinfachung ist das Resultat eines komplexen kulturellen Produktionsprozesses. Absurd ist die Frage, ob man einen schönen oder einen schlichten Hammer entwerfen soll. Und es gibt keinen Grund, warum das nicht auch für die Gestaltung eines Computers oder eines Fernsehers gelten soll. Die Zukunft wird eine zunehmende Vereinfachung bringen. Und das muss auch so sein, wenn wir eine Technologie nutzen wollen, bei der nicht die Darstellung von Komplexität zählt, sondern nur das Ergebnis. Form wird mechanisch werden und ihre Wurzeln im Alltäglichen haben. Gerade weil Designprojekte immer komplexer werden, muss der Aspekt der Wahrhaftigkeit umso deutlicher zur Geltung kommen.« SAM HECHT

SAM HECHT

BORN	1969	London, England
STUDIED	1989-91	BA Industrial Design, Central St Martin's College of Art and Design, London
	1991-93	MA Industrial Design, Royal College of Art, London
PRACTICE	1993	David Chipperfield Architects, London
	1994	Studia Design Group, Tel Aviv
	1994-99	IDEO offices, San Francisco, Tokyo
	1999	Head of Industrial Design, IDEO Europe, London
AWARDS	1997	Gold IDEA Award, IDEO San Francisco office
	1998	D&AD Exhibition Category Award, London
	2000	Watercycle Pavilion D-Line Award, London
EXHIBITIONS	1995	*Mutant Materials in Contemporary Design*, Museum of Modern Art, New York
	1997	*Whitebox*, TNProbe, Tokyo
	1998	*Printables*, Ozone Gallery, Tokyo
	2000	*Under a Fiver*, Design Museum, London
	2001	*Workspheres*, Museum of Modern Art, New York

CLIENTS

Airbus Industrie
Epson
INAX
LG Electronics
Loewe
Matsushita
NEC
Seiko
Thames Water

5

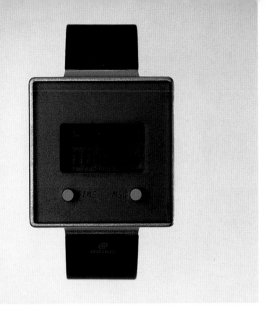

5. Desktop computer/Arbeitsplatzrechner/ordinateur
de bureau for NEC, 1998
6. **Airbus A380** window/Flugzeugfenster/hublot for Airbus
Industrie, 2000
7. **Post-It** e-mail watch/E-Mail-Armbanduhr/montre
for Seiko Communications, 1997
8. **Watercycle Pavilion**/Wasserkreislauf-Pavillon/Pavillon
du cycle de l'eau for Thames Water, 2000
9. **LG** dishwasher/Geschirrspüler/lave-vaisselle for LG
Electronics, 2000

"As a designer, there can be no greater prize, for me, than to create an object of desire."

Keith Helfet

Keith Helfet, Helfet Design, 6, Hawkesworth Drive, Kenilworth, Warwickshire CV8 2GP, England
T/F +44 1926 856 170 keith@helfet.co.uk

»Für einen Designer kann es keine höhere Auszeichnung geben, als ein Objekt der Begierde zu kreieren.«

« En tant que designer, rien ne m'est plus précieux que de créer un objet de désir. »

1.-2. **F-Type** concept sports roadster/Entwurf für einen
Roadster/projet de roadster for Jaguar, 2000

»Der Erfolg eines Designs lässt sich nach dem Wert bemessen, den es einem Produkt hinzufügt. Dieser zusätzliche Wert kann vielerlei Formen annehmen: eine Verbesserung in Funktionalität, Qualität (sowohl reale als empfundene), Kosten und Service, leichtere Fertigungsmethoden sowie eine Verstärkung oder Hervorbringung der Markenwerte und Corporate Identity. Im Idealfall sollte Design dem Produkt so viele dieser Aspekte hinzufügen wie möglich. Meiner Erfahrung nach ist das wirksamste Mittel zur Wertsteigerung, dass man die Emotionen der Käufer anspricht, indem man eine optische Anziehungskraft erzeugt. Das macht die Kaufentscheidung sowohl rational als auch emotional. Wenn ein Produkt emotional attraktiv ist, suchen die Kunden nach Gründen für den Kauf, weil sie es besitzen wollen. Emotionale Attraktivität bietet reale Wettbewerbsvorteile und folglich die Voraussetzung für Höchstpreise und/oder wachsende Umsätze. Das kann einen bedeutenden Teil der Rendite für Investitionen im Bereich Design ausmachen.

Während seiner gesamten Firmengeschichte hat das Unternehmen *Jaguar* auf die emotionale Anziehungskraft gesetzt, indem es einige der begehrtesten und wirkungsvollsten Autos ihrer Zeit produzierte. Deren Attraktivität beruhte in hohem Maße auf ihren wunderschön gestalteten fließenden Formen. Für mich als Designer schien es deshalb nur natürlich, die Form als meine Gestaltungssprache zu verwenden, zunächst für meine Jaguar-Entwürfe und später für die Konzeption meiner Produktdesigns. Die emotionale Anziehungskraft lässt Kunden Produkte kaufen, bevor sie sie ausprobiert und verstanden haben, wie sie funktionieren. Die schmeichelhafteste und befriedigendste Reaktion auf meine Arbeit ist der Satz: ›Das will ich haben‹.« KEITH HELFET

"The success of a design can be measured in terms of the value it adds to a product. This added value can take many forms: improvements in functionality, quality (both real and perceived), cost and service, easier methods of manufacture as well as the enhancement and creation of brand values and corporate identity. In an ideal world, design should add to the product in as many of these aspects as are applicable. In my experience, the most effective means of adding value is to appeal to customers' emotions by creating visual appeal. This makes the purchase decision both rational and emotional. If a product has emotional appeal, customers look for reasons to buy, because they want to own it. Emotional appeal offers real competitive advantages, and hence the opportunity for premium pricing and/or incremental volume. This can be the source of significant return on the design investment.

Throughout its history, Jaguar has relied on emotional appeal by producing some of the most desirable and evocative cars of their time. Their appeal was largely due to their beautiful sculptured flowing forms. As a designer, therefore, it seemed natural to me to use form as my design language, firstly for my Jaguar designs and later to apply this philosophy to my product design. Emotional appeal makes customers order products before they have experienced or understood the nature of their functionality. The most complimentary and satisfying response to my work that I can receive is 'I want one'." KEITH HELFET

« Le succès d'un design se mesure à la valeur qu'il ajoute à un produit. Cette valeur ajoutée peut prendre de nombreuses formes : une amélioration de sa fonctionnalité, de sa qualité (tant réelle que perçue), de son coût et de son service, des méthodes de fabrication plus simples ainsi que la mise en valeur et la création d'une image de marque et d'une identité d'entreprise. Dans un monde idéal, le design devrait enrichir le produit sous tous les aspects possibles. Mais je sais d'expérience que le moyen le plus efficace d'ajouter de la valeur est d'en appeler aux émotions du consommateur en créant un attrait visuel. Cela rend la décision d'achat à la fois rationnelle et émotive. Quand un produit présente un attrait émotionnel, on se cherche une bonne raison de l'acheter parce qu'on veut le posséder. L'attrait émotionnel offre de vraies avantages compétitifs, d'où la possibilité de vendre au prix fort et / ou d'un volume cumulatif. Cela peut générer un retour substantiel sur le budget investi dans le design.

Tout au long de son histoire, Jaguar a joué sur l'attrait émotionnel en produisant certaines des voitures les plus désirables et évocatrices de leur temps. Cet attrait était dû en grande partie à leurs superbes formes fluides et sculpturales. En tant que designer, il me semble donc naturel d'utiliser la forme comme langage de design, d'abord dans mes travaux pour Jaguar puis dans mes conceptions de produits. L'attrait émotionnel incite le consommateur a commander un produit avant même de l'avoir essayé ou d'avoir compris la nature de sa fonctionnalité. La réaction la plus flatteuse et satisfaisante à mon travail est quand j'entends dire " J'en veux un ". » KEITH HELFET

3. F-Type concept sports roadster (interior)/Entwurf für einen Roadster (Innenraum)/projet de roadster (intérieur) for Jaguar, 2000
4. Varicam nuclear medicine scanner/Nuklearmedizin-Scanner/scanner nucléaire médical for Elscint, 1995
5. Prima M. R. I. scanner/Scanner for Elscint, 1996
6. Jaguar XK8 sports roadster/Roadster for Jaguar, 1995
7. Jaguar XK180 concept sports roadster/Entwurf für einen Roadster/projet de roadster for Jaguar, 1998

KEITH HELFET		CLIENTS

BORN	1946	Cape Town, South Africa	Elscint
STUDIED	1974	BSc Mechanical Engineering, University of Cape Town	In-house designer for Jaguar
	1977	MA Automotive Design, Royal College of Art, London	
PRACTICE	1978	joined Jaguar Cars as a designer	
	1981-	Styling Management, Jaguar Cars (1981-85 Sports Cars; 1985-91 Advanced Projects; 1991-93 Exterior Design; 1993-96 Luxury Cars; 1996-99 Advanced Vehicles and Product Design)	
	1993	established Helfet Design, Kenilworth	
AWARDS	1989	Turin Prize (XJ220), Turin	
	1995	*Most Beautiful Car Award* (XJ-Series Saloon Car), Geneva Motor Show	
	1996	*Most Beautiful Car Award* (XK8), Geneva Motor Show	
	2000	*Car of the Show* (F-Type Concept Sports Roadster), Detroit Motor Show; *Design of the Year* (F-Type Concept Sports Roadster), Autocar Awards, London; Runner up for Designer of the Year, Autocar Awards, London	
EXHIBITIONS			
	1994 & 96	RSNA Medical Exhibition, Chicago	
	1995	International Nuclear Medicine Exhibition, Minneapolis	
	1999	*Moving Objects – 30 Years of Automotive Design at the Royal College of Art*, London	

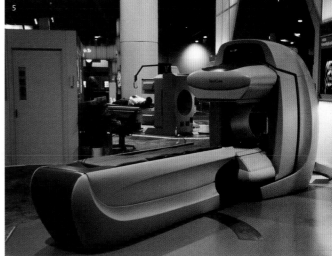

"The future of design is seduction."

Matthew Hilton

Matthew Hilton, 116, Warner Road, London SE5 9HQ, England
T: +44 20 7700 6183 F: +44 20 7700 6183 matthew.hilton@virgin.net

»Die Zukunft des Designs ist die Verführung.«

« L'avenir du design, c'est la séduction. »

1. **Havana** armchair/Sessel/fauteuil for SCP, 2000
2. ↓ **Jammy Dodger** children's desk/Kinderschreibtisch/
bureaux d'enfants from Biscuit Collection for Oreka Kids,
2000

« *2001 : L'Odyssée de l'espace*, réalisé par Stanley Kubrick il y a plus de trente ans, avait cette fantastique allure futuriste à côté de laquelle les pages des revues de design d'aujourd'hui paraissent dépassées. La réalité du nouveau monde idéal de la technologie des communications a eu de profondes implications sur la mondialisation de l'économie et des affaires, mais peu d'influence sur la maison. Au vingtième siècle, la théorie dominante en design a été alimentée par un modernisme profondément enraciné dans la production industrielle et les questions sociales. La prolifération de la technologie informatique à la fin du siècle et son énorme influence sur l'enseignement du design a naturellement eu un profond impact sur la forme du design aujourd'hui. Son influence positive est manifeste dans la croissance des liens virtuels entre le design et l'industrie.

A mon avis, nous traversons actuellement une période de transition où le design en crise se démarque du modernisme pour se tourner tantôt vers la technologie, tantôt vers la distribution, le marketing et, bien sûr, la marque. Pour ce qui est du design qui se développe en parallèle avec la production de matières synthétiques et de techniques de fabrication, nous faisons mine d'adhérer à ces progrès technologiques alors qu'en fait, nous vivons toujours comme il y a cinquante ans. Les gadgets sont là mais, pour ce qui est de la forme, nous sommes plus redevables aux frères Eames qu'à tout autre créateur de la fin du siècle. » MATTHEW HILTON

3. ← **Wait** chair/Stuhl/chaise for Authentics, 1998
4. **Converse** coffee table/Couchtisch/table basse for SCP, 2000

"Stanley Kubrick's *2001: A Space Odyssey,* made over thirty years ago, had the fantastic future edge that makes the latest amorphic shapes on the pages of today's design magazines look like has-beens. The reality of the brave new world of communications technology has had far-reaching implications within the globalization of economics and business, but this has had little impact on the domestic interior. The dominant design theory of the 20th century was fuelled by modernism with its roots firmly based in manufacturing and social issues. The proliferation of computer technology at the end of the last century and its enormous influence on design education has naturally had a strong impact on the shape of design today. Its positive influence can be seen in the growth of virtual links between design and manufacturing.

I feel that we are going through a crisis in design dealing with this transitional period which marks a shift away from modernism and in turn embraces technology, retailing, marketing and, of course, branding. In terms of design developing in parallel with the production of man-made materials and manufacturing techniques, we are only paying lip-service to these developments and realistically we are not living very differently than we were fifty years ago. The gadgets are there but in terms of form we definitely owe more to the Eameses that any other figures at the turn of the century." MATTHEW HILTON

»Der vor über vierzig Jahren fertiggestellte Film *2001: Odyssee im Weltraum* von Stanley Kubrick war von einer phantastisch futuristischen Radikalität, welche die meisten in den Designzeitschriften von heute abgebildeten Formen überholt aussehen lässt. Die ›Schöne Neue Welt‹ der Kommunikationstechnologie hatte zwar weitreichende Konsequenzen für die Globalisierung von Wirtschaft und Handel, aber nur wenig Einfluss auf unsere häusliche Umgebung.

Die vorherrschende Designtheorie des 20. Jahrhunderts basierte auf einer Moderne, die von ihren Anfängen her vor allem produktionstechnischen und sozialen Fragen verpflichtet war. Die mit dem Ende des vergangenen Jahrhunderts einhergehende Verbreitung der Computertechnologie und ihr enormer Einfluss auf die Ausbildung von Designern hatte natürlich starke Auswirkungen auf das heutige Design. Ihr positiver Einfluss zeigt sich in der Zunahme virtueller Querverbindungen zwischen Design und Produktion.

Ich habe das Gefühl, dass sich das Design in einer krisenhaften Übergangsphase befindet, die gekennzeichnet ist durch eine Abkehr von der Moderne und eine bereitwillige Hinwendung zu Technologie, Einzelhandel, Marketing und, natürlich, Markenprofilierung. Was die Entwicklung von Design im Vergleich zur Herstellung künstlicher Materialien und Fertigungstechniken betrifft, so geben wir nur Lippenbekenntnisse zu diesen Veränderungen ab, leben aber in Wirklichkeit nicht viel anders als vor fünfzig Jahren. Die technischen Vorrichtungen und Geräte sind da, aber im Hinblick auf Formgebung sind wir Charles und Ray Eames mehr verpflichtet als allen anderen Gestaltern dieser Jahrhundertwende.« MATTHEW HILTON

MATTHEW HILTON

BORN	1957	Hastings, East Sussex, England
STUDIED	1975-76	Art Foundation at Portsmouth College of Art
	1976-79	Furniture and 3-D Design (BA Hons) degree, Kingston Polytechnic
PRACTICE	1980-84	employed as an industrial designer and modelmaker at CAPA design consultancy
	1984	established own design studio/workshop
	1985-	on-going relationship with SCP, London, designing furniture and cast aluminium tableware
	2000	appointed Head of Furniture Design, Habitat
AWARDS	2000	Internationaler Designpreis Baden-Württemberg, Design Center Stuttgart; *Homes & Gardens* Classic Design Award (in association with the Victoria & Albert Museum, London)
EXHIBITIONS	1997	*British Design*, Museum für Angewandte Kunst, Cologne
	1998	Powerhouse, UK, London; *Fish and Chips,* Berlin
	2000	*Furniture for our Time* solo retrospective, Geffrye Museum, London; *Best of British Design*, Stilwerk, Berlin

CLIENTS

Authentics
Cassina
Disform
Driade
the Grosvenor Estate, London
Handles & Fittings Ltd.
Lusty Lloyd Loom
Montina
Montis
O Luce
Perobell
Sawaya & Moroni
SCP
XO
Ycami

5

6

5. **Coleridge** bed/Bett/lit for SCP, 1995
6. **Mercury** sofa/Sofa/canapé for Driade, 1997
7. **Voyager** chair/Stuhl/chaise for Driade, 1997
8. **Presshound** bookcase & magazine rack/Bücher- & Zeitschriftenständer/bibliothèque et porte-journaux for SCP, 1997
9. **Easy Chair**/Sessel/siège for SCP, 1995

7

8

9

"I see myself as a consultant who's thoughtful yet passionate, who aims to create benefits and magic for clients and consumers alike."

Geoff Hollington

Geoff Hollington, Hollington, 8th Floor, Newcombe House, 45 Notting Hill Gate, London W11 3LQ, England
T +44 20 7792 1865 F +44 20 7792 8145 geoff@hollington.co.uk www.hollington.com

»Ich sehe mich selbst als nachdenklichen und dennoch leidenschaftlichen Berater, der bestrebt ist, für Auftraggeber ebenso wie für Konsumenten Vorteile und Magie zu erzeugen.«

« Je me vois comme un consultant, à la fois prévenant et passionné, cherchant à apporter un plus et à faire rêver tant mes commanditaires que les consommateurs. »

1. **VuTable** home-office concept project/Entwurf für ein
Heimbüro/projet de bureau intégré for Herman Miller,
2000
2. ↓ **Advantix T7000** advanced Photo System camera/
APS-Kamera/appareil photo for Eastman Kodak Company,
2000

»Was ist Design? Man findet es in verschiedenen Formen. Ein großer Teil des Produktdesigns ist ›Mode‹. Dann gibt es das ernsthafte, ›problemlösungsorientierte‹ Design. Hier sind die Anforderungen komplex, und divergierende Faktoren wie Kosten, Leistung, Benutzerfreundlichkeit, Fabrikation und Nachhaltigkeit müssen miteinander in Einklang gebracht werden. Manches Design ist auch einfach (?) inspirierte ›Erfindung‹, eine brillante Idee, die ausgearbeitet und verwirklicht wurde. Und dann gibt es die Art von Design, bei der es darauf ankommt, die komplexen Neigungen und ›Leidenschaften‹, die Sehnsüchte und Wünsche anzusprechen, die für individuelle Benutzer und Konsumenten kennzeichnend sind. Meiner Ansicht nach ist dieser Bereich der härteste, und der, in dem der Produktdesigner allein operiert. Um Produkte zu entwerfen, die von Menschen begehrt und geschätzt werden, muss man sich ernsthaft mit all den Formen von Design auseinandersetzen, die ich erwähnt habe. Ansonsten wird das Produkt mit Sicherheit auf die eine oder andere Weise am Wesentlichen vorbeigehen. Aber das menschliche Wesen, das im Zentrum des Unternehmens steht, der Konsument oder Anwender, braucht oft viel mehr als eine vernünftige Lösung: Er oder sie braucht etwas, das ein wenig Leidenschaft entfacht. Und man kann keine Leidenschaft hervorrufen, ohne sie selbst zu geben. Das bedeutet, dass ich als Designer leidenschaftlich sein muss. Gegenwärtig hat das Produktdesign gewaltige soziale und kommerzielle Konsequenzen. Aber Designer werden immer noch häufig als etwas naive Kunsthandwerker betrachtet, von denen man nicht erwartet, dass sie ihre Arbeit in einem globalen Zusammenhang sehen. Diese Perspektive wird dem Management vorbehalten, und das ist schade. Ich als Produktdesigner habe mehr Erfahrungen in unterschiedlichen Wirtschaftszweigen und Märkten als die meisten meiner Klienten. Etliche von ihnen schätzen das und profitieren von unserer Erfahrung und unserem Wissen. Zu Beginn dieses neuen Jahrhunderts sollten wir dem Produktdesign jenen Rang einräumen, der ihm gebührt.« GEOFF HOLLINGTON

"What is design? It certainly comes in several flavours. A lot of product design is 'fashion'. There's serious 'problem-solving' design, where the brief is complex and issues of cost, performance, usability, manufacture and sustainability must be reconciled. Some design is simply (?) inspired 'invention', a brilliant idea worked out and made real. And then you have the kind of design that's about addressing the complex drives and 'passions', desires and needs that characterize individual users and consumers. That's the really tough arena so far as I can see and the place where the product designer operates alone. To create products that people will desire and then enjoy, you have to deal seriously with all the kinds of design I've described or the product is sure to miss the point in some fatal way. But the human being at the focus of the enterprise, the consumer, the user, often needs a lot more than a sensible solution; she or he needs something to feel a little bit passionate about. And you can't engender passion without giving of it so, as a designer, I have to be passionate. Product design is now of enormous social and commercial consequence. Designers, however, are still often regarded as somewhat naïve artisans who are not expected to see their contribution in terms of the big picture; that place belongs to management, which is unfortunate. As a product designer, I have experience of more business in more categories and more markets than most of my clients and some of them value that and make use of our experience and insights. As the new century unrolls, let's give to product design the status it deserves." GEOFF HOLLINGTON

« Qu'est-ce que le design ? On le trouve sous différentes formes. Une grande partie de la production relève de la "mode". Il y a ensuite le design sérieux qui "résout des problèmes", où les directives sont complexes et les questions de coût, de performance, de fonctionnalité, de fabrication et de rentabilité doivent être prises en compte. Certaines créations sont simplement (?) des "inventions" inspirées, une idée brillante élaborée et concrétisée. Puis il y a le design qui traite des pulsions complexes et des "passions", des désirs et des besoins des utilisateurs et des consommateurs individuels. A mon avis, c'est la branche la plus difficile, celle où le designer opère seul. Pour créer des objets que les gens désireront et apprécieront, il faut traiter sérieusement tous les types de design que je viens de décrire, autrement le produit est sûr de rater sa cible d'une manière ou d'une autre. Mais l'être humain que vise l'entreprise, le consommateur, l'utilisateur, a souvent besoin de bien plus que d'une solution astucieuse : il lui faut quelque chose qui le passionne. Or, on ne peut susciter de la passion sans en ressentir soi-même. Donc, en tant que designer, je dois être passionné. Le design de produits a aujourd'hui une énorme portée sociale et commerciale. Pourtant, les designers sont encore souvent considérés comme des artisans un peu naïfs dont on attend rarement qu'ils sachent situer leur travail dans un contexte plus grand. En tant que designer de produits, j'ai pourtant plus d'expérience dans de nombreux domaines et sur de nombreux marchés que la plupart de mes commanditaires, ce que certains d'entre eux apprécient et savent exploiter. En ce début de millénaire, donnons au design de produits le statut qu'il mérite. » GEOFF HOLLINGTON

3.-4. **Alu-1** sunglasses/Sonnenbrillen/lunettes de soleil (studio concept project), 1999
5. **Fit ... for Life** fan, torch and radio/Ventilator, Taschenlampe und Radio/ventilateur, lampe torche et radio for New Pacific Industrial, 2001

5

"Designing behaviour, not objects."

Isao Hosoe

Isao Hosoe, Isao Hosoe Design, Via Voghera 11, 20 144 Milan, Italy
T +39 02 581 05900 F +39 02 581 04927 info@isaohosoedesign.com www.isaohosoedesign.com

»Ein Design des Verhaltens, nicht der Objekte.«

« On conçoit des comportements, pas des objets. »

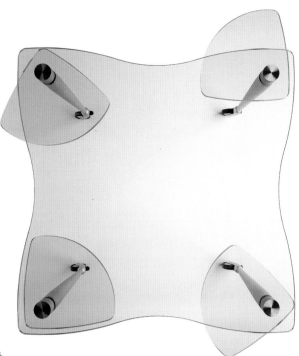

1. **Eraclito** table/Tisch for Tonelli, 1998
2. ↓ **Please** armchair/Stuhl/fauteuil for Segis,
1998 – co-designed with Etien Veeman

»Design ist ein Tätigkeitsfeld, welches das Überleben der Menschheit im 21. Jahrhundert sichern wird. Die Rolle des Designs liegt darin, zu antizipieren, vorherzusehen und eine Zukunftsvision zu vermitteln. Und sie besteht außerdem darin, auf gleiche Weise wie die Philosophie und die Wissenschaft, eine Richtgröße von Zeit und Raum zu etablieren. Im Gegensatz zur Philosophie und der Wissenschaft ist die Rolle von Design aber auf einen Bereich festgelegt, der mit der Entwicklung des Herstellungsprozesses und des Marktsystems entstanden ist. In diesem speziellen Bereich stellt Design eine Kommunikationsbrücke zwischen Anwender und Industrieprodukt, zwischen Gegenwart und Zukunft dar.
Design kann sich weder von den sozialen oder kulturellen Wertesystemen, noch von der industriellen Logik oder der Ökologie fernhalten. Kurz gesagt: Design existiert innerhalb eines hoch komplexen und interaktiven Systems, in dem die Freiräume auf ein Minimum beschränkt sind. Das heißt jedoch nicht, dass Design lediglich passiv bleiben sollte. Im Gegenteil: Gerade weil Design eine Rolle in diesem komplexen System zukommt, muss es wesentlich mehr leisten, als gegenwärtig der Fall ist. Um diese Rolle aktiver zu gestalten, muss sich das Design in kultureller Hinsicht höhere Ziele setzen und sich ein immer stärkeres Instrumentarium verschaffen. Andernfalls wird sich das Design in der Welt von morgen mit einer zweitrangigen Position zufrieden geben müssen. Das würde bedeuten, dass die Menschen in Ermangelung einer adäquaten Verbindungsbrücke zum Objekt des industriellen Systems werden, von dem alle Produkte abhängen.« ISAO HOSOE

"Design is a field of action that will ensure the survival of mankind in the 21st century. The role of design is to anticipate, to foresee, to give a vision of the future – to establish a vector of time and space in the same way that philosophy and science do. Unlike philosophy and science, however, the role of design is specific to that field which evolved only with the development of the industrial process and the market system, where design is the bridge of communication between the user and the industrial product, between the present and the future. Design cannot be extraneous to either the system of social and cultural values or to industrial logic or to the environmental world. In short, design exists in a system that is highly complex and interactive in which the margin of free movement is reduced to a minimum. This does not mean, however, that design should live only passively. On the contrary, it is precisely because design plays a role in this complex system that it must do much more than it presently does. In order to play a more active role design must set itself higher goals from a cultural point of view and must possess more and more powerful instruments. Otherwise, design will have to accept a position of secondary importance in the coming world where man, because of a lack of an adequate bridge, will become subject to the industrial system on which products depend." ISAO HOSOE

« Le design est un champ d'action qui assurera la survie de l'humanité au 21ème siècle. Son rôle est d'anticiper, de prévoir, de donner une vision du futur – d'établir un vecteur de temps et d'espace au même titre que la philosophie et la science. Toutefois, contrairement à la philosophie et à la science, le rôle du design est spécifique à un secteur qui n'évolue qu'avec le développement du processus industriel et du système de marché, où il sert de pont de communication entre l'utilisateur et le produit industriel, entre le présent et le futur.
Le design ne peut être étranger aux valeurs socioculturelles, à la logique industrielle ou à l'environnement. En bref, il existe dans un système très complexe et interactif au sein duquel sa marge de liberté est réduite à un minimum. Toutefois, cela ne veut pas dire que le design devrait rester passif. Au contraire, c'est précisément parce qu'il participe à ce système complexe qu'il doit en faire beaucoup plus qu'il n'en fait actuellement. Afin de jouer un rôle plus dynamique, il doit se fixer des objectifs culturels plus élevés et s'équiper d'outils de plus en plus puissants. Autrement, il devra se contenter d'une position secondaire dans le monde de demain où l'homme, en l'absence d'un pont adéquat, risque d'être assujetti au système industriel dont dépendent les produits. » ISAO HOSOE

3. **Vola** lamps/Lampen/luminaires for Luxo Italiana, 2000 – co-designed with Peter Solomon
4. **Arca** office lamp/Bürolampe/lampe de bureau for Luxo Italiana, 2001 – co-designed with Peter Solomon
5. **Onda** office lamp/Bürolampe/lampe de bureau for Luxo Italiana, 2001 – co-designed with Peter Solomon
6. **Hoi** table lamp/Tischlampe/lampe de table for for Luxo Italiana, 1998 – co-designed with Peter Solomon

ISAO HOSOE		**CLIENTS**
BORN	1942 Tokyo, Japan	Arflex
STUDIED	1965 BSc Aerospace Engineering, Nihon University, Tokyo	Belli e Forti
	1967 MSc Aerospace Engineering, Nihon University, Tokyo	Bernini
PRACTICE	1967 moved to Italy	Bisazza
	1967-74 collaborated with Alberto Rosselli at the Ponti-Fornaroli-Rosselli studio	Bosch Telecom
	1974-86 worked in the studio of Gruppo Professionale Pro	Bruno Magli
	1981 established the Design Research Center, Milan	Cassina
	1985 founded Isao Hosoe Design, Milan	Du Pont
	2000-01 Professor at the University of Siena and of Rome; currently Professor of Industrial Design, Politecnico di Milano	Fiat
		Fujitsu
AWARDS		Itoki
1970, 79, 87, 89 & 98	Compasso d'Oro, Milan	Iveco
1973	Gold Medal, Biennial of Industrial Design, Ljubliana; Gold Medal, Triennale, Milan	Japan Rail West
1976, 80 & 95	SMAU Award	Kartell
1988	G-Mark/Good Design Award, JIDPO, Tokyo	Luxo Italiana
1994 & 95	Roter Punkt Award, Design Zentrum Nordrhein-Westfalen, Essen	Mazda
1995, 96, 98 & 2000	Good Design Award, Chicago Athenaeum	Mitsubishi
EXHIBITIONS 1983	solo exhibition, Design Gallery, Tokyo	Philips
1987	solo exhibition, Design Concern Gallery, Seattle	Piaggio
1988	solo exhibition, Itoki Gallery, Tokyo	Sacea
1990	two solo exhibitions, Seibu Creator's Gallery and Design-Gallery, Tokyo	Segis
1990	curated *Work Encounters – Domesticity in the Office* with the Domus Academy, Milan	Steelcase Strafor
		Toshiba
		Zanussi

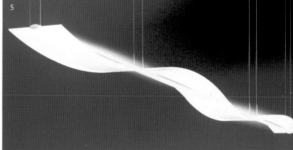

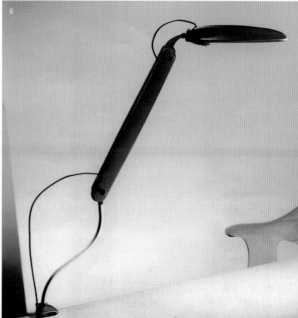

"Design is about creatively exploiting constraint."

Inflate

Inflate, 11, Northburgh Street, London EC1V 0AN, England
T +44 20 7251 5453 F +44 20 7250 0311 info@inflate.co.uk www.inflate.co.uk

»Beim Design geht es um die kreative Ausnutzung von Beschränkungen.«

« Le design, c'est exploiter les contraintes de manière créative. »

1. **Egg cup**/Eierbecher/coquetier for Inflate,
1995 – designer: Michael Sodeau
2. ↓ **Lounge chair**/Klubsessel/transat for Inflate,
1997 – designer: Nick Crosbie

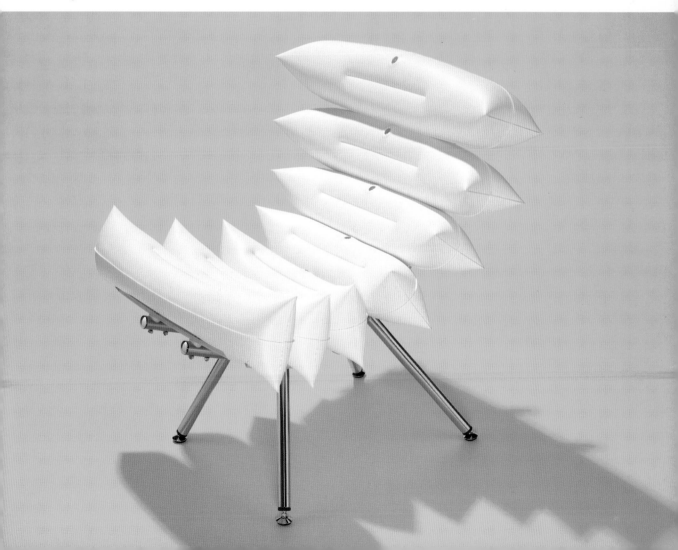

« Nous sommes spécialisés dans le développement de projets autour de processus de fabrication vieux et sous-exploités. A l'origine, toutes nos créations étaient gonflables et utilisaient des soudures à hautes fréquences. En 1997, nous avons ajouté à notre portfolio le moulage par immersion puis, en 2000, nous avons lancé nos premiers produits moulés par rotation. Nous utilisons nos propres produits de marque pour expérimenter commercialement des processus de fabrication et illustrer le potentiel de notre travail. Parallèlement, nous aimons surprendre nos clients avec des gadgets ingénieux allant des petites invitations publicitaires à l'architecture portable. Tout le monde veut laisser sa trace. Nous voulons marquer les esprits mais, pour cela, il nous faut nous démarquer des autres. Notre priorité est de présenter quelque chose de nouveau et non de capitaliser sur ce que nous avons déjà fait. Pour être reconnus en tant que source d'inspiration, nous devons aller de l'avant. C'est pourquoi nous avons monté " The Shed ", une unité à part chargée de générer de nouvelles idées et des principes inédits qui nous permettront de continuer à vendre de la surprise sans frais supplémentaires. »
INFLATE

3. ← **Fruit bowl**/Fruchtschale/coupe à fruits for Inflate, 1995 – designer: Nick Crosbie
4. **Digital Grass** cd & letter & toast holder/CD- & Brief- & Toastgestell/porte cd, lettres et toasts for Inflate, 1997 – designer: Mark Garside

"We specialise in developing projects around old, under-exploited manufacturing processes. Initially all our designs were inflatable and used high-frequency welding processes. By 1997 we had added dip moulding to our portfolio, and in 2000 our first rotational moulded products were launched. We use our own branded products as a way of commercially experimenting with manufacturing processes and illustrating the potential of our work. Alongside our branded products, we like to surprise the client with ingenious gimmicks ranging from small promotional invitations to portable architecture.
Everyone wants to make history in some sort of way. We want to make an impact, but you won't if you do the same things as everyone else. Our priority is coming up with something new, not just capitalizing on what we've already done. To be known as a source of inspiration, we need to keep moving along, and for this we've set up 'The Shed' – a separate unit for the generation of new ideas and principles that will enable us to continue selling surprise at no extra cost." INFLATE

»Wir sind auf die Entwicklung von Projekten rund um alte, wenig genutzte Herstellungsverfahren spezialisiert. Ursprünglich waren alle unsere Designs aufblasbar und verwendeten Schweißverfahren mit Hochfrequenz. 1997 fügten wir unserer Palette das Heißtauchen hinzu, und im Jahr 2000 liefen unsere ersten rotationsgeformten Produkte vom Stapel. Wir verwenden unsere eigenen Markenprodukte für das kommerzielle Experimentieren mit verschiedenen Produktionsmethoden und zur Illustration unseres Arbeitspotentials. Neben unseren Markenprodukten überraschen wir unsere Kunden gerne mit geistreichen Spielereien, die von kleinen Werbegeschenken bis zu tragbarer Architektur reichen. Jeder möchte auf die eine oder andere Art Geschichte machen. Auch wir wollen eine beeinflussende Wirkung haben, aber das schafft man nicht, indem man das Gleiche tut wie alle anderen. Unser oberstes Ziel ist, etwas Neues zu präsentieren und nicht bloß Kapital aus dem zu schlagen, was wir bereits gemacht haben. Um als Inspirationsquelle anerkannt zu sein, müssen wir uns ständig weiter vorwärtsbewegen, und deshalb haben wir ›The Shed‹ gegründet – einen gesonderten Geschäftszweig für die Entwicklung neuer Ideen und Prinzipien, die uns ermöglichen werden, auch in Zukunft Design zu verkaufen, das verblüfft, aber keine Mehrkosten verursacht.«
INFLATE

INFLATE

FOUNDED	1995	by Nick Crosbie (b. 1971 – Art Director) and Mark Sodeau (b. 1970 – Production Manager) with Michael Sodeau (see separate entry)
STUDIED		NICK CROSBIE
	1990-93	BA Industrial Design, Central St Martin's College of Art and Design, London
	1993-95	MA Industrial Design, Royal College of Art, London
		MARK SODEAU
	1989-92	B-Eng Aeronautical Engineering, City University, London
AWARDS	1996	*Blueprint*/100 % Design Award
	1998	Talente Award
	1999	*Blueprint*/100 % Design Award
	2001	Peugeot Design Award
EXHIBITIONS	1996	100 % Design, London; *Plastic Fantastic*, Frankfurt/Main
	1998	British Council, Cologne; *Light & Design – The Best of the 20th Century*, Interieur Biennial, Kortrijk
	1998-99	*Swell*, Victoria & Albert Museum, London
	1999	*British Design – 9000 Miles from Home*, Taipei; *Happening*, Tokyo

CLIENTS

Boots the Chemist
Creation Records
Habitat
Imagination
L'Oreal
Paul Smith
Virgin
also self-manufacture

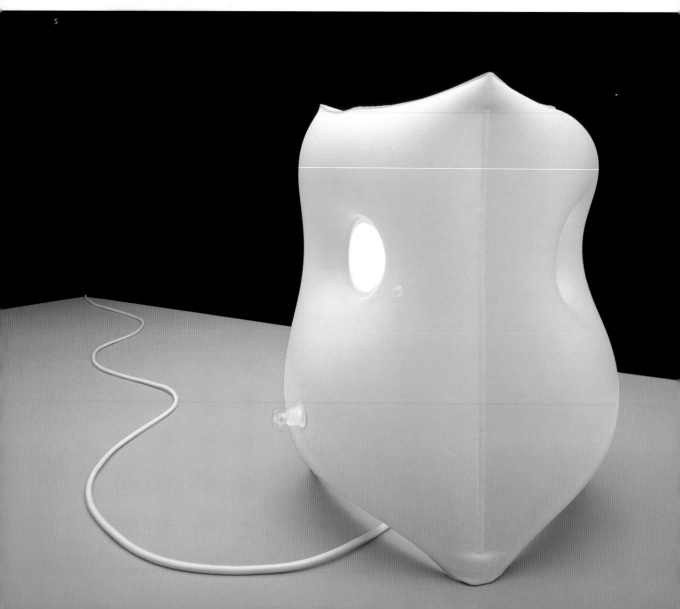

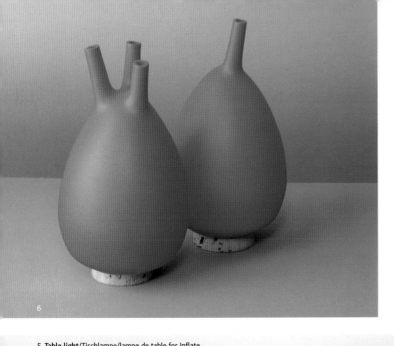

6

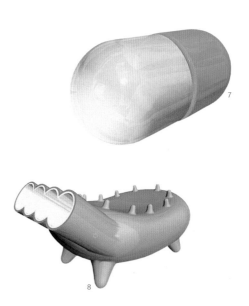

7

8

5. **Table light**/Tischlampe/lampe de table for Inflate, 1995 – designer: Nick Crosbie
6. **Mr & Mrs Prickly** salt and pepper shakers/Salz- und Pfefferstreuer/salière et poivrière for Inflate, 1997 – designer: Nick Crosbie
7. **Lozenge** storage capsule/Aufbewahrungskapsel/capsule de rangement for Inflate, 2000 – designer: Inflate Studio
8. **Soap lounger** soap and toothbrush holder/Seifen- und Zahnbürstenhalter/porte savou et brosse à dents for Inflate, 2000 – designer: Inflate Studio
9. **MEMO** bean bag/Sitzsack/pouf for Inflate, 1999 – designers: Inflate & Ron Arad

"The strength of design is that it provides a way of thinking in advance of the consequences of our actions on materials."

Massimo Iosa Ghini

Massimo Iosa Ghini, Iosa Ghini srl, Via Castiglione 6, 40 124 Bologna, Italy
T +39 051 236 563 F +39 051 237 712 info@iosaghini.it www.iosaghini.it

»Die Stärke von Design liegt darin, dass es vor die sichtbaren Folgen unserer Materialverarbeitung das Denken setzt.«

« La force du design est qu'il anticipe les conséquences de nos actes sur les matériaux. »

1. **Clone** armchair/Sessel/fauteuil from Biosphere
Collection for Bonaldo, 2000
2. ↓ **Metropolis 2000** sofa/Sofa/canapé for Roche Bobois,
2000

»In Zukunft wird es zwei Arten von Design geben: Die eine wird mit Interpretationen und neuen Ideen einhergehen, die in Zusammenarbeit mit der Großindustrie entwickelt werden. Dieser Ansatz wird immer Lösungen hervorbringen, die der Maßschneiderei gleichen, wo die äußeren Aspekte eines Objekts seine inneren Aspekte verbessern. Das Hauptziel dieser Art von Design wird die Verknüpfung von Computertechnologie mit dem eigentlichen Inhalt des Objekts sein, wodurch dieses eher die Funktion einer Schnittstelle erhält.

Die andere Art entspricht einer besonderen Eignung des Designs: Es ist die Adaptierung bereits bestehender Lösungen. Hierbei wird stets die Ressourcenknappheit mitbedacht, aus der sich die Themen Entwicklung und Innovation des materiellen Objekts ergeben, so dass es sich schließlich für die Massenproduktion eignet.

In beiden Kategorien werden jene die führenden Kräfte sein, die am ehesten imstande sind, zeitgemäße Ausdrucksformen zu finden. Die Herausforderung für alle Designer wird in der Darstellung dieser Entwicklung durch Ästhetik oder andere Kommunikationsmittel liegen.«
MASSIMO IOSA GHINI

"Design of the future will be of two kinds. One kind will involve interpretations and new ideas evolved in co-operation with large-scale industries. This approach will always produce solutions that look more like tailoring, where the outer aspects of an object can improve its internal aspects. The primary aim of this type of design will be the linking of computer technology with the body of the object, thereby allowing it to function more as an interface.

The other type will be that for which design is particularly well suited, i.e. the adaptation of existing solutions while bearing in mind the shortage of resources, from which the themes of development support and innovation of the material object will emerge, so that finally the object is suitable for mass production.

Within these two approaches, the leaders will be those who are best able to express contemporaneity. The challenge for all designers will be the presentation of this evolution through aesthetics or other means of communication."
MASSIMO IOSA GHINI

« A l'avenir, il y aura deux formes de design. L'une fera appel à des interprétations et de nouvelles idées élaborées en coopération avec des industries à grande échelle. Cette approche produira toujours des solutions proches de la confection, où les aspects extérieurs d'un objet améliorent ses aspects intérieurs. L'objectif principal de ce type de design sera de lier la technologie informatique au corps de l'objet, lui permettant de fonctionner davantage comme une interface.

La seconde forme est celle qui convient le plus au design : adapter des solutions existantes tout en tenant compte de la pénurie de ressources, faire ressortir les aspects de soutien au développement et de recherche de nouveaux matériaux afin que l'objet en question soit mieux adapté à la production de masse.

Dans ces deux approches, les leaders seront ceux qui sauront le mieux exprimer la contemporanéité. Pour tous les designers, le défi sera de présenter cette évolution à travers une esthétique ou d'autres moyens de communication. » MASSIMO IOSA GHINI

3. **Lithos** vase holder/Vasenhalterung/porte-vase from Biosphere Collection for Bonaldo, 2000
4. **Giorno** faucet/Wasserhahn/robinet for Dornbracht, 1999-2000
5. **DNA** shelves/Regale/bibliothèque from Biosphere Collection for Bonaldo, 2000
6. **T** espresso & cappuccino & chocolate maker/Espresso- & Cappuccino- & Kakaomaschine/machine à express, cappuccino et chocolat chaud for Massin Tuttoespresso, 1999
7. **H2O** table/Tisch from Biosphere Collection for Bonaldo, 2000
8. **Crio** cosmetics table/Kosmetiktisch/table cosmétique from Biosphere Collection for Bonaldo, 2000

MASSIMO IOSA GHINI		CLIENTS
BORN	1959 Borgo Tossignano, Bologna, Italy	Bonaldo
STUDIED	1983-87 Studied architecture in Florence	Cassina
	1987-89 Politecnico di Milano	Duravit
PRACTICE	1981 member of Zak-Ark group	Dornbracht
	1983 co-founded the Bolidismo movement with Pierangelo Caramia and others	Ferrari
	1985 member of Memphis design group; established Studio Iosa Ghini	Fiam
AWARDS	1987 *Young Design in Milan*	Flou
	1988 Roscoe Award, USA	Hoesch
	1990 *100 top Designers* by *Metropolitan Home*, USA	Massin Tuttoespresso
EXHIBITIONS	1986 Memphis *12 New* collection, Milan	Moroso
	1988 installation at the Centre Georges Pompidou, Paris	Roche Bobois
	1989 first solo exhibition of graphics and objects, Inspiration Gallery, AXIS Centre, Tokyo, *M. Iosa Ghini*, Design Gallery, Milan	Silhouette
		Suaidero
	1992 Design Show *M. Iosa Ghini*, Bologna	Üstra
	1995 *12 nach Memphis*, Museum für angewandte Kunst, Frankfurt/Main	Yamagiwa Lighting
	2000 train station for Expo 2000, Hanover, Essete Benessete, Milan Triennale	Zumtabel

4

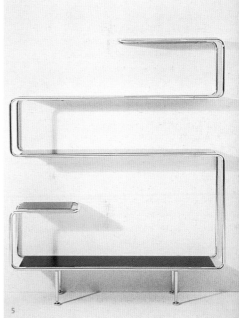

5

6

7

8

"Always question why you are doing something, unless you are being paid a ridiculous amount of money, then really question it."

James Irvine

James Irvine, Via Sirtori 4, 20 129 Milan, Italy
T +39 02 295 34532 F +39 02 295 34534 james@james-irvine.com www.james-irvine.com

»Man sollte sich immer fragen, warum man etwas tut – es sei denn, man bekommt eine absurde Summe Geld dafür bezahlt; dann sollte man es wirklich in Frage stellen.«

« Toujours remettre en question ce pour quoi on fait quelque chose, à moins d'être payé des sommes astronomiques pour le faire, auquel cas, il faut vraiment se poser des questions. »

1. **Soundwave** microwave & radio/Mikrowellenherd &
Radio/four à micro-ondes & radio for Whirlpool, 2000
2. ↓ **Üstra** city bus (Hanover)/Stadtbus(Hannover)/
autobus (Hanovre) for Mercedes Benz, 1999

« Le rôle classique du designer est destiné à
évoluer dans un futur proche. Naturellement,
la récente "guerre des styles" continuera et
deviendra de plus en plus sophistiquée. Toutefois, les designers et les industriels prennent
déjà conscience de sa futilité. Même les consommateurs s'en sont lassés. Ils commencent
à remettre en question la nécessité fondamentale de tous ces biens : " Ai-je besoin
de dépenser des milliers de livres dans une
voiture pour rester bloqué dans des embou-
teillages ? Je peux peut-être m'en passer.
Mais alors, par quoi vais-je la remplacer ? "
J'ai l'impression que beaucoup de produits
sont conçus étape par étape par des gens qui
ne se parlent pas, des spécialistes aveuglés
par leur propre spécialité. On se pose rarement les questions de base. Je suis sûr qu'une
nouvelle race de penseurs verra le jour dans
l'industrie. Ils ne seront pas designers mais
des gens capables de relier différentes disciplines afin de donner un nouveau sens aux
produits sur le plan écologique ou social. J'at-
tends avec impatience le jour où l'industrie
me demandera de participer à cette pensée.
Naturellement, en attendant, je suis prêt à
débattre de questions plus pointues telles
que le diamètre du pied de ma prochaine
chaise. » JAMES IRVINE

3. ← **Luigi** bottle opener & corkscrew/Flaschenöffner &
Korkenzieher/ouvre-bouteilles et tire-bouchons for Alfi,
1998
4. **Flik** folding chairs/Klappstühle/chaises pliantes for
Magis, 1998

"The classic role of designers is
destined to change in the near
future. The recent 'style wars' will
of course carry on and become
more and more sophisticated. However, industry and designers alike
are becoming aware that it's all
getting a bit pointless. Even consumers are starting to wise up.
They are beginning to question the
fundamental necessity of all these
things: 'Do I need to spend thou-
sands of pounds on a car then sit
in a traffic jam? Perhaps I don't
need a car. But the problem is how
do I replace it?'
I have the feeling many products
are designed in steps by people who
don't talk to each other – specialists
blinkered by their own speciality.
Basic issues are rarely discussed. I
am sure a new breed of thinkers
will become relevant to industry.
They will not be designers but
people capable of connecting different disciplines to bring a new
relevance to products whether
ecological or social. I am looking
forward to the day when my
relationship with industry will be
participating in such thinking. Of
course in the meantime, I am quite
willing to discuss the finer points
of the radii on the leg of my next
chair." JAMES IRVINE

»Die klassische Rolle von Designern wird sich
in naher Zukunft zwangsläufig verändern. Der
unlängst ausgebrochene ›Krieg der Stile‹ wird
natürlich weitergehen und sogar immer subti-
lere Formen annehmen. Industrie und Designer selbst werden sich jedoch allmählich der
Sinnlosigkeit dessen bewusst. Sogar die Konsumenten sind inzwischen schlauer geworden
und beginnen, die grundsätzliche Notwendigkeit all dieser Dinge in Frage zu stellen: ›Muss
ich wirklich Zehntausende Mark für ein neues
Auto bezahlen, nur um dann damit im Stau
zu stehen? Vielleicht brauche ich ja gar kein
Auto. Das Problem ist nur: ›Was nehme ich
stattdessen?‹
Ich habe den Eindruck, dass viele Produkte
in einzelnen Arbeitsschritten von Leuten entworfen werden, die nicht miteinander reden –
Spezialisten, die sich von ihrem eigenen Spe-
zialistentum Scheuklappen anlegen lassen.
Dabei werden grundlegende Probleme nur selten zur Sprache gebracht. Ich bin sicher, dass
eine neue Generation von Denkern für die
Industrie an Bedeutung gewinnt. Das werden
allerdings keine Designer sein, sondern Menschen, die interdisziplinär vorgehen, um Produkten eine neue Relevanz zu verleihen – sei
es auf ökologischer oder sozialer Ebene. Ich
freue mich schon auf den Tag, an dem ich in
meiner Zusammenarbeit mit der Industrie an
dieser Denkweise teilhaben werde. Bis dahin
bin ich natürlich gerne bereit, über die Fein-
heiten der Radiusberechnung für die Beine
meines nächsten Stuhls zu diskutieren.«
JAMES IRVINE

5. **Earth** planters/Übertöpfe/pots de fleurs for Arabia, 2001

JAMES IRVINE			CLIENTS
BORN	1958	London, England	Alfi
STUDIED	1978-81	BA (Des.) Kingston Polytechnic Design School, London	Asplund
	1981-84	MA (Des.) Royal College of Art, London	B&B Italia
PRACTICE	1984-92	Olivetti design studio, Milan	BRF
	1987	Toshiba Design Centre, Tokyo	Cappellini
	1988	established own studio in Milan	CBI
	1992-98	partner of Sottsass Associati, Milan	Mabeg
AWARDS	2000	iF Product Design Award, Hanover	Magis
EXHIBITIONS	1993	solo exhibition, Royal College of Art, Stockholm	Mercedes Benz
	1999	retrospective exhibition, Asplund, Stockholm	Üstra
			Whirlpool
			WMF

6

7

6. **Tubo** low chair and sofa/Couchgarnitur/chaise et canapé
bas for BRF, 1997
7. **Tubo** chairs/Stühle/chaises for BRF, 1997
8. **Spider** chair/Stuhl/chaise for Cappellini, 1996
9. **J1** sofa bed/Bettcouch/canapé-lit for CBI, 1996
10. **Lunar** sofa bed/Bettcouch/canapé-lit for B&B Italia,
1998

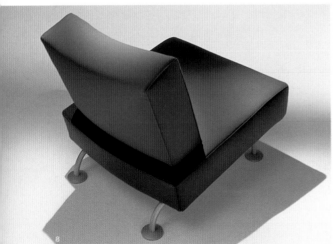

8

9

10

"Vision is not only a founding idea but necessarily the resolution to ensure its realization."

Jonathan Ive
AND THE DESIGN TEAM

Apple Computer Inc., Industrial Design,
20 730, Valley Green Drive, Cupertino, California, 95 014 USA
T + 408 996 1010 www.apple.com

»Eine Vision ist nicht nur die Grundidee, sondern notwendigerweise die Entschlossenheit, ihre Umsetzung zu realisieren.«

« La vision n'est pas seulement une idée fondatrice, elle contient nécessairement le moyen d'assurer sa réalisation. »

1. **iSub** subwoofer/Subwoofer/amplificateur
de graves for Harman Kardon, 1999
2. ↓ **Power Mac G4** computer/Computer/
ordinateur for Apple Computer, 1999

3.-4. **Apple Cinema Display** 22" flat panel/Flachbildschirm
(Vorder- und Seitenansicht)/écran plat for Apple Computer
(front and side views), 1999

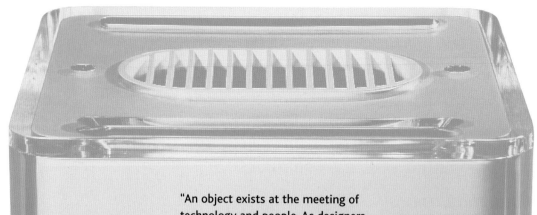

»Ein Designobjekt existiert dort, wo Technologie und Mensch zusammentreffen. Wir als
Designer beeinflussen nicht nur die Art dieses
Zusammentreffens, sondern wir verfügen –
indem wir etwas Materielles schaffen – über
ein starkes und unmittelbares Medium zur
Übermittlung der Identität und Bedeutung
eines Objekts.
Die wirkliche Herausforderung besteht für
uns nicht darin, Gehäuse für anonyme, wenn
auch mächtige Direktoren zu entwerfen, sondern darin, die technologischen Kapazitäten
leichter anwendbar und zugänglich zu machen. Die Suche nach vollkommen neuen Methoden der Gestaltung und Herstellung von
Produkten erfordert die Entwicklung grund-
legend neuer Materialien und Herstellungsverfahren.
Zukunftsweisende Lösungen ergeben sich
meistens dann, wenn neue Produktionstechniken als Mittel zu einem guten Zweck genutzt
werden – damit meine ich die handwerkliche
Gestaltung von Objekten, die mehr den Menschen als produktionstechnischen oder funktionalen Geboten verpflichtet sind.«
JONATHAN IVE

"An object exists at the meeting of
technology and people. As designers
we not only influence the nature of
that meeting but by creating something physical we have a potent and
immediate means of communicating the identity and very meaning
of an object.
Far from designing enclosures
around anonymous albeit powerful logic boards, our real challenge
is to make relevant and extend technological capability. Searching for
wholly new approaches to product
configuration and manufacturing
requires the development of funda-
mentally new materials and processes.
Significant solutions tend to
emerge when new production technologies are exploited as a means
to a greater end; the crafting of
objects that stand testament to
people rather than manufacturing
or functional imperatives." JONATHAN IVE

« Un objet existe à la rencontre entre la technologie et les hommes. En tant que designers,
non seulement nous influons sur la nature de
cette rencontre mais, en créant quelque chose
de physique, nous disposons d'un moyen puissant et immédiat de communiquer l'identité
et le sens même d'un objet.
Notre vraie mission n'est pas de décrire des
cercles concentriques autour de projets lo-
giques anonymes mais néanmoins puissants,
mais d'étendre les capacités technologiques
et de les rendre pertinentes. La recherche
d'approches radicalement nouvelles dans la
configuration et la fabrication des produits
nécessite de développer des matériaux et
des procédés fondamentalement nouveaux.
Lorsque les nouvelles technologies de production sont exploitées à de meilleures fins, des
solutions importantes émergent. Il s'agit de
concevoir des objets qui rendent hommage
aux hommes et non à des impératifs de fabrication ou de fonction. » JONATHAN IVE

5. **Power Mac G4 Cube** computer/Computer/ordinateur
for Apple Computer, 2000
6. **17" Apple Studio Display (CRT)**/Monitor/écran
d'ordinateur for Apple Computer, 2000
7. **iBook** laptop computer/Laptop/ordinateur portable
for Apple Computer, launched 2001
8. **iMac** computer/Computer/ordinateur for Apple
Computer, 1998
9. **Apple Pro Mouse**/Maus/souris for Apple Computer,
2000

JONATHAN IVE		CLIENTS
BORN	1967 London, England	In-house designer
STUDIED	1985-89 Newcastle Polytechnic	
PRACTICE	1990-92 Tangerine design consultancy, London	
	1992- leader Apple Design Team; currently Vice President of Industrial Design, Apple Computer Inc.	
AWARDS	1997 Gold and Best of Category (Consumer Products), *I. D. Magazine Annual Design Review* Award, New York; two Good Design Awards, Chicago Athenaeum	
	1998 three iF Design Awards, Hanover	
	1999 inaugural medal for design achievement, Royal Society of Arts, London; Best of Category, *I. D. Magazine Annual Design Review*, New York; D & AD Gold Award, London; *Object of the Year* Award, *The Face* magazine, London; Gold and Silver Industrial Design Excellence Awards, IDSA; three iF Design Awards, Hanover; Philadelphia Museum of Art & Collaboration COLLAB Design Excellence Award for *Designing the Future*; Winner of the inaugural World Technology Award for Design held in association with *The Economist* magazine; *Design of the Decade* Award, IDSA	
	2000 two Gold Design Excellence Awards, IDSA; D&AD Gold and Silver Product Design Awards, London; Corporate Design Achievement Award, Cooper-Hewitt National Design Museum, New York, National Design Awards; Good Design Award, Chicago Athenaeum; J. Ive awarded Honorary Doctorate, University of Northumbria, Newcastle	
	2001 nine iF Design Awards, Hanover; D & AD Gold and three Silver Product Design Awards, London; Gold Design Excellence Award, IDSA; Best of Show, *I. D. Magazine Annual Design Review*, New York	

6

7

8

9

"We believe that the combination of several strong individualities with a strong social sense gives the best results."

IXI

IXI, 6-38 Kazashi-cho, Sakaide, Kagawa 762-0038, Japan
T/F +81 877 45 3348 info@ixilab.com www.ixilab.com

»Wir glauben, dass die Verbindung mehrerer starker Individualitäten mit einem starken sozialen Verantwortungsgefühl die besten Resultate ergibt.«

« Pour obtenir les meilleurs résultats, il faut associer plusieurs fortes individualités à un puissant sens social. »

1. **Initimo+Chaise** chair with cushion & storage basket/
Stuhl mit Kissen & Korb/chaise avec coussin & panier de
rangement (self-production), 1999
2. ↓ **Tablewear** sitting pad/Sitzkissen/coussin
(self-production), 2000

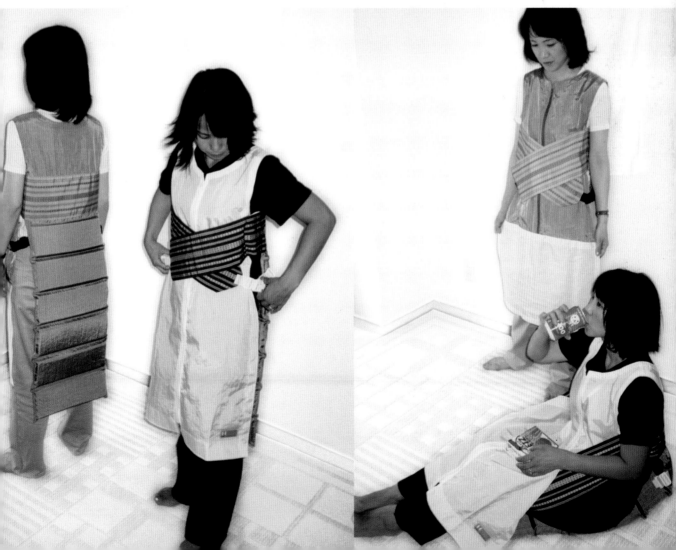

»Unser Zuhause ist eine Widerspiegelung unserer Person. Gerade der private Bereich eignet sich besonders für die Entfaltung eines persönlichen Lebensstils – einer Lebensstrategie, die eine befriedigende soziale Entwicklung erlaubt. Unsere Gesellschaften sind wie Nebelwolken. Sie sind von einer Komplexität, wo lineare Systeme nicht länger existieren sollten und wir nun lernen müssen, auf den Wellen des Chaos zu reiten, ein physisches und intellektuelles Nomadentum zu praktizieren, zu vermischen, zu kombinieren … Während unsere Wohnstätten immer noch ererbten Mechanismen verhaftet sind, sollte die Gestaltung unserer zukünftigen Behausungen von progressiven Vorhaben und neuen Lebensstilen motiviert sein.

›Smart life tools‹ sind Objekte, die eine starke Beziehung mit ihren Anwendern herstellen können. Solche Designs können zu neuen Einstellungen im privaten Bereich und als Folge auch außerhalb des eigenen Zuhauses führen. Menschen sind eher als Anwender denn als Konsumenten zu betrachten. Ein Designobjekt muss dem Anwender dienen, statt eine leblose Ikone zu sein. Es sollte die Individualität des Anwenders zelebrieren und nicht das Ego des Designers. Unsere Designprojekte sind wie japanische Großstädte. Vom ältesten Schinto-Heiligtum bis zur gigantischen Video-Bildschirmwand: Es wächst alles zusammen, voll von positiven Spannungen und Energien.«
IXI

"The home is a reflection of the person. It is the private territory that is favourable to the development of a personal way of life – a strategy for life, which allows a fulfilling social evolution. Our societies are nebulae that display their complexities, where linear systems should no longer exist and where we must now learn how to go surfing on the chaos, practise physical and intellectual nomadism, mix, juxtapose … While our homes are still fixed in ancestral mechanisms, future dwellings should be motivated by progressive propositions and new ways of living. 'Smart life tools' are objects that can establish a strong relationship with their users. Such designs can lead to new attitudes in the home and consequently outside the home. Humans must be considered as users rather than consumers. The designed object must serve the user and not be a dead icon. It should be a celebration of the user's individuality and not the designer's ego. Our design projects are just like Japanese megacities. From the oldest Shinto shrine to the ultimate super-giant video screen, it's all growing together, full of positive tensions and energy." IXI

« La maison est le reflet de l'individu. C'est un territoire privé favorable au développement d'un mode de vie personnel – d'une stratégie de vie permettant une évolution sociale épanouissante. Nos sociétés sont des nébuleuses qui exhibent leurs complexités, où les systèmes linéaires ne devraient plus exister et où nous devons désormais apprendre à surfer sur le chaos, à pratiquer le nomadisme physique et intellectuel, à mélanger, à juxtaposer … Nos maisons sont toujours figées dans des mécanismes ancestraux mais les habitations du futur devraient être motivées par des propositions progressives et de nouveaux modes de vie.
Les "outils de vie intelligents" sont des objets qui établissent des liens puissants avec leurs utilisateurs. Ils peuvent amener à de nouvelles attitudes dans la maison et, par conséquent, hors de la maison. Les êtres humains doivent être considérés comme des utilisateurs plutôt que comme des consommateurs. L'objet "design" doit servir l'utilisateur et non être un symbole inerte. Il devrait célébrer l'individualité de l'utilisateur et non l'ego du designer. Nos projets de design sont comme des mégapoles japonaises. Du plus ancien temple shintoïste au dernier écran vidéo super géant, tous les éléments se développent en même temps, riches de tensions et d'énergie positives. » IXI

3. **Baladeuses** wearable and inflatable furniture (prototype)/tragbares und aufblasbares Sitzmöbel (Prototyp)/meubles vêtements gonflables (prototypes), 2000
4. **Padybag** portable seat/tragbarer Sitz/siège portable (self-production), 1999
5. **Stoolpants** wearable and inflatable furniture/tragbares und aufblasbares Sitzmöbel/meubles-vêtements gonflables (self-production), 2000
6.-7. **Napmat** inflatable picnic mat/aufblasbare Picknickdecke/matelas de pique-nique gonflable (self-production), 2000

		IXI	CLIENTS
FOUNDED	1998	Paris by Izumi Kohama (b. 1968 Kagawa, Japan) and Xavier Moulin (b. 1969 Marseille, France)	Agip
	2000	moved to Japan	Esprit
STUDIED		IZUMI KOHAMA	French Ministry of Foreign
	1991	Interior Design Diploma, Musashiro Art University, Tokyo	Affairs, Kyoto
		XAVIER MOULIN	Habitat
	1994	Global Design Diploma, Ecole Superieure de Design Industriel, Paris	Ikea
AWARDS	2000	Second Prize *Professions Plastique* design award, Paris	Nichii
EXHIBITIONS	1998	*Smart Home Fitness*, Milan	Pirelli
	1999	*E&Y Wonder Design Exhibition*, Tokyo; *Homewear*, Paris	Sawaya & Moroni
	2000	*Big Torino 2000*, Turin; *Air-Air*, Monaco; *Future Interior*, Tokyo;	Shiseido
		My home is yours, Your home is mine, Seoul	Takashimaya
	2000-01	*Blow up – Shaped air in Design, Architecture, Fashion and Art*, Berlin, Weil am Rhein, Tokyo	Telecom Italia
	2001	*Homewear*, Tokyo Opera City Gallery, Tokyo;	also self-production
		Design 21, Fellisimo Design House, New York	
	2002	*Skin*, Cooper-Hewill National Design Museum, New York	

"Identifying the opportunity and creating the 'idea' for each and every project that will actively inspire others to believe that even the improbable is possible."

Jam

Jam Design and Communication Ltd., 4th Floor, 35-39, Old Street, London EC1V 9HX, England
T +44 20 7253 8998 F +44 20 7253 9966 all@jamdesign.co.uk www.jamdesign.co.uk

»Die Gelegenheit erkennen und für jedes neue Projekt ›die Idee‹ finden, die anderen den Glauben vermittelt, dass selbst das Unwahrscheinliche möglich ist.«

« Pour chaque nouveau projet, identifier ses possibilités et créer " l'idée " qui convaincra les autres que même l'improbable est possible. »

1. **Ringos** napkin ring/Serviettenring/ronds de serviette
de table designed in collaboration with Zotefoams Plc
(produced by Jam), 1997
2. ↓ **Panel** light/Lampe/luminaire designed in collaboration
with Zotefoams Plc (limited edition by Inflate), 2000

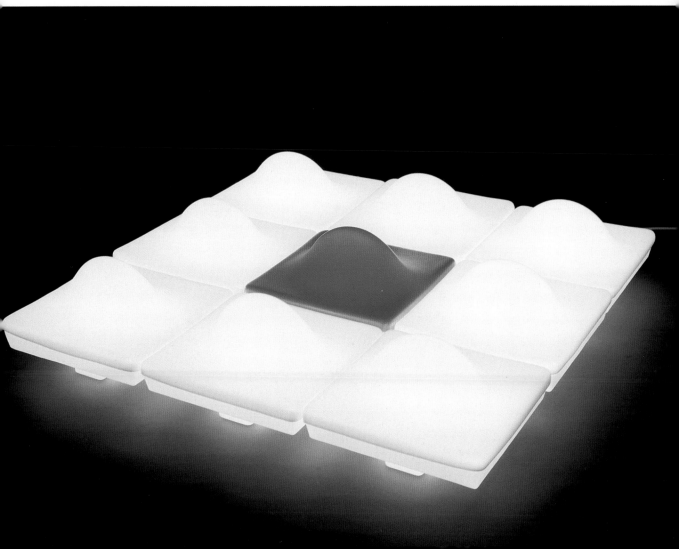

« En design, il faut sans cesse poser des questions et chercher de nouvelles perspectives. Le design prendra de plus en plus d'importance sur le plan social et économique en continuant à créer des plates-formes pour de nouvelles expériences. Il explorera de nouvelles manières de communiquer, d'intégrer et finalement d'apprécier ce qui nous entoure. Il fournira de nouvelles valeurs de responsabilité, de viabilité et d'engagement dans une société régie par le pouvoir économique. Il stimulera également la conception d'idées et de produits nouveaux, permettant l'émergence de nouvelles activités ou l'élimination de celles devenues obsolètes.

Nous traversons actuellement une passionnante période de changement culturel qui appelle une nouvelle manière de penser – à mesure que le rythme et le style de vie se modifieront, on pensera et on communiquera de façons différentes. C'est ce qui nous excite et c'est là que nous intervenons. Nous voulons inaugurer une nouvelle attitude entre nos commanditaires et leur marché cible. En se concentrant sur le design et des projets conceptuels visant à construire et communiquer des marques, nos commanditaires profitent des effets internes et externes de ces projets, qui catalysent l'innovation, le changement et de meilleures opportunités. » JAM

3. ← **Flatscreen** coffee tables using screen for Sony's widescreen Wega television/Couchtische unter Verwendung des Bildschirms für den Wega-Breitwandfernseher von Sony/tables basses utilisant les écrans du poste de télévision grand écran Wega de Sony (limited edition, produced by Jam), 1999
4. **Moving Image** stool/Hocker/tabouret (produced by Jam), 1995

"In effect, design is about asking questions and finding new opportunities. Design will gain in social and economic significance as it continues to create platforms for new experiences. It will explore different ways to communicate, integrate and ultimately relate to what surrounds us. It will bring new values of responsibility, sustainability and commitment to a society driven by economics. Design will also stimulate the conception of new products or ideas, enabling new activities to emerge or eliminating unwanted ones.

We feel people are now in an exciting period of cultural change that requires a new way of thinking – as the pace and style of life changes, people will think and communicate in new ways. This is what excites us and it is where we fit in. We want to pioneer a new attitude between our clients and their market audience. By focusing on the use of design and conceptual projects to build and communicate brands, our clients benefit from the internal and external effects of these projects, which act as a catalyst to innovation, change and increased opportunity." JAM

»Im Grunde geht es beim Design darum, Fragen zu stellen und neue Möglichkeiten zu entdecken. Design wird an sozialer und ökonomischer Bedeutung gewinnen, indem es weiterhin Plattformen für neue Erfahrungen schafft. Es wird unterschiedliche Arten erforschen, wie wir kommunizieren, anderes integrieren und uns schließlich auf das beziehen können, was uns umgibt. Design wird neue Werte der Verantwortlichkeit, Nachhaltigkeit und Verbindlichkeit in eine von der Wirtschaft gelenkte Gesellschaft einbringen. Außerdem wird es die Konzeption neuer Produkte oder Ideen stimulieren, neue Aktivitäten ermöglichen oder unerwünschte aussondern.

Wir haben das Gefühl, dass sich die Menschen gegenwärtig in einer aufregenden Periode kultureller Veränderung befinden, die neue Denkweisen erfordert. Während sich Tempo und Stil des Alltagslebens verändern, werden die Leute auch auf neue Arten denken und kommunizieren. Das ist der Punkt, den wir spannend finden, und wo wir ansetzen. Wir wollen den Weg bahnen für eine neue Haltung im Verhältnis zwischen unseren Klienten und deren Zielgruppen. Indem wir uns auf den Einsatz von Design und konzeptionellen Projekten konzentrieren, um neue Marken aufzubauen und bekannt zu machen, profitieren unsere Auftraggeber von den internen und externen Auswirkungen dieser Projekte, die als Katalysatoren für Innovation, Veränderung und erweiterte Möglichkeiten fungieren.« JAM

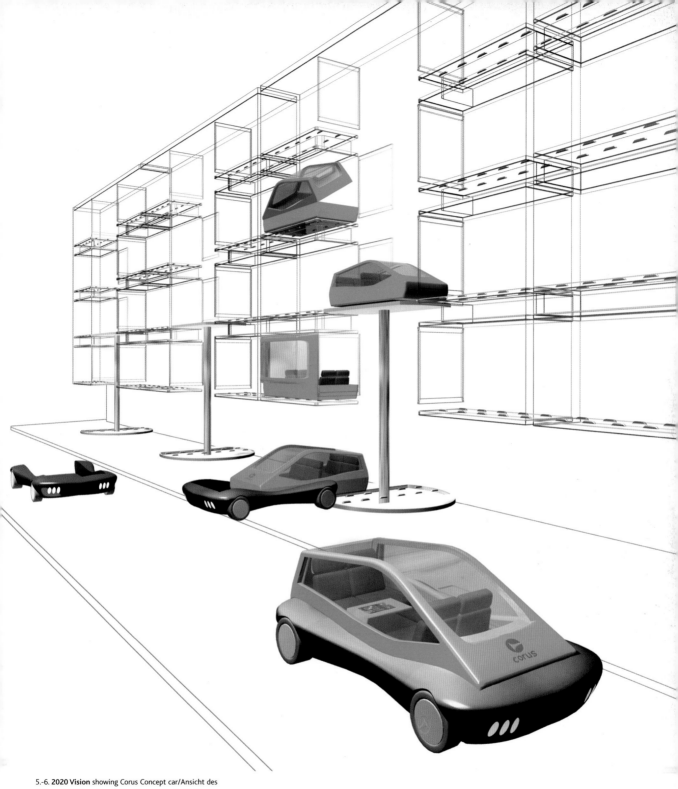

5.-6. **2020 Vision** showing Corus Concept car/Ansicht des
Automodells Corus/vue de la voiture conceptuelle Corus
for Corus, 2000

		JAM		CLIENTS

		JAM	CLIENTS
FOUNDED	1995	in London by Jamie Anley (b. 1972) and Astrid Zala (b. 1968) (with Mathieu Paillard who left Jam in 1998)	Audi Breitling
STUDIED		JAMIE ANLEY	Corian
	1995	graduated from Bartlett School of Architecture, London	Corus
		ASTRID ZALA	Evian
	1991	graduated from Goldsmith's College, London, also studied Fine Art at Wimbledon School of Art, London	Guinness Philips Lighting
EXHIBITIONS	1999	installation at The Building Design Centre, London	Softroom Sony UK Whirlpool Europe Zotefoams

7

8

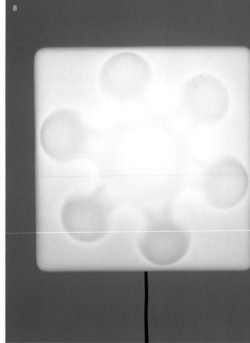

9

7. **Saturn** light/Lampe/luminaire designed in collaboration with Zotefoams, 1999

8. **Panel** light/Lampe/luminaire designed in collaboration with Zotefoams (produced by Jam), 2000 – original concept for the series/Originalentwurf für die Serie/concept original de la série: Andrea Grey

9. **Ladder** chair and stool/Stuhl und Hocker/chaise et tabouret in collaboration with SGB Youngman (produced by Jam), 1996

10. **Foam Dome**/Schaumkuppel/dôme en mousse designed in collaboration with Zotefoams (produced by Jam), 1998

11. **Three-door** concept washing machine/dreitürige Modellwaschmaschine/concept machine à laver trois portes for Whirlpool, 1999

12. **Concept kitchen**/Modellküche/concept de cuisine for Whirlpool and Corian (shown at 100 % Design exhibition), 1999

"Objects designed by trial and error have more soul."

Hella Jongerius

Hella Jongerius, JongeriusLab, Schietbaanlaan 75b, 3021 LE Rotterdam, The Netherlands
T +31 104 770 253 F +31 104 778 300 jongeriuslab@planet.nl

»Objekte, die durch praktisches Herum-probieren entstanden sind, haben mehr Seele.«

« Les objets conçus sur le tas ont plus d'âme. »

1. **Wash-basin**/Waschbecken/lavabo for JongeriusLab, 1997

»Meine schlichten und bodenständigen Entwürfe verfügen über eine Art ›schmutzigen Realismus‹. Sie sind eine Verherrlichung der Unvollkommenheiten des industriellen Produkts. Seelenlose Massenartikel befinden sich nicht länger im Einklang mit einer Ära, die von Veränderung, Tempo und Mühelosigkeit der Fabrikation beherrscht wird. Das Konzept des ›Industriellen‹ erlebt zur Zeit eine Umwandlung.

Indem ich meine Arbeit von einer konzeptionellen Perspektive aus angehe, bin ich mehr an den sozialen und menschlichen Implikationen von Design interessiert als an der äußeren Form oder an den Objekten selbst. Meiner Ansicht nach kommuniziert ein Designprodukt mit seinem Umfeld und erfüllt seinen Besitzer mit einer Identität. Aus diesem Grund suche ich nach dem Charakter, der im Inneren verborgen liegt. Damit sind meine Entwürfe in erster Linie ein Mittel, um mit dem zukünftigen Besitzer in einen Dialog zu treten. Die persönliche Note – oder auch: die Seele – verleiht Industrieprodukten eine Aura, die sie wie individuelle Einzelstücke wirken lässt. Ebenso wie in der avantgardistischen Designermode die Materialprüfung entscheidend für die Endgestaltung ist, so bestimmen die in meinen Designs verwendeten Werkstoffe häufig schon in einem frühen Stadium Form und Funktion des Endprodukts. Die Designer von heute sollten als hyper-moderne Alchemisten traditionelle Techniken nutzen und ausnutzen, um neue und bessere Lösungen zu kreieren.« HELLA JONGERIUS

"My plain and down-to-earth designs have a 'dirty realism'; they are a celebration of the imperfections of the industrial product. Soulless, mass-produced objects are no longer in tune with an era that is dominated by change, speed and ease of manufacture. The concept of 'what is industrial' is undergoing transformation.

By approaching my work from a conceptual perspective, I am interested in the social and human implications of designs rather than in their form or in the objects themselves. From my point of view, a product communicates with its environment and imbues its owner with an identity. Because of this, I search for the character that lurks within so that my designs are first and foremost a means of creating a dialogue with the future user. The personal touch – the soul – will bestow on industrial designs a sense of being individual one-offs. Just as material research is crucial to final creations in avant-garde fashion, so the materials used in my designs often determine the final product's form and function at an early stage. As hyper-modern alchemists, today's designers should use and abuse traditional techniques so as to create new and better solutions." HELLA JONGERIUS

« Mes créations simples et terre à terre sont "vulgairement réalistes". Elles célèbrent les imperfections du produit industriel. Les objets sans âme, produits en masse, ne sont plus en harmonie avec une époque dominée par le changement, la vitesse et la fabrication facile. Le concept de " ce qui est industriel " est en mutation.

En abordant mon travail dans une perspective conceptuelle, je m'intéresse aux implications sociales et humaines des produits plutôt qu'à leurs formes ou aux objets eux-mêmes. De mon point de vue, un produit communique avec son environnement et imprègne son propriétaire d'une identité. Pour cela, je cherche à insuffler une personnalité dans mes créations pour qu'elles soient avant tout un moyen d'instaurer un dialogue avec leurs futurs utilisateurs. La note personnelle – l'âme – conférera aux designs industriels la qualité d'un exemplaire unique.

Toute comme la recherche de matières est vitale aux créations de la mode d'avant-garde, les matériaux utilisés dans mes designs déterminent souvent très tôt la forme et la fonction du produit final. Tels des alchimistes ultramodernes, les designers devraient user et abuser des techniques traditionnelles afin de créer des solutions nouvelles et meilleures. » HELLA JONGERIUS

2. **Kasese Foam chair**/Stuhl/chaise produced by JongeriusLab for Cappellini, 1999
3. **Kasese Foam chair** (folded)/Stuhl (zusammengeklappt)/chaise (pliée) produced by JongeriusLab for Cappellini, 1999
4. **Felt stool**/Hocker/tabouret for Cappellini, 2000
5. **Soft Urn vases**/Vasen for JongeriusLab, 1999

HELLA JONGERIUS			CLIENTS
BORN	1963	de Meern, the Netherlands	Arabia
STUDIED	1988-93	Academy for Industrial Design, Eindhoven	Cappellini
PRACTICE	1997	workshops at Staatliche Akademie für Bildende Künste, Karlsruhe	Donna Karan
	1998	summer workshop Domus Academy, Milan	Droog Design
	1998-99	taught design at the Design Academy, Eindhoven	Iittala
	2000	director of *Het Atelier*, Design Academy, Eindhoven	Maharam NY
AWARDS	1997	Incentive Award Industrial Design, Amsterdam Foundation of Art	Rosenthal
	1999	World Technology Award for Design, World Technology Network, London	
EXHIBITIONS	1994	Droog Design exhibition, Milan	
	1995	*Mutant Materials in Contemporary Design*, Museum of Modern Art, New York	
	1996	*Self Manufacturing Designers*, Stedelijk Museum, Amsterdam; *Thresholds in Contemporary Design from the Netherlands*, Museum of Contemporary Art, New York	
	1997	*5 Years Droog Design*, Central Museum, Utrecht, Droog Design, Milan	
	1998	*Do Normal*, San Francisco Museum of Modern Art, Droog Design Milan; *Inevitable Ornament*, Milan	
	1999	Droog Design, Oranienbaum, Milan	
	2000	*Pseudofamily*, Het Princessehof, Leeuwarden, ICA, Philadelphia; *Design World 2000*, Museum of Art and Design, Helsinki	
	2001	*Workspheres*, Museum of Modern Art, New York	

"Design must balance ethics and
aesthetics for the good of society."

Kazuo Kawasaki

Kazuo Kawasaki, c/o Ouzak Design Formation, International Design Center Nagoya,
7F Design Lab Studio 1, 3-18-1 Sakae Naka-ku, Nagoya Aichi-ken, 460-0008 Japan
T +81 52 249 2466 F +81 52 249 2467 info@ouzak.co.jp www.ouzak.co.jp

»Design muss Ethik und Ästhetik zum
Nutzen der Gesellschaft ausbalancieren.«

« Le design doit équilibrer l'éthique et
l'esthétique pour le bien de la société. »

1. **Flex Scan L675** display/Bildschirm/écran for Eizo Nanao
Corporation, 2001
2. ↓ **Anti-Tension Frame** glasses/Brillengestelle/lunettes
for Masunaga Optical Mfg. Co., 2000

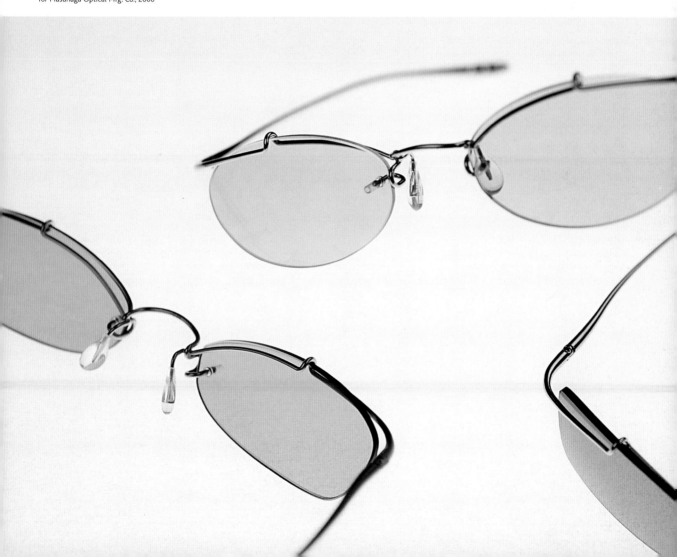

»Rolle und sozialer Einfluss von Design haben sich durch die Entwicklung der Informationsgesellschaft in einem solchen Maße gewandelt, dass wir nun die Ziele, Anwendungsgebiete und Techniken des Designs neu bewerten müssen. Erstens: Was die Techniken betrifft, so können wir Computer als ein Hilfsmittel für Design nutzen. Es sollte aber nicht unser Ziel sein, nur mittels Computer zu gestalten. In diesem Zusammenhang sind 3D-CAD/CAM und *Rapid Prototyping* die effektivsten Werkzeuge, die uns derzeit zur Verfügung stehen. Zweitens: Die zahlreichen Anwendungsbereiche für Design, von der Grafik über die Produktgestaltung bis zur Architektur und sogar dem Kunsthandwerk, welche die Gestalter in der Vergangenheit mit einem jeweils eigenen Ausdrucksmittel versorgten, werden sich unvermeidlicherweise stärker vermischen. Und zuletzt: Die Ziele von Design sollten nicht nur außerhalb des menschlichen Körpers realisiert werden, sondern auch innerhalb des Körpers – und das heißt hier, nicht nur auf die Entwicklung künstlicher Herzen und anderer menschlicher Organe beschränkt. Das alles bedeutet, dass Design die Rolle einer Vermittlungsinstanz einnehmen wird, durch die unsere idealistischen Vorstellungen von einem längeren und besseren Leben konkretisiert werden. Schließlich ist das Design eine Widerspiegelung der gesellschaftlichen Einstellungen und Standpunkte.« KATSUO KAWASAKI

"The role and social impact of design have been transformed to such an extent with the emergence of the information society that we must now reassess the objectives, areas and techniques of design. First, concerning techniques, we can use the computer as an implement of design, but it should not be our aim to design using a computer. In this regard 3D-CAD/CAM and Rapid Prototyping are the most effective tools currently available to us. Second, the many areas of design, from graphics to product to architecture and even crafts, which have historically provided designers with a means of expression, will inevitably become more closely integrated. Lastly, the objectives of design should not only be realized on the outside or around the human body but inside the living body – and here, not only in the development of artificial hearts and other internal organs. What all this means is that design will provide the agency through which our idealistic notions of a prolonged and better life will be brought to fruition – design, after all, is a reflection of the attitudes of society." KAZUO KAWASAKI

« Le rôle et l'impact social du design ont été tellement transformés par l'émergence de la société de l'information que nous devons désormais réévaluer ses objectifs, ses domaines et ses techniques. Tout d'abord, pour ce qui est des techniques, nous pouvons utiliser l'ordinateur comme un instrument de design à condition que la création sur ordinateur ne devienne pas un objectif. A cet égard, le 3D-CAD/CAM et le Prototypage Rapide sont les outils les plus efficaces dont nous disposons actuellement. Ensuite, les nombreux domaines du design qui ont depuis toujours permis aux créateurs de s'exprimer – des graphiques aux produits en passant pas l'architecture et même l'artisanat – deviendront inévitablement plus étroitement intégrés. Enfin, les objectifs du design ne devraient pas être réalisés en dehors ni autour du corps humain mais à l'intérieur, et pas uniquement à travers le développement de cœurs artificiels ou d'autres organes internes. Tout ceci signifie que le design sera l'instance au travers de laquelle nos notions idéalistes d'une vie meilleure et plus longue se concrétiseront. Après tout, le design est le reflet des attitudes de la société. » KATSUO KAWASAKI

3. **Scissors**/Schere/ciseaux for TAKEFU Knife Village Association, 2000
4. **Flex Scan 80A** bedside television/Bett-Fernseher/télévision de chevet for Eizo Nanao Corporation, 1999
5. **Two-Dimensional** barcode reader/Strichcode-Lesegerät/lecteur de codes-barres for Nippon Chemi-Con Corporation, 1999

		KAZUO KAWASAKI	CLIENTS
BORN	1949	Fukui, Japan	AISIN AW Co.
STUDIED	1992	graduated (Industrial Design), Kanazawa College of Art	Denso Corporation
	1999	M.D., Nagoya City University; Ph.D. (Medical Science), Nagoya City University	Eizo Nanao Corporation
PRACTICE	1977-79	Creative Director, Product Design Department, Toshiba	Fujitsu
	1979-80	freelance consultant designer	Japan Industrial Design
	1995	founded Ouzak Design Formation, Nagoya	KYODEN Corporation
	1996-2000	professor of School of Design & Architecture, Nagoya City University	Kyoto Prefecture
	2000-	professor of Graduate School of Design & Architecture, Nagoya City University	Masunaga Optical Mfg. Co.
AWARDS	1991	Mainichi Design Award, Japan	Nippon ChemiCon Corp.
	1992	Special Award for excellence, ICSID (International Council of Societies of Industrial Design Group)	NTT DoCoMo Promotion Organization
	1994	Kunii Kitaro Industrial Crafts Award, Japan	Sabae city
EXHIBITIONS	1993	BIO 13 Biennial of Industrial Design, exhibition, Ljubliana	TAKATA LEMNOS
	1994	*Japanese Design* exhibition, Philadelphia Museum of Art	TAKEFU Knife Village Association
	1995	*Mutant Materials in Contemporary Design*, Museum of Modern Art, New York	
	1998	*Japan 2000*, Chicago Museum of Art	

4

5

"If the job we do has a future it lies in the victory of those who think of design as the constituent factor of a product, the heart of the creative process."

King-Miranda

Perry King & Santiago Miranda, King-Miranda Associati, Via Forcella 3, 20 144 Milan, Italy
T +39 02 839 4963 F +39 02 836 0735 mail@kingmiranda.com www.kingmiranda.com

»Falls unsere Arbeit eine Zukunft hat, so liegt sie im Sieg jener, die Design als den konstituierenden Faktor eines Produkts und als das Herz des kreativen Prozesses betrachten.«

« Si notre travail a un avenir, celui-ci réside dans la victoire de ceux qui considèrent que le design est le facteur constituant d'un produit, le cœur du processus créatif. »

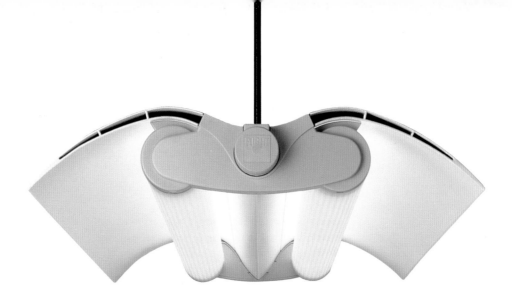

1. **Soft** light fitting/Lampenfassung/luminaire for Flos,
1999
2. ↓ **Miss Moneypennie** task lamp/Arbeitslampe/
lampe d'architecte for CBS Products, 1998

»Wir sind davon überzeugt, dass Design ein wichtiger Teil der Kultur ist, in der wir leben und arbeiten. Und deshalb ist es notwendig, unserer Arbeit mit Respekt für jene Werte zu begegnen, die für eine Vision von Design in einem größeren Zusammenhang unerlässlich sind, statt nur pragmatisch und mit Respekt vor der Technologie zu agieren.
Wir sind außerdem der Meinung, dass es für das Design zunehmend wichtig ist, jedes Objekt als einen Übermittler strukturierter und kultureller Signale zu betrachten, die bei all denen, die dieses Objekt gebrauchen, funktionale und emotionale Reaktionen hervorrufen.« KING-MIRANDA

"We are convinced that design is an ever more important part of the culture in which we live and work. If this is true, as we believe, then it becomes necessary to approach our work with respect for those values that are inherent in a vision of design as an integral part of a much wider context and not just with pragmatism and a respect for technology.
We also believe that it is increasingly important for design to consider each object as a transmitter of structured and cultural signals which stimulate functional and emotional responses in all those who use that object."
KING-MIRANDA

« Nous sommes convaincus que le design occupe une place de plus en plus importante dans la culture dans laquelle nous vivons et travaillons. Il devient donc nécessaire d'aborder notre travail en respectant les valeurs inhérentes à une vision d'un design intégré dans une contexte beaucoup plus vaste et pas seulement avec pragmatisme et respect pour la technologie.
Il est de plus en plus important de considérer chaque objet comme le transmetteur de signaux structurés et culturels qui stimulent des réactions fonctionnelles et émotionnelles chez tous ceux qui l'utilisent. » KING-MIRANDA

3. **Lisa** stacking chairs/Stapelstühle/chaises encastrables for Baleri Italia, 2000
4. **XCose** shelving system/Regalsystem/étagères for Monnalisa, 2000
5. **Diogenes** floor lamp/Stehlampe/lampadaire for Belux, 2000

		KING-MIRANDA	CLIENTS
FOUNDED	1975	Milan by Perry King (b. 1938 London, England) and Santiago Miranda (b. 1947 Seville, Spain)	Ahrend
STUDIED		PERRY KING	Akaba
	-1965	Birmingham School of Art	Applicazioni
		SANTIAGO MIRANDA	Arteluce
	1971	graduation Escuela de Artes Aplicadas y Oficions Artisticos, Seville	Atelier International
AWARDS			Baleri Italia
	1990, 91, 94 & 98	Compasso d'Oro selection, Milan	Belux
	1996	iF Design Award, Hanover; AEPD Premios de Diseño, Madrid	Black & Decker
	1997	Janus de l'industrie, Paris and Trophée du Design 97; Bronze medal, Interclima, Paris	CBS Products
	2000	Architektur- und Innovationspreis, Cologne; Good Industrial Design Award,	Fiat
		Foundation Good Industrial Design, the Netherlands	Flos
EXHIBITIONS	1990	*Lonely Tools*, Barcelona, Amsterdam & Tokyo	Fratelli Fantini
	1992	*Drawings by King and Miranda*, Economist Building, London	iGuzzini
	1996	*King-Miranda Designers*, Istituto Europeo di Diseño, Madrid	Louis Poulsen
	1999	*The Fifth Quarter*, Seville	Luxo
	2000	*The Fifth Quarter*, Madrid	Marcatré
			Olivetti
			Tecno

"Inquisitive and practical, combining traditional techniques with technology and a unique aesthetic."

Tom Kirk

Tom Kirk, 13c, Camberwell Church Street, London SE5 8TR, England
T/F +44 20 7780 9288 tomkirk@excite.co.uk

»Wissbegierig und praktisch, eine Kombination traditioneller Techniken mit neuer Technologie und einer unverwechselbaren Ästhetik.«

« Recherché et pratique, associant des techniques traditionnelles à la technologie et à une esthétique qui lui soit propre. »

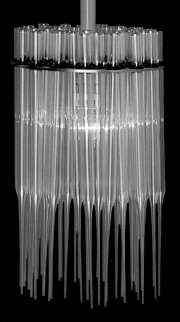

1. **GS Series** lamp/Lampe/lustre (self-production), 2000
2. . **Spike No. 2** wall light/Wandleuchte/appliques
(self-production), 2000

»In dem Maße, in dem der industrielle Sektor durch die fortschreitende Computerisierung immer vielseitiger wird, verringert sich die Zahl der in Produkten verwendeten Komponenten. In Kombination mit der Einführung neu entwickelter Materialien bedeutet diese spannende Technologisierung, dass wir mit einer zunehmenden Zahl an miniaturisierten Apparaten und Objekten leben. In Zukunft werden wir zunehmend vertrauter mit alternativen Lebensräumen, wie es sie früher nur auf der Filmleinwand zu sehen gab. In Bezug auf Inneneinrichtung und Architektur bedeutet diese Entwicklung, dass wir ein vermindertes Bedürfnis nach unordentlich vollgestopften Räumen haben werden. Wir werden mehr und mehr von multifunktionalen Objekten umgeben sein, und Design wird bei der Herstellung von Alltagsprodukten eine weit größere Rolle spielen als bisher.« TOM KIRK

"As computerization continues to add versatility to industry, we are seeing a continual shrinkage in the scale of components used in products. Combined with the introduction of newly developed materials, this technology is exciting to work with and means that we are living with an increasing number of miniaturised gadgets and objects. We will be living nearer to the alternative environments that have previously been limited to celluloid. Within interiors and architecture, this will reduce our everyday need for clumsy and cluttered living spaces. We will be surrounded more and more by multifunctional objects, and design will have a far greater scope within the everyday products around us." TOM KIRK

« A mesure que l'informatisation continue de rendre l'industrie de plus en plus polyvalente, la taille des composants utilisés dans les produits se réduit. Associée à l'introduction de nouvelles matières, cette technologie excitante signifie que nous vivons avec un nombre croissant d'objets et de gadgets miniaturisés. Nous habiterons dans des environnements alternatifs comme en n'en voyait jusque-là qu'au cinéma. Dans les intérieurs et en architecture, nos espaces de vie seront mieux adaptés et moins encombrés. Nous serons de plus en plus entourés d'objets aux fonctions multiples et le design jouera un rôle beaucoup plus important dans les produits quotidiens autour de nous. » TOM KIRK

3. CS2 table lamp/Tischlampe/lampe (self-production), 2000
4. Turf table light/Lampe/luminaire (self-production), 2000
5. CS3 table lamp/Tischlampe/lampe (self-production), 2000

TOM KIRK

BORN	1972	Manchester, England
STUDIED	1990-91	Foundation Studies, Middlesex University
	1991-94	BA (Hons) Silversmithing and Metalwork, Camberwell College of Arts, London
PRACTICE	1991-94	exhibition construction for Crafts Council, London
	1994-95	lighting department Heal's, London
	1995-97	sales consultant, London Lighting Company, London
AWARDS	1992	Johnson and Matthey silver bursary
	1994	sponsored by Goldsmith's Hall
	1997	Setting-up grant awarded by Crafts Council, London
	1998	Crafts Council and 100 % Design exhibition bursary, London
	1999	winner *Ergonom* product development Award
EXHIBITIONS	1994	*New Designers*, Business Design Centre, London
	1997	*Trans-Forms*, Cable Street Gallery, London; *One Year On*, Business Design Centre, London
	1998	*New British Design*, London; *Interior*, British Embassy, Paris
	1999	*Create Britain*, Taiwan; *Design Resolutions*, Royal Festival Hall, London
	2000	*Creative Britain*, Stilwerk, Berlin; *New British Design*, Paris; *Decorative Arts 2000*, Sotheby's, London; *British Design*, Arango, Florida

CLIENTS

Annexe Bar and Restaurant, London (installation)
Boss Models
The End Bar, London (installation)
Jerusalem Bar, London (installation)
Nambe
Ozer Restaurant, London (installation)
Smirnoff Vodka
St. Lukes Communications
also self-production

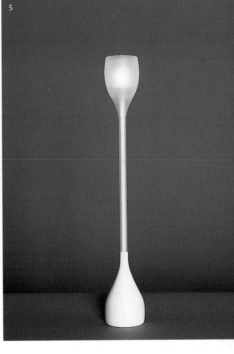

"Every new product development must involve innovation."

Ubald Klug

Ubald Klug, 33, Rue Croulebarbe, 75013 Paris, France
T +33 1 43 31 38 82 F +33 1 45 35 31 54

»Jede neue Produktentwicklung muss
innovativ sein.«

« Le développement de chaque nouveau
produit doit être innovateur. »

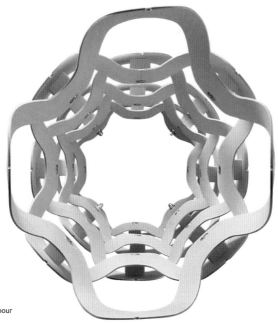

1. **Spiga** clothes stand/Kleiderständer/portant pour
vêtements for Röthlisberger Kollektion, 1999
2. ↓ **100531** carpet/Teppich/moquette from Jour et Nuit
Collection for Lantal Textiles, 1994

»Design ist nicht eine Stilrichtung, eine
Formensprache.
Design ist eine Haltung – heute nicht anders
als gestern und morgen.
Design löst Probleme.
Design heißt Hinterfragen, Kritik von Gewohn-
heiten, Suchen nach neuen Lösungsmöglich-
keiten.
Die Möglichkeiten sind in permanenter
Entwicklung.
Design folgt ihnen, ist im Stande, ihnen zu
folgen.
Design ist zeitlos aktuell.
Zeitlos, ohne Bindung an Trends.
Kann Trends setzen, geht ihnen aber voraus.
Design ist frei nach vorne, erfüllt von Erfah-
rungen aus Vergangenem.
Design kann nur aktuell sein, jetzt, hier, nicht
in der Zukunft.« UBALD KLUG

"Design is not a stylistic direction,
a formal language.
Design is an attitude – no different
today than it was yesterday or will
be tomorrow.
Design solves problems.
Design means asking questions,
challenging conventions, seeking
new solutions.
Design is timeless, not tied to
trends.
Design is open to the future, filled
with experiences from the past.
Design can only be contemporary,
here now, not in the future."
UBALD KLUG

« Le design n'est une orientation stylistique,
un langage formel.
Le design est une attitude – il n'est pas différent aujourd'hui de ce qu'il était hier et de ce
qu'il sera demain.
Le design résout des problèmes.
Le design est atemporel, non lié à des tendances.
Le design est ouvert au futur, rempli d'expériences du passé.
Le design ne peut être que contemporain, ici
et maintenant, il ne se situe pas dans
l'avenir. » UBALD KLUG

3.-5. **+&+** glass panel system/Glaswandschirm/cloisons
en verre for Glaströschdesign, 1998
6.-7. **Shell** trunk cupboard/Schrankkoffer/placard – malle
for Röthlisberger Kollektion, 1997

UBALD KLUG		CLIENTS
BORN	1932	St. Gallen, Switzerland	Airbus
STUDIED	1952-55	interior design Kunstgewerbeschule, Zurich (under Willy Guhl)	deSede
	1958-60	François Stahly's studio, Paris (taught by Jean Prouvé)	Glasträsch
PRACTICE	1962-65	technical director of Troesch & Co., Berne	Lantal Textiles
	1966	moved to Paris	Laufen, Plastra
	1968-72	Mafia design studio	Röthlisberger
	1972	established own product/interior design office	Ruckstuhl
AWARDS	1998	iF Product Design Award, Hanover	Swatch
EXHIBITIONS	1997	Swiss Design Prize exhibition, Solothurn	Swissflex
	1998	iF (Industrie Forum), Hanover	Wogg
	1999	Internationaler Designpreis Baden-Württemberg exhibition, Stuttgart; Swiss Design Prize exhibition, Langenthal	

6

7

"The fundamental purpose of design is to either answer or formulate essential questions."

Harri Koskinen

Harri Koskinen, c/o Hackman Designor Oy Ab, Iittala Glass, 14 500 Iittala, Finland
T +358 204 39 6318 F +358 204 39 6303 harri.koskinen@designor.com

»Der grundlegende Zweck von Design ist, essentielle Fragen entweder zu beantworten oder zu formulieren.«

« L'objectif fondamental du design est de formuler des questions essentielles ou d'y répondre. »

1. **Tools** outdoor cooking utensils/Grill-Utensilien/
ustensiles de cuisine pour l'extérieur for Hackman,
2000
2. ↓ **Block** lamp/Lampe/lampe for Design House
Stockholm, 1998

« J'écris sur le futur du design, mon futur et celui de nous tous. A l'heure actuelle, je conçois des produits de consommation qui me sont commandés par des sociétés qui les fabriquent. Ces produits sont destinés à être utilisés quotidiennement dans un avenir proche. Lorsqu'elles me passent une commande, les entreprises m'expliquent une situation qu'elles veulent voir se réaliser au plus tôt : ce dont le consommateur a besoin et ce dont on a décidé qu'il aurait besoin. Les problèmes sont très réalistes, impliquant des améliorations aux produits déjà disponibles ainsi que de nouvelles perspectives. Ce qui m'intéresse dans mon travail ce sont mes intuitions, les moments où je trouve une solution qui débouchera sur des produits plus fonctionnels et plus faciles à fabriquer. A l'avenir, nous occuperons l'instant présent plus que nous le faisons actuellement. Nos victoires personnelles nous donneront davantage de raisons de nous battre. Nous développons une nouvelle conscience en la cherchant. Satisfaire nos besoins de base reste encore notre activité principale. De l'autre côté de l'océan, il y a peut-être encore des terres arables à cultiver.
Le design joue un rôle dans tout ceci, mais, d'un autre côté, il en est également très éloigné. A l'avenir, nous réfléchirons davantage à l'avenir. » HARRI KOSKINEN

"I'm writing about the future of design, my future and the future of us all. At present, I'm working as a designer of consumer goods under commission from companies that produce them. The designs I create are meant for everyday use in the near future. When commissioning work from me, companies outline a situation envisioned for the near future: what the consumer needs and is allowed to need. The problems are very realistic, involving improvements to the products that are available now as well as new perspectives. My interest in my work lies in insights, in the moments when I figure out a solution that leads to products that are more functional and easier to manufacture.
In the future, we'll occupy the *now* more than we do at present. The things we win for ourselves will give us more to fight for. We evolve a new consciousness by searching for it. The fulfilling of basic needs remains the most important activity. Over the ocean, there might still be arable fields to farm.
Design plays a part in all of this — but, on the other hand, it is also very far removed from it. In the future, we'll give more thought to the future." HARRI KOSKINEN

»Ich schreibe über die Zukunft von Design, meine Zukunft und die Zukunft von uns allen. Gegenwärtig arbeite ich als Designer von Konsumartikeln im Auftrag der Hersteller. Die Designs, die ich entwerfe, sind für den alltäglichen Gebrauch in der nächsten Zukunft bestimmt. Wenn Firmen mich mit einer Arbeit beauftragen, skizzieren sie für mich eine Situation, die sie für die nächste Zukunft anvisieren: was der Konsument braucht, und was er brauchen darf. Die Problemstellungen sind sehr realistisch und beinhalten Verbesserungen für bereits erhältliche Produkte sowie neue Perspektiven. Was mich in meiner Arbeit interessiert, sind Einsichten und Erkenntnisse. Damit meine ich jene Momente, in denen mir eine Lösung einfällt, die zu Produkten führt, die zweckmäßiger und leichter zu handhaben sind.
In Zukunft werden wir das *Jetzt* mehr ausfüllen, als wir es gegenwärtig tun. Die Dinge, die wir für uns selbst gewinnen, werden uns mehr bieten, wofür wir kämpfen können. Wir entwickeln ein neues Bewusstsein, indem wir danach suchen. Dabei bleibt die Erfüllung elementarer Bedürfnisse die wichtigste Aktivität. Jenseits des Ozeans mag es noch urbares Ackerland zu bebauen geben.
Design spielt bei all dem eine Rolle. Auf der anderen Seite ist es aber auch sehr weit davon entfernt. In Zukunft werden wir mehr Gedanken auf die Zukunft verwenden.«
HARRI KOSKINEN

8

5. **Air** food container/Vorratsdose/récipient for Arabia, 2001
6. **Slow** lamp/Lampe/lampe (one-off), 2000
7. **Shelf** system (prototype)/Regalsystem (Prototyp)/ étagères (prototype), 2000
8. **Atlas** candleholder & vase/Kerzenhalter & Vase/ bougeoir & vase for Iittala, 1996
9. **Alue** bowls/Schalen/bols for **Pro Arte Collection**, Iittala, 2000

9

BORN	1970	Karstula, Finland
STUDIED	1993	BA, Lahti Design Insitute
	1994	MA studies Product and Strategic Design, University of Industrial Arts and Design, Helsinki
PRACTICE	1996	Designor Oy (Nuutajärvi Glass), Finland
	1998-	Hackman Designor Oy (Iittala Glass), Finland
AWARDS	1997 & 98	grant University of Art and Design, Helsinki
	1999	grant Häme Region, Finland; grant Finnish Cultural Foundation
	2000	winner Absolut Helsinki Prize, Helsinki Awards
EXHIBITIONS	1997	*PTTY 90 Years*, Museum of Fine Arts, Pori, Finland
	1998	*International Design Forum*, Singapore; *Empty Spaces*, Alvar Aalto Museum, Jyväskylä; *Talente '99*, Munich
	1999	*Artificial Nature*, Milan; *New Scandinavia*, Museum für Angewandte Kunst, Cologne; *Finnish Modern Design*, Göteborg, Hamburg; *Empty Spaces*, Munich
	2000	*Design World 2000*, Museum of Art and Design, Helsinki; *Privacy*, solo exhibition, Miyake Design Studio Gallery, Tokyo

CLIENTS

Arabia
Design House Stockholm
Genelec
Hackman
Iittala
Issey Miyake
Källemo
Nuutajärvi Glass
Schmidinger-Modul

10

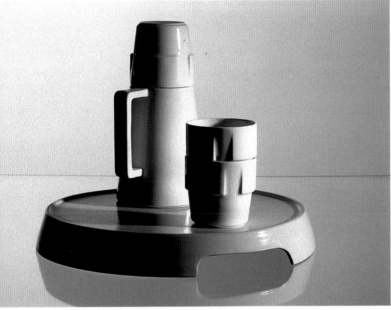

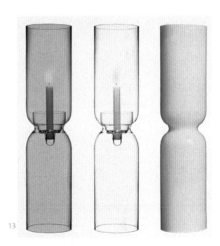

10. **Kämppä** installation/Installation at Iittala glassworks, 1999-2000
11. **Klubi** glassware/Glasware/verres for Iittala, 1996-98
12. **Ceramic** thermos set (prototype)/Thermoskanne und Tassen (Prototyp)/service Thermos (prototype), 1998-2000
13. **Relations** storm candleholder/Windlichter/photophores for Iittala, 1999
14. **Sofa bed** (prototype)/Bettcouch (Prototyp)/canapé-lit (prototype), 2000

"Design has gone through a transition from hard, material, status products to soft, immaterial, spiritual products – from extreme masculinity to extreme femininity."

Kristiina Lassus

Kristiina Lassus, Villa Rosa, Via Rosmini 7, 28010 Miasino (NO), Italy
T +39 0323 868 611 F +39 0323 63 739 kristiina.lassus@alessi.com

»Design hat sich von harten, materiellen, statussymbolisierenden Produkten zu weichen, immateriellen, spirituellen Produkten gewandelt – vom extrem Männlichen zum extrem Weiblichen.«

« Le design est passé des produits de prestige, concrets et matériels, à des produits spirituels, doux et immatériels, d'une masculinité à une féminité extrêmes. »

1. **Clea** armchair/Sessel/fauteuil for Zanotta, 1998
2. ↓ **Strawbowls**/Strohschalen/coupes en paille
for Alessi, 2000

»Die 90er Jahre waren eine Dekade der Träume, der Poesie, des Mystizismus, einer positiven Lebenseinstellung, des Ausgleichs, der Sanftheit, des Instinkts, des Immateriellen, des Ätherischen … und letztlich der Weiblichkeit. Wahrscheinlich befinden wir uns jetzt in der stärksten Phase von Weiblichkeit, und der Trend wird sich allmählich wieder zur Männlichkeit hinwenden. Was wird Männlichkeit diesmal bedeuten? Wie wird sie sich manifestieren? Durch Effizienz, Kontrolle, Macht, Zeitmanagement, Programmierung … neue intelligente, technische Lösungen werden uns hauptsächlich aus zwei Richtungen erreichen: der Wohnräume und der Werkzeuge. Diese ›neue‹ Männlichkeit wird sich nicht in harten und aggressiven Formen darstellen (wie es in den 80er Jahren der Fall war), sondern höchstwahrscheinlich in ziemlich neutralen und reinen, noch weicheren und weiblich-runderen Formen. Diesmal, so glaube ich, wird sich Männlichkeit in vollkommen neuen technologischen Lösungen zeigen oder sich in ihnen bilden. Diese Lösungen – Systeme und elektronische Produktkategorien (Werkzeug) – werden zu den ›neuen Musts‹ in unserem Alltagsleben, und sie werden uns durch ihre männlichen Eigenschaften beeinflussen. Kontinuierliche Forschungen über die Systeme alltäglicher Gebrauchsartikel (Architektur, Innenraumgestaltung, Industriedesign, Beleuchtung, Transportmittel, Kleidung) werden mittels ausgefeilter Technologie neue Dimensionen eröffnen, die uns ermöglichen, unsere private und soziale Umwelt besser zu programmieren, zu kontrollieren und zu regulieren. Dadurch können wir Bedingungen und ›Klimaverhältnisse‹ schaffen, die auf unsere persönlichen Wünsche und Bedürfnisse zugeschnitten sind. In vielen Fällen wird das eine radikale Veränderung der Konsumartikel bedeuten, eine Umwandlung ihrer Formen und Funktionen sowie deren Ersatz durch vollkommen neue Lösungen – häufig weniger sichtbare, beinah immaterielle Lösungen.«
KRISTIINA LASSUS

"The 1990s was a decade of dreams, poetry, mysticism, positivism, equilibrium, softness, instinctiveness, immaterialism, etherealism … and ultimately femininity. It is likely that as we are now in the strongest phase of femininity, that the trend will start slowly turning again towards masculinity. What will masculinity mean this time? How will it manifest itself? Efficiency, control, power, time management, programming … new intelligent technological solutions that will approach us from two main directions: living environments and tools.
This 'new' masculinity will not demonstrate itself in hard aggressive forms (as it did in the 1980s) but most likely in fairly neutral and essential forms that will adopt even softer and more rounded feminine shapes. This time around, I believe that masculinity will mostly take form in completely new technological solutions – systems and electronic product categories (tools) that will become the 'new musts' in our everyday lives and that will influence us with their masculine characteristics.
On-going research into everyday product intelligence systems (architecture, interiors, industrial design, lighting, transport, clothing etc.) will provide new dimensions with sophisticated technology enabling us to better programme, control and tune our intimate and social environment, so as to create conditions and 'climates' according to our personal wishes and needs. In many cases it will mean a radical alteration of consumer products, changing their forms and functions and replacing them with completely new solutions – often less visible, almost immaterial." KRISTIINA LASSUS

« Les années 90 furent une décennie de rêves, de poésie, de mysticisme, de positivisme, d'équilibre, de douceur, d'instinct, d'immatérialité, de légèreté … en somme, de féminité. Maintenant que nous avons atteint le point culminant de cette féminité, la tendance s'inversera probablement à nouveau, s'acheminant lentement vers la masculinité. Que signifiera-t-elle, cette fois ? Comment se manifestera-t-elle ? Efficacité, contrôle, pouvoir, gestion du temps, programmation … de nouvelles solutions intelligentes qui nous touchent sur deux fronts : nos espaces de vie et nos outils.
Cette " nouvelle " masculinité ne se manifestera pas par des formes dures et agressives (comme c'était le cas dans les années 80) mais, plus probablement, par des lignes assez neutres et essentielles qui adopteront des silhouettes féminines encore plus douces et rondes. Cette fois, je pense qu'elle s'inspirera principalement ou découlera directement de solutions technologiques totalement nouvelles – des systèmes et des catégories de produits électroniques (outils) qui deviendront les nouveaux " musts " de nos vies quotidiennes et nous influenceront par leurs caractéristiques masculines. La recherche de systèmes de produits intelligents d'usage quotidien (architecture, intérieurs, design industriel, éclairage, transport, vêtement, etc.) fournira de nouvelles dimensions avec une technologie sophistiquée nous permettant de mieux programmer, contrôler et régler notre environnement intime et social, afin de créer des conditions et des " climats " comblant nos souhaits et nos besoins individuels. Dans de nombreux cas, cela entraînera une altération radicale des produits de consommation, changeant leurs formes et leurs fonctions et les remplaçant par des solutions totalement nouvelles, souvent moins visibles, presque immatérielles. » KRISTIINA LASSUS

3. **Tundra** trivet set/Untersetzer-Set/ensemble de dessous-de-plat for Alessi, 1995
4. **Sosta** armchair and ottoman/Sessel und Fußbank/fauteuil et repose-pied for Poltronova, 1997

KRISTIINA LASSUS			CLIENTS

KRISTIINA LASSUS

			CLIENTS
BORN	1966	Helsinki, Finland	Alessi
STUDIED	1992	MA Design Leadership, University of Industrial Arts and Design (UIAH), Helsinki	Harmonia
	1993	Specialization Course of Product Development, Helsinki Polytechnic	Poltronova
	1995	MA Interior Architecture and Furniture Design, University of Industrial Arts and Design (UIAH), Helsinki	Zanotta
PRACTICE			
	1987-88 & 90	Studio Antti Nurmesniemi, Helsinki	
	1989	Studio Bligh Robinson Interiors, Brisbane	
	1991	Studio Sistem, Helsinki	
	1993	founded D'Imago design office; Product Manager, Silva Wetterhoff, Hameenlinna, Finland	
	1994-97	Design Coordinator, Artek Oy, Helsinki	
	1998-99	Project Manager, Alessi Spa, Crusinallo	
	1999-	Design Manager, Alessi Spa, Crusinallo	
AWARDS	2000	Third Prize in *Fair to Nature*, Frankfurt/Main	
	2001	Design Plus Award, Frankfurt/Main	
EXHIBITIONS	2000	*Find* (Finnish Design 2000 exhibition), Avignon, Bergen, Bologna, Brussels, Helsinki, Kraców, Prague, Reykjavik, Santiago de Compostela; *Finnish Design – 125th anniversary exhibition*, Design Forum, Helsinki, *Young Nordic Design*, Scandinavian House, New York	

"I seek 'sentimental' design that exists somewhere between the past and the future."

Roberto Lazzeroni

Roberto Lazzeroni, Studio Lazzeroni, Via G. Cei 125, C. A. P. 56 021, Cascina (Pisa), Italy
T +39 050 701 457 F +39 050 710 079 studiolazzeroni@hlnt.it

»Ich strebe nach einem ›sentimentalen‹ Design, das irgendwo zwischen Vergangenheit und Zukunft existiert.«

« J'aspire à un design " sentimental " qui existe quelque part entre le passé et le futur. »

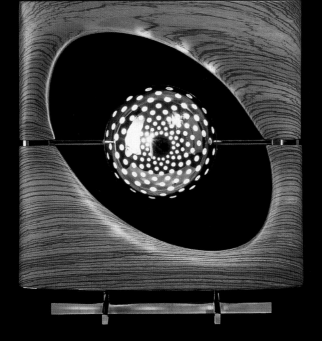

1. **Sun Ra** light/Lampe/luminaire for Luminara, 2000
2. ↓ **Surfing** sofa/Sofa/canapé for Frighetto, 1998

»Meine Designentwürfe pendeln zwischen der Vergangenheit und der Zukunft, ohne nostalgisch zu sein und ohne vor der Zukunft davonzulaufen. Sie stellen die Verbindung mit einer Erinnerungskraft her, die genügend ausgereift ist, um subjektive und emotionale Themen in die Welt der industriellen Fertigung einzuführen. All dieser Aktivität liegt die Vorstellung von Geschichte zugrunde, die nicht chronologisch oder linear wahrgenommen wird, sondern eher als ein Hypertext, der aufgesucht und durchlaufen werden kann, indem ›Fenster‹ auf Formen, Emotionen und Zeichen geöffnet werden. Design als das Ergebnis einer Abtastung und Neuverknüpfung der ›Datenbank‹ meines Gedächtnisses ... Es ist gleichzeitig Vergangenheit, Gegenwart und Zukunft.« ROBERTO LAZZERONI

"My design work shuttles between the past and the future, without nostalgia, and without running away from the future. It is capable of establishing a relationship with the memory that is mature enough to introduce subjective and emotional themes into the world of production. Underlying all this activity is the notion of history, perceived not as a chronology or linearity, but rather as a hypertext to be visited and passed through by opening 'windows' onto forms, emotions and signs. Design as the result of a sampling and remix of the 'data base' of my memory ... It is simultaneously past, present and future."
ROBERTO LAZZERONI

« Mon travail va et vient entre le passé et le futur, sans nostalgie et sans fuir l'avenir. Il est capable d'entretenir une relation suffisamment mature avec la mémoire pour introduire des thèmes subjectifs et émotionnels dans le monde de la production. Toute cette activité recouvre la notion d'histoire perçue non pas d'une manière chronologique ou linéaire mais comme un hypertexte que l'on visite et que l'on se transmet en ouvrant des "fenêtres" sur des formes, des émotions et des signes. Le design comme le résultat d'un sampling et d'un remix de la "base de données" de ma mémoire ... Il est simultanément passé, présent et futur. » ROBERTO LAZZERONI

3. **Dulittle Ghost** wall-light/Wandleuchte/lampe for Luminara, 2000
4. **ICS Gran Sofa**/Sofa/canapé for Ceccotti, 1999
5. **Bloody Mary** table lamp/Tischlampe/lampe for Luminara, 1999
6. **ICS Mix** chairs/Sessel/sièges for Ceccotti, 1999
7. **Makassar** floor lamp/Stehlampe/lampadaire for Luminara, 1999

ROBERTO LAZZERONI			CLIENTS
BORN	1950	Pisa, Italy	Acerbis
STUDIED	1970s	art and architecture, Florence	Ceccotti
PRACTICE	1980	established Studio Lazzeroni	Ciatti
	1988-	art director of Ceccotti	Confalonieri
	1998-	art director of Levante	Driade
	1999-	art director of Luminara	Frighetto
EXHIBITIONS	1991	*Techniques Discrètes*, Paris	Gervasoni
	1992	*Conran Foundation Selection*, London; *Elegant Techniques*, Chicago	Gufram
	1993	*La Fabbrica Estetica*, Paris; *Dall'Albergo all Nave*, Genoa	Levante
	1999	*Costruire il Mobile*, Milan	Luminara
			Moroso
			Rapsel

"Design makes rubbish superfluous."

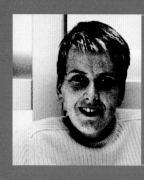

Isabelle Leijn

Isabelle Leijn, Vrolikstraat 355-c, 1092 TB Amsterdam, The Netherlands
T/F +31 20 675 1654 isabelle-leijn@planet.nl www.leijn.com

»Design macht Müll überflüssig.«

« Le design rend la camelote superflue. »

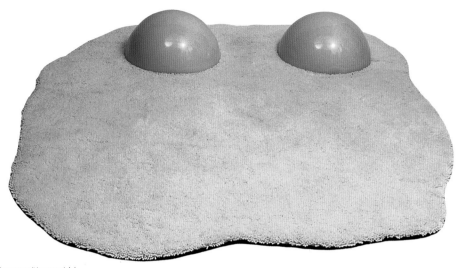

1. **Sunny Side Up** relax carpet/Liegeteppich/
tapis de détente (self-production), 2000
2. ↓ **Bollamp** lights/Lampen/luminaires (self-production),
2000

»Eine Gesellschaft ist wie eine Geleemasse. Teile davon bewegen sich, und die Masse folgt. Andere Teile wieder werden absorbiert. Die Masse bewegt und verändert sich fortwährend. Ideen und Werte verändern sich auf politischer, ökonomischer und sozialer Ebene. Neue Erfindungen verlangen neue Bräuche. Neue Bräuche verlangen neue äußere Umstände und nehmen alte Bräuche mit sich, die der Veränderung bedürfen. All dies erfordert Formgebung, und mit diesem Bedürfnis sind viele Designer beschäftigt. Sie entwerfen schöne und hässliche Objekte, entweder in futuristischem oder altmodischem Stil, aus umweltfreundlichen oder umweltschädlichen Materialien hergestellt. Was gekauft wird, wird produziert! Auf diese Weise diktiert die Masse den Weg, den die Gesellschaft einschlägt. Nicht die Designer, sondern die Leute bestimmen, was ›hip‹ ist und was nicht. *Wer kann die Massen formen?*« ISABELLE LEIJN

"Society is like a moving jelly mass. Parts of it grow and the mass follows. Other parts get drawn in again. The mass moves, it is ever-changing. On political, economical and social levels, ideas and values change. New inventions demand new customs. New customs demand new surroundings, taking with them old customs for want of change.
All this needs shape, a need that many designers busy themselves with. They design beautiful and ugly objects in a style that is either futuristic or old-fashioned, made from environmentally correct or polluting material. What will be bought shall be produced! Thus the mass dictates the road society takes. Not the designer but the people decide what's hot and what's not. *Who can shape the masses?*" ISABELLE LEIJN

« La société est comme une masse gélatineuse en mouvement. Des parties se développent et la masse suit. D'autres parties sont réabsorbées dans la masse. La masse bouge, se transformant sans cesse. Sur les plans politiques, économiques et sociaux, les idées et les valeurs changent. Les nouvelles inventions exigent de nouvelles habitudes. Les nouvelles habitudes exigent de nouveaux environnements, entraînant avec elles les vieilles habitudes qui ont besoin d'évoluer.
Tout ceci nécessite une mise en forme, qui occupe de nombreux designers. Ils conçoivent des objets qui sont beaux ou laids, dans un style qui est soit futuriste soit désuet, fabriqués avec des matériaux qui respectent l'environnement ou qui le polluent. Ce qui sera acheté sera produit ! Ainsi la masse dicte-t-elle la voie que la société doit prendre. Ce n'est pas le designer mais le peuple qui décide de ce qui est dans le coup ou pas. *Qui peut modeler les masses ?* » ISABELLE LEIJN

3. **Chair 00**/Stuhl/chaise (self-production), 2000
4. **Cocoon** sofa/Sofa/canapé (self-production), 1999
5. **Statement 2** shelving system/Regalsystem/bibliothèque (self-production), 1995
6. **Bed 01**/Bett/lit (self-production), 1999

ISABELLE LEIJN

			CLIENTS
BORN	1964	Nijmegen, the Netherlands	Artifort
STUDIED	1982-85	Art Academy, Arnhem	Creafort
PRACTICE	1994	began career as an industrial and furniture designer	Harvink
EXHIBITIONS	1995	solo exhibition, Metri, Amsterdam	MBH
	1996	Interieur Biennial, Kortrijk	also self-production
	1997	Gallery Kis, Amsterdam	
	1998	Meubelbeurs RAI, Amsterdam	
	1999	Perles & Fracas, Brussels	
	2000	*Places and Spaces*, London; Salone del Mobile, Gallery Pit, Milan	
	2001	*Baby*, Amsterdam; Salone del Mobile, SaloneSatelitte, Milan	

5

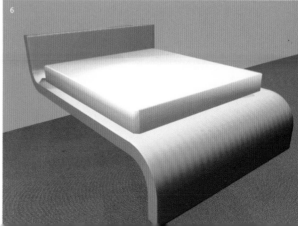

"Design is a way to and from life. Like giving birth, it can be painful but it is also the greatest feeling making real ideas."

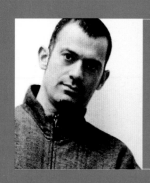

Arik Levy

Arik Levy, L Design, 5 bis, Rue des Haudriettes, 75 003 Paris, France
T +33 1 44 78 61 61 F +33 1 44 78 00 46 arik@ldesign.fr www.ldesign.fr

»Design führt zum und kommt vom Leben. Wie bei einer Geburt kann es schmerzhaft sein, wirkliche Ideen zu erzeugen, aber es ist auch ein großartiges Gefühl.«

« Le design mène à et provient de la vie. Comme un accouchement, créer de vraies idées peut être douloureux mais c'est également une sensation inouïe. »

1. **Light Pocket** pendant lamp/Hängelampe/plafonnier
for Ligne Roset, 1998
2. ↓ **Infinite Light** lamp/Lampe/luminaire
for Snowcrash, 1999

»Ich erforsche und analysiere den ›genetischen Code‹ von Strukturen, Firmen und Werkstoffen, damit ich ein neues Element in ihre ›DNS‹ einfügen kann. Indem ich das tue, kreiere ich neue Materialien, Aktivitäten, Firmen und Konzepte. Dadurch dass ich sowohl in molekularem als auch in ›über-dimensionalem‹ Maßstab arbeite, kann ich unsichtbare Aspekte erschließen und sichtbar machen. Der innere Zusammenhang zwischen meiner Herangehensweise und der Art meiner Reaktionen ist von großer Wichtigkeit für mich und meine Beziehung zum Auftraggeber. Offene Konzepte eröffnen den Unternehmen von heute neue Möglichkeiten für Wachstum und Entwicklung. Durch Ideen, die geeignet sind, zum gemeinsamen Nenner zu werden und sich in unterschiedliche Sphären und Aktivitäten übertragen zu lassen, können wir die Zukunft gestalten. Design muss sich mit dem Neuen befassen, Innovationen schaffen und Probleme lösen.« ARIK LEVY

"I investigate and analyse the 'genetic codes' of structures, companies and materials so as to be able to insert a new element into their 'DNA'. By doing this, I create new materials, activities, companies and concepts. Working on a molecular scale as much as on an 'over dimensional' scale, I can explore and make visible invisible aspects. The coherence of my approach and the quality of my responses are of great importance to me and to my relationship with the client.
Open-ended concepts permit today's companies the possibilities for growth and development. By creating ideas that can become the common denominator and which translate themselves into different domains and activities, we can create the future. Design has to touch the new, innovate and solve problems." ARIK LEVY

« J'étudie et j'analyse les " codes génétiques " des structures, des compagnies et des matériaux afin d'insérer un nouvel élément dans leur " ADN ". Ce faisant, je crée des matériaux, des activités, des compagnies et des concepts nouveaux. Travaillant à l'échelle moléculaire ainsi qu'à une échelle " sur-dimensionnelle ", je peux explorer et rendre visibles des aspects invisibles. La cohérence de ma démarche et la qualité de mes réponses sont importantes pour moi et pour ma relation avec mon client. Les concepts ouverts permettent aux entreprises d'aujourd'hui de grandir et de se développer. En créant des idées capables de servir de dénominateur commun et se traduisant dans différents domaines et activités, nous pouvons créer l'avenir. Le design doit toucher le nouveau, innover et résoudre des problèmes. » ARIK LEVY

3. **Alchemy** light/Leuchte/luminaire for Tronconi, 1997
4. **Life View** information system watch/Computer-Armbanduhr/montre avec système informatique for Seiko, 1996
5. **O-Ring** bracelet/Armreif/bracelet (self-production), 1999
6. **Need** recycled-cardboard lamps/Recycling-Lampen aus Karton/lampes en carton recyclé for L-Design, 1997

ARIK LEVY

BORN	1963	Tel Aviv, Israel
STUDIED	1991	graduated Industrial Design, Art Center College of Design, Switzerland
PRACTICE	1986-88	focused on graphic design and sculpture
	1991	designer for Seiko Epson Inc., Japan
	1992-94	taught at École Nationale Supérieure de Création Industrielle, Paris
	1995	founded L Design with Pippo Lionni
AWARDS	1991	Seiko Epson (International Art Center Award), Japan
	1997	Mouvement Français de la Qualité, Paris
	1999	Design Plus Award, Frankfurt/Main; Grand Prix International de la Critique section luminaire, Salon du Meuble, France
	2000	iF Design Award, Hannover
	2001	George Nelson Award, *Interiors Magazine*, USA
EXHIBITIONS	1991	*Design Thinking*, AXIS Gallery, Tokyo
	1996	*Design and Identity*, Louisiana Museum, Humlebæk
	1997	*Terra*, Frankfurt/Main and Ozone Gallery, Tokyo
	1998	*Light Light*, Gallery Passage de Retz, Paris
	1999	*Label 99*, Gallery Via, Paris
	2000	*Snowcrash*, Milan, *Virtual Light*, Isart Gallerie, Munich
	2001	Museum of Modern Art, New York

CLIENTS

Ligne Roset
Seiko
Snowcrash
Tronconi
Vitrashop
also self-production

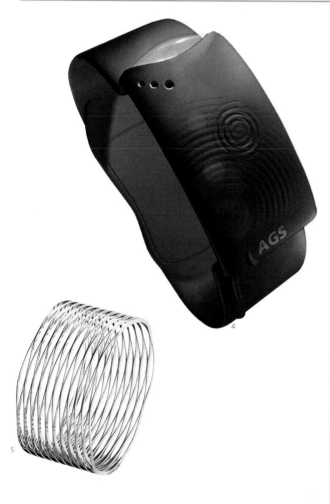

"There's something I hate in the world of design: the excess of protagonism, which can make designed objects so difficult to live with."

Piero Lissoni

Piero Lissoni, Lissoni Associati srl, Via Goito 9, 20 121 Milan, Italy
T +39 026 571 942 F +39 026 571 918 lissoni@mclink.it

»Was ich an der Welt des Designs hasse, ist die Profilierungssucht, die es so schwierig machen kann, mit Design-objekten zu leben.«

« Ce que je déteste dans le monde du design : le manque d'humilité, qui rend parfois si difficile de vivre avec certains des objets conçus. »

1. **Metro2** sofa/Sofa/canapé for Living Divani, 2000
2. ↓ **Frog** chair/Stuhl/chaise for Living Divani, 2000

»Ich glaube, das Design der Zukunft wird dank technischer Fortschritte hauptsächlich durch eine bessere Qualität in der industriellen Massenfertigung gekennzeichnet sein, was zu einem Rückgang des Handwerks auf Kosten ungewöhnlicher, individueller Objekte führen wird. Designer werden stärker in die Verbesserung und Entwicklung von Materialien einbezogen, und sie werden über neuartige, kreative Produktionsmittel verfügen (z. B. Elektronik und Biotechnik). Was Möbel und die Ausstattung von Innenräumen betrifft, so werden die ›Schlüsselworte‹ lauten: Eklektizismus, Schlichtheit, Erinnerungskraft, Innovation, ethnisch, unsichtbar und elektronisch. Die Käufer werden bewusster den wirklichen Wert der Dinge erkennen und jeden Aspekt eines Objekts bedenken, statt nur dessen Marke oder den jeweils aktuellen Trend. Die Leute werden Produkte kaufen, weil sie ihnen gefallen und weil sie zufriedenstellend funktionieren. Ich glaube nicht, dass unser Übergang in das neue Jahrtausend ›die eine große Veränderung‹ mit sich bringen wird: Es wird keine plötzlichen Umwandlungen geben, sondern einen evolutionären Prozess, eine allmähliche Entwicklung, die – auf lange Sicht – einen Unterschied machen wird. Ich kann nur phantasieren, wie es sein wird ...« PIERO LISSONI

"I think that design in the future will be mainly characterized by better quality in industrial mass production thanks to technological advances, leading to a decline in craftwork at the cost of special, individual pieces. Designers will become involved in the improvement and development of materials and will have new creative means at their disposal (eg. electronics and biotechnology). As far as furniture and the use of internal spaces go, the 'keywords' will be eclecticism, simplicity, memory, innovation, ethnic, invisible and electronics. Buyers will be more conscious of where real value lies and will consider every aspect of an object rather than just its brand or the current trend. Products will be chosen because people like them and are satisfied by their function. I do not think that our passage into the new millennium will create 'the big change': there will be no sudden transformation, but a process of evolution, a gradual development that in the long term will make a difference. I can only imagine how it will be ..." PIERO LISSONI

« A mon avis, le design sera surtout marqué par une meilleure qualité de la production industrielle de masse grâce aux progrès technologiques, entraînant une déclin de l'artisanat au détriment des pièces uniques, spéciales. Les designers s'impliqueront dans l'amélioration et le développement des matériaux et disposeront de nouveaux moyens créatifs (comme l'électronique et la biotechnologie). Pour ce qui est du mobilier et de l'aménagement des intérieurs, les mots clefs seront "éclectisme", "simplicité", "mémoire", "innovation", "ethnique", "invisible" et "électronique". Les acheteurs seront davantage conscients des vraies valeurs et prendront en compte chaque aspect d'un objet plutôt que sa marque ou la tendance du moment. Ils choisiront les produits parce qu'ils leur plaisent et parce qu'ils seront satisfaits de leur fonction. Je doute que notre passage au prochain millénaire crée "le grand chambardement": il n'y aura pas de transformations soudaines mais une évolution, un développement progressif qui, à long terme, fera la différence. Je ne peux qu'imaginer comment ce sera ... » PIERO LISSONI

3. **Spin** chair/Stuhl/chaise for Porro, 2000
4. **HT** shelving & cabinet system/Regal- & Schranksystem/ meuble bibliothèque for Porro, 1999
5. **Pavillon** table/Tisch for Porro, 1993
6. **Basics** bed/Bett/lit for Porro, 1998
7. **Modern** shelving & cabinet system/Regal- & Schranksystem/meuble bibliothèque for Porro, 1995

PIERO LISSONI		CLIENTS
BORN	1956 Seregno, Italy	Allegri
STUDIED	1985 Architectural degree, Politecnico di Milano	Artemide
PRACTICE	1986 founded Studio Lissoni with Nicoletta Canesi	Benetton
	1995 appointed art director for Cappellini	Boffi
AWARDS	1991 Compasso d'Oro selection, Milan	Cappellini
	1999 third prize TKTS Time Square competition, New York	Cassina
EXHIBITIONS	1997 *30 Years of Italian Design*, Palazzo della Triennale di Milano, Milan	Iren Uffici
	2000 *Design 4:3 – Fünfzig Jahre italienisches und deutsches Design*, Kunst- und Ausstellungshalle der Bundesrepublik Deutschland, Bonn	Kartell
		Living Divani
		Matteograssi
		Nemo
		Porro
		Wella

"It's only the future if it can't be made."

Ross Lovegrove

Ross Lovegrove, Studio X, 21, Powis Mews, London W11 1JN, England
T +44 20 7229 7104 F +44 20 7229 7032 studiox@compuserve.com

»Zukunft ist alles das, was noch nicht
gemacht wurde.«

« Ce n'est l'avenir que si c'est irréali-
sable. »

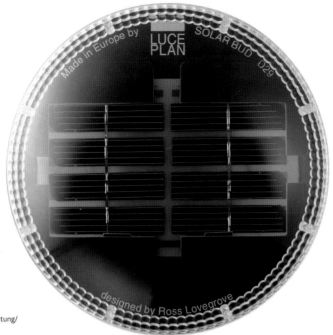

1. **Solar Bud** outdoor light/Außenbeleuchtung/
luminaire for Luceplan, 1998
2. ↓ **Bioform** wooden sculpture/Holzskulptur/
sculpture en bois (studio project), 2000

« En ce début de nouveau millénaire, nous entrons dans une ère unique de réévaluation de nous-mêmes et de notre habitat. Nous avons atteint un niveau de confiance en nos capacités créatives qui alimente un degré sans précédent de recherche dans tous les domaines, du génie génétique aux ressources énergétiques, de la médecine aux profondeurs abstraites de notre univers organique. Le processus qui nous permet de découvrir de nouvelles possibilités est rapidement accéléré par la technologie informatique, une technologie dont nous avons toujours su qu'elle ouvrirait nos esprits. De fait, c'est ce concept d'inexorabilité qui m'intrigue, surtout quand il est appliqué au monde que nous voyons et touchons ... notre monde physique. A mesure que les frontières deviennent floues, ce monde deviendra de plus en plus étrange et imprévisible – une perspective fabuleuse pour ceux d'entre nous qui croient que l'étrangeté est une conséquence de la pensée innovatrice. L'ironie de tout ceci est que, au bout du compte, la créativité engendrée par une telle liberté ramènera l'homme à la nature, à sa composition organique, à ses objectifs et à ses formes qui ne seront plus limitées par l'imagination de l'homme. Le design organique découle de la pensée organique. Il émeut les gens de l'intérieur vers l'extérieur, stimulant de profondes résonances primordiales qui transcendent les tendances superficielles. Jusqu'ici, nous ne faisions que deviner, mais la beauté extraordinaire et impérissable des œuvres d'art organiques produites par des artistes tels que Henry Moore ou Frei Otto suggère que l'association d'intuition brute et d'un degré de logique cellulaire, fractale, influencera inévitablement la forme et la matérialité du monde fabriqué par l'homme, des automobiles à l'architecture. » ROSS LOVEGROVE

"As we begin a new millennium we are entering a unique era of re-evaluation of ourselves and our habitat. We have reached a level of confidence in our creative abilities that is fuelling an unprecedented level of inquiry in all fields, from genetic engineering to fuel cells and medicine to the abstract depths of our organic universe.
The process by which we are discovering new possibilities is being rapidly accelerated by computing technology – a technology that we always knew would open our minds. Indeed, it is this concept of inevitability that intrigues me especially when applied to the world we see and touch ... our physical world. As boundaries blur, this world will become stranger and less predictable – a fabulous prospect for those of us who believe that strangeness is a consequence of innovative thinking. The irony of all this is that ultimately, creativity generated by such soup-like freedom will lead mankind full circle back to nature, its organic composition, its purpose and with it forms that will no longer be limited by man's imagination.
Organic design comes from organic thinking. It moves people from the inside out, stimulating deep primordial resonances that transcend superficial trends. So far we have only been guessing, but the extraordinary and enduring beauty of the organic works of art produced by the likes of Henry Moore and Frei Otto tends to suggest that the combination of raw intuition combined with a degree of cellular, fractal logic will inevitably begin to greatly influence the form and physicality of our man-made world from cars to architecture."
ROSS LOVEGROVE

»Zu Beginn des neuen Jahrtausends treten wir in ein einzigartiges Zeitalter der Neubewertung unserer selbst und unserer Lebensräume ein. Wir haben ein solches Vertrauen in unsere kreativen Fähigkeiten erreicht, das in einem noch nie da gewesenen Maß die Forschung in allen Bereichen anspornt, von der Gentechnik über Brennstoffelemente und Medizin bis zu den dunklen Tiefen unseres organischen Universums. Dieser Prozess, der uns neue Möglichkeiten eröffnet, wird durch die Computertechnologie stark beschleunigt – eine Technologie, von der wir immer wussten, dass sie unseren Horizont erweitern würde. Tatsächlich ist es das Konzept des Unvermeidlichen, das mich fasziniert, besonders in seiner Anwendung auf die Welt, die wir sehen und berühren – also unsere sinnlich wahrnehmbare Welt. In dem Maß, in dem sich die Grenzen verwischen, wird diese Welt fremder und weniger berechenbar, was phantastische Aussichten für jene von uns bietet, die Fremdheit für eine Folge innovativen Denkens halten. Es ist die Ironie dieser Situation, dass eine von solch unbegrenzter Freiheit hervorgebrachte Kreativität die Menschheit letzten Endes im Zirkelschluss zurück zu einer Natur führen wird, deren organische Struktur, Zweck und damit Formen nicht länger von der menschlichen Vorstellungskraft begrenzt sein werden. Organisches Design kommt von organischem Denken. Es berührt die Menschen in ihrem Innersten und stimuliert tiefverwurzelte, archaische Reaktionen, die über oberflächliche Trends hinausgehen. Das alles sind nur Vermutungen. Aber die außerordentliche und bleibende Schönheit der organischen Kunstwerke, die von Künstlern wie Henry Moore und Frei Otto geschaffen wurden, legt nahe, dass die Verbindung von unverfälschter Intuition und einem gewissen Grad an zellularer, fraktionierter Logik zwangsläufig die Form und physische Beschaffenheit unserer durch Menschenhand geschaffenen Welt stark beeinflussen wird – und zwar vom Autodesign bis hin zur Architektur.« ROSS LOVEGROVE

3. ← **Solar Seed** – product architecture concept for a wholly autonomous nomadic structure/Produktarchitektur-Entwurf für eine vollkommen autarke nomadische Konstruktion/concept de structure itinérante entièrement autonome, 1999
4. **Go** magnesium chair/Stuhl/chaise for Bernhardt Design USA, 2001

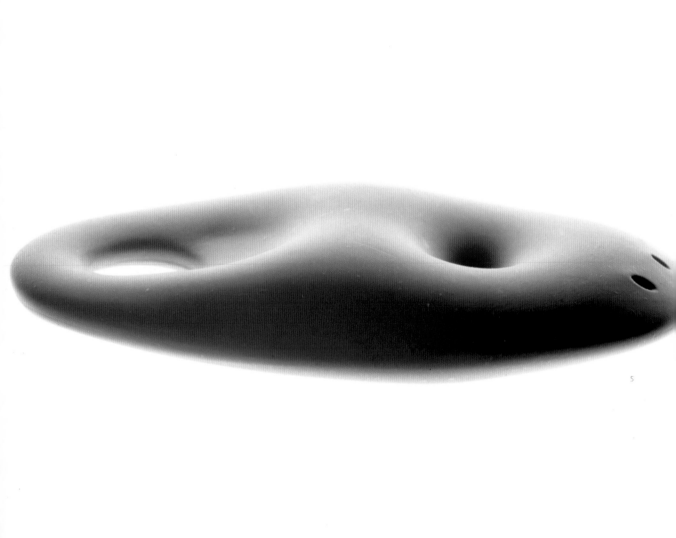

5

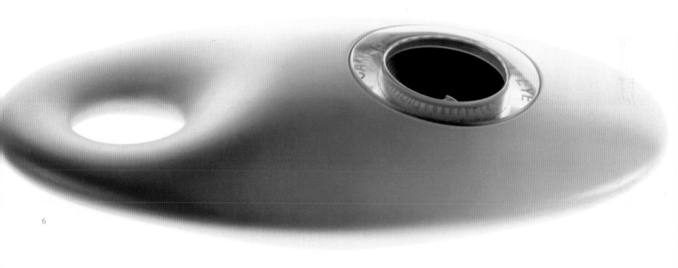

6

5.-6. **Elastomeric digital camera** (prototype)/Elastomer-
Digitalkamera (Prototyp)/appareil photo numérique en
élastomère (prototype), 1989-93

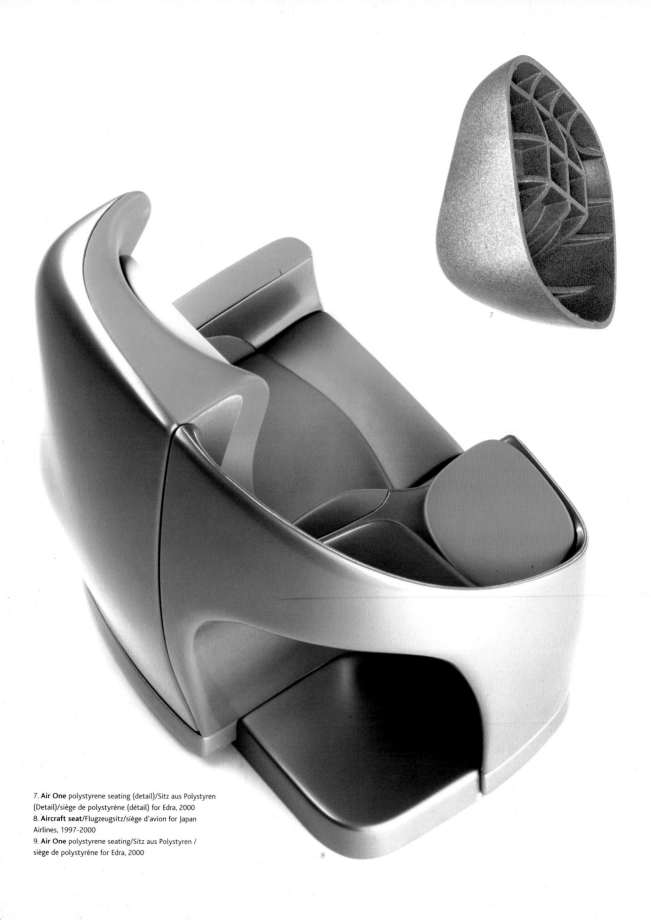

7. **Air One** polystyrene seating (detail)/Sitz aus Polystyren (Detail)/siège de polystyrène (détail) for Edra, 2000

8. **Aircraft seat**/Flugzeugsitz/siège d'avion for Japan Airlines, 1997-2000

9. **Air One** polystyrene seating/Sitz aus Polystyren / siège de polystyrène for Edra, 2000

8

		ROSS LOVEGROVE	CLIENTS

		ROSS LOVEGROVE	**CLIENTS**
BORN	1958	Cardiff, Wales	Apple Computer
STUDIED	1980	BA (Hons) Industrial Design, Manchester Polytechnic	Bernhardt
	1983	MA Industrial Design, Royal College of Art, London	Biomega
PRACTICE	1983-84	worked at Frogdesign, Altensteig	Cappellini
	1984-87	worked as an in-house designer for Knoll International, Paris	Ceccotti
	1986-90	established a design partnership in London	Connolly Leather
	1990	established own design office, Studio X, London	Driade
AWARDS	1998	George Nelson Award, USA; iF Design Award, Hanover	Edra
	1999	Medaille de la Ville de Paris	Fratelli Guzzini
	2000	*I. D. Magazine Annual Design Review* Award, New York	Frighetto
	2001	nominated Designer of the Year by the magazine *Architektur & Wohnen*, Hamburg	Hackman
EXHIBITIONS	1996	*Ross Lovegrove Objects*, Stockholm	Hansgrohe
	1997	*Ross Lovegrove – Design*, Danish Museum of Decorative Art, Copenhagen; *Organic Dreams*, IDÉE, Tokyo	Herman Miller
	1999	*Sensual Organic Design*, Yamagiwa Corporation, Tokyo	Japan Airlines
			Junghans
			Kartell
			Knoll International
			Loom
			Luceplan
			Matoso
			Moroso
			Motorola
			Olympus Cameras
			Tag Heuer
			Toyo Architects
			Zanotta

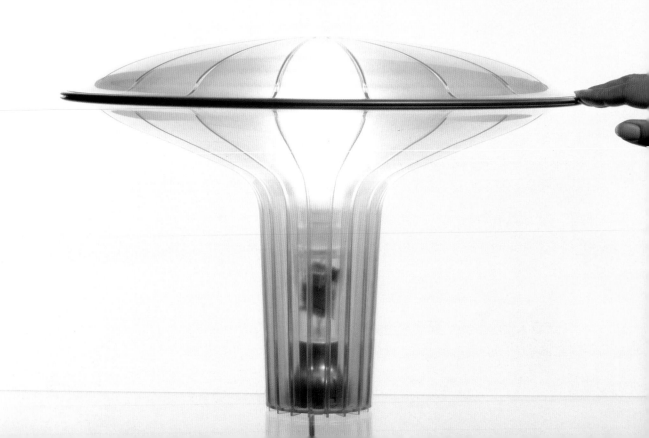

11

10. **Agaricon** table lamp/Tischlampe/
lampe de table for Luceplan, 2001
11. **Water bottle**/Wasserflasche/
bouteille d'eau for Ty Nant, 2001

"Our goal is to solve business problems by connecting brand, technology and people in innovative and compelling ways."

Lunar Design

Lunar Design, 537, Hamilton Avenue, Palo Alto, California 94 301, USA
T + 650 326 7788 F +650 326 2420 info@lunar.com www.lunar.com

»Unser Ziel ist es, Probleme im Unter-nehmensbereich zu lösen, indem wir Marke, Technologie und Menschen auf innovative und unwiderstehliche Weise in Verbindung bringen.«

« Notre objectif est de résoudre des problèmes commerciaux en reliant les marques, la technologie et les consom-mateurs par des moyens innovateurs et irrésistibles. »

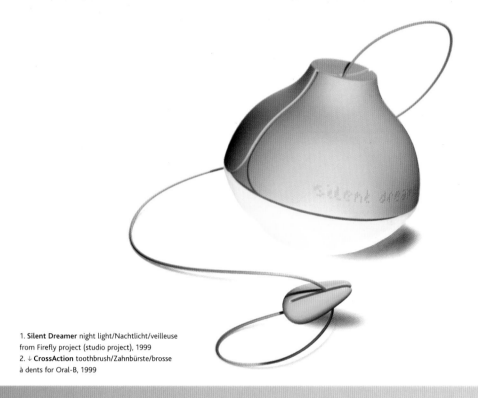

1. **Silent Dreamer** night light/Nachtlicht/veilleuse
from Firefly project (studio project), 1999
2. ↓ **CrossAction** toothbrush/Zahnbürste/brosse
à dents for Oral-B, 1999

« En quelques années, l'Internet a révolutionné la manière de faire des affaires. Il a déjà déclenché la transition de la "production de masse" au "sur mesure de masse". Quiconque ayant une idée de produit peut le vendre directement sur le Net. Les entrepreneurs n'ont plus besoin d'attendre qu'un détaillant présente leurs produits. Les consommateurs ne sont plus limités à la marchandise en stock dans les magasins. Pour les designers, le "sur mesure de masse" représente un sérieux défi : celui de développer des produits souples et des systèmes modulaires qui offrent des choix censés aux consommateurs. A mesure que la technologie devient de plus en plus transparente et compacte, les produits servent des objectifs toujours plus complets. La taille et l'aspect des articles de demain refléteront de plus en plus leur capacité à rendre un service, à informer sur les avantages de telle ou telle marque, à traduire les préférences des consommateurs. De fait, pour se différentier, les marques s'attacheront surtout à relier les gens à la technologie de façons simples et attrayantes.
Les designers d'aujourd'hui sont investis d'une lourde responsabilité : ils doivent créer des produits qui communiquent les promesses d'une marque, qui puissent être fabriqués de manière efficace à un haut niveau de qualité, et qui "parlent" de manière convaincante à ceux qui les achèteront et les utiliseront. Les produits du futur devront également respecter davantage l'environnement. C'est d'autant plus important que des marchés de consommateurs émergent dans les pays en voie de développement, ce qui ne manquera pas d'étirer encore les ressources naturelles. »
LUNAR DESIGN

3. ← **HP Pavilion FX70** flat panel display/Flachbildschirm/écran plat for Hewlett Packard, 1999
4. **Sprout** night light/Nachtlicht/veilleuse from Firefly project (studio project), 1999

"In just a few years, the Internet has revolutionized the way the world does business. It has already triggered the move from 'mass production' to 'mass customization'. In fact, almost anyone with a product idea can sell goods directly over the Web. Entrepreneurs don't have to wait for a retailer to carry their products. And consumers are no longer limited to merchandise that stores have in stock. For product designers, mass customization presents a compelling challenge: to develop flexible products and modular systems that give consumers meaningful choices.
Just as technology is becoming increasingly transparent and compact, the purpose of products is becoming increasingly comprehensive. The size and appearance of tomorrow's products will, more and more, reflect their ability to deliver a service, to inform consumers of their brand's benefit proposition, and to reflect customers' preferences. Indeed, connecting people to technology in easy and engaging ways will become the primary way to differentiate a brand.
Designers today carry a great responsibility. They must create products that communicate a brand promise, that are efficient to manufacture at high quality levels, and that resonate strongly with the people who will buy and use them. Anything less thoughtful won't attract the emerging generation of discerning consumers. Future products will soon have to be more ecologically friendly, too. This need is particularly important as consumer markets emerge in developing countries, further straining natural resources." LUNAR DESIGN

»Innerhalb weniger Jahre hat das Internet die Form des globalen Wirtschaftens revolutioniert. Bereits jetzt hat es den Aufbruch von der ›Massen-Produktion‹ zur ›Massen-Kundenauftragsfertigung‹ in Gang gesetzt. Fast jeder, der eine Produktidee hat, kann seine Waren direkt über das ›World Wide Web‹ verkaufen. Unternehmer brauchen nicht mehr darauf zu warten, dass ein Einzelhändler ihre Produkte ins Sortiment nimmt. Und die Verbraucher sind nicht länger auf Waren beschränkt, die in den Geschäften vorrätig sind. Für Produktdesigner stellt die Anpassung an den speziellen Kundenbedarf die faszinierende Herausforderung dar, flexible Produkte und modulare Systeme zu entwickeln, die den Konsumenten sinnvolle Wahlmöglichkeiten bieten.
In gleichem Maß, wie Technologien zunehmend transparent und kompakt werden, wird der Zweck von Produkten umfassender. Größe und Aussehen der Produkte von morgen werden immer stärker deren Fähigkeit widerspiegeln, eine Dienstleistung zu bieten, über den Nutzwert einer Marke zu informieren und sich den Vorlieben der Konsumenten anzupassen. Tatsächlich wird die Frage, inwieweit es gelingt, Menschen auf einfache und attraktive Weise mit Technologie in Verbindung zu bringen, zu einem der wichtigsten Profilierungsmerkmale für eine Marke.
Die Designer tragen heutzutage eine große Verantwortung. Die von ihnen entworfenen Produkte müssen die Verheißungen einer Marke übermitteln, effizient und auf hohem Qualitätsniveau herzustellen sein und eine starke, ansprechende Wirkung auf die Menschen ausüben, die sie kaufen und benutzen. Produkte, die weniger durchdacht sind, können die aufkommende Generation urteilsfähiger Konsumenten nicht für sich gewinnen. Darüber hinaus müssen zukünftige Produkte auch umweltfreundlicher sein. Diese Notwendigkeit ist besonders wichtig im Hinblick darauf, dass in den Entwicklungsländern neue Märkte entstehen, wodurch die natürlichen Ressourcen noch weiter belastet werden.«
LUNAR DESIGN

		LUNAR DESIGN	CLIENTS
FOUNDED	1985	co-founded by Jeff Smith (b. 1953 Springfield, IL) and Gerard Furbershaw (b. 1952 New York, NY)	Apple Computer
STUDIED		JEFF SMITH	Acuson
		BA Industrial Design, University of Illinois	Cisco Systems
		GERARD FURBERSHAW	Electrolux
		BA Architecture, University of Southern California and BA Industrial Design,	Glad Products
		San Hosé University	Hewlett-Packard
AWARDS	1995	D&AD Award, London; Good Design Award, Chicago Athenaeum;	Microsoft Corporation
		Grand Prize, Absolut Design Competition	Motorola
	1996	Appliance Manufacturer Excellence in Design Best Overall And Winner; People's Choice	Oral-B
		Award, Society of Plastics Engineers; SMAU Cadd Industrial Design Award;	Palm, Inc.
		iF Design Award, Hanover	Philips
	1997	two Silver Industrial Design Excellence Awards, IDSA; three Good Design Awards, Chicago	SGI
		Athenaeum; SMAU Cadd Industrial Design Award	Sony
	1998	two Design Distinction Awards, *I. D. Magazine Annual Design Review*, New York;	
		Silver Industrial Design Excellence Award, IDSA; two Good Design Awards, Chicago	
		Athenaeum	
	1999	three Gold Medical Design Excellence Awards; Gold and Silver Industrial Design Excellence	
		Awards, IDSA; five Good Design Awards, Chicago Athenaeum; two Silver *Design of the Decade*	
		awards, IDSA	
	2000	Good Design Award, Chicago Athenaeum; Silver Industrial Design Excellence Award, IDSA;	
		four iF Design Awards, Hanover	
EXHIBITIONS	1996	*The Dumb Box – Designing the Desktop CPU*, San Francisco Museum of Modern Art	
	1997	Showplace for Excellence in Industrial Design, Georgia Institute of Technology, Atlanta	
	2000	*Design Matters*, Museum of Contemporary Art, Miami; *National Design Triennial –*	
		Design Culture Now, Cooper-Hewitt National Design Museum, New York	
	2001	*Global Tools*, Künstlerhaus, Vienna	

5

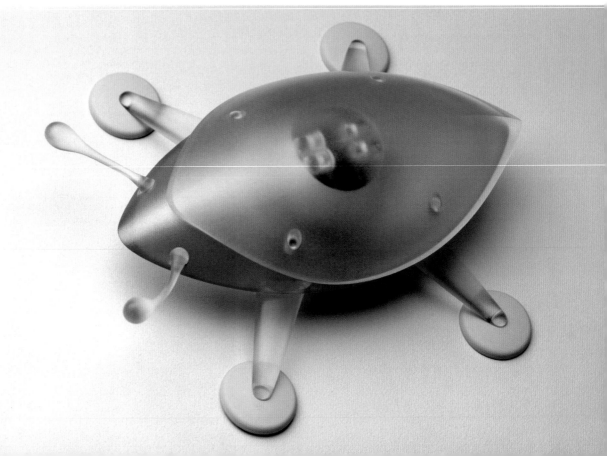

5. **Glimo** night light/Nachtlicht/veilleuse from Firefly project (studio project), 1999
6. **HMD-A200, FD Trinitron** monitor/Monitor/écran d'ordinateur for Sony, 1999
7. **Daisy Glow** night light/Nachtlicht/veilleuse from Firefly project (studio project), 1999
8. **Travel Tote**/Reise-Organizer/guide personnel de voyage from *Service-as-Product* range (studio project), 1998
9. **PoP** night light/Nachtlicht/veilleuse from Firefly project (studio project), 1999

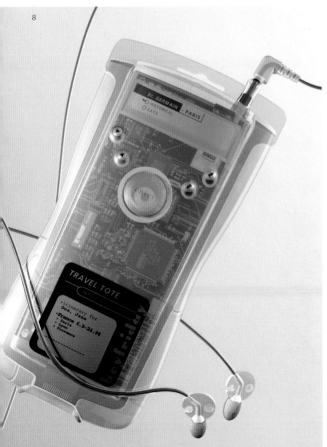

"Form is what is there – not what seems to be there; therefore, we must speak in terms of the work that brings it into being."

Enzo Mari

Enzo Mari, Enzo Mari e Associati, Piazzale Baracca 10, 20 123 Milan, Italy
T +39 02 481 7315 F +39 02 469 3651

»Form ist das, was da ist – nicht das, was da zu sein scheint. Deshalb müssen wir über die Arbeit reden, die eine Form erschafft.«

« La forme est ce qui est là, pas ce qui semble être là. Par conséquent, nous devons parler en termes de travail qui crée la forme. »

1. **Alta Pressione** pressure cooker/Dampfkochtopf/
Cocotte-minute for Zani e Zani, 1998
2. ↓ **Ypsilon** table/Tisch for Magis, 1999

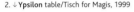

« Nous devons retrouver la puissance originelle du design à créer une utopie. S'il s'agit
d'une allégorie de la transformation poten-
tielle, le message doit parvenir au plus grand
nombre. Ceux qui savent que notre environnement est aliéné doivent continuer à guider
cette transformation. Aujourd'hui, les mécanismes dirigés par la révolution de l'information engloutissent toutes les idées vomies
sous la forme de marchandises. Au cours des
décennies à venir, il faudra avant tout découvrir les démarches adéquates capables d'isoler
la notion de transformation des questions su-
perflues. Pour ce faire, le concept idéal devra
se distinguer de tous ceux générés par des
anarchies irresponsables, qui rejettent ou ba-
nalisent l'élan vers l'utopie en rendant impossible toute implication du peuple. Pendant ce
temps, il vaudrait la peine de promouvoir une
acceptation générale du principe selon lequel
" l'éthique doit guider tout forme de design "
(un code similaire au serment d'Hippocrate). »
ENZO MARI

3. ← **Miss Tea** pot and warmer/Teekanne und Stövchen/
théière et chauffe-théière for Leonardo, 1998
4. **Brocca** jug/Krug/cruche for Arnolfo di Cambio, 1999

"The original power of design to
create a utopia must be recovered.
If this is the allegory of the potential transformation, the message
must reach as many people as possible. The people who are aware
that our environment is being alien-
ated, must continue as leaders in its
transformation. At present, mechanisms driven by the information
revolution will swallow any idea
that is vomited up in the form of
merchandise. Over the coming
decades, the first requirement will
be to discover suitable approaches
capable of isolating the idea of
transformation from superfluous
issues. To do this, the ideal concept
will have to be distinguished from
all those generated by irresponsible
anarchies, which reject or trivialize
the impulse towards utopia and in
so doing render any involvement of
the people impossible. In the meantime, it would be well worth the
effort to promote a general accept-
ance of the principle that 'ethics
must guide all design' (a code similar to the Hippocratic Oath)."
ENZO MARI

»Wir müssen die ursprüngliche Macht des
Designs wiederfinden, eine Utopie zu erschaffen. Wenn man Veränderungen anstrebt, dann
muss die Botschaft so viele Menschen wie
möglich erreichen. Die Menschen, denen bewusst ist, dass unsere Umwelt entfremdet
wird, müssen auch in Zukunft bei Veränderungen vorangehen. Gegenwärtig schlucken die
von der Informationsrevolution angetriebenen
Mechanismen jede Idee, die kommerziell ver-
wertbar ist. Während der kommenden Jahr-
zehnte wird die vorrangige Aufgabe darin bestehen, geeignete Ansätze zu finden, damit
das Konzept für Veränderungen nicht von
überflüssigen Themen und Ansätzen überla-
gert wird. Dazu muss man das ideale Konzept
von all jenen unterscheiden, die, von verant-
wortungslosen Anarchien hervorgebracht, den
Impuls zur Utopie ablehnen oder trivialisieren
und damit jede Einbeziehung der Menschen
unmöglich machen. In der Zwischenzeit wäre
es lohnend, sich für die allgemeine Anerkennung des Prinzips einzusetzen, dass ›Ethik die
Richtschnur für jedes Design sein muss‹ (eine
dem hippokratischen Eid ähnliche Regel).«
ENZO MARI

ENZO MARI

			CLIENTS
BORN	1932	Novara, Italy	Adelphi
STUDIED	1952-56	Accademia di Belle Arti di Brera, Milan	Agape
PRACTICE	1957	began designing for Danese	Alessi
	1963	joined the Nuove Tendenze movement and taught at the Scuola Umanitaria, Milan	Arnolfo di Cambio
	1970	published *Funzione della ricerca estetica*	Arte e Cuoio
	1974-96	wrote another eight publications on design	Artemide
	1976-79	President of ADI (Associazione per il Disegno Industriale)	Boringhieri
	1989	founded Enzo Mari e Associati	Castelli
AWARDS			Danese
	1967, 79 & 87	Compasso d'Oro, Milan	Driade
	1997	Barcelona Award	Fantini
EXHIBITIONS			Gabbianelli
	1967, 79 & 86	Venice Biennale	Ideal Standard
	1972	*Design and Plastic*, Museum of Decorative Arts, Prague	Interflex
	1983-84	*Design Since 1945*, Philadelphia Museum of Art	KPM
	1988	*Modelli del Reale*, San Marino	Le Creuset
	1991	*Mobili Italiani 1961-91 – Le Varie Età dei linguaggi*, Milan	Leonardo
	1996	*Arbeiten in Berlin*, Schloß Charlottenburg, Berlin	Olivetti
	1999	*Enzo Mari. Il lavoro al Centro*, Barcelona & Madrid	Robots
	2000	Galleria Nazionale d'Arte, Modena; *Tre mostre di Enzo Mari*, Faenza	Zani e Zani
			Zanotta

5. **Spartha** and **Athene** vases/Vasen for Arnolfo di Cambio, 1998
6. **Trieste** shelving system/Regalsystem/étagères for Robots, 1999
7. **Sigmund** daybed/Liege/lit de repos for Arte e Cuoio, 1999
8. **Elastica** fruit bowl/Obstschale/coupe à fruits for Zani e Zani, 1999
9. **Dama** pouf/Sitzpolster for Arte e Cuoio, 1999

"I hope to produce objects which are quietly enigmatic, that function beauti-fully, communicate well, mature well and last longer."

Michael Marriott

Michael Marriott, Unit F2, 2-4, Southgate Road, London N1 3JJ, England
T/F +44 20 7923 0323 marriott.michael@virgin.net

»Ich hoffe, Objekte herzustellen, die auf ruhige Art rätselhaft sind, die ausgezeich-net funktionieren, gut kommunizieren, gründlich reifen und länger halten.«

« J'espère créer des objets discrètement énigmatiques, qui fonctionnent à mer-veille, savent communiquer, vieillissent bien et durent plus longtemps. »

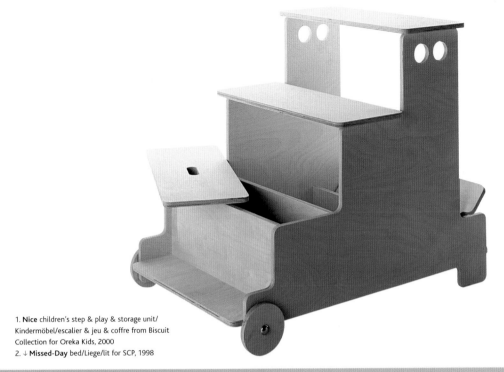

1. **Nice** children's step & play & storage unit/
Kindermöbel/escalier & jeu & coffre from Biscuit
Collection for Oreka Kids, 2000
2. ↓ **Missed-Day** bed/Liege/lit for SCP, 1998

»Als Kind war ich von einer Sendung im Kinderfernsehen fasziniert, die so ähnlich hieß wie ›Durch das Rundbogenfenster‹. Darin bekam man einen kurzen Einblick in ein spezielles Fabrikationsverfahren, wie z. B. das Herstellen, Sterilisieren, Füllen und Versiegeln von Dosen für gebackene Bohnen. Das Faszinierende an diesem Schauspiel war für mich, dass es mich verstehen ließ, wie Objekte entstanden, und wie Gebrauchsgegenstände mittels einer mir unbekannten Technik hergestellt wurden. Es ist diese anhaltende Faszination, wie man aus Materialien Objekte formt, die mich zum Designer macht.
Ich sehe das Wesentliche in meiner Rolle als Designer in der Problemlösung, d. h. in der Suche nach intelligenten, einfallsreichen und geschickten Lösungen, die den Objekten ein langes, reiches und zufriedenstellendes Leben verleihen. Was mich ebenso fasziniert, ist das Wesen, die Präsenz und der Charakter von Objekten. Ich verbringe viel Zeit damit, die Welt der Dinge zu beobachten und zu studieren. Dabei analysiere ich die Objekte, bewusst oder unbewusst, im Hinblick auf Material, Funktion, Gebrauch, Missbrauch, Form, Farbe, Oberfläche, Ausführung, Befestigung, Alter, Patina, Verbindung von Linienführung und Material ...
Wenn ich neue Objekte entwerfe, beziehe ich mich unbewusst (oder nicht) auf diese Informationen, woraus Dinge entstehen können, die vertraut aussehen oder sich vertraut anfühlen. Das geschieht als Ergebnis meines Bestrebens, wirklich moderne Objekte zu gestalten (im Sinne einer ehrlichen und adäquaten Verwendung von Material, Methode und Funktion). Die eigentliche Form des Endprodukts ist dann mehr das Resultat einer Verarbeitung von Ideen als einer Anwendung von Stilen.«
MICHAEL MARRIOTT

"As a child, I was always fascinated with one particular part of a children's television programme, called something like 'through the round window'. In it, you were offered a glimpse of a factory production line (i. e. the manufacturing, sterilization, filling and sealing of tins of baked beans). What intrigued me about this spectacle was the opportunity to understand how foreign objects came into being, how things were made using technology beyond that of the garden shed. It is this continuing fascination with the manipulation of materials into objects that makes me a designer.
I see this role primarily as a problem-solving one, to find intelligent, resourceful and cunning solutions that will provide objects with a long, rich and satisfying life.
I am also intensely intrigued by the nature, presence and character of objects. I spend a lot of time observing and studying things and the world, analysing objects consciously and unconsciously in terms of material, function, use, misuse, form, colour, texture, finish, fixings, age, patina, junctions of line and material etc.
When designing new objects, I draw subconsciously (or not) on this gathered information, which can produce things that look or feel familiar. This happens as a result of aiming to design truly modern objects (in terms of the honest and appropriate use of material, process and function). The literal form of the end result is the outcome of a processing of ideas rather than an application of styles." MICHAEL MARRIOTT

« Petit, j'étais fasciné par une des rubriques d'une émission de télévision pour enfants, un programme qui s'appelait quelque chose comme " à travers la fenêtre ronde ". On y voyait une chaîne d'assemblage dans une usine (plus précisément, la fabrication, le remplissage, la stérilisation et la fermeture hermétique de boîtes de flageolets en conserve). Ce qui m'intriguait, c'était comment on fabriquait les choses, comment on les créait en utilisant une technologie autre que les outils de notre remise au fond du jardin. C'est cette même fascination pour la manipulation des matières pour en faire des objets qui fait de moi un designer.
Mon rôle consiste à résoudre des problèmes, à trouver des solutions intelligentes, ingénieuses et astucieuses qui assureront aux objets une vie longue, riche et satisfaisante. Je suis également très intrigué par la nature, la présence et le caractère des objets. Je passe un temps considérable à observer et étudier les choses et le monde, analysant les objets consciemment et inconsciemment en termes de matière, de fonction, d'usage, de mauvais usage, de forme, de couleur, de texture, de finition, de garniture, d'âge, de patine, de jonctions de lignes et de matériaux, etc. Lorsque je conçois un nouvel objet, je m'inspire inconsciemment (ou non) de ces informations, qui peuvent déboucher sur quelque chose qui paraît familier. C'est ce qui se passe quand je cherche à créer des objets vraiment modernes (en termes d'utilisation honnête et adéquate du matériau, du procédé et de la fonction). La forme littérale du résultat final découle du traitement des idées plutôt que de l'application de styles. » MICHAEL MARRIOTT

3. **Bedside** table/Nachttisch/table de chevet for the exhibition *Living Rooms*, 100 % Design, London, sponsored by Cappellini, 1999
4. **Croquet** shelving system/Regalsystem/étagères for SCP, 2000
5. **Ferret** bench/Sitzbank/banc for the exhibition *Lost + Found*, British Council, London, 1999
6. **Fast** flat-pack table/Tisch/table (self-production), 1997

MICHAEL MARRIOTT			CLIENTS
BORN	1963	London, England	20/21
STUDIED	1985	HND London College of Furniture	DIM
	1993	MA Royal College of Art, London	Inflate
PRACTICE	1993	established own studio	Mathmos
	2000	co-directed first Oreka Kids furniture collection; currently tutor on Product Design course, Royal College of Art, London	Oreka Kids
			SCP
AWARDS	1999	Jerwood Furniture Prize, London	SMAK
EXHIBITIONS	1998	*Living Rooms*, London; *Oggetti Onesti*, Milan; Powerhouse UK, London	Trico
	1999	*Identity Crisis – The 90s Defined*, The Lighthouse, Glasgow; *Stealing Beauty*, Institute of Contemporary Arts, London	also self-production
	2000	*Bring Me Sunshine*, Tokyo; *Industry of One*, London & Edinburgh	

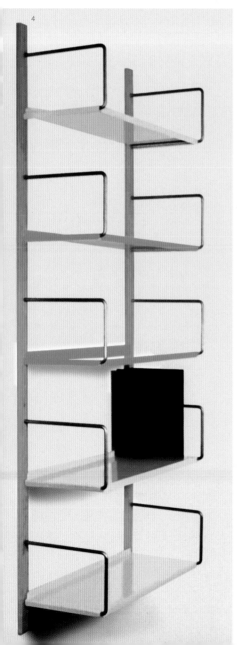

4

5

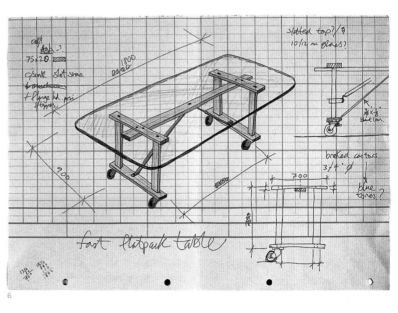

6

"Exploring the properties of materials in order to create forms which have organic and sculptural qualities that are enhancing and enhanced by light."

Sharon Marston

Sharon Marston, Studio 38, 21, Clerkenwell Green, London EC1R 0DP, England
T/F +44 20 7490 7495 enquiries@sharonmarston.com www.sharonmarston.com

»Die Eigenschaften von Materialien erforschen, um organische und skulpturale Formen zu gestalten, die durch Licht intensiviert werden.«

« Explorer les propriétés des matériaux afin de créer des formes ayant des qualités organiques et spirituelles qui rehaussent et sont rehaussées par la lumière. »

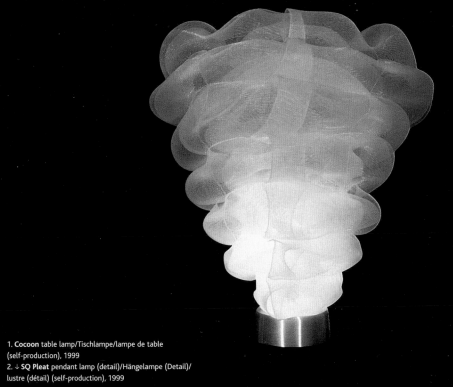

1. **Cocoon** table lamp/Tischlampe/lampe de table
(self-production), 1999
2. ↓ **SQ Pleat** pendant lamp (detail)/Hängelampe (Detail)/
lustre (détail) (self-production), 1999

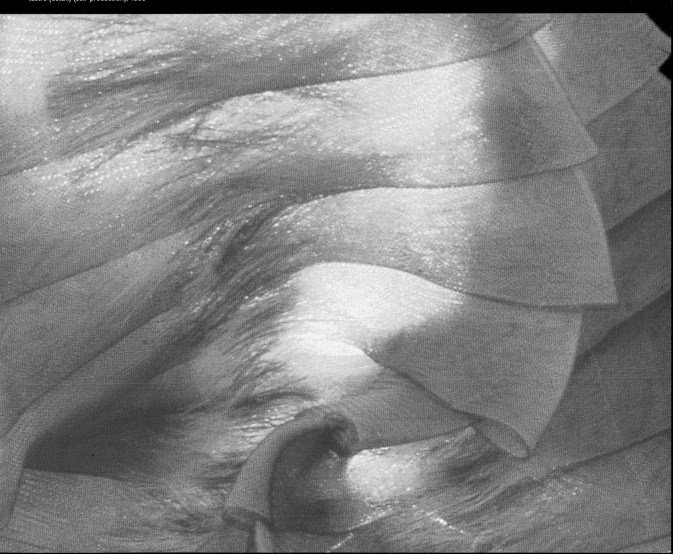

»Designer lassen sich in zwei Kategorien ein-
ordnen: Die einen arbeiten auf einer logischen
Ebene, die anderen auf einer emotionalen. Ich
selbst würde mich zur zweiten Kategorie
zählen. Zentraler Aspekt meiner Entwürfe ist
ein Gefühl, das sich auf eine zunehmend kon-
fus und unsicher werdende Zukunft bezieht.
Das ist eine sehr spannende Position für Designer, da die gegenwärtigen technischen For-
schritte viele neue Räume schaffen, in denen
sich Design entwickeln kann.
Als Konsumenten bewegen wir uns heute auf
eine Welt zu, die das Grundkonzept von Design im Sinne von ›Weniger ist Mehr‹ in Frage
stellt. Damit sind wir mit einer Welt voller
Wahlmöglichkeiten konfrontiert. Diese Ver-
mehrung resultiert teilweise aus den Fort-
schritten im Bereich der Fertigungstechniken
und aus dem massiven medialen Bombardement durch multinationale Konzerne.
Ich halte das für eine positive Entwicklung,
weil auf diese Weise eine reiche Auswahl an
verschiedenen Farben, Materialien, Größen,
Funktionen und Preise geboten wird. Und da
wir menschliche Wesen sind, betrachten wir
uns als Individuen und wollen unsere unterschiedlichen Geschmäcker und Vorlieben gel-
tend machen. Die Auswahl der Objekte, mit
denen wir uns umgeben, definiert und prägt
unsere Identität, indem wir uns unterscheiden.
Die Designer der Zukunft müssen sich dieser
Aspekte bewusst sein, wenn sie neue Produkte
entwickeln. Dabei müssen sie gleichermaßen
auf unsere körperlichen wie auf unsere emotionalen Bedürfnisse eingehen.« SHARON MARSTON

"Designers can be said to fall into
two categories: those who design on
a logical level and those who design
on an emotional level. I would put
myself in the latter of these two
categories. I create designs that are
built around emotion for a future
that is becoming increasingly con-
fused and uncertain. This is a very
exciting position to be in as current
advances in technology are creating
many new spaces in which design
can develop.
As consumers, we are now moving
forward into a world that challenges
the fundamental concept of design
based on the idea of 'Less is More'.
Now we are faced with a world of
choices. This proliferation is partly
the result of advances in manufacturing processes and the massive
media bombardment by multi-
national companies.
I believe that this is a positive step,
for people are now offered the op-
tions of different colours, materials,
sizes, functions and price variations.
As humans, we consider ourselves
individuals and like to assert our
different tastes. Our decisions on
the objects we surround ourselves
with define who we are and provide
us with identity through difference.
Designers in the future will have to
be aware of these issues when developing new products. They must
design not only for our physical
needs but for our emotional needs
as well." SHARON MARSTON

« On distingue deux catégories de designers :
ceux qui créent sur un plan logique, et ceux
qui créent sur un plan émotionnel. Je me
place dans la seconde. Je crée des lampes
construites autour de l'émotion pour un avenir de plus en plus confus et incertain. C'est
une situation passionnante car les progrès
technologiques actuels nous offrent de nombreux nouveaux espaces dans lesquels le
design peut se développer.
En tant que consommateurs, nous nous diri-
geons vers un monde qui remet en question
le concept fondamental du design, à savoir
" moins il y en a, mieux c'est ". Nous sommes
confrontés à un monde de choix. Cette prolifération résulte en partie des progrès des procédés de fabrication et du bombardement
médiatique des multinationales.
C'est une étape positive, car on peut désormais opter entre différents prix, couleurs, matières, tailles et fonctions. En tant qu'êtres
humains, nous nous considérons comme des
individus et aimons affirmer nos goûts personnels. Nos décisions sur les objets qui nous
entourent définissent qui nous sommes et
nous offrent une identité par le biais de la
différence. Les créateurs du futur devront en
tenir compte en développant de nouveaux
produits. Ils devront répondre à nos besoins
physiques mais également à nos besoins
émotionnels. » SHARON MARSTON

3. **SQ Pleat** pendant lamp/Hängelampe/lustre
(self-production), 1999
4. **Aqua** floor lamp/Stehlampe/lampadaire
(self-production), 1998
5. **Cocoon** floor lamp/Stehlampe/lampadaire
(self-production), 1998
6. **Spiral Pleat** table lamp/Tischlampe/lampe de table
(self-production), 1998

SHARON MARSTON

BORN	1970	Hereford, England
STUDIED	1986-88	Btec Diploma Art & Design, Herefordshire College of Art & Design
	1988-92	BA (Hons) Jewellery Design, Middlesex University
PRACTICE	1997-	independent designer/maker
EXHIBITIONS	1997	*Design Resolutions*, Royal Festival Hall, London
	1998	*UK 98 British Festival*, Tokyo; *British and Hungarian Jewellery Design*, Vienna; 100 % Design, London
	1999	*Sotheby's Decorative Arts*, London
	2000	*British Design Excellence*, Manila; International Contemporary Furniture Fair, New York

CLIENTS

Harvey Nichols
Jaeger
The Metropolitan Hotel
also self-production

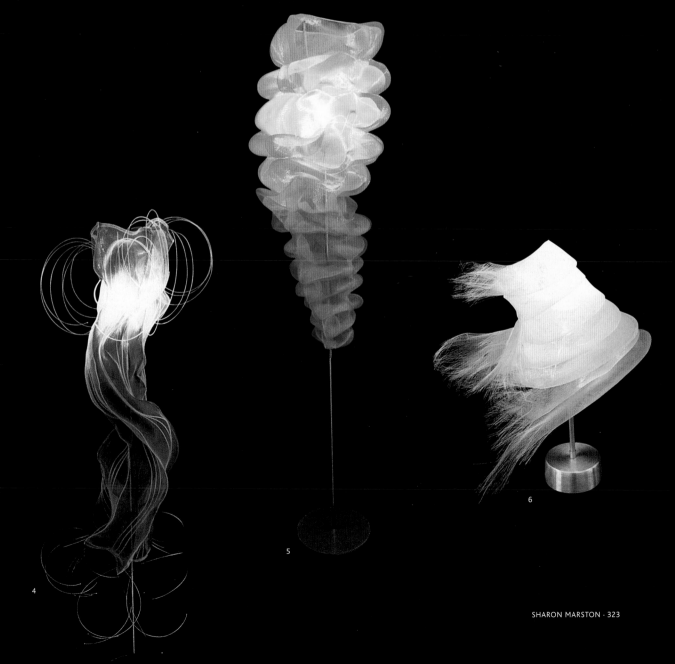

4

5

6

"My favourite design is in my mind,
not yet born."

Ingo Maurer

Ingo Maurer, Ingo Maurer GmbH, Kaiserstrasse 47, 80 801 Munich, Germany
T +49 89 381 6060 F +49 89 381 60620 postmaster@ingo-maurer.com www.ingo-maurer.com

*»Mein Lieblingsdesign existiert in mei-
nem Kopf, es ist noch nicht geboren.«*

« Mon design préféré est dans ma tête,
pas encore né. »

»Kunst ist das, was eine Person in einem Objekt sieht. Kunst kann ein Nagel oder ein Stück
Natur sein, je nach persönlicher Empfindung.
Ich kann keine Grenze zwischen Kunst und
Design erkennen. Und ich habe auch keine
Philosophie. Ich versuche, meiner Intuition,
meinem Instinkt, meinen zwanzig Verpflich-
tungen zu folgen. Wobei das Wichtigste natürlich die Qualität ist. In Zukunft wird die
größte Herausforderung für Designer darin
liegen, verantwortlich gegenüber den Menschen und der Umwelt zu handeln und mit
Sinn und Verstand zu entwerfen.« INGO MAURER

"Art is what a person sees in an
object. Art could be a nail or a piece
of nature, depending on one's perception. I cannot see any borderline
between art and design. I do not
have a philosophy. I try to follow my
intuition, my instinct, my twenty
responsibilities, and, of course, most
important is quality. The main challenge for a designer in the future
will be to act responsibly towards
human beings and the environment
and to design with sense." INGO MAURER

« L'art est ce que la personne voit dans un
objet. Il peut s'agir d'un clou ou d'un fragment
de la nature, selon la perception de chacun.
Je ne vois aucune frontière entre l'art et le
design. Je n'ai pas de philosophie. J'essaie de
suivre mon intuition, mon instinct, mes vingt
responsabilités. Bien sûr, ce qui compte avant
tout, c'est la qualité. A l'avenir, le plus grand
défi du designer sera d'agir de manière responsable envers les êtres humains et l'environnement et de créer en se servant de sa
raison. » INGO MAURER

1. page/Seite 223 **XXL Dome** pendant lamps in
Westfriedhof subway station, Munich/Hängelampen
in der Münchner U-Bahn-Station Westfriedhof/
plafonniers de la station de métro Westfriedhof, Munich
(self-production), 1999
2. **Bob** table light/Tischlampe/lampe (self-production),
2000
3. **Paragaudi** lamp/Lampe/luminaire (self-production),
1997

INGO MAURER	CLIENTS
	self-production

BORN	1932	Reichenau island, Lake Constance
STUDIED		Typography courses in Germany and Switzerland
	1954-58	Graphics Diploma, Munich
PRACTICE	1960-63	freelance designer in New York and San Francisco
	1966	founded "Design M" in Munich
AWARDS	1986	created *Chevalier des arts et des lettres* by the French Ministry of Culture
	1998	nominated Designer of the Year by the magazine *Architektur & Wohnen*, Hamburg
	1999	prize for design, City of Munich
	2000	prize for design, City of Barcelona; Lucky Strike Designer Award, Raymond Loewy Foundation, Switzerland
EXHIBITIONS	1985	installation for *Lumières – Je pense à vous*, Centre Georges Pompidou, Paris
	1986	*Ingo Maurer Lumière aha Soho*, Institut Français d'Architecture, Paris; light show for *Design à la Villa Medici*, Rome
	1988	installation for *Design heute. Maßstäbe – Formgebung zwischen Industrie und Kunst-Stück*, Deutsches Architekturmuseum, Frankfurt/Main
	1989	*Ingo Maurer – Lumière Hasard Réflexion*, Fondation Cartier, Paris
	1991	*Münchener Räume*, Stadtmuseum, Munich
	1993	*Licht licht*, Stedelijk Museum, Amsterdam
	1998	*Projects 66* (with Fernando and Humberto Campana), Museum of Modern Art, New York
	1999	installation for Issey Miyake, La Villette

"Every new product development must contain innovation."

J Mays

J Mays, c/o Product Development Center, Ford Motor Company,
20 901 Oakwood Blvd., Dearborn MI 48 124-4077, USA
T +313 621 6089 F +313 845 1119 media@ford.com www.media.ford.com

»Jede neue Produktentwicklung muss Innovation enthalten.«

« Tout produit nouveau doit innover. »

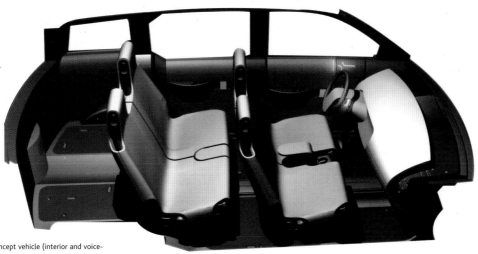

1.-2. **24.7 Wagon** concept vehicle (interior and voice-activated reconfigurable projected image display)/ Konzept-Fahrzeug (Innenraum und sprachgesteuertes neu-konfigurierbares Wiedergabe-Bild)/concept de véhicule (intérieur et image projetée reconfigurable commandée à la voix) for Ford Motor Company, 2000

« Un bon design repose sur trois éléments : la simplicité, la crédibilité et les attentes du consommateur. Le designer a pour tâche de créer un design qui communique la nature du produit, établit un lien émotionnel avec le consommateur et, dans le meilleur des cas, élargit le vocabulaire du genre. C'est une philosophie relativement facile à exprimer, mais un peu plus compliquée à mettre en œuvre. Par exemple, communiquer la nature d'un produit ne signifie pas simplement refléter ce que fait le produit, sa fonction. Cela implique de transmettre de manière crédible le caractère du produit : son intégrité, ses qualités essentielles et la promesse de sa marque. En bref, les attributs critiques qui le distinguent des autres. Un bon design exprime tout ceci visuellement, de manière simple et spectaculaire afin qu'il puisse être immédiatement compris parmi la masse chaotique des produits similaires.

La seconde tâche est d'établir un lien émotionnel avec le consommateur. Cela nécessite de traduire une fonction en un concept qui éveille l'intérêt et stimule. Il s'agit de sentiments qui évoquent des formes, de concocter ce que John Galsworthy appelle " le vin de leurs aspirations ". En fin de compte, il s'agit de passer au crible les valeurs, le mode de vie et les aspirations d'un individu pour fabriquer un reflet de ses désirs en trois dimensions. La troisième tâche est d'élargir le vocabulaire, le langage du design. L'une des caractéristiques de l'industrie automobile — elle n'est sans doute pas la seule — est d'être très insulaire. Au lieu de chercher de nouveaux moyens de communiquer avec le consommateur, on est trop souvent en train d'espionner ce que fait le voisin sur sa planche à dessin. Résultat, nous passons régulièrement par des cycles où le travail de tout le monde se ressemble. Je vois deux remèdes à cela. Tout d'abord, nous devons être prêts à explorer de nouvelles idées sur l'aspect des produits en nous basant sur d'autres éléments importants du mode ↓

"I believe that good design rests on three elements: simplicity, credibility and the aspirations of the customer. The task for a designer is to create a design that communicates the nature of the product, connects emotionally with the customer and, on a good day, expands the vocabulary of the genre. It's a relatively easy philosophy to articulate — a bit more complicated to execute.

Communicating the nature of the product, for example, means more than reflecting what the product does — its function. It also includes credibly communicating the character of the product — its integrity, the essential qualities it represents and the brand promise — in short, the critical attributes that uniquely distinguish the product. Good design is the visual communication of all these things — and doing it simply and dramatically so that it can be immediately grasped in the confusion of similar products.

The second task is the creation of an emotional connection with the customer. That requires translating a functional thing into a concept that arouses and excites people. It's about form creating feelings — about concocting what John Galsworthy referred to as 'the wine of their aspirations'. Ultimately, it is about sifting through a person's values, lifestyle and aspirations to fabricate a three-dimensional reflection of their desires.

The third task is to expand the vocabulary, the language of product design. One of the characteristics of the automotive industry — and I suspect some others — is that it is very insular. Too often we seem to be peeking at each other's drawing boards rather than searching out new ways of communicating ↓

»Ich glaube, dass gutes Design auf drei Elementen beruht: Einfachheit, Glaubwürdigkeit und den Erwartungen des Käufers. Die Aufgabe für einen Designer besteht darin, ein Design zu entwickeln, das die Eigenart des Produkts mitteilt, das eine emotionale Verbindung mit dem Käufer herstellt und, im Idealfall, das Vokabular des Genres erweitert. Diese Philosophie ist relativ einfach zu formulieren — aber ein bisschen komplizierter umzusetzen. Das besondere Wesen des Produkts mitzuteilen, bedeutet zum Beispiel mehr, als nur widerzuspiegeln, was ein Produkt macht — also seine Funktion. Dazu gehört nämlich auch, glaubwürdig den Charakter des Produkts zu vermitteln: seine Integrität, die essentiellen Qualitäten, die es repräsentiert, und das Versprechen der Marke. Kurz gesagt: die entscheidenden Attribute, die das Produkt von anderen unterscheidet. Gutes Design ist der sichtbare Ausdruck all dieser Elemente — in ebenso einfacher wie spektakulärer Form, so dass es in dem Durcheinander ähnlicher Produkte sofort wahrgenommen werden kann. Die zweite Aufgabe besteht darin, eine emotionale Verbindung mit dem Käufer herzustellen. Dazu muss ein funktionaler Gegenstand in ein Konzept übertragen werden, das die Leute neugierig macht und stimuliert. Es geht darum, durch Form Gefühle zu erzeugen — oder, anders ausgedrückt, um die Zubereitung dessen, was John Galsworthy den ›Wein ihrer Hoffnungen‹ nannte. Im Grunde kommt es also darauf an, die Werte, Lebensstile und Hoffnungen der Leute ausfindig zu machen und daraus ein dreidimensionales Spiegelbild ihrer Wünsche zu fabrizieren. Die dritte Aufgabe für Designer liegt in der Erweiterung des Vokabulars bzw. der Sprache des Produktdesigns. Eines der charakteristischen Merkmale der Automobilindustrie — und sicherlich einiger anderer Industriezweige — ist, dass sie eine Art Inseldasein führt. Statt nach neuen Möglichkeiten zu suchen, wie wir mit den Kunden kommunizieren können, schielen wir Gestalter nur allzu oft auf die ↓

3.-4. ← **(My) Mercury** concept vehicle (opening-back rear doors)/Konzept-Fahrzeug (mit rückwärtig zu öffnenden Hintertüren)/concept de véhicule (ouverture des portières arrière) for Ford Motor Company, 1999
5. **Thunderbird** concept vehicle (front grill)/Konzept-Fahrzeug (Kühlerhaube)/concept de véhicule (calandre) for Ford Motor Company, 1999

	J MAYS		CLIENTS
BORN	1954	Pauls Valley, Oklahoma, USA	in-house designer for Ford Motor Company
STUDIED	1980	Art Center College of Design, Pasadena	
PRACTICE	1983	designer, BMW AG, Munich	
	1984-89	senior designer Audi AG, Ingolstadt	
	1989-93	chief designer Volkswagen of America's Design Center, California	
	1993-95	design director, Audi AG, Ingolstadt	
	1995-97	vice president of Design Development SHR Perceptual Management, Scottsdale	
	1997-	vice president-Design, Ford Automotive Operations, Dearborn	

6

du vie du consommateur. Eero Saarinen a suggéré un jour qu'on devrait toujours concevoir un objet en le plaçant dans un contexte plus large – une chaise dans une pièce, une pièce dans une maison, une maison dans un paysage. Nous devons regarder au-delà du produit et examiner tout l'éventail des possibilités. Ensuite, nous devons reconnaître qu'un design ne communique pas uniquement à travers sa forme. Plus nous stimulerons nos sens, plus l'expérience du produit sera forte.
Quant à l'avenir, plus notre culture deviendra complexe, plus nous apprécierons les messages simples et crédibles qui feront appel à nos émotions et refléteront nos aspirations. »
J. MAYS

6. **24.7 PickUp** concept vehicle/Konzept-Fahrzeug/concept de véhicule for Ford Motor Company, 2000
7. **Ford Equator** concept pick-up/Konzept-Pickup/concept de camionnette for Ford Motor Company, 2000
8. **Thunderbird** concept vehicle/Konzept-Fahrzeug/concept de véhicule for Ford Motor Company, 1999
9. **Thunderbird** concept vehicle (front door)/Konzept-Fahrzeug (Vodertür)/concept de véhicule (portière avant) for Ford Motor Company, 1999

with the customer. As a result, we cycle through periods when everybody's work looks the same.
I see two remedies for this. First, we need a willingness to explore new ideas of what a product could look like based on other important things in the customer's lifestyle. Eero Saarinen once suggested you should always design a thing by considering it in its next largest context – a chair in a room, a room in a house, a house in an environment. We need to look beyond the product and examine the spectrum of possibilities. Second, we need to recognize that design does not communicate through shape alone. The more senses we engage the stronger the product experience.
As to the future, the more complicated our culture becomes, the more we will value simple, credible design messages that engage our emotions and reflect our aspirations." J MAYS

Zeichenbretter der anderen. Das Ergebnis ist, dass wir regelmäßig Perioden durchmachen, in denen alle Entwürfe gleich aussehen.
Ich sehe zwei Lösungen für dieses Problem: Als erstes müssen wir bereit sein, neue Ideen für das Aussehen von Produkten zu erforschen, indem wir von anderen wichtigen Aspekten im Lebensstil der Käufer ausgehen. Von Eero Saarinen stammt der Vorschlag, einen Gegenstand zu gestalten, indem man ihn in seinem nächstgrößeren Kontext betrachtet – einen Stuhl in einem Raum, einen Raum in einem Haus, ein Haus in einer Umgebung. Wir müssen über das Produkt hinausschauen und das ganze Spektrum der Möglichkeiten studieren. Zweitens müssen wir erkennen, dass sich Design nicht allein durch die äußere Form mitteilt. Je mehr Sinne ein Produkt anspricht, desto stärker wirkt es auf uns.
Was die Zukunft betrifft: Je komplizierter unsere Kultur wird, desto höher werden wir einfache, glaubwürdige Designbotschaften schätzen, die unsere Gefühle ansprechen und das widerspiegeln, was wir erhoffen.« J. MAYS

"The attempt to achieve simple things meets what you might call a 'biological' need for simplicity. Since we are complicated beings, let us at least be surrounded by simple objects."

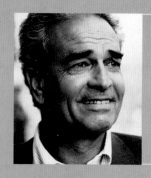

Alberto Meda

Alberto Meda, Via Savona 97, 20 144 Milan, Italy
T +39 02 422 90157 F +39 02 477 16169 a.meda@planet.it

»Das Bemühen um Einfachheit in der Gestaltung von Objekten entspricht einer Art ›biologischem‹ Bedürfnis: Da wir komplizierte Wesen sind, sollten wir uns zumindest mit einfachen Dingen umgeben.«

« La tentative d'accomplir des choses simples répond à ce qu'on pourrait appeler un besoin " biologique " de simplicité. Puisque nous sommes des êtres complexes, entourons-nous au moins d'objets simples. »

1. **Floating Frame** chair/Stuhl/chaise for Alias, 2000
2. ↓ **Fortebracco** task lamp/Arbeitslampe/lampe
d'architecte for Luceplan (designed with Paolo Rizzatto),
1998

« Le design n'est pas un processus linéaire, c'est une activité assez complexe qui ressemble à un jeu stratégique mais où, bizarrement, les règles changeraient constamment. C'est ce qui le rend si fascinant et mystérieux. Le designer puise ses idées dans différentes sources au sein de son propre monde de références où il cherche des suggestions créatives. Personnellement, je m'intéresse à la technologie, parce qu'elle me paraît être l'expression actuelle de la capacité imaginative de l'homme, de son ingéniosité nourrie de connaissance scientifique. La technologie élargit le champ de la connaissance, mais son développement ne doit pas avancer sans justification, sans prendre en considération ses répercussions. La technologie pour la technologie peut être très dangereuse.
La technologie doit être apprivoisée afin de réaliser des objets qui aient avec l'homme la relation la plus simple possible. Nous devons rejeter les produits industriels qui ne prennent pas en compte les besoins humains, qui n'ont aucune rationalité communicative. La technologie n'est pas une fin en soi mais un moyen de produire des objets capables d'améliorer de manière expressive l'espace autour d'eux. Paradoxalement, plus la technologie devient complexe, plus elle est en mesure de générer des objets à l'image simple, unitaire, " quasi organique ".
Le design devrait être considéré comme une stratégie s'inspirant du domaine de l'imaginaire technologique. Son but n'est pas d'invoquer une image mettant en avant la pensée scientifique et technique, et donc la technologie en soi, mais d'utiliser cette dernière comme un moyen esthétique et figuratif ↓

3. ← **Meda** conference chair/Konferenzstuhl/fauteuil de conférence for Vitra, 1996
4. **Meda** chair (work drawings)/Stuhl (Entwurfsskizzen)/chaise (dessins) for Vitra, 1997

"The design process is not linear, it is rather a complex activity similar to a game's strategy, but strangely it is a game where the rules are continuously changing and that is what makes it so fascinating and mysterious.
The designer collects his ideas from various sources within his own world of reference where he looks for creative suggestions. I am personally interested in the world of technology, because it seems to me to be the contemporary expression of the imaginative capability of man, of his ingenuity fed by scientific knowledge. Technology widens the scope of knowledge, but it is necessary to understand that technological development must no longer proceed without justification, without consideration of its repercussions. Self-directed technology can be very dangerous. Technology must be tamed in order to realize things that have the simplest possible relation with man – we must reject technologically driven industrial goods that have no regard for human needs and no communicative rationality. Technology is not an end in itself, but a means of producing simple things capable of enhancing expressively the space around them. Paradoxically, the more complex technology becomes, the better it can generate objects with a simple, unitary, 'almost organic' image.
Design should be seen as a strategy that fishes in the realms of techno- ↓

»Der Designprozess verläuft nicht linear, sondern stellt eine komplexe Aktivität dar, die einer Spielstrategie ähnelt. Komischerweise ist es ein Spiel, dessen Regeln sich ständig ändern. Aber genau das ist es, was es so faszinierend und geheimnisvoll macht.
Designer beziehen ihre Ideen aus verschiedenen Quellen innerhalb ihres eigenen Bezugssystems, wo sie nach kreativen Anregungen suchen. Mein persönliches Bezugssystem ist die Welt der Technik, weil mir die Technik der zeitgemäße Ausdruck des Vorstellungsvermögens des Menschen, seiner von wissenschaftlicher Erkenntnis gespeisten Erfindungsgabe zu sein scheint. Die Technik erweitert das Spektrum unseres Wissens. Wir müssen jedoch einsehen, dass die technische Entwicklung nicht länger ohne Rechtfertigung und ohne Rücksicht auf ihre Auswirkungen fortschreiten darf. Eine Technologie, deren Zweck nur in sich selber liegt, kann sehr gefährlich werden.
Die Technik muss gezähmt werden, damit man Objekte realisieren kann, die eine einfache Beziehung zum Menschen ermöglichen. Abzulehnen sind rein technisch orientierte Industrieerzeugnisse, die keine Rücksicht auf menschliche Bedürfnisse nehmen und keiner kommunikativen Logik folgen. Technologie ist kein Selbstzweck, sondern ein Mittel zur Herstellung einfacher Dinge, die auf ausdrucksvolle Weise ihre Umwelt bereichern können. Je komplexer die Technik wird, desto besser ist sie paradoxerweise geeignet, Objekte mit einer einfachen, einheitlichen und beinahe ›organischen‹ Erscheinungsform zu erzeugen. Man sollte Design als eine Strategie betrachten, mit der man sich Anregungen aus dem ↓

		ALBERTO MEDA	CLIENTS
BORN	1945	Lenno Tremezzina, Como, Italy	Alfa Romeo
STUDIED	1969	MA Mechanical Engineering, Politecnico di Milano	Alessi
PRACTICE	1973-79	technical manager, Kartell	Alias
	1979	established own design office	Ansaldo
	1983-87	lecturer, industrial technology Domus Academy, Milan	Carlo Erba
	1995-	lecturer Politecnico di Milano	Cinelli
AWARDS	1989	Compasso d'Oro, Milan	Colombo Design
	1992	Design Plus Award, Frankfurt/Main	Fontana Arte
	1994	Compasso d'Oro, Milan; European Design Prize, Frankfurt/Main	Gaggia
	1995	iF Design Award, Hanover	Ideal Standard
	1996	iF Design Award Hanover	Italtel Telematica
	1997	Best of Category, *I. D. Magazine Annual Design Review*, New York	Kartell
	1999	Designer of the Year, Salon du Meuble, Paris	Luceplan
EXHIBITIONS	1990	*Creativitalia* and solo exhibition, Design Gallery, Tokyo	Legrand
	1992	*Il Giardino delle Cose*, Triennale, Milan; *Mestieri d'Autore*, Siena	Mandarina Duck
	1993	*Design, Miroir du Siècle*, Paris	Mondedison
	1995	*Mutant Materials in Contemporary Design*, Museum of Modern Art, New York	Omron Japan
	1996	*Meda-Rizzatto*, Amsterdam; *Lighting Affinities*, Milan	Philips
	1999	Salon du Meuble, Paris	Vitra

5

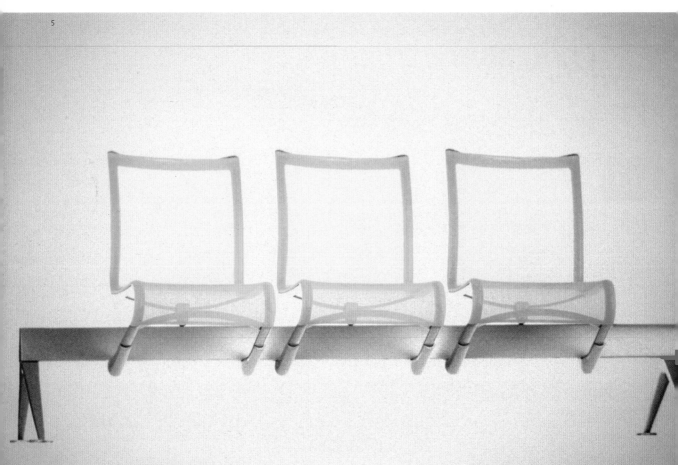

d'interpréter et d'explorer les performances possibles. Je ressens le besoin de produire des objets ayant une qualité culturelle reconnaissable, qui aient un " sens " en plus d'une " forme ". En d'autres termes, le design devrait servir à fabriquer des produits résolvant des problèmes irrésolus. » ALBERTO MEDA

logical fantasy. Its purpose is not to conjure up an image that emphasizes scientific and technical thinking, and therefore technology for its own sake, but to use technology as a means of aesthetic-figurative interpretation and exploration of possible performances. I feel the necessity to produce things with a recognizable cultural quality – things that make 'sense', in addition to 'shape'. In other words, design should be approached with a view to making products capable of solving unsolved problems."
ALBERTO MEDA

Reich der technischen Phantasie holt. Es geht nicht darum, ein Image zu erzeugen, das wissenschaftliches und technisches Denken ins Zentrum stellt – und damit die Technologie zum Selbstzweck macht. Design sollte vielmehr bewirken, Technik als Instrument einer ästhetisch-figurativen Interpretation und Erforschung möglicher Funktionen einzusetzen. Ich halte es für notwendig, Dinge mit einer erkennbaren kulturellen Qualität herzustellen – Dinge, die einen ›Sinn‹ haben, und nicht nur eine ›Form‹. Mit anderen Worten: Man sollte an die Gestaltung von Design mit dem Ziel herangehen, Produkte anzufertigen, die ungelöste Probleme lösen können.« ALBERTO MEDA

5. **Floating Frame** bench seating system/Sitzbanksystem/système de banquette for Alias, 2000
6. **Partner** shelving system/Regalsystem/système d'étagères for Kartell (designed with Paolo Rizzato), 1999 (exploded to show components/explodiert, um die einzelnen Komponenten sichtbar zu machen/décomposé pour montrer les différents composants)
7. **Words of Light** table lamp/Tischlampe/lampe de table for Luceplan (designed with Paolo Rizzato), 2000

6

7

"Keep a thing for seven years and you'll find a use for it." (IRISH PROVERB)

Jasper Morrison

Jasper Morrison, Office for Design

»Behalte einen Gegenstand sieben Jahre lang, und du wirst eine Verwendung dafür finden.« (IRISCHES SPRICHWORT)

« Conservez un objet pendant sept ans et vous finirez par lui trouver une utilité. » (PROVERBE IRLANDAIS)

1. **Glo-ball** pendant lamp/Hängelampe/plafonnier
for Flos, 1998
2. ↓ **Three** sofa/Sofa/canapé for Cappellini, 1992

Il y a plusieurs avenirs possibles pour le design, mais imaginons d'abord le meilleur. Le design (le vrai) sature progressivement tous les domaines de l'industrie, apportant une qualité esthétique et matérielle exceptionnelle aux produits, qui peuvent être commercialisés à des prix abordables, enrichissant notre quotidien au-delà de toute espérance. A présent, un avenir moins désirable : les gens du marketing s'emparent de l'industrie et le saturent avec leur idée du design (pas le vrai), inondant le monde d'articles inutiles dont personne ne sait quoi faire, à part les offrir à d'autres. Comme d'habitude, le futur réside quelque part entre ces deux extrêmes. »
JASPER MORRISON

3. ← **Air-Chair**/Stuhl/chaise for Magis, 1999
4. **Tin Family** kitchen containers/Behälter für die Küche/
récipients de cuisine for Alessi, 1998

"There are many possible futures of design, but let's imagine an ideal one first. Design (the real thing) gradually saturates all areas of industry bringing exceptional aesthetic and material quality to products, which can be marketed at affordable levels, enriching our daily lives beyond imagination. And now a less desirable future: marketing people take over industry and saturate it with their idea of design (not the real one), flooding the world with useless articles that nobody needs, which can only be bought as gifts for others. As usual, the future lies somewhere between these extremes." JASPER MORRISON

»Es gibt viele Zukunftsmöglichkeiten für das Design, aber lassen Sie mich zunächst eine Idealversion beschreiben: Design (das wahre) durchdringt allmählich alle Industriebereiche und verleiht den Produkten eine außergewöhnliche ästhetische und materielle Qualität. Diese Produkte werden dann zu vernünftigen Preisen vermarktet und bereichern unser Alltagsleben mehr als man es sich heute vorstellen kann. Und jetzt ein weniger wünschenswertes Zukunftsszenario: Marketing-Manager übernehmen die Herrschaft über die Industrie und durchdringen sie mit ihrer Vorstellung von Design (nicht das wahre). Sie überschwemmen die Welt mit nutzlosen Waren, mit denen niemand etwas anzufangen weiß, außer, sie zu verschenken. Wie immer liegt die Zukunft irgendwo zwischen diesen beiden Extremen.« JASPER MORRISON

UP IN THE TREE

DOWN ON THE GROUND

5.-7. ← **Luxmaster** standing lamps/Stehlampen/
lampadaires for Flos, 2000
8. **Bird-Table**/Tisch/table for Magis, 2000

JASPER MORRISON

BORN	1959	London, England
STUDIED	1979-82	BA (Des) Kingston Polytechnic Design School, London
	1982-85	MA (Des) Royal College of Art, London
	1984	scholarship studies Hochschule der Künste, Berlin
PRACTICE	1986	established Office for Design, London
	1992	co-directed *Progetto Oggetto* for Cappellini
	1999	edited *International Design Year Book*
AWARDS	1992	Bundespreis Produktdesign, Frankfurt/Main; iF *Top Ten* Design Prize, Hanover; International Design Prize, Design Zentrum Nordrhein-Westfalen, Essen
	1997	iF Transportation Design Prize and Ecology Award, Hanover; (has also won numerous Design Plus Awards, Frankfurt/Main, and nominations for Compasso d'Oro awards, Milan)
EXHIBITIONS	1987	*documenta 8*, Kassel
	1988	*Design Werkstadt*, Berlin
	1994	solo exhibition, Interieur Biennial, Kortrijk
	1995	group exhibition, Museum für Kunsthandwerk, Frankfurt/Main; solo exhibition, Arc en Rêve Centre d'Architecture, Bordeaux
	1999	*Jasper Morrison, Marc Newson, Michael Young – Design*, Reykjavik Art Museum
	2000	solo exhibition, AXIS GALLERY, Tokyo
	2001	solo exhibition, Yamagiwa Centre, Tokyo

CLIENTS

Alessi
Alias
Artifort
BETTE
Bree Collection
Bute Fabrics
Canon Camera Division
Cappellini
Colombo Design
Flos
FSB
Mabeg
Magis
Rosenthal
SCP
Sony Design Centre Europe
Üstra
Vitra

9. **Lima** folding outdoor chair/Klappstuhl für draußen/
chaise de jardin pliable for Cappellini, 1996
10. **Hi Pad** chairs/Stühle/chaises for Cappellini, 1999
11. **Low Pad** lounge chair/Klubsessel/trausat for Cappellini,
1999
12. **Plan** drawers/Schubladen/tiroirs for Cappellini, 1999

"Think Right – *Penser Juste*"

Pascal Mourgue

Pascal Mourgue – Patrice Hardy, 2, Rue Marcelin Berthelot, 93 100 Montreuil-Sous-Bois, France
T +33 1 48 51 59 38 F +33 1 48 51 59 51 mourgue.hardy@wanadoo.fr

»Richtig denken«

« Penser juste »

1. **Le Paresseux** armchair/Sessel/fauteuil for Cinna-Ligne
Roset, 1999
2. ↓ **Smala** sofa/Sofa/canapé for Cinna-Ligne Roset, 2000

»Ein gutes Designprodukt ist immer mit einer konzeptionellen Innovation verknüpft. Dabei reicht es nicht, nur auf die Form abzuzielen. Alle guten Produkte, d. h. alle Produkte, die kommerziell erfolgreich sind, sind auf die eine oder andere Weise innovativ. Es ist ziemlich einfach, einer Idee Form zu verleihen. Auf der anderen Seite ist es jedoch sehr schwierig, ohne gedankliche Auseinandersetzung eine Form zu gestalten. Meine Arbeit als Designer besteht darin, Ideen zu formulieren, die auf Innovation beruhen.« PASCAL MOURGUE

"A good product is always linked to a conceptual innovation. Researching only through form is not enough. All good products, meaning those that are commercially successful, have a subtle touch of innovation. It is quite easy to get an idea into shape. On the other hand, with no thoughts it is very difficult to create a form. As a designer, my work lies in formulating ideas based on innovation."
PASCAL MOURGUE

« Un bon produit est toujours lié à une innovation conceptuelle. La recherche uniquement formelle n'est pas suffisante. Tous les bons produits en termes commerciaux ont ce subtil dosage d'innovation. Il est très facile de donner forme à une idée. D'un autre côté, sans pensée, il est très difficile de créer une forme. En tant que designer, mon travail consiste à formuler des idées basées sur l'innovation. »
PASCAL MOURGUE

3. **10 Line** chair/Stuhl/chaise for Artelano, 1997
4. **Dune** chair/Stuhl/chaise for Fermob, 1995
5. **Smala** table/Tisch for Cinna-Ligne Roset, 2000
6. **Câlin** armchair/Sessel/fauteuil for Cinna-Ligne Roset, 1994

"The basic idea is the legitimization
of new products."

N2 Design

N2 – Design, Postfach 6330, 6000 Lucerne 6, Switzerland
T/F +41 41 360 8665 n2@n2design.ch www.n2design.ch

*»Die Grundidee ist die Legitimation für
neue Produkte.«*

« L'idée de base est de légitimer les
nouveaux produits. »

1. **Ajax** desk/Schreibtisch/bureau for ClassiCon,
1998 – designers: Jörg Boner & Christian Deuber
2. ↓ **Pac Man** mirrors/Spiegel/miroirs (self-production),
2001 – designers: Jörg Boner & Christian Deuber

»Jedes Mitglied unserer Gruppe arbeitet an seinen eigenen Ideen, holt sich jedoch Rat bei den anderen vier Designern. Für einige Aufträge arbeiten wir als Gruppe zusammen. Diese Form der Partnerschaft ist nicht immer leicht zu handhaben, aber sie erzeugt eine Menge Synergie. Wir wollen, dass unsere Arbeiten leicht verständlich sind und immer ein überraschendes Moment oder eine ironische Seite enthalten. Unser Anliegen ist, Möbel zu entwerfen, bei denen die Qualität und nicht bloß die Quantität im Vordergrund steht. Als Gruppe sind wir daran interessiert, mit neuen Materialien und Technologien zu experimentieren. Unsere Hauptmotivation besteht in der Realisierung unserer Ideen mit Hilfe des Potentials neuer Produktionsmethoden, gepaart mit der Kenntnis industrieller Fertigungsprozesse und Tradition. Wir wollen etwas ›wirklich Neues‹ schaffen, statt immer nur das Rad wieder neu zu erfinden.« N2 DESIGN

"Each member of our group works on his own ideas yet seeks advice from the other four designers. For some commissions we work together as a team. This form of partnership is not always easy to handle but it creates a lot of synergy. We want our work to be clearly understood and to always have a surprising moment or an ironic side. We want to create furniture that emphasizes quality and not just quantity. As a group, we are all interested in exploring new materials and technologies. Our central motivation is our vision of realizing our ideas through the potential of new production methods twinned with a knowledge of manufacturing and tradition. We want to create 'new stuff' and not just reinvent the wheel over and over again!" N2 DESIGN

« Chaque membre de notre groupe travaille ses propres idées tout en demandant conseil aux quatre autres designers. Pour certaines commandes, nous travaillons en équipe. Cette forme de partenariat n'est pas toujours facile à gérer mais elle crée une grande synergie. Nous voulons que notre travail soit clairement compris et qu'il ait toujours un côté surprenant ou ironique. Nous souhaitons créer des meubles qui mettent en avant la qualité, pas uniquement la quantité. En tant que groupe, nous sommes tous intéressés par l'exploration de technologies et de matériaux nouveaux. Notre principale motivation est de concrétiser nos idées au travers du potentiel des nouvelles méthodes de production associées à une connaissance de la fabrication et de la tradition. Nous voulons créer du " nouveau " et pas réinventer la roue une énième fois ! » N2 DESIGN

3.-4. **Wegtauchen** chaise longue& bookcase/Liege & Büchergestell/chaise longue & bibliothèque for Hidden, 2000
5. **Tube** light/Röhrenlampe/lampe tubulaire for Palluccoitalia, 1997
6. **Cotton** shelves/Regale/étagères (self-production), 1998
7. **Olma** shelves/Regale/étagères (self-production – limited edition), 1998 – designer: Jörg Boner

N2 DESIGN		CLIENTS
FOUNDED	1997 Basle, Switzerland by Jörg Boner (b. 1968 Uster), Christian Deuber (b. 1965 Lucerne), Paolo Fasulo (b. 1965 Lucerne), Valerie Kiock (b. 1971 Munich) & Kuno Nüssli (b. 1970 Niederrohrdorf)	ClassiCon Driade Hidden Palluccoitalia also self-production
AWARDS	1997 Appreciation Design-Preis Schweiz, Switzerland	
	1998 Appreciation Design for Europe Award, Kortrijk	
	1999 Design-Preis Schweiz, Switzerland	
	2000 Förderpreis 2000, Zurich	
EXHIBITIONS	1997 *Mustermesse*, Basle; *Interni*, Milan	
	1998 *Salone Satellite*, Milan; *Designer's Saturday*, Langenthal, Switzerland; *N2*, Lucerne	
	1999 *Salone Satellite*, Milan; *N2*, Vienna	
	2000 *Waschtag*, Cologne; *Submeet*, Zurich; *Talente*, Munich; *Big Torino*, Turin	

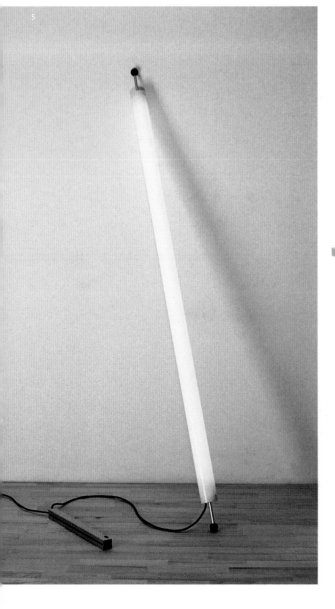

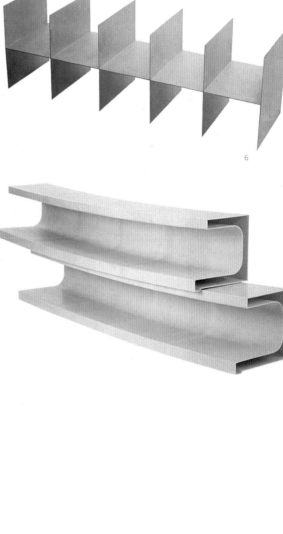

"I approach design in a fairly subliminal way, which is lucky because I don't have time to think about it too much ..."

Marc Newson

Marc Newson, Marc Newson Ltd., 1, Heddon Street, London W1R 7LE, England
T +44 20 7287 9388 F +44 20 7287 9347 pod@marc-newson.com www.marc-newson.com

»Mein Zugang zu Design ist ein ziemlich unbewusster. Glücklicherweise, denn ich habe keine Zeit, besonders viel darüber nachzudenken ...«

« J'aborde le design d'une manière assez subliminale, ce qui est aussi bien parce que je n'ai pas le temps de trop y penser ... »

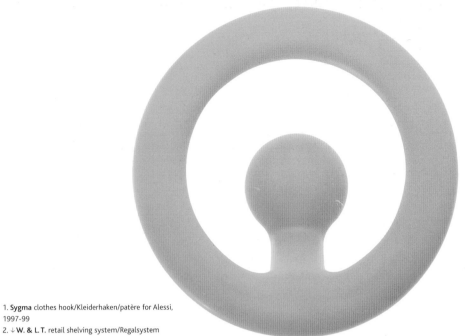

1. **Sygma** clothes hook/Kleiderhaken/patère for Alessi, 1997-99
2. ↓ **W. & L. T.** retail shelving system/Regalsystem für Geschäfte/présentoir de boutique for Walter Van Beirendonck, 1996-97

4

« Il ne fait aucun doute que le design jouera un rôle plus important dans notre vie à l'avenir, que ça nous plaise ou non. Il jouera certainement un rôle plus important dans les grandes entreprises. Dans un sens, c'est comme s'il renaissait en ce moment même, coïncidant étrangement avec le nouveau millénaire. De même, je suppose que le terme " design " deviendra de plus en plus familier pour tout le monde. J'espère seulement qu'il ne sera pas uniquement une accroche commerciale mais qu'il sera synonyme de qualité et d'amélioration. » MARC NEWSON

"Without doubt, design will play a more important role in our lives in the future whether we like it or not. Certainly, it will play a much bigger role in large companies. In a sense, it's as if design is being re-born as we speak, strangely coinciding with the new millennium. As well, I suppose the word 'design' will become increasingly familiar to most people. My hope is that it will not simply become a commercial catch-phrase, but come to define something that implies quality and improvement." MARC NEWSON

5

»Zweifellos wird Design in Zukunft eine wichtigere Rolle in unserem Leben spielen, ob uns das gefällt oder nicht. Und ganz sicher wird es eine wesentlich größere Bedeutung für große Unternehmen haben. In gewissem Sinne scheint es, als werde Design gerade jetzt neu geboren, was eigenartigerweise mit dem Beginn des neuen Jahrtausends zusammenfällt. Außerdem nehme ich an, dass der Begriff ›Design‹ den meisten Menschen immer vertrauter wird. Ich hoffe nur, dass es sich dabei nicht einfach zu einem kommerziellen Schlagwort entwickelt, sondern dass es etwas definieren wird, das Qualität und Verbesserung beinhaltet.« MARC NEWSON

3. ← **W. & L.T.** retail shelving system/Regalsystem für Geschäfte/présentoir de boutique for Walter Van Beirendonck, 1996-97
4. **Megapode** watch/Armbanduhr/montre for Ikepod, 1998
5. **Stavros** bottle opener/Flaschenöffner/ouvre-bouteilles for Alessi, 1997-99
6. **Titan** soap dish/Seifenschale/porte-savon for Alessi, 1997-99
7. **Hi, Med, Low** drinking glasses/Trinkgläser/verres for littala, 1998

6

7

8

9

10

8. & 10. **Interior** for Syn recording studio in Tokyo/
Inneneinrichtung für das Syn-Aufnahmestudio in Tokio/
décoration intérieure de studio d'enregistrement Syn à
Tokyo, 1996
9. **Interior** for Andoni shop/Inneneinrichtung für den
Andoni-Laden/intérieur de boutique Andoni, 1988
11. **Orgone** plastic chair/Plastikstuhl/chaise en plastique
for Pod, 1998
12. **Bath Plug**/Badewannenstöpsel/bouchon de baignoire
for Alessi, 1997
13. **David Gill** chair/Stuhl/chaise for B&B Italia, 1998

12

11

13

14

15

16

17

14.-19. **021C** concept vehicle for Ford (exterior and interiors)/Konzept-Fahrzeug für Ford (Innen- und Außenansichten)/concept de véhicule pour Ford (intérieur et extérieur), 2000

18

19

MARC NEWSON

BORN	1963	Sydney, Australia
STUDIED	1984	BA jewellery and sculpture, Sydney College of Arts
PRACTICE	1987-91	lived and worked in Tokyo
	1991	established design studio in Paris
	1997	established Marc Newson Ltd. in London
AWARDS	1984	Australian Crafts Council Award
	1989	George Nelson Award, USA
	1990	First Prize Salon du Meuble Creator of the Year Award
	1999	Sydney Design Convention Award
	2001	shortlisted for Perrier-Jouët Selfridges Design Award, London
EXHIBITIONS	1990	*Fresh Produce by Marc Newson*, Gold and IDÉE, Tokyo
	1991 & 92	solo exhibitions, Carla Sozzani, Milan
	1995	*Marc Newson & Bucky*, Fondation Cartier, Paris
	1997	*Marc Newson*, Villa de Noailles, France
	1998	solo exhibition, Museum Boijmans Van Beuningen, Rotterdam
	1999	*Marc Newson*, McLellan Gallery, Glasgow; *Jasper Morrison, Marc Newson, Michael Young*, Reykjavik Art Museum

CLIENTS

Alessi
Biomega
Cappellini
Flos
Ford
IDÉE
Iittala
Ikepod Watch Company
Magis
Moroso

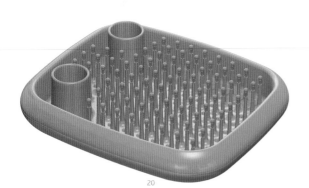

20

21

22

23

24

25

26

20. **Dish Doctor** drainer/Abtropfgestell/égouttoir
for Magis, 1997
21. **Gemini** salt grinder and pepper mill/Salz- und
Pfeffermühle/salière et poivrière for Alessi, 1999
22.-23. **Falcon 900B** long-range executive jet (interior)/
Langstreckenflieger (Innenausstattung)/jet privé long-
courrier (intérieur), 1998-99
24.-25. **MN01** bicycle/Fahrrad/bicyclette for Biomega,
1998-99
26. **Rock** doorstop/Türstopper/butoirs de porte for Magis,
1997
27. **IO** table/Tisch for B&B Italia, 1998

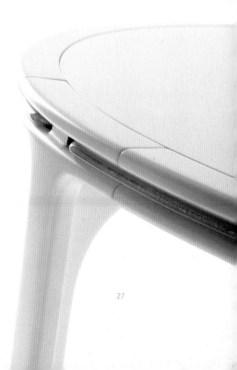

27

"Our design aspirations: surprise, beauty, invention, curiosity, intelligence and joy."

PearsonLloyd

Luke Pearson & Tom Lloyd, PearsonLloyd, 42 -46, New Road, London E1 2AX, England
T +44 207 377 0560 F +44 207 377 0550 mail@pearsonlloyd.co.uk www.pearsonlloyd.co.uk

»Mit unserem Design streben wir Über-
raschung, Schönheit, Erfindung, Neugierde, Intelligenz und Freude an.«

« En tant que designers, nous recher-
chons la surprise, la beauté, l'inventivité,
la curiosité, l'intelligence et la joie. »

1. **Camouflage** table/Tisch for Poltronova, 2000
2. ↓ **Camouflage Collection** seating, tables, cabinets, rugs and vases/Sitzmöbel, Tische, Kabinettschränke, Teppiche und Vasen/sièges, tables, meubles de rangement , tapis et vases for Poltronova, 2000

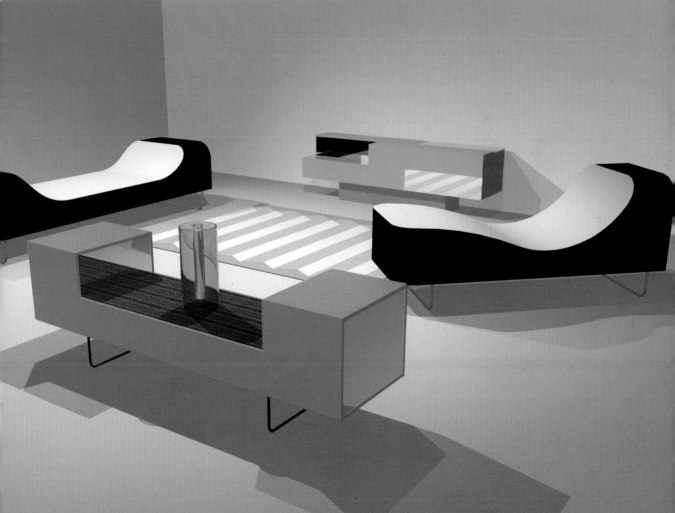

« Nous présentons un design " industriel " qui nourrit et encourage la pollinisation croisée des cultures et des technologies en mélangeant les domaines, les techniques et les fonctions. Cela nous vient de notre goût des matières, des procédés et de la manière dont les choses s'assemblent. En travaillant dans divers secteurs avec des procédés qui ne sont pas " les nôtres ", nous pouvons jouer et expérimenter sans jamais être enchaînés par la perception traditionnelle de la manière dont ces matières " devraient " fonctionner ensemble. Le fait de conjuguer différents domaines du design nous permet d'échanger des idées sur le plan culturel mais également en termes de langage et de technologie.
La gamme du design de produits manufacturés s'étend de l'artisanat à la production de masse. Nous tâchons de situer nos objets sur cette gamme à l'endroit qui leur convient le mieux, en fonction de besoins technologiques et culturels. Cela renvoie également à une responsabilité au sein de l'économie mondiale telle qu'on la perçoit : concevoir des produits viables dans un système viable.
Notre objectif est de créer des objets qui expriment ou transmettent un sens et une émotion au-delà de leur forme, de leur structure et de leur fabrication. Nous voulons éviter de souscrire à un dogme ou à une mode en produisant, non pas des archétypes, mais des objets innovateurs qui soient universellement compréhensibles et satisfaisants. A l'avenir, nous aspirons à servir d'interprètes entre l'industrie et le consommateur, les traducteurs de nos univers changeants. Les progrès technologiques permettront au design industriel de devenir une discipline vraiment expressive. L'afflux toujours croissant de matériaux et de procédés permettra de conjuguer les moyens et les idées, de créer des objets meilleur marché, plus efficaces et mieux adaptés à un monde en mutation. » PEARSONLLOYD

3. ← **Homer** personal mobile hot-desking unit/mobiles Büromöbel/unité de travail personnelle et mobile for Knoll International, 1997-98
4. **Ilos** table lamp/Tischlampe/lampe for ClassiCon, 2000

"We present an 'industrial' design, which entertains and encourages cultural and technological cross-pollination by working across diverse scales, technologies and functions. This comes from a love of materials and processes and how things are put together. By working across different industries and processes that are not 'ours', we can play and experiment, never becoming slaves to the traditional understanding of how those materials 'should' go together. Working in varied areas of design allows an exchange of ideas either in terms of cultural ideas or in terms of language and technology. The spectrum of design for manufacture exists from craft to mass production. Our design work attempts to place objects appropriately and sympathetically within this spectrum, as a response to both technological and cultural needs. This also relates to a responsibility within the perceived global economy, to design sustainable goods within a sustainable system.
Our aim is to provide objects that express or relay meaning and emotion and go beyond their appropriate form, structure and manufacture. Our desire is to avoid subscribing to dogma or fashion and to create innovative rather than archetypal objects that are universally understandable and enjoyable. Our aspiration is to act as an interpreter of our changing worlds between industry and the user. The embracing of technological advances will allow industrial design to become a truly expressive discipline. The expanding flow of materials and processes available will provide an opportunity to mix mediums and ideas, and create objects which are cheaper, more efficient and appropriate within a changing world." PEARSONLLOYD

»Wir präsentieren ein ›industrielles‹ Design, das unterhaltsam ist, und das die gegenseitige Befruchtung zwischen Kultur und Technologie fördert, indem wir unterschiedliche Dimensionen, Technologien und Funktionen miteinander verbinden. Das kommt von unserer Faszination für Materialien und Prozesse und für die Art, wie Dinge zusammengesetzt werden. Durch unsere Arbeit mit unterschiedlichen Fertigungsprozessen, die nicht ›unsere eigentlichen‹ sind, können wir spielen und experimentieren und werden nie zu Sklaven der traditionellen Auffassung davon, wie diese Werkstoffe zusammenpassen ›müssten‹. Die Tatsache, dass wir in gemischten Designbereichen tätig sind, ermöglicht uns einen Austausch von Ideen entweder in kultureller Hinsicht oder im Sinne von Formensprache und Technologie.
Das für die Fabrikation geeignete Spektrum des Designs reicht vom Handwerk bis zur Massenproduktion. Mit unseren Entwürfen versuchen wir, den Objekten einen angemessenen und günstigen Platz innerhalb dieses Spektrums zu geben, als eine Reaktion sowohl auf technische als auch auf kulturelle Bedürfnisse. Das bezieht sich auch auf eine Verantwortung, die wir im Rahmen der globalen Wirtschaft darin sehen, nachhaltige Produkte für ein nachhaltiges System zu gestalten.
Unser Ziel ist es, Objekte anzubieten, die Bedeutung und Emotion ausdrücken oder vermitteln und die über ihre jeweilige Form, Struktur und Herstellungsweise hinausgehen. Wir wollen vermeiden, uns einem Dogma oder einer Mode zu verschreiben und eher innovative als archetypische Objekte kreieren, die allgemein verständlich, brauchbar und befriedigend sind. Für die Zukunft streben wir an, als Interpreten unserer sich wandelnden Welt zwischen Industrie und Verbraucher zu fungieren. Industriedesign wird durch den technologischen Fortschritt zunehmend ausdrucksstärker. Mit der immer weiter ansteigenden Flut von Materialien und Fertigungstechniken bietet sich uns die Gelegenheit, Gestaltungselemente und Ideen zu mischen und Objekte zu entwerfen, die billiger, effizienter und für die sich wandelnde Umwelt passender sind.« PEARSONLLOYD

		PEARSONLLOYD		CLIENTS
FOUNDED	1997	London, England by Luke Pearson (b. 1967 Portsmouth) and Tom Lloyd (b. 1967 London)		Acco
STUDIED		LUKE PEARSON		The Body Shop
	1991	BA (Hons) Industrial Design, Central St Martin's College of Art and Design, London		Carhartt
	1993	MA Furniture Design, Royal College of Art, London		ClassiCon
		TOM LLOYD		Dockers
	1991	BA (Hons) Furniture Design, Nottingham Trent University		Ettinger
	1993	MA Industrial Design, Royal College of Art, London		Hitch Mylius
AWARDS	1999	First Prize *Millennium Street Furniture Competition*, Westminster City Council, London		Knoll International
	2000	FX Design Award, London; *Gift of the Year Award*, London; iF Design Award, Hanover		Levis Europe
EXHIBITIONS	1999	*Identity Crisis – The 90s Defined*, The Lighthouse, Glasgow		Poltronova
	2001	*Workspheres*, Museum of Modern Art, New York		Walter Knoll
				Westminster City Council, London
				Urban Splash

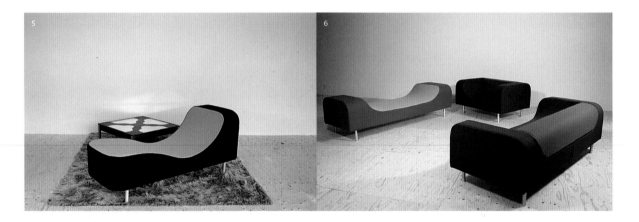

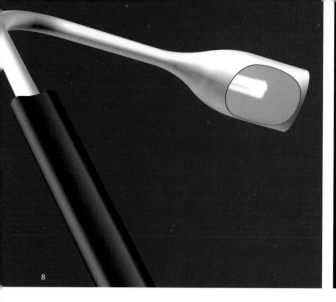

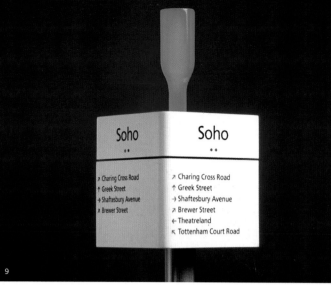

5.-6. **Camouflage** sofa, chaise longue and armchair/
Sofa, Liege und Sessel/canapé, chaise longue et fauteuil
for Poltronova, 2000

7. **Knollscope** office storage system/Büro-Aufbewahrungs-
system/meuble de rangement de bureau for Knoll
International, 2000

8. **Westminster Eye** street light and canopy light/
Straßenlaterne und Lampengehäuse/réverbère et

luminaire avec auvent for Westminster City Council,
1999-2001

9. **Westminster Eye** street light/Straßenlaterne/réverbere
for Westminster City Council, 1999-2001

10. **HNB** desking program/Schreibtischsystem/système
de bureau for Walter Knoll, 2001

"Reality is what we make it."

Stephen Peart

Stephen Peart, Vent Design, Unit 15, 1436, White Oaks Road, Campbell, California, 95008 USA
T +408 559 4015 F +408 559 4036 vent1design@earthlink.net

»Realität ist das, was wir dazu machen.«

« La réalité est ce qu'on en fait. »

1. **Computercap**/Computerhelm/casque ordinateur
for Virtual Vision, 1996
2. ↓ **Animal** wetsuit/Tauchanzug/combinaison de plongée
for O'Neill, 1990

»Wir befinden uns mitten in einer ökono-
mischen und spirituellen Revolution, wobei
Design heute mehr auf Entdeckungen und
Visionen basiert als auf den Kosten von Waren. Wir konstruieren Dinge, weil wir es können und nicht, weil wir sie brauchen. Dinge
sollten als Werkzeug, Gebäude, Möbel, Produkte oder Medien angesehen werden – und
wir sollten nicht zum Werkzeug für die Existenz von Dingen werden. Die Leute halten
Design für cool, und das ist es auch. Aber im
Gestalten von Design liegt auch eine Verantwortung. Indem wir etwas herstellen, billigen
wir persönlich dessen Existenz und beeinflussen das Schicksal zahlreicher Ressourcen.
Wenn wir Dinge konstruieren, sollten wir die
verwendeten Werkstoffe und deren Neben-
wirkungen in Betracht ziehen. Die meisten
der heute hergestellten Chemikalien kommen
ungeprüft auf den Markt. Nehmen Sie zum
Beispiel die von Mobiltelefonen ausgehende
Elektronenemission: Sie mag nicht tödlich für
Sie sein, aber sie könnte Ihr Leben sehr beein-
trächtigen. Das Entsorgen all dieser Dinge
auf Mülldeponien ist vielleicht unser gering-
stes Problem. Das heißt nicht, dass wir eine
Revolution anzetteln sollten statt als Designer
zu arbeiten. Aber wir sollten uns darüber im
Klaren sein, welche Konsequenzen die von
uns gestalteten Produkte haben. Wir müssen
unsere natürlichen Spielräume schützen. Sie
sind zu kostbar, um sie zu verlieren.«
STEPHEN PEART

"We are in the midst of an economic and spiritual revolution with
design now being based more on
discovery and vision than on the
cost of goods. We build things because we can, not because we need
to. Things should be tools, buildings,
furniture, products or media – we
should not become tools for the
existence of things.
People think of design as cool and
it is, but there is responsibility in
design. By creating something,
you are personally approving its
existence and directing the fate
of many resources.
When we build things we should
consider their side effects and the
substances used. Most chemicals
made today are untested. Take, for
example, the electronic hardware
emissions produced by cell phones:
They may not kill you but they
could make you very unhappy.
Throwing things into landfill sites
may be the least of our worries.
This doesn't mean that we should
start a revolution and stop designing, but we must be aware of the
consequences of the products we
create. We need to protect our
physical playground, it's too much
fun to lose." STEPHEN PEART

« Nous sommes au beau milieu d'une révolution économique et spirituelle où le design
est désormais basé davantage sur la décou-
verte et la vision que sur le coût des produits.
Nous construisons des choses parce que nous
le pouvons, pas parce que nous en avons besoin. Les choses devraient être des outils, des
bâtiments, des meubles, des produits ou des
médias. Nous ne devons pas devenir les outils
des choses. Les gens pensent que le design,
c'est cool, et ils ont raison, mais il implique
également une responsabilité. En créant quelque chose, on approuve son existence et on
influe sur le sort de nombreuses ressources.
Quand on construit quelque chose, on devrait
tenir compte de ses effets secondaires et des
composants utilisés. La plupart des substances chimiques fabriquées aujourd'hui ne sont
pas testées. Prenez par exemple les émissions
des matériaux électroniques utilisés dans
les téléphones cellulaires : elles ne vous tue-
ront peut-être pas mais elles peuvent sérieusement vous gâcher la vie. On ne se soucie
guère des dépotoirs dans lesquels on déverse
tous ces déchets. Ça ne veut pas dire qu'il faut
faire la révolution et bannir le design, mais
qu'on doit être conscient des conséquences
des produits qu'on crée. Nous devons protéger
notre terrain de jeux, il est trop beau pour
qu'on le perde. » STEPHEN PEART

3. **Shoe of the Future** concept project/Projekt für Schuhe/
projet de chaussure for Reebok, 1996
4. **EMMA** floor system/Bodensystem/système de fixation
de carrelage for Herman Miller (concept project, designed
with Ross Lovegrove), 1995-1999
5. **Enterprise** ear-mounted telephone headset/am Ohr
befestigter Telefonhörer/oreillettes pour téléphone
for Plantronics, 1993
6. **Persona** Internet answering machine/Internet-Anruf-
beantworter/répondeur Internet for Sun Microsystems,
1998

STEPHEN PEART

BORN	1958	Durham, England
STUDIED	1975-79	BA (Hons) Industrial Design, Sheffield City Polytechnic
	1979-82	MA Industrial Design, Royal College of Art, London
PRACTICE	1982-87	Design Director Frogdesign, Altensteig and California
	1987	founded Vent Design, Campbell, California
AWARDS	1985	Best of Category, *I. D. Magazine Annual Design Review* Award, New York
	1986	Gold Industrial Design Excellence Award, IDSA
	1991	Gold Industrial Design Excellence Award, IDSA
	1993	iF Design Award, Hanover; Special Award for Design Innovation in the Field of Computer and Communication Technology, Roter Punkt Award, Design Zentrum Nordrhein-Westfalen, Essen; Silver Industrial Design Excellence Award, IDSA
	1994	American Society of Interior Designers (ASID) Interior Design Product Award; Roter Punkt Award, Design Zentrum Nordrhein-Westfalen, Essen; *I. D. Magazine Annual Design Review* Design Distinction Award and Best of Category, New York
	1995	shortlisted for BBC Design Awards
	1996	Good Design Award, Chicago Athenaeum; Best of Category, *I. D. Magazine Annual Design Review* Award, New York
	1997	Industrial Design Excellence Award, IDSA
EXHIBITIONS	1995	*Mutant Materials in Contemporary Design*, Museum of Art, New York; *National Design Triennial – Design Culture Now*, Cooper-Hewitt National Design Museum, New York

CLIENTS

Apple Computer
GE Plastics
Herman Miller
Jetstream
Knoll Group
Nike
O'Neill
Plantronics
Sun Microsystems
Virtual Vision
Visioneer

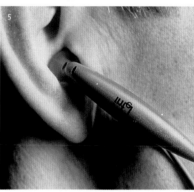

"The best is yet to come."

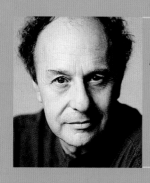

Jorge Pensi

Jorge Pensi, Jorge Pensi Diseño, Pza. Berenguer 1, 08 002 Barcelona, Spain
T +34 93 310 3279 F: +34 93 315 1370 pensi@idgrup.ibernet.com

»Das Beste kommt erst noch.«

« Le meilleur est encore à venir. »

1. **Peppermint** armchair/Sessel/fauteuil for Kron, 2000
2. ↓ **Chocolate** sofa/Sofa/canapé for Perobell, 1999

« Un designer aborde un objet un peu comme un auteur, tissant une histoire visuelle et conceptuelle à partir d'une image originale qu'il a dans la tête. La principale différence est que le designer travaille généralement avec un commanditaire qui spécifie le thème et le cadre dans lequel le processus créatif doit se dérouler. Le client est la pierre d'achoppement du processus créatif, celui qui fera " croire " au designer à son inspiration avant même que n'apparaissent les premières images mentales (qui aient un sens). Dans certains projets, l'image est créée d'avance, alors que dans d'autres, il ne s'agit que d'un concept brut et flou qui doit être étayé par plusieurs modèles tridimensionnels et des prototypes. En ce sens, le design ressemble à l'architecture et repose sur l'expérimentation.

Le designer vit entre deux mondes, le subjectif et l'objectif. Le premier se base sur des symboles, l'originalité et la nature relativement immuable et intrinsèque des objets. Il est lié à la magie de la créativité, à l'influence de l'histoire et de la mémoire, aux grands maîtres et visionnaires du design. Le second est le monde réel, qui dépend des marchés, des investissements, des coûts, des calendriers des fabricants et de la production. Le premier monde représente le désir et l'autre, la réalité. Plus nos désirs se rapprochent de la réalité, plus le design sera bon. La capacité d'un objet à susciter des émotions vient d'un processus de développement, où les désirs ne peuvent être trahis par la réalité et où le lien entre les deux mondes reste intact. » JORGE PENSI

3. ← **Duna** chair/Stuhl/fauteuil for Cassina, 1998
4. **Splash** armchair/Stuhl/fauteuil for Amat, 1999

"A designer approaches an object in a similar way to an author – visually and conceptually weaving a story from an original mind's eye image. The most important difference, however, is that the designer usually works with a client, who specifies the theme and framework in which the creative process must take place. The client is the first input of the creative process, the person responsible for making the designer 'believe' in the inspiration before the first mental images (that make any sense) appear. In some projects the image is created in advance, while in others it is merely a rough, fuzzy concept that needs to be verified by several three-dimensional models and prototypes. In this sense, design is similar to architecture in that it relies on a process of trial and error.

The designer lives between two worlds – the subjective and the objective. The first world is based on symbols, originality and the relatively immutable and intrinsic nature of objects. It is connected to the magic of creativity, the influence of history and memory, and the great masters and visionaries of the design field. The second world is the real world, which is related to markets, investments, costs, the manufacturer and the production schedule. One world represents desire and the other, reality. The closer our desires are to reality, the better the design will be. The ability of an object to stir emotions comes from a process of development, where desires cannot be betrayed by reality and where the connection between the two worlds remains intact." JORGE PENSI

»Ein Designer geht in seiner Arbeit an einem Objekt ähnlich vor wie ein Schriftsteller – indem er aus einem ursprünglich geistigen Bild visuell und konzeptionell eine Geschichte entwickelt. Der wichtigste Unterschied ist jedoch, dass Designer in der Regel mit Auftraggebern zusammenarbeiten, die das Thema und den Rahmen vorgeben, in dem der kreative Prozess stattzufinden hat. Der Auftraggeber gibt den ersten Impuls für den kreativen Prozess und ist verantwortlich dafür, dass der Designer an die Inspiration ›glaubt‹, noch bevor die ersten (einigermaßen sinnvollen) mentalen Bilder auftauchen. Bei einigen Projekten entsteht das Bild vorher, während es bei anderen lediglich ein grobes, vages Konzept gibt, das durch mehrere dreidimensionale Modelle und Prototypen verifiziert werden muss. In diesem Sinne lässt sich Design auch mit Architektur vergleichen, da es ebenso wie diese auf einem Prozess des Experimentierens beruht.

Designer leben im Wechsel zwischen zwei Welten – der subjektiven und der objektiven. Die erste Welt basiert auf Symbolen, Originalität und der relativ unveränderlichen und spezifischen Natur von Objekten. Sie steht in Verbindung mit der Magie der Kreativität, dem Einfluss von Geschichte und Erinnerung sowie mit den großen Meistern und Visionären des Designs. Die zweite Welt ist die reale Welt, die mit Handelsmärkten, Investitionen, Kosten, dem Hersteller und dem Produktionsplan verbunden ist. Die eine Welt repräsentiert das Begehren und die andere die Realität. Je näher unsere Begierden der Realität sind, desto besser wird das Design sein. Die Fähigkeit eines Objekts, Emotionen zu wecken, ist auf einen Entwicklungsprozess zurückzuführen, in dem die Begierden nicht von der Realität verraten werden können und die Verbindung zwischen beiden Welten intakt bleibt.« JORGE PENSI

JORGE PENSI			CLIENTS
BORN	1949	Buenos Aires, Argentina	Akaba
STUDIED	1965-73	architecture, Facultad de Arquitectura, UBA, Buenos Aires	Amat
PRACTICE	1975	emigrated to Spain and adopted Spanish nationality	Andreu World
	1977-84	collaborated with Alberto Liévore as part of Group Berenguer in Barcelona	B.Lux
	1985	established own design practice in Barcelona	Cassina
AWARDS	1988	Award Selection from SIDI	Ciatti
	1987 & 95	Silver Delta Award, Assoziazione del Diesegno Industriale	Disform
	1990	*Design-Auswahl 90* Award, Design Center Stuttgart	Driade
	1997	*National Design Prize*, Spanish Ministry of Industry and BCD (Barcelona Design Centre),	Inno Interior
		Golden Delta Award, Assoziazione del Diesegno Industriale	Knoll International
EXHIBITIONS	1984	*SIDI (Salón Internacionale de Diseño para el Habitát) ON Diseño*	Kron
	1988-94	*Design in Catalonia*, touring exhibition, Milan, Tokyo, Singapore and USA	Kusch+Co
			Perobell
			Punt Mobles
			Santa & Cole
			SIDI
			Thonet

5. **Gimlet** stools/Hocker/tabouret for Mobles 114, 1998
6. **Techne** office seating system/Büromöbel/sièges de bureau for Kitto, 2000
7. **Nite** table & pendant lamp/Tisch- & Hängelampe/lampe suspendue for B. Lux, 1998
8. **Hega** table & sideboard/Anrichte & Tisch/table & console for Azcue, 2000
9. **Goya** wall-bookcase/Wand-Buchregal/bibliothèque for Casprini, 1998

"A good designer has to be part artist, part engineer, psychologist, sociologist, planner, marketing man and communicator: part everything, and part nothing!"

Roberto Pezzetta

Roberto Pezzetta, c/o Electrolux Zanussi S. P. A.,
Uffici di Corso Lino Zanussi 30, 33 080 Porcia (Pordenone), Italy
T +39 0434 39 6215 F: +39 0434 39 6045 roberto.pezzetta@notes.electrolux.it www.zanussi.com

»Ein guter Designer muss ein bisschen Künstler, ein bisschen Ingenieur, Psychologe, Soziologe, Planer, Marketing-Experte und Vermittler sein: ein bisschen alles ... und ein bisschen nichts!«

« Un bon designer doit être un peu artiste, ingénieur, sociologue, planificateur, expert en marketing et en communication : un peu tout ... et n'importe quoi ! »

1. **ZHC95ALU** extractor fan/Abzugshaube/hotte de cuisine
from **Aluminium Range** for Zanussi, 2000
2. ↓ **Softech** built-in electric oven/elektrischer Einbauherd/
four électrique encastrable for Zanussi, 1996

»Ein Kollege sagte einmal zu mir, Design re-
präsentiere eine elitäre Wahl. Das ist wahr.
Und es trifft ebenfalls zu, dass jeder Berufs-
stand von einer Ideologie getragen wird, die
man nicht ignorieren kann. Es ist keine leichte
Aufgabe, Konflikte zu klären und Ideologien
auf ein neues, gemeinsames Ziel auszurichten.
Ein charakteristisches und inhärentes Merk-
mal des ›Handwerks‹ von Designern ist deren
Bewusstsein, sich nicht im Besitz einer absoluten Wahrheit zu befinden. Gerade die Tatsache, dass dieser Beruf von anderen Berufen
häufig nicht zu unterscheiden ist oder mit
ihnen in Deckung gebracht werden kann, bedeutet, dass Designer – mehr als andere Leute – eine Neigung zu Zweifel und Relativismus
haben, was sie beständig über die Grenzen
ihrer eigenen Wahrheiten hinaus forschen
lässt.
Hier ein Rat, zuallererst an mich selbst und
dann an alle gerichtet, die es interessiert:
Man muss in dynamischen Begriffen denken;
man darf es sich nicht zu leicht machen, indem man immer nur festen Regeln und be-
währten Lösungen folgt, sondern man muss
aus der Perspektive kontinuierlichen For-
schens und Experimentierens handeln, den
Mut zu unerwarteten Vorschlägen haben
und – zusätzlich zum Bleistift – diese essentielle Eigenschaft der Designer gebrauchen:
die Neugierde.« ROBERTO PEZZETTA

"A colleague once told me that
design represents an aristocratic
choice. This is true, and it is also
true that every profession is sus-
tained by an ideology that you
cannot ignore. Settling conflicts
and reorienting ideologies towards
a common goal are not easy tasks
to accomplish. A peculiar and inherent characteristic of the designer's
'craft' is the awareness of not being
in possession of absolute truth.
The very fact that this profession
is often indistinguishable from and
superimposable on others means
that, more than other people, the
designer is predisposed to doubt
and relativism, and is capable of
continuously searching beyond
his own truths.
A piece of advice directed first and
foremost to myself and then to anyone who is willing to listen: think in
dynamic terms, do not take the easy
way out by following the rules and
approved solutions, act in the perspective of continuous research, find
the courage to make unexpected
proposals, and, in addition to your
pencil, use that quintessential quality of designers – curiosity."
ROBERTO PEZZETTA

« Un collègue m'a dit une fois que le design
représentait un choix aristocratique. C'est
vrai, comme il est également vrai que chaque
profession est soutenue par une idéologie
qu'on ne peut ignorer. Régler des conflits et
réorienter les idéologies vers un objectif commun ne sont pas des tâches faciles. Une des
caractéristiques singulières et inhérentes à
" l'art " du designer est la conscience de ne pas
être le détenteur d'une vérité absolue. Le seul
fait que la profession elle-même soit souvent
indissociable et superposée à d'autres signifie
que les designers sont particulièrement pré-
disposés au doute et au relativisme, et qu'ils
sont capables de chercher continuellement
au-delà de leurs propres vérités.
Un petit conseil, tout d'abord à moi-même
puis à tous ceux que cela intéresse : il faut
penser en termes dynamiques, ne pas chercher une porte de sortie facile en suivant les
règles et les solutions établies, agir dans la
perspective de recherches continues, trouver
le courage de faire des propositions inatten-
dues et, outre son crayon, utiliser cette qualité
fondamentale des designers : la curiosité. »
ROBERTO PEZZETTA

3. **Oz** refrigerator/Kühlschrank/réfrigérateur for Zanussi,
1994-98
4. **Ambience 9** electric oven/Elektroherd/four électrique
from **Aluminium Range** for Zanussi, 2000
5. **ZD699ALU** dishwasher (detail)/Spülmaschine (Detail)/
lave-vaisselle (détail) from **Aluminium Range** for Zanussi,
2000

ROBERTO PEZZETTA

BORN	1946	Treviso, Italy
STUDIED		self-taught
PRACTICE	1967-69	worked in R&D for Zoppas
	1969-74	product designer for Zoppas
	1974-77	product designer for Zanussi
	1977-78	product designer for Nordica
	1978-82	product designer for Zanussi
	1982-	head of industrial design, Zanussi Electrodomestici Industrial Design Center
	1993-	Director of Design, Electrolux European Design Management Team
AWARDS	1981	Compasso d'Oro, Milan
	1987, 89 & 91	Compasso d'Oro selection, Milan
	1987, 91 & 99	*Goed Industrieel Ontwerp* Award, Netherlands
	1988	Gold Medal, BIO 12 Biennial of Industrial Design, Ljubliana
	1990	Sami du Design Award, Salon des Arts Ménagers, Paris
	1997	Design Prestige Award, Brno
	1997	conferred *Master of Labour* by the President of the Italian Republic
	1998	Premio De Diseño award, Cuba; Honour Selection for Compasso d'Oro, Milan
	1999 & 2000	Good Design Award, Chicago Athenaeum
EXHIBITIONS	1990	*Civiltà delle Macchine*, Turin
	1992	*Organic Design*, Design Museum, London
	1997	Expo L'ocio, Madrid
	1998	Biennale Internationale du Design de Saint-Etienne
	1999	*Roberto Pezzetta*, Forum for Form, Stockholm; *The Shape of Colour Red*, Glasgow; *Design in the Digital Age*, Victoria & Albert Museum, London
	2000	*Les Bons Génies de la Vie Domestique*, Centre Georges Pompidou, Paris

CLIENTS

Nordica
Zanussi/Electrolux
Zoppas

4

5

"Design must offer people an alternative way of living – it must answer the aspirations of people in terms of well-being and happiness."

Christophe Pillet

Christophe Pillet, 81 Rue Saint-Maur, 75011 Paris, France
T +33 1 48 06 78 31 F +33 1 48 06 78 32 cpillet@club-internet.fr

»Design muss den Menschen eine alternative Lebensform anbieten. Es muss den Sehnsüchten der Menschen im Hinblick auf Wohlbehagen und Glück entsprechen.«

« Le design doit offrir aux gens une autre manière de vivre. Il doit répondre à leurs aspirations de bien-être et de bonheur. »

1. **Sunset Lounge** armchair/Sessel/fauteuil for Cappellini,
1998
2. ↓ **Ultra Living** sofa/Sofa/canapé for E&Y, 1998

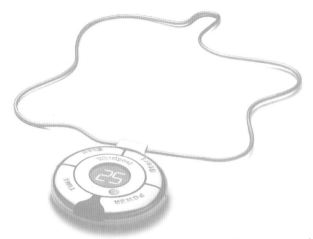

« Si, par le passé, le design s'est concentré principalement sur des solutions à des problèmes spécifiques de fonction, d'ergonomie et d'esthétique, à l'avenir, il tendra de plus en plus à se libérer de ces préoccupations pour se consacrer avant tout à l'invention d'environnements pour des particuliers. S'émancipant des systèmes qui l'ont généré, il travaillera à une échelle plus globale sur des modes de vie alternatifs et innovateurs, sur des scénarios imaginaires motivés par le désir d'un meilleur style de vie. » CHRISTOPHE PILLET

3. ← Saucepan/Kochtopf/faitout for the **Pots and Pans** microwave experimental project for Whirlpool, 2000
4. Remote control/Fernbedienung/télécommande for the **Pots and Pans** microwave experimental project for Whirlpool, 2000
5. Pasta cooker/Nudelkocher/cuit-pâtes for the **Pots and Pans** microwave experimental project for Whirlpool, 2000
6. Kettle/Kessel/bouilloire for the **Pots and Pans** microwave experimental project for Whirlpool, 2000

"If in the past design has concentrated mainly on producing solutions for specific problems of function, ergonomics, economy and aesthetics, it will tend in the future to liberate itself more and more from these specific concerns in order to become a discipline primarily devoted to the invention of environments for individuals. Freeing itself from the systems that generated it, design will work on a more global scale on alternative and innovative lifestyles, on scenarios imagined that are driven by the desire for a better way of living."
CHRISTOPHE PILLET

»War das Design in der Vergangenheit hauptsächlich darauf konzentriert, Lösungen für bestimmte Probleme im Hinblick auf Funktion, Ergonomie, Ökonomie und Ästhetik anzubieten, so wird es sich in Zukunft mehr und mehr von diesen spezifischen Anliegen befreien und zu einer Disziplin werden, die sich in erster Linie dem Erfinden von individuellen Umwelten widmet. Indem es sich von den Systemen verselbstständigt, die es hervorgebracht haben, wird Design auf einer globaleren Ebene an alternativen und innovativen Lebensformen arbeiten, an imaginativen Szenarios, die von dem Wunsch nach einer besseren Lebensform motiviert werden.« CHRISTOPHE PILLET

CHRISTOPHE PILLET			CLIENTS
BORN	1959	Montrajes, near Paris, France	Artelano
STUDIED	1985	Design diploma, Ecole des Arts Décoratifs, Nice	Bally
	1986	MA Design, Domus Academy, Milan	Cappellini
PRACTICE	1986-88	collaborated with Martine Bedine in Milan	Daum
	1988-93	collaborated with Philippe Starck in Paris	Domeau & Perès
	1993	established own design practice	E&Y
AWARDS	1995	Designer of the Year, France	Ecart International
EXHIBITIONS	1988	*Memphis*, Milan	Fiam
	1989	group exhibition, Paris, Bordeaux	JCDecaux
	1991	*Les Capitales du Design*, Paris; group show, Athens	Lancôme
	1992	*Exposition Gitane*, La Villette, Paris	L'Oréal
	1993	*VIA-carte blanche*, solo exhibition, Paris	Magis
	1994	*Lucerna*, Paris; *Cartons à Dessins*, Paris	Mazzega
	1995	solo exhibition, Düsseldorf; *Créateur de l'Année*, Paris	Moët & Chandon
	1997	*E&Y*, Tokyo; *Parism*, Osaka; *10 ans de création*, Bologna; *20 ans de Création en France*, Paris	Moroso
	1998	*E&Y*, Osaka	Schopenhauer
	1999	*Dososcuola*, Milan; *Deluxe*, Lisbon	Shiseido
	2000	*Forum*, Paris	Trussardi
			Whirlpool

7

8

9

10

11

12

7. **Air Can** lamp/Lampe/lampe for AV Mazzega, 1999
8. **Nath's Sofa**/canapé for Domeau & Perès, 1998
9. **Marie Claire** 2000 virtual project/virtuelles Projekt/projet virtuel for the magazine *Marie Claire*, 2000
10. **Video Lounge** chaise longue/Liege for Domeau & Perès, 1998
11. **C&C** table on castors/Tisch auf Rollen/table à roulettes for Fiam, 2000
12. **C&C** table/Tisch for Fiam, 2000

"We jumble up typologies, mix references, manipulate codes, usages, techniques, forms and enjoy re-inventing
our everyday habits."

RADI DESIGNERS

RADI Designers, 89, rue de Turenne, 75 003 Paris, France
T +33 1 42 71 29 57 F +33 1 42 71 29 62 radi@worldnet.fr www.radidesigners.com

*»Wir werfen Typologien durcheinander,
vermischen Bezüge, manipulieren Regeln, Anwendungen, Techniken, Formen
und genießen es, unsere alltäglichen
Gewohnheiten neu zu erfinden.«*

« Nous brouillons les typologies, mélan-
geons les références, manipulons les
codes, les usages, les techniques et les
formes. Nous nous amusons à réinventer nos habitudes quotidiennes. »

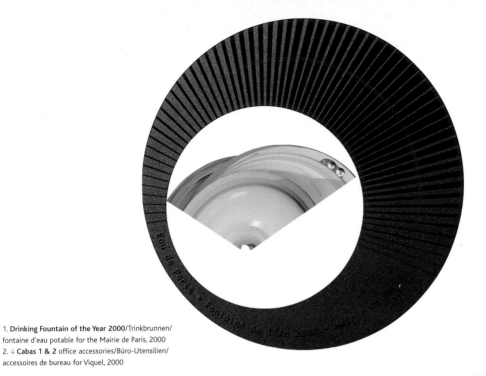

1. **Drinking Fountain of the Year 2000**/Trinkbrunnen/
fontaine d'eau potable for the Mairie de Paris, 2000
2. ↓ **Cabas 1 & 2** office accessories/Büro-Utensilien/
accessoires de bureau for Viquel, 2000

« Nous travaillons ensemble sur une variété de projets tels que le design de produits, l'aménagement d'expositions et l'architecture d'intérieur. Avec chacune de nos créations, nous cherchons à repenser nos environnements domestiques, professionnels et publics, à renouveler l'histoire de nos vies quotidiennes en réinventant les objets les plus usuels ou en trouvant de nouvelles manières amusantes de les utiliser. En tant que groupe, nous avons développé une série de produits simples et drôles dont l'éventail de matières se distingue par une texture lisse, des couleurs vives et une douce translucidité qui évoquent une sorte de monde fantastique visuel. Avec nos produits, nous aimons brouiller les typologies, mélanger les références, manipuler les techniques et doter les objets de combinaisons et de possibilités inédites.

En cultivant la malice et le non-sens, en détournant les clichés de manière poétique et en réinventant des manières d'interpréter et de toucher les choses autour de nous, notre groupe de design tente de rendre spirituels les objets les plus humbles. En transposant notre philosophie du design dans des formes qui sont humoristiques et subtilement décalées tout en restant profondément humaines, nous tentons de projeter une manière douce mais profonde d'imaginer demain. » RADI DESIGNERS

3.-4. ← **Fabulation** installation/Installation for the Fondation Cartier pour l'art contemporain, Paris, 1999
5. **Do Cut-Stool**/Hocker/tabouret from **Do Create** collection, Robert Stadler/RADI DESIGNERS, Do Foundation, 2001

"We work together on a variety of projects such as product design, exhibition design and interior architecture. In each of our creations, we seek to rethink our home, work and public environments, to renew the history of our day-to-day lives by reinventing the most common objects or by finding new, amusing ways of using them. As a group, we have developed a series of simple fun products whose array of materials is distinguished by a smooth texture, bright colours or a soft translucence so as to frequent a kind of visual fantasy. With our products, we enjoy jumbling typologies, mixing references, manipulating techniques and furnishing objects with unprecedented combinations and possibilities. By cultivating mischief and nonsense, poetically twisting clichés, and reinventing ways of interpreting and touching the things around us, our design group attempts to give wit to the most humble of objects. By transposing our philosophy of design into forms that are at once humorous and subtly out-of-step but also thoroughly humanized, we try to project a gentle yet profound way of imagining tomorrow."
RADI DESIGNERS

»Unsere Zusammenarbeit umfasst eine Vielfalt von Projekten, wie Produktdesign, Ausstellungsdesign und Innenarchitektur. Mit jedem unserer Entwürfe versuchen wir, unsere häusliche, berufliche und öffentliche Umgebung zu überdenken und die Geschichte unseres Alltagslebens zu beleben, indem wir die alltäglichsten Gegenstände neu erfinden oder uns neue, amüsante Verwendungsarten dafür ausdenken. Als Gruppe haben wir eine Serie einfacher, unterhaltsamer Produkte entwickelt, die sich aufgrund der gewählten Werkstoffe durch glatte Oberflächen, helle Farben und eine sanfte Durchsichtigkeit auszeichnet und damit eine Art visuelle Phantasie hervorruft. Mit unseren Produkten werfen wir gerne Typologien durcheinander, vermischen Bezüge, manipulieren Techniken und versehen Objekte mit vollkommen neuen Kombinationen und Möglichkeiten.

Indem wir Unfug und Verrücktheit kultivieren, Klischees poetisch verzerren und neue Möglichkeiten erfinden, die Dinge in unserer Umgebung zu interpretieren und zu berühren, versucht unsere Designgruppe, selbst den banalsten Objekten Esprit und Witz zu verleihen. Wir setzen unsere Designphilosophie in Formen um, die gleichzeitig humoristisch und leicht schräg, aber auch zutiefst menschlich sind. Damit versuchen wir, eine sanfte und doch tiefgründige Zukunftsvorstellung zu entwerfen.« RADI DESIGNERS

		RADI DESIGNERS		CLIENTS
FOUNDED	1992	Paris by Florence Doleac (b. 1968), Laurent Massaloux (b. 1968), Olivier Sidet (b. 1965) and Robert Stadler (b. 1966)		Air France
				Galerie Kréo
AWARDS	2000	Designer of the Year, Salon du Meuble, Paris		Ricard
EXHIBITIONS	1997	*Made in France*, Centre Georges Pompidou, Paris		Schweppes
	1998	solo exhibition, Galerie Emmanuel Perrotin, Paris		Tarkett Sommer
	1999	*Fabulation*, solo exhibition, Fondation Cartier, Paris		
	2000	*RADI ROOM*, solo exhibition, IFA, Paris		
	2001	Musée Magnelli, Musée de la Céramique, Grégoire Gardelle, Vallauris; solo exhibition, Sandra Gering Gallery, New York		

6

7

8

6. **Drinking Fountain of the Year 2000**/Trinkbrunnen/
fontaine à boire for the Mairie de Paris, 2000
7. **Whippet Bench**/Sitzbank/banc, courtesy Galerie
Emmanuel Perrotin & FNAC (Fonds National d'Art
Contemporain, Puteaux), 1998
8. **Patrizia** pneumatic and phosphorescent door bell/
pneumatische und phosphoreszierende Türglocke/
sonnette pneumatique phosphorescente for Galerie
Emmanuel Perrotin, 1998
9. **Do Cut-Big Rocking Vase**/vase from **Do Create**
collection, Robert Stadler/RADI DESIGNERS,
Do Foundation, 2001
10. **Do Cut-Lamp**/Lampe/lampe from **Do Create**
collection, Robert Stadler/RADI DESIGNERS,
Do Foundation, 2001

"My work is always a link between simplicity, function and aesthetic values."

Ingegerd Råman

Ingegerd Råman, Bergsgatan 53, 11231 Stockholm, Sweden
T/F +46 8 650 2824 per.larsson@orrefors.se

»Meine Arbeit ist immer eine Verbindung von Einfachheit, Funktion und ästhetischen Werten.«

« Mon travail relie toujours la simplicité, la fonction et les valeurs esthétiques. »

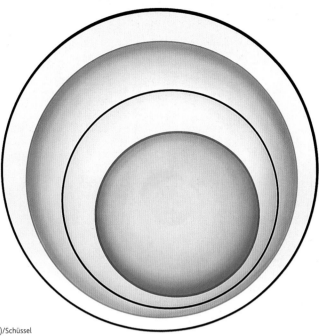

1.-2. **Babuschka** bowls and jug (prototypes)/Schüssel und Krug (Prototypen)/coupes et carafe (prototypes) for Orrefors, 2000

« A l'avenir, les origines culturelles et géographiques du designer deviendront de plus en plus pertinentes. L'héritage et la tradition seront des stimulations importantes dans la création et l'interprétation des objets concrets. Toutefois, les qualités d'un objet particulier ne seront pas jugées sur ses seules formes et fonctions. Les designers devront prendre une part active à l'ensemble du processus industriel et s'investir dans la production de leur œuvre. Ils devraient participer au développement de nouveaux matériaux et techniques, tout en veillant à leur impact sur l'environnement et aux besoins énergétiques de leur production. Ils devraient être conscients de tous les aspects du processus complexe par lequel passent leurs créations pour être produites. Le rôle du designer sera donc semblable à celui d'un chercheur. Pour les jeunes artistes, le travail d'équipe sera d'une importance capitale dans la création d'un design indépendant et innovateur ».
INGEGERD RÅMAN

3. ← **Skyline** vases/Vasen for Orrefors, 2000
4. **Tanteralla** carafe/Karaffe for Orrefors, 2000

"In the future, a designer's cultural and geographical background will become increasingly significant. Heritage and tradition will be important stimuli in the creation and interpretation of concrete objects. However, the qualities of a particular object will not be judged on the basis of form and function alone. Designers will have to take an active part in the entire industrial process and become stakeholders in their works' production. Designers should participate in the development of new techniques and materials, remaining alert to the environmental impact and energy demands of production. They should be aware of every aspect of the complicated process by which their pieces are realised. The role of a designer will therefore be akin to that of a researcher. For young artists, teamwork will be paramount in the creation of independent, innovative design." INGEGERD RÅMAN

»In Zukunft wird der kulturelle und geographische Hintergrund des Designers zunehmend bedeutsam werden. Kulturelles Erbe und Tradition werden zu wichtigen Stimuli für die Gestaltung und Interpretation konkreter Objekte. Die Qualität eines bestimmten Objekts wird sich jedoch nicht allein auf der Basis von Form und Funktion beurteilen lassen. Designer werden eine aktive Rolle im gesamten industriellen Prozess übernehmen und ihre Interessen in der Produktion ihrer Arbeiten vertreten müssen. Designer sollten sich an der Entwicklung neuer Techniken und Materialien beteiligen und dabei wachsam bleiben für die ökologischen Auswirkungen und den Energieverbrauch der Produktion. Sie sollten sich über jeden Aspekt des komplizierten Prozesses bewusst sein, durch den ihre Entwürfe realisiert werden. Die Rolle eines Designers wird folglich der eines Forschers gleichen. Für junge Künstler wird bei der Gestaltung von unabhängigem, innovativem Design die Teamarbeit an erster Stelle stehen.« INGEGERD RÅMAN

7

8

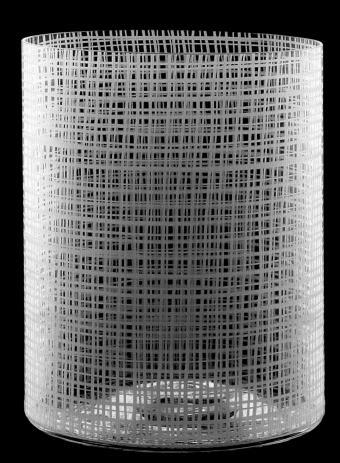

"Design is the whole experience
of living."

Karim Rashid

Karim Rashid, 357, W 17th Street, New York, NY 10011, USA
T +1 212 929 8657 F +1 212 929 0247 office@karimrashid.com www.karimrashid.com

*»Design ist das ganze Erlebnis des
Daseins.«*

« Le design est l'expérience de la vie. »

1. **Pendant** lamp/Hängelampe/lustre from
Soft Collection for George Kovacs Lighting, 1999
2. ↓ **Omni** reconfigurable seating object/variables Sitz-
objekt/banquette modulable for Galerkin Furniture, 1999

« Les produits doivent être en rapport avec nos émotions et enrichir l'imagination et l'expérience populaire. La diversité, la variété, la multiplicité et le changement font partie d'un ensemble de concepts. Le design industriel est un acte créatif, politique et physique. C'est un procédé interactif qui dépasse la forme physique elle-même. Son résultat se manifeste par des lignes esthétiques, son contenu s'inspirant de toutes les possibilités de notre monde moderne.

Les nouveaux objets qui façonnent nos vies sont des hybrides transconceptuels, multiculturels. Ils peuvent exister n'importe où dans différents contextes, naturels et synthétiques, inspirés par les télécommunications, l'information, le ludique et le comportement. Notre culture de l'objet capte l'énergie et le phénomène de cette nouvelle ère numérique universelle. Ce qui m'intéresse le plus en design, c'est l'apparition de nouveaux procédés industriels, de nouveaux matériaux, de nouveaux marchés planétaires. Ils nous permettent d'espérer remodeler nos vies. Les nouvelles cultures exigent de nouvelles formes, de nouvelles matières et de nouveaux styles. Je définis mon travail en termes de minimalisme sensuel ou de " sensualisme ", où les objets communiquent, attirent et inspirent tout en restant relativement dépouillés. Ils parlent simplement et directement, sans superflu. Mon travail est un mariage de géométrie pure et organique.

Pour ce qui est des arguments controversés d'excès, de durabilité et de séduction du marché, j'estime que chaque nouvel objet devrait en remplacer trois. *La qualité des produits détermine le marché.* Les objets ne devraient pas être des obstacles mais des capteurs d'expérience. J'essaie d'en développer qui luttent contre le stress, qui apportent de la joie et simplifient nos tâches tout en augmentant notre degré d'implication et ↓

"Products must deal with our emotional ground and increase the popular imagination and experience. Diversity, variance, multiplicity and change are part of every whole construct. Industrial design is a creative act, a political act, a physical act and a socially interactive process that is greater than the physical form itself – its result is manifested in aesthetic forms, the content inspired by all the possibilities of our contemporary conditions.
I believe that the new objects that shape our lives are trans-conceptual, multi-cultural hybrids, objects that can exist anywhere in different contexts, that are natural and synthetic, that are inspired through telecommunications, information, entertainment and behaviour. Our object culture can capture the energy and phenomena of this contemporary universal culture of the digital age. The birth of new industrial processes, new materials, global markets are my great interests in design that all lend hope to reshaping our lives. I feel that new culture demands new forms, material and style. I define my work as sensual minimalism, or 'sensualism', where objects communicate, engage and inspire yet remain fairly minimal. They can speak simply and directly, without superfluousness. My work is a marriage of organic and pure geometry.
In the controversial arguments about excess, sustainability and market seduction, I believe that every new object should replace three. *Better products edit the marketplace.* I believe objects should not be obstacles in life but raptures of experience. I try to develop objects as de-stressers – objects that bring enjoyment and simplify tasks while increasing ↓

»Designprodukte müssen sich mit unserer emotionalen Grundhaltung befassen, sowie Vorstellungskraft und Erfahrungsschatz der Allgemeinheit bereichern. Mannigfaltigkeit, Verschiedenheit, Vielfalt und Veränderung sind Bestandteile jeder Gesamtkonzeption. Die Gestaltung von Industriedesign ist ein kreativer, politischer, physischer Akt und ein sozial interaktiver Prozess, der über die sinnlich wahrnehmbare Form hinausgeht. Das Resultat manifestiert sich in ästhetischen Gestaltungsformen, während der Inhalt durch all die Möglichkeiten unserer modernen Lebenswelt inspiriert wird.
Neue Objekte, die unser Leben formen, sind konzeptübergreifende und multikulturelle Mischformen. Sie können überall und in verschiedenartigen Zusammenhängen existieren. Sie sind natürlich und synthetisch und werden durch Telekommunikation, Information, Unterhaltung und Verhaltensweisen angeregt. Unsere Kultur des Objekts fängt die Energie und Phänomene dieses neuen und universellen digitalen Zeitalters ein. Ich interessiere mich besonders für das Aufkommen neuer Produktionsmethoden, neuer Materialien und globaler Märkte – Aspekte, die alle zur Hoffnung auf eine Umgestaltung unserer Lebenswelten berechtigen. Meiner Ansicht nach erfordert eine neue Kultur die Entwicklung neuer Formen, Werkstoffe und Stile. Ich definiere meine Arbeit als sinnlichen Minimalismus oder ›Sensualismus‹, wobei die Objekte kommunizieren, berühren und inspirieren und doch ziemlich minimalistisch bleiben. Ihre Sprache ist einfach und direkt, ohne Überflüssiges. Ich sehe meine Arbeit als eine Verschmelzung des Organischen mit dem rein Geometrischen.
In der Kontroverse über die Themen Überfluss, Nachhaltigkeit und die Verlockungen des Marktes, vertrete ich den Standpunkt, dass jedes neue Objekt drei andere ersetzen sollte. *Bessere Produkte ordnen und korrigieren den Markt.* Ich finde, Designprodukte sollten keine Hindernisse für das Alltagsleben darstellen, sondern mit Begeisterung wahrgenommen und erlebt werden. Ich versuche, Objekte zu entwickeln, die ›ent-spannend‹ wirken. Sie sollen Freude bereiten und Tätigkeiten vereinfachen, während sie gleichzeitig unser Engagement und unser ästhetisches Niveau erhöhen. Unser Alltag wird bereichert durch das Erlebnis, dass Schönheit, Komfort, Luxus, Funk- ↓

3. ← **OH** stacking chair/Stapelstuhl/chaise encastrable for Umbra, 1999
4. **Softscape** conceptual environment for future living/ Entwurf für zukünftige Lebensraumgestaltung/environnement conceptuel pour la vie de demain, 1998

d'appréciation de la beauté. Lorsque nous vivons dans une alliance parfaite de beauté, de confort, de luxe, de performance et d'utilité, nos vies s'en trouvent enrichies. La beauté est une relation profonde entre l'intérieur et l'extérieur, une osmose d'esthétiques. Elle n'est pas une question de goût mais une appréciation acquise, un processus empirique. Cette profondeur sous-jacente signifie que le contenu joue un rôle primordial dans la beauté des choses. Les peintures, les objets d'art, l'architecture, l'espace, tous expriment leur esthétique au travers de leur contenu. Le visuel et le concept ne font qu'un. Tout ce qui est beau a un contenu. » KARIM RASHID

5. **Blobject** chairs/Stühle/chaises (limited edition of 10), 1999
6. **Syntax** chairs/Stühle/chaises from **Decola Vita Furniture Collection** for Idée, 1998
7. **Sofa Two**/Sofa/canapé for Galerkin Furniture, 1999

our level of engagement and of beauty. Our lives are elevated when we experience beauty, comfort, luxury, performance and utility acting seamlessly together. Beauty is a deeper, inseparable relationship between the inner and the outer, an osmosis of aesthetics. Beauty is not a question of taste, or personal likes and dislikes but a learned appreciation, an experiential process. This underlying depth of beauty means that content plays a primary role in the beauty of things. Paintings, objects, art, architecture, space, all manifest their aesthetics through their content. The visual effect and the concept are one. Something beautiful has content." KARIM RASHID

tionalität und Zweckmäßigkeit nahtlos ineinander greifen. Schönheit ist eine tiefere, unauflösbare Verbindung zwischen dem Inneren und dem Äußeren, eine Osmose der Ästhetik. Schönheit ist keine Frage des Geschmacks oder der persönlichen Vorlieben und Abneigungen, sondern ein erlerntes Verständnis, ein Erfahrungsprozess. Diese tiefere Dimension von Schönheit bedeutet, dass bei der Schönheit von Dingen der Inhalt eine entscheidende Rolle spielt. Gemälde, Objekte, Kunst, Architektur, Räume – in all diesen Dingen manifestiert sich ihre Ästhetik durch ihren Inhalt. Optische Wirkung und Konzept sind eins. Alles, was schön ist, besitzt Inhalt.« KARIM RASHID

KARIM RASHID

BORN	1960	Cairo, Egypt (Canadian national)
STUDIED	1978-82	BA Industrial Design (Distinction), Carleton University, Ottawa
	1983	post-graduate design studies, Massa Lubrense, Italy sponsored by ADI/ISIA, Rome
PRACTICE	1981-82	Mitel Corporation, Kanata, Canada
	1984	Rodolfo Bonetto Industrial Design Studio, Milan
	1984-91	senior designer/partner, KAN Industrial Designers, Toronto
	1985-91	senior designer/co-founder, Babel Inc. and North Studio, Toronto
	1992-	principal designer, Karim Rashid Inc., New York
	1993-95	Visiting Associate Professor, Industrial Design, Pratt Institute, New York
	1993-	Associate Professor, Industrial Design, The University of the Arts, Philadelphia
AWARDS	1993	Best of Year in Product Design, *I. D. Magazine Annual Design Review* Award, New York
	1995-2000	11 Good Design Awards, Chicago Athenaeum
	1999	Design Journal Gold Award; two Good Design Awards, Chicago Athenaeum; George Nelson Award, USA; DaimlerChrysler Design Award
	2001	Designer of the Year, Interior Design Show, Toronto; Gold IDEA Award, IDSA; 3 *I. D. Magazine Annual Design Review* Distinctive Awards, New York
EXHIBITIONS	1998	*Decola Vita* solo show, IDÉE Gallery, Tokyo
	1999	*Collab Award* exhibition, Philadelphia Museum of Art
	2000	*National Design Triennial – Design Culture Now*, Cooper-Hewitt National Design Museum, New York
	2001	*Pleasurscape*, Rice University Gallery, Houston; *Workspheres*, Museum of Modern Art, New York; *010101*, San Francisco Museum of Art

CLIENTS

Black & Decker
Canada Post Corporation
Citibank
ClassiCon
Estée Lauder
Fasem
Fujitsu
Giorgio Armani
Guzzini
IDÉE
Issey Miyake
Sony
Swid Powell
Tommy Hilfiger
Zanotta
Zeritalia

8

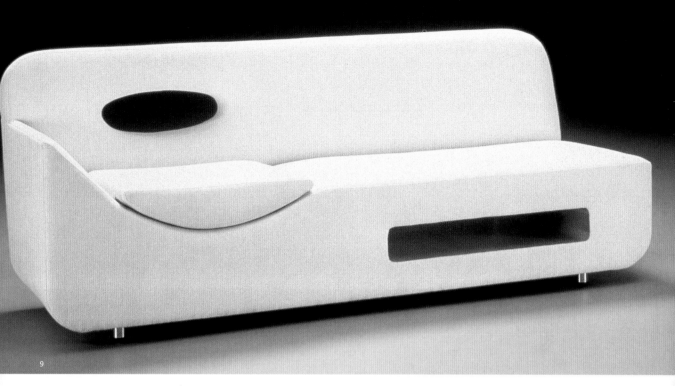

9

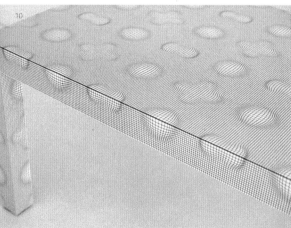

10

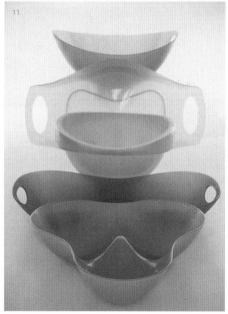

11

12

8. **Ribbon** future desktop landscape/Arbeitsplatz
der Zukunft/bureau du futur for Totem, 1999
9. **Sofa One**/Sofa/canapé for Galerkin Furniture, 1999
10. **Morphscape** table/Tisch (one-off), 2000
11. **Sumo** bowl/Schale/bol, **Jambo** tray/Tablett/plateau,
Rimbowl and **Tribowl** bowls/Schalen/bols for Umbra, 1999
12. **Garbo** and **Garbino** wastepaper baskets/Papierkörbe/
corbeilles à papier for Umbra, 1996

"Exact/precise/intensive observation
and planning are the preconditions
for designing objects that have
visible souls."

Prospero Rasulo

Prospero Rasulo, Via Sebenico 13, 20 124 Milan, Italy
T +39 02 668 8840 F +39 02 668 8842 prrasulo@tin.it

»Intensive Beobachtung und Planung
sind die Vorbedingungen für das Gestalten von Objekten, die eine sichtbare
Seele haben.«

« L'observation et une planification
exactes/précises/intensives sont les
conditions préalables à la conception
d'objets pourvus d'une âme visible. »

1. **Alma** chair/Stuhl/chaise for BRF, 2000
2. ↓ **Skinny** table/Tisch/table basse for Zanotta, 1999

»Mein künstlerischer Hintergrund kennzeichnet und beeinflusst die Art, wie ich Dinge wahrnehme und verstehe. Indem wir die materiellen Güter, die uns umgeben, mit Aufmerksamkeit und Neugier betrachten, können wir den für unsere Inspiration notwendigen Wunsch in uns entdecken, Objekte mit Herz und Gefühl zu entwerfen. Ein bestimmtes Material, ein Zeichen oder eine Farbe kann als Katalysator für die emotionale Beziehung zwischen Objekten und Menschen fungieren. Für mich muss jedes Produkt eine autonome Ausdruckskraft haben. Zusammen mit seiner klaren Funktionalität wird das Produkt damit zu einem dauerhaften Objekt, denn es wird auch mit der Zeit verblüffend präsent bleiben. Beim Design kommt es in erster Linie auf das Spiel der Anziehung an.« PROSPERO RASULO

"My artistic background characterizes and influences the way I observe and comprehend things. By looking with attention and curiosity at the material goods that surround us, we are able to find the necessary desire that inspires us to create objects with heart and emotion. A certain material, sign or colour can act as a catalyst for an emotional relationship between objects and people. I believe that every product should have an autonomous expressive energy. With this, together with an obvious usefulness, the product will become a durable object because over time it will continue to offer the surprise of its presence. Design is ultimately about the game of attraction."
PROSPERO RASULO

« Ma formation artistique caractérise et influence la façon dont j'observe et je comprends les choses. C'est dans l'examen attentif et curieux des biens matériels qui nous entourent que nous puisons le désir nécessaire qui nous inspire la création d'objets avec cœur et émotion. Une certaine matière, une couleur ou un signe servent parfois de catalyseur à une relation émotionnelle entre les objets et les hommes. Pour moi, chaque produit devrait avoir une énergie expressive autonome. Ceci, associé naturellement à son utilité, en fait un objet durable parce que, avec le temps, il continue d'offrir la surprise de sa présence. Le design est avant tout un jeu de séduction. »
PROSPERO RASULO

3. **Alma** chairs/Stühle/chaises for BRF., 2000
4. **Bone** table/Tisch for BRF, 2000
5. **Qua** lamp/Lampe/applique for Foscarini, 1998

PROSPERO RASULO			CLIENTS
BORN	1953	Stigliano, Matera, Italy	Antonio Lupi
STUDIED	1973	graduated (art & design), Accademia di Belle Arti di Brera, Milan	Arcade
PRACTICE	1980-82	designed for Studio Alchimia and collaborated with Alessandro Mendini researching "redesign" and the "banal object"	Arflex
			BRF
	1982	began working as an industrial designer	Fiam Italia
	1987	founded Oxido Gallery, Milan	Foscarini
EXHIBITIONS			L'Oca Nera
	1986-88	*Sexy Design*, Milan & Parma; *L'Immagine Imprudente*, Milan, Reggio Emilia and Mantova; *Abitare con Arte*, Verona, Paris	Mandelli
			Poltronova
	1994	*Piatto Fax*, Milan; *Trash Furniture*, Milan	Rosenthal
	1998	*Eco Mimetico*, Milan	Zanotta

4

5

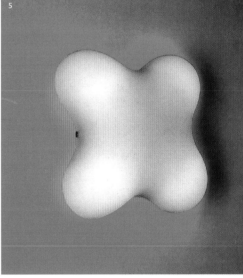

"Thrill by balance, please with courage."

Rivieran Design Studio

Olof Söderholm & Buster Delin, Rivieran Design Studio,
Sankt Eriksgatan 48B, 112 34 Stockholm, Sweden
T +46 8 653 08 88 F +46 8 650 75 55 olof@rivieran.com

»Spannung durch Balance, Gefallen durch Mut.«

« Séduire par son équilibre, plaire par son courage. »

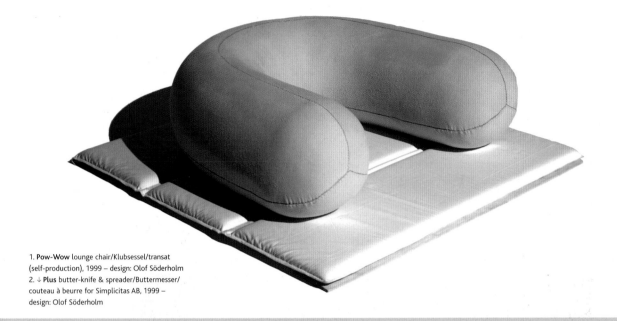

1. **Pow-Wow** lounge chair/Klubsessel/transat
(self-production), 1999 – design: Olof Söderholm
2. ↓ **Plus** butter-knife & spreader/Buttermesser/
couteau à beurre for Simplicitas AB, 1999 –
design: Olof Söderholm

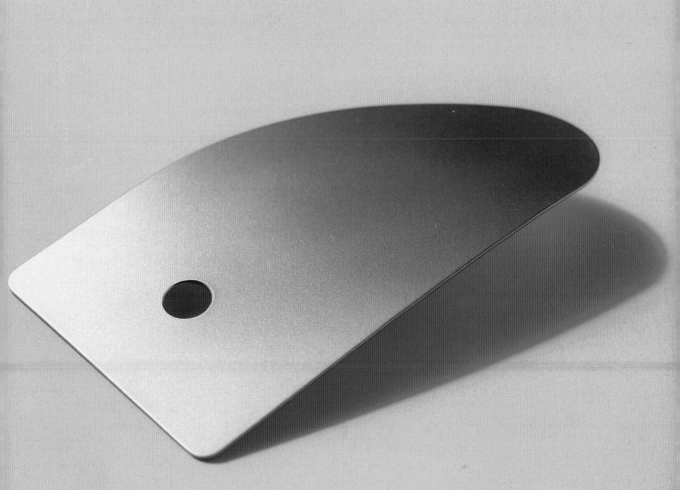

»In Zukunft wird das in den westlichen Ländern vorherrschende Design internationaler sein. Zwar wird es noch Spuren kultureller oder geographischer Herkunft geben, aber sie werden schwieriger auszumachen sein. In immer größerem Maß wird Design durch die Entwicklung unentbehrlicher Hilfsmittel für unser Alltagsleben in die Gesellschaft integriert. Diese Tatsache wird vermutlich dazu führen, dass Design als Unterrichtsfach größere Verbreitung an den Schulen findet. Die funktionalistische Herangehensweise an Design wird fortbestehen, doch ästhetische Kriterien werden eine gleichwertige Bedeutung erlangen. Man wird vermehrt mit neuen und alten Werkstoffen, mit Proportionen und Konstruktionsmethoden experimentieren. Und Design wird, als notwendiger Bestandteil der Markenidentität und der Identifizierung von Strukturen innerhalb der ›New Economy‹, in stärkerem Maß in Unternehmensprojekte einbezogen.

Das Herstellen von Querverbindungen zu anderen Wissenszweigen wird sich ausweiten, und Design wird plötzlich an Orten auftauchen, an denen man es vorher nicht erwartet hätte. Es könnte gut sein, dass einige Länder der so genannten ›Dritten Welt‹ in Sachen Design und Technologie mit neuen und innovativen Strategien aufwarten werden – jedenfalls wird das Design nicht mehr so wie bisher von den westlichen Nationen dominiert sein. Bei all dem ist zu hoffen, dass menschliche Werte und das Bedürfnis nach einfachen Lösungen weiterhin oberste Priorität haben werden.« RIVIERAN DESIGN STUDIO

"In the future, design in the West will be more international – the marks of cultural or geographical origin will still be there but will be harder to spot. To an ever increasing extent, design will be integrated into society through the development of essential tools for living – a fact of life, one might say, that will lead to the subject being taught more widely in schools.

The functionalistic approach to design will remain but aesthetics will achieve parity in importance. There will be more experimentation with new and old materials, proportions and construction. The incorporation of design into business projects will increase as a necessary part of branding and identification of structures in the 'new economy'. Cross-linking with other disciplines will become more prevalent and design will pop up from formerly unexpected parts of the world. Some so-called 'Third World' nations may well emerge in design and technology with new and innovative strategies – design will not be as Western-centred as it has been. In all this, it is hoped that humanistic values and the need for simplified solutions will remain of paramount importance." RIVIERAN DESIGN STUDIO

« A l'avenir, le design occidental sera plus international. L'empreinte de l'origine culturelle ou géographique sera toujours présente mais plus difficile à discerner. Le design s'intégrera toujours plus dans la société à travers le développement d'outils essentiels à la vie quotidienne – un état de fait qui en fera une discipline enseignée plus communément dans les écoles.

L'approche fonctionnaliste du design perdurera mais l'esthétique deviendra aussi importante. On expérimentera davantage les matériaux nouveaux et anciens, les proportions et la construction. L'intégration du design dans les projets des entreprises augmentera, devenant une partie nécessaire du marketing et de l'identification des structures de la " nouvelle économie ".

L'interaction avec les autres disciplines sera plus répandue et le design fera son apparition dans des régions du globe où on ne l'attendait pas. Certains pays dits du " Tiers-monde " pourraient développer de nouvelles stratégies innovatrices en design et en technologie. Le design sera moins dominé par l'Occident que par le passé. Dans tout ceci, il faut espérer que les valeurs humanistes et le besoin de solutions simplifiées resteront au premier plan. » RIVIERAN DESIGN STUDIO

3. **Sn** metal pencil/Metall-Bleistift/crayon en métal (self-production), 2000 – design: Buster Delin
4. **Chaise Courte**/Liege (self-production), 1999 – design: Olof Söderholm
5. **Springtime** floor lamps/Stehlampen/lampadaires (self-production), 1999 – design: Buster Delin
6. **Armchair-Blue**/Sessel/fauteuil (self-production), 1999 – design: Buster Delin
7. **Office** table/Bürotisch/table de bureau for the Rivieran Design Studio, 1999 – design: Clara von Zweigbergk, Buster Delin and Olof Söderholm

RIVIERAN DESIGN		CLIENTS
FOUNDED	1997	in Stockholm by Olof Söderholm (b. 1962 Sjaelevad), Buster Delin (b. 1967 Stockholm) & Clara von Zweigbergk (b. 1970 Stockholm)	Forum Lustrum
STUDIED		OLOF SÖDERHOLM	Maxibit World Wide
	1993-96	Beckman's School of Design, Stockholm	Nelli Rodi Scandinavia
		BUSTER DELIN	Simplicitas
	1993-96	Beckman's School of Design, Stockholm	Stockholm Furniture Fair
AWARDS	1998	Excellent Swedish Design Award, Stockholm	Swedish Society for Arts
EXHIBITIONS	1998	Design Biennial, St Etienne; Swedish Pavillion, Expo '98, Lisbon; *Sagor, a Lifestyle Story*, Antwerp	& Design
	1999	*The Nordic Transparency*, Stedelijk Museum, Amsterdam	

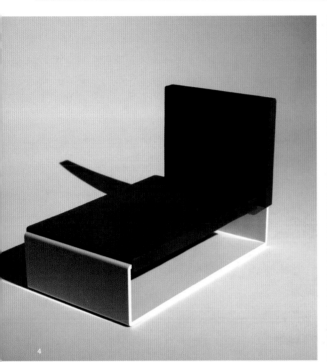

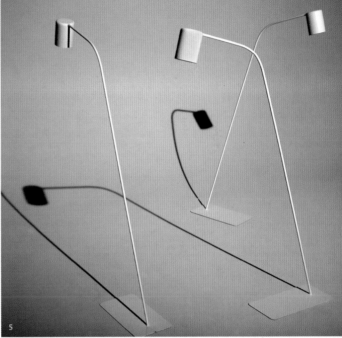

"Low-tech choices for a digital era."

Timo Salli

Timo Salli, Muotoilutoimisto Salli Ltd., Meritullinkatu 11, 00 170 Helsinki, Finland
T +358 9 681 37700 F +358 9 278 2277 salli@timosalli.com

»Low-tech-Alternativen für ein digitales
Zeitalter.«

« Des choix non technologiques pour
une ère numérique. »

1. **Jack in the Box** television set/Fernseher/meuble de
télévision (self-production), 1997
2. ↓ **Zik Zak** collapsible chair/Klappstuhl/chaise pliante
(one-off for Snowcrash exhibition), 1997

« Je m'interroge sur la manière dont nous regardons les choses et me demande si ce comportement justifie la création d'objets fonctionnels. Une cheminée peut elle remplacer une télévision ? Lorsqu'on les fixe du regard, toutes deux ont un but plus profond : elles effacent notre mémoire jusqu'à être téléchargées. Associer la fonction d'un miroir à celle d'une lampe est une manière de produire un double sens pour un même objet. Lorsque la lampe est éteinte, elle sert de miroir en réfléchissant la lumière du jour, tandis que le soir, elle sert à la fois de source lumineuse et de miroir, pour voir et être vu. Nos maisons sont saturées d'objets que nous ne remarquons plus. En réinterprétant les reliques du foyer, je vise un contact plus direct et profond entre les gens et les meubles. » TIMO SALLI

"I question how we look at things and whether this behaviour can be a motive to make functional objects. Could a fireplace replace a television? When stared at, both have a deeper purpose – they erase your memory until it is downloaded. Connecting the function of a mirror with that of a lamp is a way of producing a double meaning for one object. When the light is turned off it can be used as a mirror to reflect daylight, while during the evening it can be used both as a light-source and as a mirror, to see with and to be seen. Our homes are saturated with objects that we no longer notice. By reinterpreting the relics in the home, I aim for a more direct and meaningful contact between people and furniture." TIMO SALLI

»Ich hinterfrage die Art, wie wir Dinge ansehen und denke darüber nach, ob dieses Verhalten ein Motiv für die Herstellung funktionaler Objekte sein kann. Könnte ein Kamin an die Stelle eines Fernsehers treten? Wenn man sie länger ansieht, haben beide Gegenstände einen tieferen Zweck: Sie löschen das eigene Gedächtnis, bis es heruntergeladen ist. Indem man die Funktion eines Spiegels mit der einer Lampe verbindet, kann man einem einzelnen Objekt eine doppelte Bedeutung verleihen. Wenn das Licht ausgeschaltet ist, kann man es als Spiegel benutzen, der das Tageslicht reflektiert, während man es am Abend sowohl als Lichtquelle wie als Spiegel verwenden kann, um damit zu sehen und gesehen zu werden. Unsere Wohnungen sind voller Objekte, die wir nicht mehr bewusst wahrnehmen. Mit meiner Neuinterpretation häuslicher Relikte bezwecke ich einen direkteren und tiefer gehenden Kontakt zwischen Mensch und Möbel.« TIMO SALLI

3. ← **Tramp** easy chair (prototype)/Sessel (Prototyp)/ chauffeuse (prototype) for Cappellini, 1997
4. **Meccano** chair/Stuhl/chaise (one-off material study), 1995

TIMO SALLI

BORN	1963	Helsinki, Finland
STUDIED	1992	BA Furniture Design, Lahti Design Institute
	1996	MA Craft & Design, University of Industrial Arts and Design, Helsinki
PRACTICE	1993	established own design studio
AWARDS	1993	honourable mention, IKEA mötet, Helsinki
	1997	Young Finland Prize, Helsinki
	1998	Young Design Prize, Hamburg
	1999-2001	State Grant, Helsinki
EXHIBITIONS	1997	*Young Forum*, Nagoya Design Centre; *Snowcrash*, Milan; *New Simplicity?*, Helsinki
	1998	*Finnish Design*, Design Forum, Helsinki; *Nomadhouse*, Milan; *Alvar Aalto Symposium*, Jyväskylä
	1999	*New Scandinavia*, Museum für Angewandte Kunst, Cologne; *Snowcrash*, Milan; *Biennale dei Giovani Artisti Dell Europa e Mediteraneo*, Rome; *Taivas Kattona*, Tampere; *Italy-Europa*, Verona; *Empty Spaces*, Munich
	2000	*Objects and Concepts*, Museum of Applied Arts, Helsinki; *100*, Helsinki; Designers Block, London

CLIENTS

Designium
Fat Douglas
Helsinki Cultural Capital 2000
SITRA
Sandgate
Snowcrash
Stanza
Suomen Messut
TEKES

5

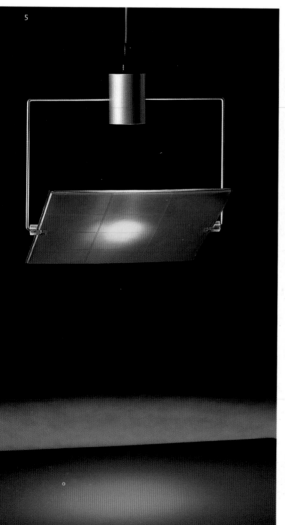

6

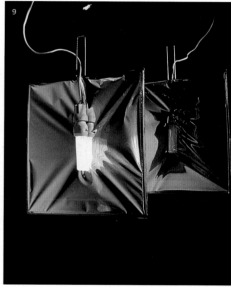

5. **ScreenLamp** light (prototype)/Leuchte (Prototyp)/
luminaire (prototype), 1998
6. **Firecase** fireplace (prototype)/Kamin (Prototyp)/
cheminée (prototype), 2000
7. **LampLamp** mirror lamp/Spiegel-Lampe/lampe miroir
(self-production), 2000
8. **Power Ranger** chair/Stuhl/chaise (one-off), 1996
9. **TimoTimo** lamp (prototype)/Lampe (Prototyp)/
lustre (prototype), 1999

"Use your sense and have fun ..."

Thomas Sandell

Thomas Sandell, Sandell Sandberg, Riddargatan 17 D 11, 114 57 Stockholm, Sweden
T +46 8 506 21700 F +46 8 506 21707 info@sandellsandberg.se www.sandellsandberg.se

*»Gebrauchen Sie Ihren Verstand und
haben Sie Spaß ...«*

« Sers-toi de ta tête et amuse-toi ... »

1. **PS** sofabed/Bettsofa/canapé-lit for IKEA, 1999
2. ↓ **Skar** carpet/Teppich/moquette for Kasthall, 1999

»Meiner Meinung nach wird nichts die Bedingungen für Design jemals mehr verändern als die Globalisierung. Sie wird dazu führen, dass Design nicht länger an eine nahegelegene Industrie gebunden ist. Bestimmte Nationen und Regionen werden sich auf die Konzeption und andere auf die Produktion von Design spezialisieren. Bereits heute kennen wir italienische Hersteller, die von ›ausländischen‹ Designern entworfene Möbel produzieren, und dieses Phänomen wird sich weltweit verbreiten.

Diese Entwicklung wird die alte Regel außer Kraft setzen, dass ein guter Designer per definitionem eng mit den Arbeitern im Fertigungsbetrieb verbunden ist. In Zukunft werden die Produzenten und die Designer in Symbiose arbeiten, wobei die Hersteller für die Aspekte Konstruktion und Technik verantwortlich sein werden. Designer werden für eine Marke wie Cappellini oder B&B tätig sein. Und wie in der Mode wird die Marke wesentlich wichtiger werden als die Designer – wie schon heute die Tatsache zeigt, dass der Name Tom Ford nicht halb so bekannt ist wie der Name Gucci.

Das hat zur Folge, dass die Designer immer anonymer werden. Natürlich wird das für sie ein wenig betrüblich sein. Aber es bedeutet hoffentlich auch, dass die Produzenten mit Verantwortungsgefühl und Verstand handeln ... denn dann können die Designer ihre Zeit damit verbringen, Spaß zu haben.«
THOMAS SANDELL

"I believe that nothing will ever change the conditions for design more than globalization. Globalization will mean that design no longer has to be connected to an industry close by. Certain nations and geographical areas will be specialized in design, while others will specialize in production. We already see Italian producers manufacturing furniture designed by 'foreign' designers, and this phenomenon will become common worldwide.

This development will replace the old truth that a good designer by definition is close to the workers on the shop floor. The producers and the designer will work in symbiosis and the producer will be responsible for the engineering and technical aspects. Designers will work for a brand, like Cappellini or B&B Italia. As with fashion, the brand will become a lot more important than the designer – like the fact that Tom Ford's name is not half as important as Gucci's.

As a result, the designer will become more and more anonymous. Which of course will be a little sad for the designer, but hopefully will mean that the producer will take responsibility for having sense. ... and then the designer can spend his time having fun!" THOMAS SANDELL

« Rien ne changera davantage les conditions du design que la mondialisation. Grâce à elle, le design n'aura plus besoin d'être lié à une industrie locale. Certaines nations et zones géographiques seront spécialisées dans la conception, d'autres dans la production. Nous voyons déjà des producteurs italiens fabriquant des meubles dessinés par des designers " étrangers ", et ce phénomène se répandra dans le monde entier.

Ce développement remplacera l'ancienne vérité selon laquelle un bon designer était, par définition, proche des ouvriers de l'atelier. Les producteurs et le designer travailleront en symbiose et le producteur sera responsable des aspects d'ingénierie et techniques. Les designers travailleront pour une marque, comme Cappellini ou B&B Italia. Comme dans la mode, la marque deviendra beaucoup plus importante que le créateur – ce qui est déjà le cas de Tom Ford dont le nom est beaucoup moins connu que celui de Gucci.

Par conséquent, les designers deviendront de plus en plus anonymes. Ce qui, bien sûr, sera un peu triste pour eux. Mais, espérons-le, cela signifiera également que ce sera au producteur de garder toujours la tête claire pendant que le designer pourra passer son temps à s'amuser ! » THOMAS SANDELL

3. **PS** bureau/Schreibpult for IKEA, 1999
4. **Miami** tables/Couchtische for B&B Italia, 1997
5. **Elena** chair and ottoman/Sessel und Fußhocker/ fauteuil et repose-pied for B&B Italia, 1999
6. **Honey Pye** bed/Bett/lit for Mobileffe, 2000

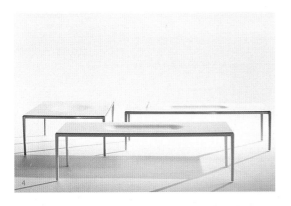

"... Places to live in will become temples,
and objects will be their idols."

Marta Sansoni

Marta Sansoni, Via S. Spirito 11, 50 125 Florence, !taly
T/F +39 055 218 932 martasansoni@yahoo.it

»... Wohnstätten werden zu Tempeln,
und Objekte werden ihre Idole sein.«

«... Les lieux à vivre deviendront des
temples et les objets seront leurs
idoles. »

1. **Tralcio Muto** tray/Tablett/plateau for Alessi, 2000
2. ↓ **Folpo** hand mixer/Handmixer/fouet for Alessi, 1998

»Ich stelle mir Objekte vor, die sich, obgleich durch eine starke formale Persönlichkeit gekennzeichnet, nicht aufdrängen. Objekte, die hergestellt wurden, um aktuelle Bedürfnisse zu befriedigen, die aber über den Gebrauch hinaus auch zur Kontemplation einladen. Objekte, die sich in die häusliche Umgebung einfügen, die nicht allzu selbstverliebt, arrogant oder prätentiös sind. Objekte, die wir niemals müde werden anzusehen oder fürchten zu berühren.

Nichtsdestoweniger glaube ich, dass das Design der Zukunft nicht auf die konventionelle Kombination aus Ästhetik, Funktion, Produktion und Kommerzialisierung angewiesen sein wird. Stattdessen sollte es Objekte realisieren, die neben den genannten Merkmalen mit wirklich therapeutischen Eigenschaften ausgestattet sind: der Fähigkeit zu trösten, zu beschützen und ein Gefühl von Wohlbefinden und Friedfertigkeit zu erzeugen. Folglich möchte ich gerne Objekte entwerfen, die nicht nur zweckmäßig sind, sondern die sich auch zum Spielen und zum Liebkosen eignen. Dinge, die man umarmen, die man auf einen Altar stellen kann, in einen von der Außenwelt abgeschirmten, kostbaren und stillen häuslichen Schrein, den allerletzten Ort individueller Freiheit.

Ich liebe Objekte, die provokative Emotionen und Empfindungen hervorrufen. In zunehmendem Maße müssen die emotionalen Bedürfnisse ebenso befriedigt werden wie die praktischen. In diesem Kontext kann die ästhetische Planung einen wesentlichen Beitrag für den Schutz der menschlichen spirituellen Integrität leisten. Vielleicht kann ich an den Bedingungen für Wohlbefinden, Glück und emotionale Stabilität mitarbeiten, indem ich eine spirituelle Konzeption von Orten entwerfe, in denen man leben und von Objekten, mit denen man leben kann.« MARTA SANSONI

"I imagine objects that, although characterized by a strong formal personality, are not intrusive; objects made to meet contemporary needs, that invite use beyond contemplation; objects that can fit in with the domestic environment; objects that are not too self-celebrating, arrogant or pretentious; objects that we are never tired of seeing or afraid of touching.

Nevertheless, I believe that future design will not have to rely on the conventional combination of aesthetics, function, production and commercialization, but rather should realize objects that, together with these characteristics, are provided with real therapeutic qualities: the capacity for reassuring, protecting and generating a feeling of well-being and peacefulness ... Thus, I would like to design objects that are suitable not only for use but also for playing with, to be caressed; things to be embraced, things to be put on an altar in a secluded, precious and quiet domestic shrine, the very last place of individual freedom.

I love objects that are capable of evoking emotions and feelings that are provocative. Increasingly, emotional needs have to be satisfied as much as the practical ones; in this context, aesthetic research can play a crucial role in protecting human spiritual integrity. Perhaps the only thing that remains for me to do is to help create those conditions that are essential to well-being, happiness and emotional stability, through a projection toward a spiritual conceptualization of places to live in and of objects to live with." MARTA SANSONI

« J'imagine des objets qui, bien que caractérisés par une forte personnalité formelle, ne sont pas envahissants ; des objets conçus pour satisfaire des besoins contemporains ; qui nous invitent au-delà de la contemplation ; qui s'intègrent dans l'environnement domestique ; que nous ne nous lassons jamais de voir et n'avons pas peur de toucher.

Néanmoins, je pense que le design du futur ne dépendra plus du mélange conventionnel d'esthétique, de fonction, de production et de commercialisation, mais qu'il réalisera des objets qui, aux côtés de toutes ces caractéristiques, seront dotés de véritables vertus thérapeutiques : la capacité à rassurer, à protéger et à générer un sentiment de bien-être et de paix ... J'aimerais donc créer des objets qui soient non seulement utiles, mais également ludiques, que l'on aime caresser, des choses à étreindre, à placer sur un autel dans une châsse domestique isolée, précieuse et tranquille, le dernier retranchement de la liberté individuelle.

J'aime les objets capables d'évoquer des émotions et des sentiments provocants. Nos besoins émotionnels doivent de plus en plus être pris en compte au même titre que nos besoins pratiques. Dans ce contexte, la recherche esthétique peut jouer un rôle crucial pour protéger l'intégrité spirituelle de l'homme. La seule chose qui me reste peut-être à faire est d'aider à créer ces conditions essentielles au bien-être, au bonheur et à la stabilité émotionnelle, au travers d'une projection vers une conceptualisation spirituelle des lieux à vivre et des objets avec lesquels vivre. » MARTA SANSONI

3. **Evoluzioni** two-sectioned silver candelabrum/ zweiteiliger Kandelaber/chandelier en argent en deux parties for Pampaloni, 1998
4. **Evasioni** silver vase/Silbervase/vase en argent for Pampaloni, 1998
5. **Evoluzioni** silver salt and pepper cruet/silberner Salz- und Pfefferstreuer/salière et poivrière en argent for Pampaloni, 1998
6. **Mother and Son** ceramic centrepiece/Keramik-Tafelaufsatz/centre de table en céramique for Flavia, 1998

MARTA SANSONI

BORN   1963   Florence, Italy
STUDIED   1990   graduated in Architecture, University of Florence
PRACTICE   1990-98 assistant to Professor Remo Buti, Architecture Faculty, University of Florence
EXHIBITIONS 1990   *Memory Containers-Alessi*, Crusinallo
            1991   *Square with a Monument at the Keihanna Interaction Plaza* design competition,
                    Kansai Science City, Osaka; *Una Porta per Venezia* competition, Biennale di Venezia
            1994   *I Designers per la Ceramica*, Museum for Archeology and Ceramics, Florence
            1995   *Assopiastrelle*, Palazzina Ducale della Casiglia, Modena
            1996   *Evasioni* project, Pampaloni Argenterie, Florence
            1998   *Evoluzioni* project, Pampaloni Argenterie, Florence

CLIENTS

Alessi
Ceramica Bardelli
Flavia Bitossi
Gruppo Colorobbia
Pampaloni
Stayer

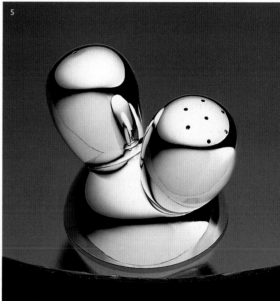

"An innovative approach is needed for modern textile and surface design, while new and existing methods of application and production need to be continuously explored."

Santos & Adolfsdóttir

Leo Santos-Shaw & Margrét Adolfsdóttir, 4, Middle Ground, Fovant, Salisbury, Wiltshire SP3 5LP, England
T/F +44 1722 714 669 sa-tex@dircon.co.uk

»Modernes Textil- und Oberflächen-design erfordert einen innovativen Ansatz, während bestehende Methoden der Anwendung und Fertigung konti-nuierlich erforscht werden müssen.«

« Le textile moderne et le design de surface ont besoin d'une approche innovatrice tandis que les méthodes d'application et de production exis-tantes doivent être continuellement explorées. »

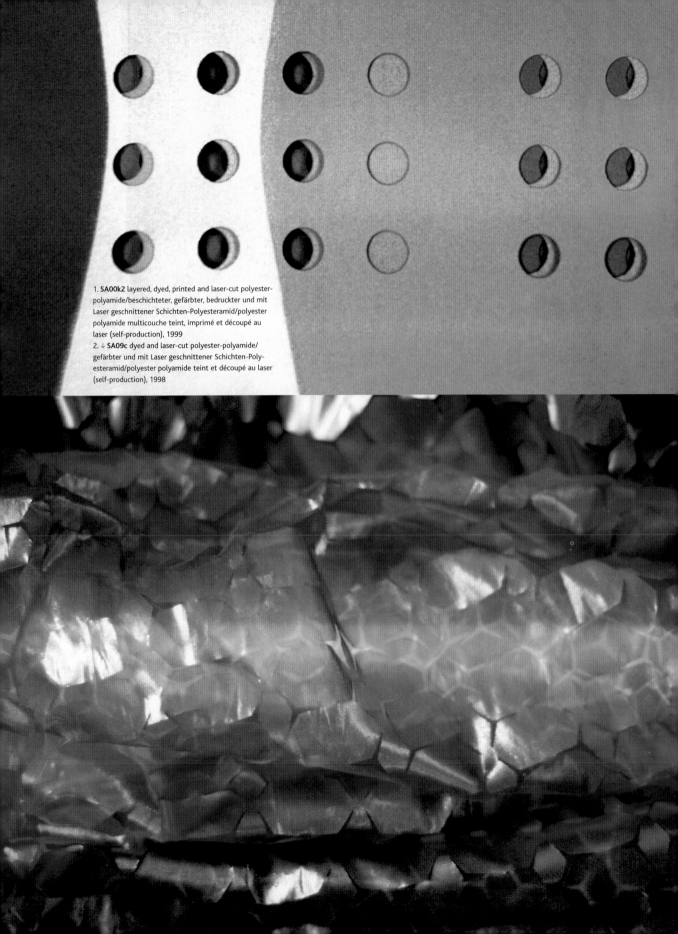

1. **SA00k2** layered, dyed, printed and laser-cut polyester-polyamide/beschichteter, gefärbter, bedruckter und mit Laser geschnittener Schichten-Polyesteramid/polyester polyamide multicouche teint, imprimé et découpé au laser (self-production), 1999

2. ↓ **SA09c** dyed and laser-cut polyester-polyamide/gefärbter und mit Laser geschnittener Schichten-Polyesteramid/polyester polyamide teint et découpé au laser (self-production), 1998

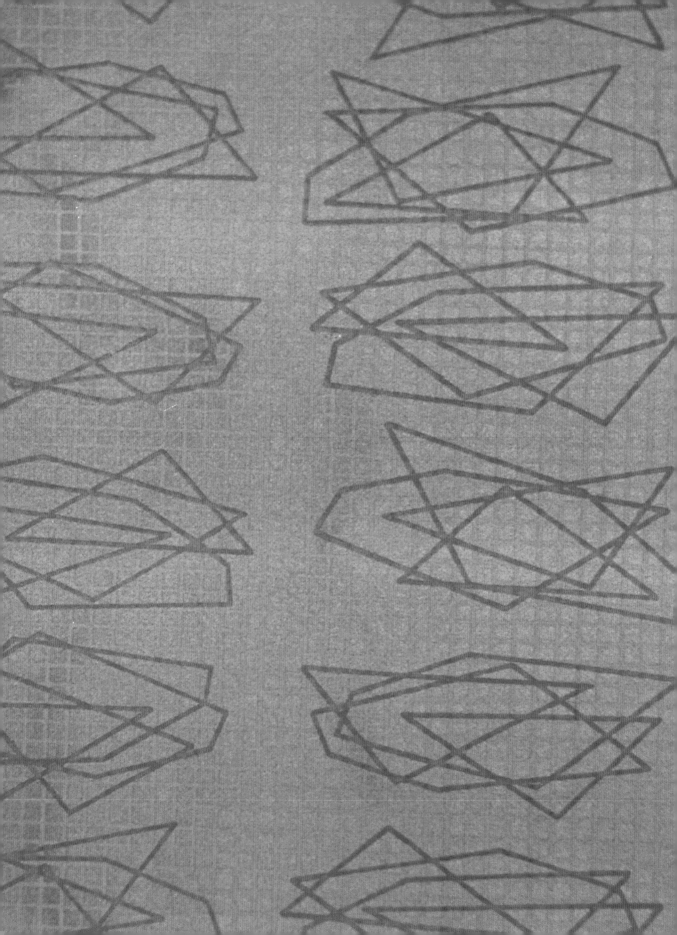

« Les développements expérimentaux et les progrès technologiques rapides de la dernière décennie ont abouti à des matières nouvelles et excitantes dans tous les domaines du design. A l'avenir, celui-ci sera toujours aussi passionnant mais chargé de considérations plus sociales, économiques, écologiques et technologiques. L'utilisation croissante et l'influence de l'informatique commencent dès les premières étapes de la création et se poursuivent tout au long de la fabrication et de la réalisation. Du fait du développement de matériaux et de techniques de plus en plus sophistiqués, les designers doivent sans cesse remettre en question leurs méthodes de travail. L'ordinateur a sans doute entraîné le changement le plus visible en introduisant un effet tridimensionnel dans les images en deux dimensions en même temps qu'une nouvelle esthétique visuelle et, naturellement, la vitesse.

Les exigences écologiques du 21ème siècle modifieront considérablement l'aspect et la fonction du design dans de nombreux domaines. Grâce à une meilleure prise de conscience des effets nocifs des matériaux utilisés dans la fabrication, les entreprises font désormais de l'environnement une de leurs préoccupations majeures, se rendant compte que les ressources mondiales seront bientôt épuisées si des mesures ne sont pas prises rapidement. Les déchets seront de plus en plus recyclés et exploités d'une manière utile. Les substances toxiques utilisées dans la fabrication de produits et de matériaux seront progressivement remplacés par des alternatives moins nocives. Travailler avec l'environnement plutôt que contre lui deviendra également un facteur extrêmement important sur le plan esthétique et " humain ".

L'enseignement du design connaîtra aussi d'importants développements. Dans les ate- ↓

3. ← **SA08d2** printed silk taffeta/bedruckter Seidentaft/taffetas de soie imprimé (self-production), 1999
4. **SA08f** printed acetate taffeta/bedruckter Azetat-Taft/taffetas d'acétate imprimé (self-production), 1999

"Experimental developments and rapid advances in technology over the last decade are producing new and exciting materials in all areas of design. The future of design will be as exciting as ever but with more social, economic, environmental and technological considerations. The increasing use and influence of the computer begins at the very initial stages of design, continuing through manufacturing and realization. Owing to the increasing development of sophisticated materials and techniques, designers are continuously re-examining areas of working practices. The computer has brought about probably the most visible change in design, introducing the sense of three-dimensions into two-dimensions into real three-dimensions, together with a new visual aesthetic and of course, speed.

The ecological requirements of the 21st century will greatly affect the appearance and function of design in many areas. Because of an increasing awareness of the harmful environmental effects of manufacturing materials, companies are making ecology a prime concern — being aware that the world's resources will soon be depleted if major changes are not made. Waste products will increasingly be recycled and reused positively. Toxic chemicals used in the production of products and materials are gradually being replaced by less harmful alternatives. Ecology and working with the environment rather than against it will be an extremely important factor in future design also on an aesthetic and 'human' level. ↓

»Die experimentellen Entwicklungen und raschen technologischen Fortschritte der letzten Dekade bringen in allen Bereichen des Designs neue und aufregende Materialien hervor. Das Design der Zukunft wird weiterhin spannend bleiben, allerdings werden soziale, ökonomische, ökologische und technische Überlegungen eine größere Rolle spielen. Der zunehmende Gebrauch und Einfluss des Computers beginnt bereits im Anfangsstadium jeder Gestaltung und setzt sich durch alle Phasen der Realisierung und Produktion fort. Aufgrund der Weiterentwicklung immer ausgeklügelter Materialien und Techniken müssen Designer ihre Arbeitsmethoden fortwährend überprüfen. Der Computer hat zweifellos die sichtbarste Veränderung im Design bewirkt, indem er eine reale Dreidimensionalität in die bildnerische Gestaltung einführte, zusammen mit einer neuen visuellen Ästhetik und Geschwindigkeit.

Die ökologischen Anforderungen des 21. Jahrhunderts werden Erscheinungsform und Funktion des Designs in vielen Bereichen stark beeinflussen. Dank eines gewachsenen Bewusstseins für die umweltschädlichen Auswirkungen von Industriestoffen machen Unternehmen die Ökologie zu einem Hauptanliegen, da sie sich darüber im Klaren sind, dass die natürlichen Ressourcen der Erde bald erschöpft sein werden, wenn nicht entscheidende Maßnahmen ergriffen werden. Deshalb werden Abfallstoffe immer öfter einem Recycling zugeführt und für positive Zwecke wiederverwendet. Giftige, für die Herstellung von Produkten und Werkstoffen eingesetzte Chemikalien werden allmählich durch weniger schädliche Alternativen ersetzt. Die Ökologie und das Bemühen, für die Umwelt statt gegen sie zu arbeiten, wird für das zukünftige Design zu einem äußerst wichtigen Faktor werden, und zwar auch auf ästhetischer und ›menschlicher‹ Ebene.

Ebenfalls von großer Bedeutung ist die Entwicklung der Designausbildung. Eine am Ausbildungsplatz praktizierte und auf Forschungs- und Entwicklungsanstalten ausgeweitete Teamarbeit wird den ›individuellen Schöpfer‹ eines Produkts oder Konzepts ↓

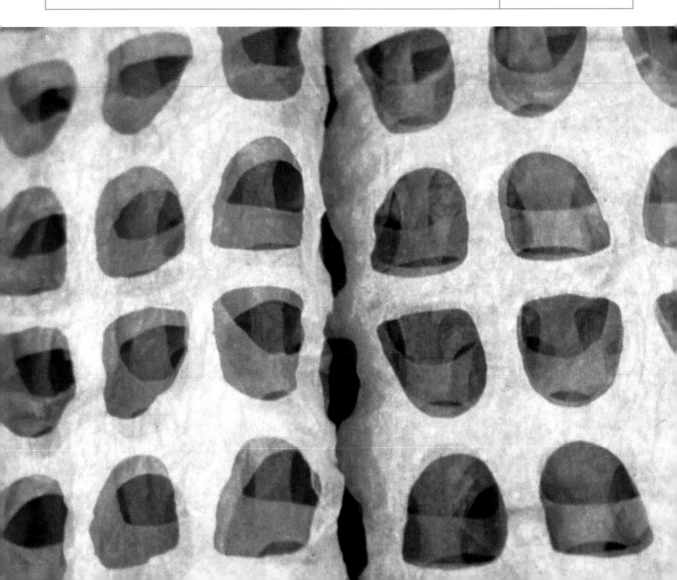

liers des écoles, y compris dans la recherche plastique, le travail d'équipe remplacera le " créateur individuel " d'un produit ou d'un concept. L'accent mis sur la formation professionnelle dans les écoles et les universités ainsi que la participation croissante de designers de tous les horizons venant donner des conférences encouragera une culture pluridisciplinaire, le travail d'équipe et la créativité dans le bureau de design. L'avenir du design est entre les mains des générations à venir. »
SANTOS & ADOLFSDÓTTIR

5. **SA092** three layer laser-cut polyester-polyamide/ dreischichtiger, mit Laser geschnittener Polyesteramid/ polyester polyamide trois couches, découpé au laser (self-production), 1998
6. **SA08el** printed silk taffeta/bedruckter Seidentaft/ taffetas de soie imprimé (self-production), 1999
7. **SA09f** two layer dyed and laser-cut polyester-polyamide/zweischichtiger, gefärbter und mit Laser geschnittener Polyesteramid/polyester polyamide deux couches, teint et découpé au laser (self-production), 1999

The development of design education is also of great importance. Teamwork in the educational workplace, extending into design research practices will replace the 'individual creator' of a product or concept. The emphasis on vocational learning in colleges and universities and the increasing engagement of a broad range of designers from varying disciplines as visiting lecturers, will encourage a multi-disciplinary culture, teamwork and creativity in the design studio. The future of design is in future generations." SANTOS & ADOLFSDÓTTIR

ablösen. Der Schwerpunkt auf berufsbezogenes Lernen an den Schulen und Universitäten sowie das wachsende Engagement von Designern aus unterschiedlichen Disziplinen als Lehrende werden die interdisziplinäre Kultur, Teamarbeit und Kreativität in den Designstudios fördern. Die Zukunft des Designs liegt bei den kommenden Generationen.«
SANTOS & ADOLFSDÓTTIR

"Our work strives for understanding beyond our reach; every piece another step in a journey exploring the richness of human experience; a journey that can never be completed."

Schamburg + Alvisse

Schamburg + Alvisse, Level 1, 116, Kippax Street, Surry Hills, NSW 2010, Australia
T +612 9212 7644 F +612 9212 7844 sa@sadesign.com.au www.schamburgalvisse.com.au

»Unsere Arbeit strebt nach einem Verständnis über das Naheliegende hinaus. Jedes Objekt ist ein weiterer Schritt auf einer Forschungsreise zu den Reichtümern der menschlichen Erfahrung – einer Reise, die niemals abgeschlossen werden kann.«

« Notre travail aspire à une compréhension qui nous dépasse. Chaque nouvelle pièce est un pas de plus dans l'exploration de la richesse de l'expérience humaine ; une exploration qui ne s'achève jamais. »

1. **Bummegg** stool/Hocker/tabouret (self-production),
2000
2. ↓ **Mango** lounge chair/Klubsessel/fauteuil, design:
Michael Tyler (Sydney 612) (self-production), 2000

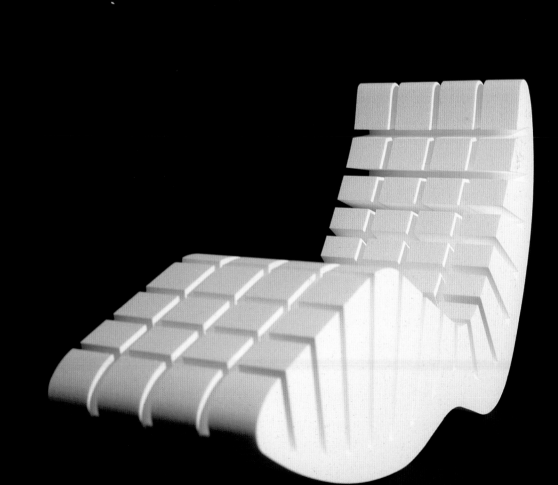

»Geschwindigkeit ist ätzend! Unsere schweiß-treibende Affäre mit der Maschine rast auf ihr Verfallsdatum zu, und wir fragen uns, wie wir es zulassen konnten, von dieser Manie ange-steckt zu werden, in der die Maschine als Ret-ter der Menschheit betrachtet wird. Selbst die Naturwissenschaftler bezweifeln inzwischen, dass mechanistische Weltanschauungen im-stande sind, die Komplexität der natürlichen und menschlichen Systeme ganz zu begreifen. Unsere Krisen des 21. Jahrhunderts betreffen ebenso sehr den Zustand des menschlichen Geistes wie den Zustand unserer Umwelt. Einige von uns glauben sogar, dass es einen tieferen Zusammenhang zwischen den Dilem-mata unserer inneren und äußeren Welten gibt.

›FutureDesign‹ lehnt sowohl die von der Mo-derne vorgenommene Reduktion der mensch-lichen Erfahrung auf das Quantifizierbare ab, wie auch das Angewiesensein des Kapitalis-mus auf inhärente kulturelle Verkümmerung. ›FutureDesign‹ erforscht eine neue Rolle als Mediator zwischen dem Menschen und dem neuen Universum, das wir beginnen zu ent-decken. Diese Rolle ermöglicht eine tiefere Einsicht in die Komplexität der Welt und op-tiert für die Instandsetzung unserer zerbro-chenen Beziehung zu ihr.« SCHAMBURG + ALVISSE

"Speed sucks! Our sweaty affair with the machine is hurtling to-wards its 'use by' date and we're wondering why we allowed our-selves to be sucked in by the machine-as-saviour hype. Even science is questioning whether mechanistic views of the world are capable of fully understanding the complexity of natural and human systems.
Our crises of the 21st century are as much about the state of the human spirit as the state of the environment we live in. Some of us even suspect a profound con-nection between the dilemmas of our inner and outer worlds. FutureDesign rejects both Mod-ernism's reduction of the human experience to the quantifiable and Old Capitalism's dependence on in-built cultural obsolescence. Fu-tureDesign explores a new role as mediator between man and the new universe we're discovering. It facilitates a deeper understanding of the world's complexity and pre-empts the repair of our fractured relationship with it." SCHAMBURG + ALVISSE

« La vitesse, ça craint ! Notre laborieuse his-toire d'amour avec la machine atteint bientôt sa date de péremption et nous nous deman-dons comment nous avons pu nous laisser aspirer dans cette mode de la machine vue comme le messie. Même les scientifiques se demandent si les visions mécanistes du monde sont capables de comprendre totale-ment la complexité des systèmes naturels et humains. Nos crises du 21ᵉ siècle concer-nent autant l'état de l'esprit humain que celui de l'environnement. Certains d'entre nous soupçonnent même qu'il existe un lien pro-fond entre les dilemmes de nos mondes inté-rieurs et extérieurs.
Le FutureDesign rejette à la fois la réduction moderniste de l'expérience humaine au quan-tifiable et la dépendance du vieux capitalisme à l'obsolescence culturelle intégrée. Le Future-Design explore le rôle inédit de médiateur entre l'homme et le nouvel univers que nous sommes en train de découvrir. Il facilite une compréhension plus profonde de la com-plexité du monde et anticipe la réparation de la relation fracturée que nous entretenons avec lui. » SCHAMBURG + ALVISSE

3. **Smooth** lounge chair/Klubsessel/fauteuil for interior commission, 1998
4. **Regalo di Canto** floor lamp/Stehlampe/lampadaire (limited edition, self-production), 2000
5. **Icon** sofa/Sofalandschaft/canapé (self-production), 1998

		SCHAMBURG + ALVISSE	CLIENTS
FOUNDED	1995	Sydney, Australia by Marc Schamburg (b. 1966 Southport, Queensland) and Michael Alvisse (b. 1963 Singapore)	Australian Embassy, Tokyo
STUDIED		MARC SCHAMBURG	Australian Consulate, Berlin
	1987	BA Design, Sydney College of Arts	Museum of Melbourne
		MICHAEL ALVISSE	Australian National Gallery
	1985	BA Architecture, Western Australia Institute of Technology	
AWARDS	1994	*Australis Cognita Award* for design excellence (Marc Schamburg)	
EXHIBITIONS	1999	*4 plus 1*, Powerhouse Museum, Sydney	
	2000	*Salone Satellite*, Salone del Mobile, Milan; *Designing Minds*, Olympic Arts Festival, Sydney, Adelaide	

4

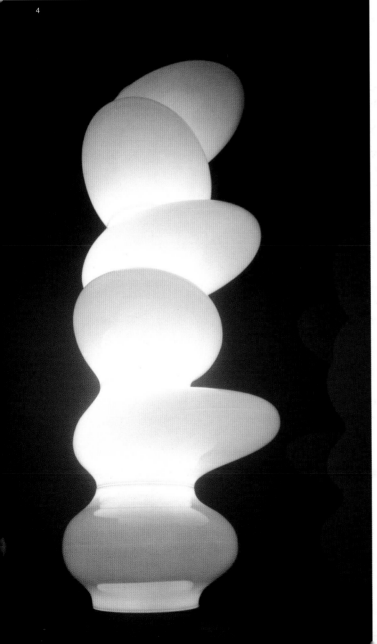

5

"Only the visionary is the real realist."

Peter Schreyer

Peter Schreyer, c/o Audi Design, Audi AG, 85045 Ingolstadt, Germany
T +49 841 89 33575 F +49 841 89 33585 peter.schreyer@audi.de www.audi.com

*»Nur der Visionär ist der wirkliche
Realist.«*

« Seul le visionnaire est un vrai réaliste. »

1. **TT Roadster** for Audi, 1999
2. ↓ **TT Roadster** interior/Innenausstattung/
intérieur for Audi, 1999

»In Zukunft wird die Identifikation der Marke mehr und mehr durch das Design definiert. Die technischen Voraussetzungen sämtlicher Produkte werden zunehmend ähnlicher. Gegenwärtig ist dies bereits bei Autos, Computern, Armbanduhren und sogar Staubsaugern der Fall. Design formt nicht nur das Produkt selbst, es steht auf gleicher Stufe mit der Marke, und es ist Teil der charakteristischen Werte einer Marke.

Die mannigfaltige Warenwelt ist ein Kennzeichen unserer Freiheit. Design hat seinen Platz mehr auf der psychologischen Ebene. Gutes Design verkauft Emotionen, stellt die Identifikation mit einer Marke her und beeinflusst unsere Position in der Gesellschaft. Ein Beispiel dafür ist die Alessi-Zitronenpresse von Philippe Starck: Neben ihrer perfekten Funktionalität kommt auch ihrem Design eine starke Bedeutung zu. Wenn man dieses Objekt bei jemandem zu Hause sieht, weiß man sofort, dass diese Person ein Interesse für Design hat und nicht bloß gerne Zitronen auspresst. Es ist schlichtweg ein außerordentliches Design. Ein derartiger Entwurf gelingt nur mit Visionen, die über die Vorstellungskraft der heutigen Käufer hinausgehen. Es sind die Visionäre, die seit jeher zu den kulturellen, wissenschaftlichen und sozialen Errungenschaften unserer Gesellschaft beigetragen haben. Ohne sie würden wir wahrscheinlich immer noch in der Steinzeit leben.«
PETER SCHREYER

"In the future, identification by label will be granted more and more through design. The technical prerequisites of all products are becoming increasingly similar. At present, this is the case with cars, computers, watches and even vacuum cleaners. Design forms not only the product itself, it stands equal to the label. And is a part of defining label-values.
The diverse world of products is an indication of our liberty. Design has its place more on the psychological level. Good design sells emotions, creates identification with a label and ultimately influences someone's position in society. As an example I could mention the Alessi lemon-press by Philippe Starck – next to its perfect function, the design also has a strong meaning. If you see this object in someone's house you immediately know that this person is design-oriented and not just someone who likes to squeeze lemons. It is just an extraordinary design. You can reach that type of design only with visions, which exceed the imagination of today's customer. It is visioneers that have always contributed to the cultural, scientific and sociological successes of our society. We would still be living in the Stone Age if it were not for visionaries." PETER SCHREYER

« A l'avenir, l'identification de la marque se fera de plus en plus au travers du design. Les critères techniques de tous les produits se ressemblent de plus en plus. C'est le cas aujourd'hui des automobiles, des ordinateurs, des montres et même des aspirateurs. Le design ne donne pas seulement sa forme au produit, il occupe la même place que la marque ; il fait partie des valeurs qui la définissent.
Le monde varié des produits est une indication de notre liberté. Le design se place davantage au niveau psychologique. Le bon design vend des émotions, crée une identification à la marque et, au bout du compte, influe sur notre position dans la société. Prenons par exemple le presse-citron dessiné par Philippe Starck pour Alessi : outre sa fonction parfaite, ce design véhicule un message puissant. Quand on voit cet objet chez quelqu'un, on sait immédiatement que cette personne aime le citron pressé et s'intéresse au design. C'est un objet extraordinaire. Pour atteindre ce type de design, il faut avoir une vision qui surpasse l'imagination du client d'aujourd'hui. Les visionnaires ont toujours contribué aux succès culturels, scientifiques et sociologiques de notre société. Sans eux, nous en serions probablement encore à l'âge de pierre. »
PETER SCHREYER

3. **A4** for Audi, 2000
4. **Rosemeyer** project/Projekt/projet for Audi, 2000
5. **A2** for Audi, 1999
6. **Steppenwolf** project/Projekt/projet for Audi, 2000
7. **Allroad** estate car/Kombi/break for Audi, 1999

PETER SCHREYER		CLIENTS
BORN	1953 Bad Reichenhall, Germany	in-house designer for Audi AG
STUDIED	1975-79 Diploma Industrial Design, Fachhochschule, Munich	
	1979 sponsorship from Audi AG, Royal College of Art, London	
PRACTICE	1978 student at design department of Audi AG	
	1980-90 exterior and interior car designer at Audi Design	
	1991-92 Volkswagen Design Studio, California (New Beetle concept)	
	1992-93 Audi Design Concept Studio	
	1993 Head of Volkswagen Exterior Design	
	1994 Head of Audi Design	
AWARDS	1994 IBCAM British Steel Design Award	
1994, 98 (two) & 2000	iF Design Award, Hanover	
1994 (two)	Bundespreis Produktdesign, Frankfurt/Main; Best Concept Car, *Autoweek* magazine, UK	
1995 (two), 96 & 97	Roter Punkt Award, Design Zentrum Nordrhein-Westfalen, Essen	
1997 & 2000	Good Design Award, Chicago Athenaeum	
1998 & 99	Autocar Award, USA	
1999	*Design Team of the Year*, Design Zentrum Nordrhein-Westfalen, Essen	
2001	Best of Category, iF Design Award, Hanover	

"Live fast, die young, reincarnate, live happily ever after."

Jerszy Seymour

Jerszy Seymour, Via Vigevano 39, 20 144 Milan, Italy
T +39 02 894 22 105   F +39 02 894 25924   jerszyseymour@tin.it

»Schnell leben, jung sterben, wieder-
geboren werden und glücklich bis in alle
Ewigkeit leben.«

« Vivre à toute allure, mourir jeune, se
réincarner, être ensuite éternellement
heureux. »

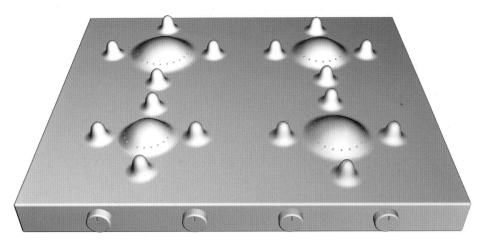

1. **Easy Clean** gas hob (prototype)/Gasherd-Kochplatte
(Prototyp)/plaque de cuisson à gaz (prototype) for Smeg,
1995
2. ↓ **Playstation LE** armchair with footrest/Sessel mit
Fußstütze/fauteuil avec repose-pied for Original Sin, 2001

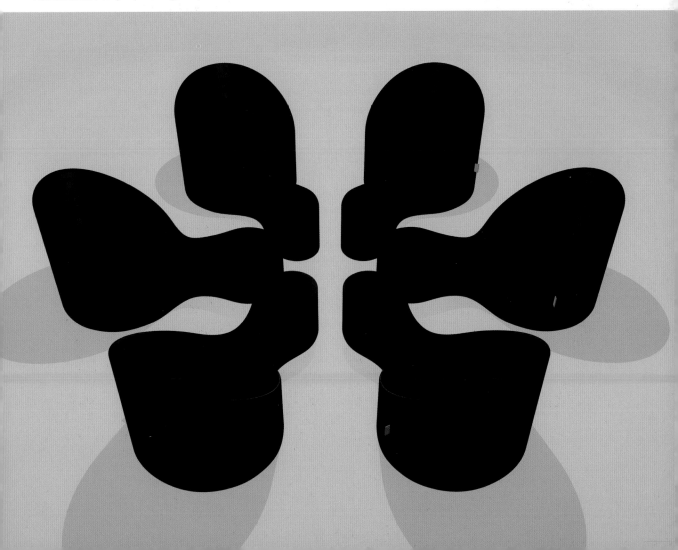

»Ich glaube, in Zukunft wird Design von ›intelligenter‹ Auswahl und ›fleischlichen‹ Begierden gekennzeichnet sein. Dabei wird die Loyalität der Konsumenten gegenüber sinnlichen und intellektuellen Statuswerten den Fokus des Designs von der materiellen Gestaltung zum ›ideologischen Inhalt‹ verschieben.

Da die moderne Industrie immer sensibler für die Grundbedingungen von Qualität, Funktionalität, Preis, ökologischen Belangen etc. sein muss, wird die Fähigkeit eines Produkts, seine charakteristischen Eigenschaften zu vermitteln, zunehmend an Bedeutung gewinnen. Tatsächlich muss das Objekt selbst zum Kommunikationsmittel werden, damit Design in einer Welt, die von Unternehmensmarketing und einem medialen Überangebot beherrscht wird, ohne Integritätsverlust weiterbestehen kann: Wenn ein Stuhl bequem ist, muss er die Vorstellung von Bequemlichkeit vermitteln und zu einer Art Super-Abbild seiner selbst werden, zu einem Super-Stuhl mit den Eigenschaften eines Super-Stars, zu denen auch Sex-Appeal gehört.

Die Zukunft des Designs wird fabelhaft, flauschig, furios und fröhlich sein. Design wird ein Instrument der Liebe sein, ein Superheld, der bereit ist, für das Gute und das Böse zu kämpfen. Das Design wird fragen, warum es auf der Welt ist und was sein Lebenszweck ist. Es wird den Stinkefinger hochhalten, nackt durch die Wälder rennen und die Welt retten.«
JERSZY SEYMOUR

"In the future, I believe design will be characterized by 'intelligent' choice and 'carnal' desire, where consumer allegiance to sensual and intellectual status values will change the focus of design from material styling to 'ideological content'.

As the fundamentals of quality, functionality, price, ecological issues etc. become ever more sensitive to modern industry, the ability of a product to communicate its attributes becomes more important. Indeed, for design to continue to exist with integrity in a world dominated by corporate marketing and media saturation, the object must become the communication medium itself – if a chair is comfortable it must communicate comfort and become a kind of super-representation of itself, a super-chair with super-star qualities that include sex.

The future of design is going to be fabulous, furry, furious and fun. It will be a tool of love, a superhero ready to do battle for good and evil. It will ask why it exists and what its purpose in life is. It will stick its middle finger up, run through the woods naked, and save the world." JERSZY SEYMOUR

« A l'avenir, je crois que le design se caractérisera par des choix "intelligents" et un désir "charnel", où l'allégeance du consommateur aux valeurs sensuelles et intellectuelles déplacera le centre d'intérêt du design de la conception matérielle au "contenu idéologique". A mesure que l'industrie moderne est de plus en plus sensible aux règles de base de la qualité, de la fonctionnalité, du prix, des questions écologiques, etc., la capacité d'un produit à communiquer ses attributs devient plus importante. De fait, pour que le design conserve son intégrité dans un monde dominé par le marketing et la saturation des médias, l'objet doit lui-même devenir un moyen de communication : une chaise confortable doit communiquer l'idée de confort et devenir une sorte de super représentation d'elle-même, une super chaise avec des qualités de super star qui incluent le sexe.

L'avenir du design sera fabuleux, flou, furieux et fou. Il sera un outil d'amour, un super héros prêt à combattre pour le bien et le mal. Il se demandera pourquoi il existe et interrogera sa raison d'être. Il fera des bras d'honneur, courra nu dans les bois et sauvera le monde. »
JERSZY SEYMOUR

3. **FreeWheelin'Franklin** remote control side tables/ Beistelltische mit Fernbedienung/dessertes contrôlées par télécommande (limited edition) for Sputnik/IDÉE, 2000
4. **Jelly Fish** watch (prototype)/Armbanduhr (Prototyp)/ montre (prototype) for Seiko, 1998
5. **Pipe Dreams** watering can/Gießkanne/arrosoir for Magis, 2000
6. **Xylo** collapsible handbag/faltbare Handtasche/sac à main pliable for Original Sin, 2001
7. **Captain Lovetray** serving tray/Tablett/plateau for Magis, 1999

JERSZY SEYMOUR			CLIENTS
BORN	1968	Spandau, Berlin, Germany	BRF
STUDIED	1989	BSc Engineering Design, South Bank Polytechnic, London	Magis
	1994	MA Industrial Design, Royal College of Art, London	Original Sin
PRACTICE	1996	collaborated with Stefano Giovannoni, Milan	Smeg
	1997	collaborated with Smart Design, New York	Sputnik/IDÉE
	1999	established own design studio, Milan	Swatch
AWARDS	2000	Dedalus Award for European Design	
EXHIBITIONS	2000	*2nd edizione del Premio Dedalus per il design europeo*, Bra, Italy; *Carrefour de la création*, Centre Georges Pompidou, Paris	

"If you don't remember that design is about creating things that make people's lives better, then you're part of the problem, not the solution ..."

Seymour Powell

Seymour Powell, The Chapel, Archel Road, London W14 9QH, England
T +44 20 7381 6433 F +44 20 7381 9081 design@seymourpowell.co.uk www.seymourpowell.co.uk

»Wenn man vergisst, dass es beim Design darauf ankommt, Dinge herzustellen, die das Leben der Menschen verbessern, ist man Teil des Problems, nicht der Lösung ...«

« Si vous avez oublié que le design consiste à créer des choses qui améliorent la vie des gens, c'est que vous faites partie du problème, pas de la solution ... »

1. **Infinium** bagless vacuum cleaner/
beutelloser Staubsauger/aspirateur
sans sac for Rowenta, 2000
2. ↓ **Domestic Range cooker**/Herd/
cuisinière for Mercury, 2000

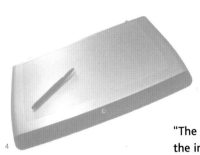

"The boundaries that contained the individual disciplines of design are dissolving and mutating, driven largely by the shift of emphasis away from the physical (product) towards the intangible (the 'meta'-product). We cling to the old definitions because the 'new order' is, as yet, undefined and in flux. With the metaproduct come the additional dimensions of depth and time, which graphic designers are unfamiliar with. But beyond the much-vaunted convergence will come divergence. And only designers can tell us what this will mean. Fasten your seatbelts. ..."
SEYMOUR POWELL

« Les frontières qui délimitaient les différentes disciplines du design se dissolvent, muent, entraînées en grande partie par le déplacement de l'intérêt général du (produit) physique vers l'intangible (le " méta " produit). Nous nous raccrochons aux vieilles définitions car le " nouvel ordre " est encore indéfini et en mutation. Le métaproduit apporte avec lui les dimensions supplémentaires de profondeur et de temps, auxquelles les graphistes ne sont pas encore habitués. Mais après la convergence tant vantée viendra la divergence. Seuls les designers peuvent nous dire ce que cela signifiera. Accrochez vos ceintures ... » SEYMOUR POWELL

»Die Grenzen zwischen den einzelnen Disziplinen des Designs lösen sich auf und verändern sich. Diese Entwicklung wurde hauptsächlich von einer Akzentverlagerung weg vom Materiellen (Produkt) hin zum Immateriellen (›Meta‹-Produkt) ausgelöst. Wir halten an den alten Definitionen fest, weil die ›neue Ordnung‹ noch unbestimmt und im Fluss ist. Mit dem Meta-Produkt kommen die zusätzlichen Dimensionen von Tiefe und Zeit hinzu, mit denen sich Grafikdesigner noch nicht auskennen. Aber jenseits der vielgerühmten Konvergenz wird sich Divergenz einstellen. Und nur die Designer werden uns sagen können, was das bedeuten wird. Schnallen Sie sich an ...« SEYMOUR POWELL

3. ← **Cyborg** joystick/Joystick for Saitek, 1998
4.-7. **Wacom-board, Setup, Rat** and **Hub** elements from Post Production Editing Station/Computer-Editierstation für Nachbearbeitung/unité de montage post-production for Quantel, 2000

SEYMOUR POWELL

FOUNDED	1984	London by Richard Seymour (b. 1953 Scarborough, England) and Dick Powell (b. 1951 Great Kingshill, England)
STUDIED		RICHARD SEYMOUR
	1971-74	BA (Hons) Graphic Design, Central St Martin's College of Art and Design, London
	1974-77	MA Graphic Design, Royal College of Art, London
		DICK POWELL
	1970-73	BA Industrial Design, Manchester Polytechnic
	1973-76	MA Industrial Design, Royal College of Art, London
AWARDS	1990	Best Overall Design & Product Design Awards, *Design Week* Awards, London
	1991 & 93	D&AD Silver Award, London
	1994	BBC Design Award for *Most Outstanding Product Design*, London
	1995	D&AD President's Award for *Outstanding Contribution to Design*, London
	1997	Special Commendation, Prince Philip Design Prize, London
	1998	Janus Award, France
EXHIBITIONS		
	1999-2000	The Glasgow Collection, Glasgow
	2000	Millennium Dome, London; The Ideal Home Show, London

CLIENTS

Addis
Aqualisa
BMW
Calor
Casio
Charnos
Cathay Pacific
Coleman Europe
Connolly
Dell
Ford
Four Square
General Motors
Hasbro Toys
Hewlett-Packard
Jaguar
London Underground
Minolta
MuZ
Nissan
Nokia
Panasonic
Renault
Rowenta
Shimano
SmithKline Beecham
Sun Microsystems
Tefal SA
Toyota
Waterman
Yamaha Motors

8

9

11

12

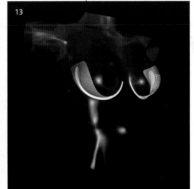

13

8. **Linn** watch/Armbanduhr/montre for Linn, 2000
9. **Avanti** toaster/Toaster/grille-pain for Tefal, 1998
10. **Avantis** iron/Bügeleisen/fer à repasser for Tefal, 1999
11. **DP 154-EX** mobile phone/Handy/téléphone portable
for Nokia, 1998
12. **Luxury Luggage** attaché-case/Aktentasche
for Connolly, 2000
13. **Bioform** bra/Büstenhalter/soutien-gorge for Charnos,
2000

"Design objects with simplicity and personality."

Michael Sodeau

Michael Sodeau Partnership, Studio 26, 26, Rosebery Avenue, London EC1R 4SX, England
T +44 20 7833 5020 F +44 20 7833 5021 michael@msp.uk.com

*»Objekte mit Einfachheit und Persönlich-
keit gestalten.«*

« Concevoir des objets avec simplicité
et personnalité. »

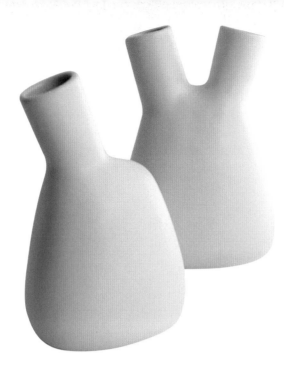

1. **Single** and **Twin** vases/Vasen for MSP, 1998
2. ↓ **RedRug/BlueRug** three-dimensional carpets/
dreidimensionale Teppiche/tapis tridimensionnels
for Christopher Farr, 2000

« Tandis que nous entrons dans le 21e siècle, ma vision du design est celle de la simplicité. Il est essentiel qu'en tant que créateur, je sois conscient des différents aspects du design liées à l'environnement, aux matériaux et à la fabrication ainsi qu'aux besoins des consommateurs du 21e siècle.
Ce dernier facteur change constamment : si les environnements domestiques et professionnels évoluent et fusionnent, il en va de même pour les objets qui sont censés y fonctionner. A mesure que le design avance dans le futur, c'est le monde tel qu'il se déroule et les moyens de vivre confortablement dans cet environnement toujours changeant qui deviennent les principales préoccupations des créateurs. Les designers de l'ère de la communication ont désormais à leur disposition des lignes ISDN qui transmettent leurs images et leurs dessins directement aux fabricants sur une simple pression d'un bouton, ainsi que des systèmes capables de faire des prototypes d'objets en quelques heures afin que designers et fabricants puissent détecter tous les problèmes avant que l'objet en question n'entre dans la chaîne de production. Tout ceci a accéléré le passage du concept au produit fini et a considérablement influencé l'offre proposée aux consommateurs. Si tous ces facteurs ont modifié le design, il est essentiel de ne pas perdre de vue le " pourquoi " de notre travail. Je m'intéresse avant tout à la relation entre l'objet et son utilisateur ; à ce qu'on attend d'un objet (en terme de fonctionnalité) et à la manière dont celui-ci doit fonctionner pour améliorer la vie quotidienne de l'utilisateur. J'aspire à donner à l'objet un certain degré de personnalité et de caractère afin de créer un lien entre lui et son utilisateur. » MICHAEL SODEAU

3. ← **Woven** floor lights/Stehlampen/lampadaires for MSP, 1998
4. **Line** stacking chairs/Stapelstühle/chaises encastrables (prototype), 1999

"My vision for design as we enter the 21st century is one of simplicity. It is essential that as a designer I am aware of the various issues that are associated with design in terms of the environment, materials and manufacturing coupled with the needs of the 21st-century consumer.
This last factor is a constantly changing one: as domestic and work environments change and merge so do the associated objects required by consumers to perform within them. As design progresses into the future, it is the world as it unfolds that is the designer's major concern, and what is required to live with comfort in this changing environment. In this, the communication-age designers now have at their disposal ISDN lines that can send drawings and images direct to the manufacturer at the touch of a button as well as rapid prototyping facilities that can prototype objects in a matter of hours so that designers and manufacturers can access any problems before the object goes into production. This has speeded up the process of design concept to manufacture and greatly impacted on what is available to the consumer.
While all these factors have had an impact on design it is essential that 'what' and 'why' we design is not lost. My interest lies in the relationship between objects and users. What is required from the object (in terms of functionality) and how the object needs to perform to enhance the user's day-to-day life. My aim is to give objects a degree of personality and character so as to create a bond between object and user." MICHAEL SODEAU

»Meine Vision vom Design im beginnenden 21. Jahrhundert ist eine der Einfachheit. Für mich als Designer ist es wesentlich, dass ich mir der verschiedenartigen Probleme bewusst bin, die mit Design verknüpft sind – Probleme im Hinblick auf Umwelt, Materialien und Fabrikation, verbunden mit den Bedürfnissen der Konsumenten des 21. Jahrhunderts. Der letztgenannte Faktor ist einer, der sich kontinuierlich verändert: Ebenso wie sich unsere Wohn- und Arbeitswelten wandeln und miteinander verschmelzen, tun dies auch die Objekte, die benötigt werden, um in der jeweiligen Umgebung zu funktionieren. In dem Maße, in dem Design in die Zukunft fortschreitet, wird die sich entfaltende Welt und die Frage, was notwendig ist, um komfortabel in ihr zu leben, zum Hauptinteresse für Designer. Hierfür stehen den Gestaltern des Kommunikationszeitalters nun ISDN-Verbindungen zur Verfügung, mit denen sie per Knopfdruck Zeichnungen und Bilder direkt an den Hersteller senden können, sowie Computerprogramme, die innerhalb weniger Stunden Prototypen von Objekten anfertigen, so dass Gestalter und Hersteller jedes eventuelle Problem abschätzen können, bevor das Objekt in Serienproduktion geht. All das hat den Gestaltungsprozess von der Konzeption bis zur Fabrikation beschleunigt und das den Konsumenten zur Verfügung stehende Warenangebot verändert. Neben dem großen Einfluss dieser Faktoren auf das Design der Vergangenheit und Gegenwart dürfen wir nicht die Frage aus den Augen verlieren, ›was‹ und ›warum‹ wir designen. Mein Interesse gilt der Beziehung zwischen Objekten und ihren Anwendern: Was wird vom Objekt verlangt (im Sinne von Funktionalität), und wie muss das Objekt funktionieren, um das Alltagsleben des Benutzers zu bereichern? Mein Ziel ist es, Objekten ein gewisses Maß an Persönlichkeit und Charakter zu verleihen, so dass eine emotionale Verbindung zwischen Objekt und Anwender entsteht.« MICHAEL SODEAU

		MICHAEL SODEAU	CLIENTS
BORN	1969	London, England	Asplund
STUDIED	1994	BA (Hons) Product Design, Central St Martin's College of Art and Design, London	Christopher Farr
PRACTICE	1995	co-founded Inflate, London	Dinny Hall
	1997	co-founded Michael Sodeau Partnership, London with Lisa Giuliani	Gervasoni
AWARDS	2000	winner Best Design Award, 100% Design, London	Inflate
EXHIBITIONS	1998	*Interior*, Paris; *New British Design*, Athens; *Caned*, London; *Happening*, Tokyo; *Landed*, New York	Isokon Plus
	1999	*Premillennium Tension*, British Council, Cologne; *Being There*, Tokyo, London; *Child's Ply*, London	SCP
	2000	*Michael Sodeau*, Stockholm; *TWIST*, London; Child's Form, London	Wedgwood
	2001	*Michael Sodeau*, New York	also self-production

5

5. **Wing** storage unit and **Flip** tables and shelves/Schrank, Tische und Regale/buffet, tables et étagères for Isokon Plus, 1999 & 2000

6. **Wing** storage unit/Schrank/buffet for Isokon Plus, 1999

7. **Satellite** tables/Tische for MSP, 1997

8. **Tea Time** teaset/Teeservice/service à thé (prototype), 1999

9. **Walking on Water** hand-knotted rug/handgeknüpfter Teppich/tapis noué à la main for Christopher Farr, 1998

10. **Lounge chairs**/Sessel/fauteuils (prototype), 1999

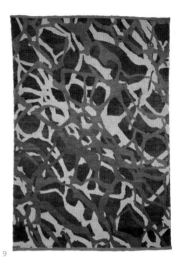

"One-byte design – to create forms
that go beyond functional beauty to
heart-touching designs that fascinate
our instincts the minute they are held
or seen."

Sony Design Center

Design Center, Sony Corporation, 6-7-35 Kitashinagawa, Shinagawa-ku, Tokyo 141-0001, Japan
www.world.sony.com

»One-Byte-Design: Die Gestaltung von
Formen, die über die funktionale Schönheit hinaus zu Herzen gehen und in dem
Moment, in dem wir sie berühren oder
sehen, unsere Instinkte fesseln.«

« Le design d'un octet: créer des formes
qui vont au-delà de la beauté fonctionnelle, qui émeuvent, qui fascinent nos
instincts dès qu'on les tient ou qu'on
les voit. »

1. **Cybershot DSC-F505** digital camera/
Digitalkamera/appareil photo numérique
for Sony, 1999, design: Kaoru Sumita
2. ↓ **SDM-N50** LCD monitor/Bildschirm/écran à cristaux
liquides for Sony, 1999, design: Masakazu Kanatani

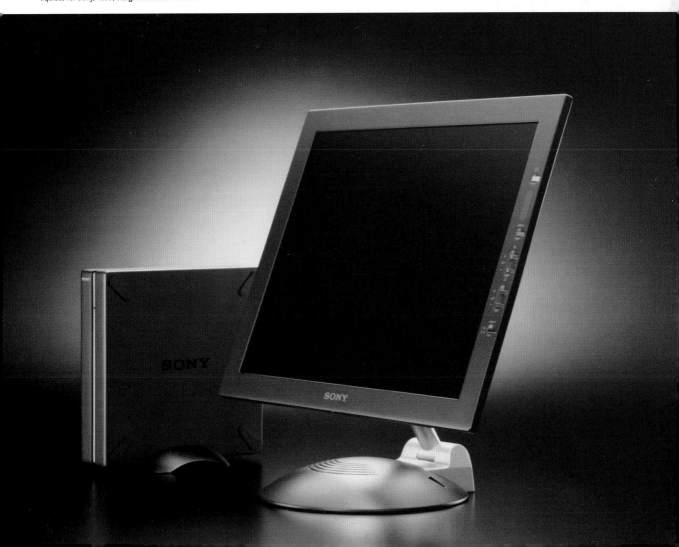

»Design lässt sich als eine Sprache definieren, die Menschen ermöglicht, mit innovativen Technologien zu kommunizieren. Als Interpreten menschlicher Bedürfnisse und Anliegen müssen Designer bejahen, dass wir – als menschliche Wesen – die Richtung kontrollieren, in die sich Technologie entwickelt, anstatt von ihr beherrscht zu werden. Darüber hinaus entspricht es unserer menschlichen Natur, dass sich mit der Zeit Vernunft und Emotionen der Umwelt entsprechend verändern. Folglich müssen wir das gegenwärtige System der Massenproduktion erneuern, das nur der Effizienz Rechnung trägt und die verschiedenen Arten von Konsumenten alle als eine einzige Gruppe betrachtet. Um Produkte und Dienstleistungen hervorzubringen, welche die individuelle Vernunft ansprechen, muss die höchste soziale Infrastruktur – die Verschmelzung von Handwerk und Massenproduktion – entworfen werden.«

MITSURU INABA, CORPORATE VICE PRESIDENT, CREATIVE (DESIGN) CENTER

"Design can be referred to as the language that enables people to communicate with innovative technologies. As interpreters of people's needs and concerns, designers must affirm that we, as human beings, control the direction that technology is headed – rather than being ruled by it. Furthermore, it is in our human nature that rationality and human emotions change over time according to environment. Thus, we need to renovate the current mass-production system that only takes into consideration efficiency and classifies the various types of consumers all in one group. To originate products and services that appeal to the rationale of individuals, the ultimate social infrastructure – the fusion of handcraft and mass-production – needs to be designed."

MITSURU INABA, CORPORATE VICE PRESIDENT, CREATIVE (DESIGN) CENTER

« Le design peut être défini comme un langage qui permet à l'homme de communiquer avec les technologies innovatrices. Interprètes des besoins et des préoccupations des gens, les designers doivent affirmer qu'en tant qu'êtres humains, nous contrôlons la direction que prend la technologie et que ce n'est pas elle qui nous gouverne. En outre, notre nature humaine fait que le rationalisme et les émotions varient avec le temps et selon l'environnement. Par conséquent, nous devons rénover l'actuel système de production de masse qui ne prend en considération que l'efficacité et qui range tous les types de consommateurs dans le même sac. Pour créer des produits et des services qui parlent à la logique des individus, il convient de concevoir l'infrastructure sociale ultime : la fusion de l'artisanat et de la production de masse. »

MITSURU INABA, CORPORATE VICE PRESIDENT, CREATIVE (DESIGN) CENTER

3. **Playstation 2** for Sony, 1999, design: Teiyu Goto
4. **VAIO LX Series** personal computer/Personalcomputer/ordinateur PC for Sony, 1999, design: Haruo Oba
5. **Handycam DCR-PC100** camcorder/Videokamera/vidéocaméra for Sony, 1999 – design: Hiroki Oka
6. **VAIO SR Series** laptop computer/Laptop/ordinateur portable for Sony, 1999, design: Shinichi Ogasawara

	SONY DESIGN CENTER	CLIENTS
FOUNDED	1961 Tokyo, Japan	Sony Corporation
SINCE	1997 Sony Corporation Design Center has been headed by Mitsuru Inaba (b. 1942 Tokyo), who graduated from Musashino Art University (1968), Rhode Island School of Design (1969). The current design team includes: Teiyu Goto (b. 1953), Kaoru Sumita (b. 1946), Shinichi Ogosawara (b. 1954), Haruo Oba (b. 1962), Masakazu Kanatani (b. 1956), Shin Miyashita (b. 1955), Takuya Niitsu (b. 1955), Hiroki Oka (b. 1956) and Junichi Nagahara (b. 1966)	
AWARDS	2000 Grand Prize, Gold Prize and four G-Mark/Good Design Awards, JIDPO, Tokyo; Packaging Design Award, Japan Packaging Competition; nine iF Design Awards, Hanover; *Design team of the Year* and ten Roter Punkt Awards, Design Zentrum Nordrhein-Westfalen, Essen; SMAU (Salone Macchine Attrezzature Ufficio) Industrial Design Award, Milan	
EXHIBITIONS	2000 *Sony Digital Dream*, Tokyo, Osaka; *Design Innovation (Roter Punkt) Design Team of the Year*, Design Zentrum Nordrhein-Westfalen, Essen	

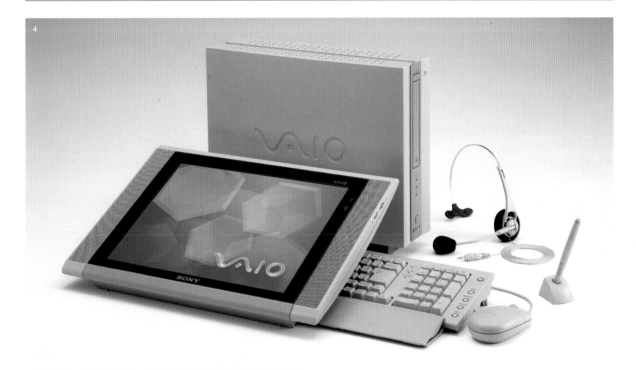

"We live in a society that accepts uncertainty as a principle and disregards the security that accompanies ideology."

SowdenDesign

Georg J. Sowden & Hiroshi Ono, SowdenDesign, Corso di Porta Nuova 46, 20 121 Milan, Italy
T +39 02 653 089 F +39 02 657 0228 milan@sowdendesign.com www.sowdendesign.com

»Wir leben in einer Gesellschaft, die Ungewissheit als ein Prinzip akzeptiert und Sicherheit als eine Begleiterscheinung von Ideologien gering schätzt.«

« Nous vivons dans une société qui accepte l'incertitude comme un principe et ne s'attache pas à la sécurité qui accompagne l'idéologie. »

1. **Toaster**/grille-pain for Guzzini, 2001
2. ↓ **Public Internet Terminal** for American
Airports (kiosk arrangement)/Öffentliche Internetstation für amerikanische Flughäfen (Kiosk-Version)/
terminal internet public pour aéroports américains
(aménagement des cabines) for Get2Net, 1999

« Le travail de notre studio se caractérise par le fait que nous traitons en même temps le design et l'ingénierie – les séparer serait artificiel. La manière dont les différents éléments sont assemblés est très importante, comme dans la couture ou la musique. L'ingénierie est aux produits ce que la précision de la coupe est au vêtement ou la sensibilité du doigté à la musique. L'ingénierie régie les industries de la fabrication. Celle-ci doit être réalisée avec soin : l'esthétique moderne, comme les modes de vie modernes, est très fragile. Je ne veux pas dire par là qu'elle est faible, mais qu'elle évolue rapidement, ne supporte pas le monumental et se nourrit de diversité. Il me semble tout à fait irréaliste de chercher à mettre de l'ordre dans notre environnement mais, si quelque chose peut donner un sens à cette fragilité, il faut le chercher dans la qualité de la fabrication tandis que nous construisons un collage toujours changeant d'objets non apparentés, qui devient le monde dans lequel nous vivons. » GEORGE J. SOWDEN

3. ← **Wide-screen television set** (study)/Breitwand-Fernseher (Entwurf)/télévision grand écran (étude) for McPerson, 1999
4. **Joe** telephone/Telefon/téléphone for Alessi, 1998
5. **Hand-blender**/Mixer/mixeur for Guzzini, 2001

"The nature of the studio's work is determined by the fact that we do the design and the engineering at the same time – to divide them would be artificial. The way that things are assembled is so important, as it is in fashion and music. The engineering in products is like the precision of the cut in clothes or the sensitivity of the touch in music. Engineering is the execution that directs manufacturing industries. Manufacturing needs to be done carefully: modern aesthetics, like modern lifestyles, are very fragile. I do not mean this in a weak sense: I mean they are fast, they disregard monumentality, they thrive on diversity. I believe that it is quite unrealistic to try to put order into our environment but, if one thing can give sense to its fragility, the key is the *quality* of our manufacturing as we build an ever-changing collage of unrelated objects, which becomes the world in which we live." GEORGE J. SOWDEN

»Die Arbeitsweise unseres Studios kennzeichnet sich durch die Tatsache, dass wir Gestaltung und technische Ausführung der Designs gleichzeitig machen – beides voneinander zu trennen wäre künstlich. Die Art und Weise, wie Dinge konstruiert werden, ist im Design ebenso wichtig wie in Mode und Musik. Die technische Ausführung von Produkten lässt sich mit der Präzision des Schnitts bei Kleidern oder dem Taktgefühl in der Musik vergleichen. Die Fertigungstechnik gibt in der verarbeitenden Industrie die Richtung an. Die Fabrikation muss sorgfältig durchgeführt werden: Die moderne Ästhetik ist – ebenso wie moderne Lebensstile – sehr fragil. Ich meine das nicht im Sinne von Schwächlichkeit. Sondern ich meine, Ästhetik und Lebensstil sind schnelllebig, geben nichts auf Monumentalität und gedeihen in der Vielfältigkeit. Ich glaube, dass der Versuch, unserer Umwelt eine feste Ordnung zu geben, ziemlich unrealistisch ist. Wenn jedoch etwas ihrer Fragilität Sinn verleihen kann, dann ist er in der *Qualität* unserer Produktion zu suchen, während wir eine sich stetig wandelnde Collage einzelner Objekte konstruieren, die zu der Welt wird, in der wir leben.« GEORGE J. SOWDEN

6

7

6. **Rotor 2000** outdoor public telephone/öffentliches Telefon/téléphone public for I.P.M., 1998
7. **Web payphone**/Öffentliches Internet-Telefon/ Poste public de télépone-Internet for Nextera, 2000
8. **Rotor 2000** outdoor public web access telephone/ öffentliches Telefon mit Internetanschluss/téléphone public connecté à internet for I.P.M., 1998
9. **Calculator**/Rechenmaschine/calculatrice (study for Olivetti), 1999

8

9

SOWDENDESIGN		CLIENTS
FOUNDED	1980	Milan by George J. Sowden (b. 1942 Leeds)	Alessi
	1994	Hiroshi Ono (b. 1968 Okayama, Japan) joined the studio as partner	Ace Hardware
STUDIED		GEORGE SOWDEN	Bodum
	1960-64 & 66-68	Architecture, Gloucester College of Art, Cheltenham	C. T. S. Systems
AWARDS	1988 & 95	Compasso d'Oro selection, Milan	e-Products
	1989, 96 & 98	SMAU (Salone Macchine Attrezzature Ufficio) Industrial Design Award, Milan	Get2Net
	1995	Compasso d'Oro selection, Milan	I. P. M.
	1991	Compasso d'Oro, Milan	Mattel
	1998 & 99	selected twice for ADI Design Index	McPerson
	1999	special mention, Design-Preis Schweiz, Switzerland; selected for D&AD Award, London	Memphis
EXHIBITIONS			OLOMilano
	1981-87	Memphis exhibitions, Milan, London, Paris, Düsseldorf, Hanover, Geneva, New York, Chicago, Los Angeles, Tokyo	Olivetti
	1990-91	*George J. Sowden Design: 1970-1990*, Musée des Arts Décoratifs, Bordeaux, Marseille, Lyons	Rancilio
	1988, 91 & 95	Compasso d'Oro exhibitions, Milan	Steelcase
			Swatch
			Telecom Italia
			Urmet

10

11

12

13

10.-11. **Flat screen monitor**/Flachbildschirm/écran plat
(research program), 1999
12. **ST 2000** banking terminal/Bankomat/distributeur
automatique de banque for C. T. S. Systems, 1999
13. **Automatic coffee machine**/Kaffeemaschine/machine
à café for Rancilio, 2000
14. **Public Internet Terminal** (free-standing version)/
Öffentliche Internetstation (freistehende Version)/
terminal Internet public (version sur pied) for Get2Net,
1999
15. **Chair**/Stuhl/chaise (study project), 2000

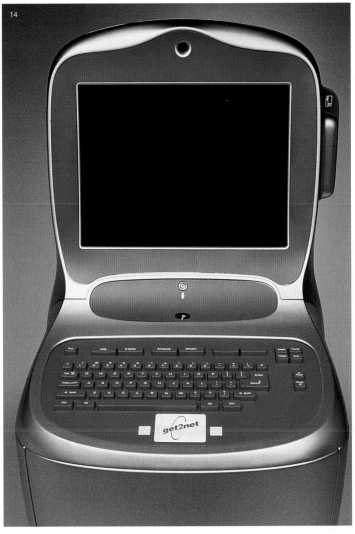

14

15

"The 21st century will be immaterial and human."

Philippe Starck

Philippe Starck, Agence Philippe Starck, 27, rue Pierre Poli, 92 130 Issy les Moulineaux, France
T +33 1 41 08 82 82 F +33 1 41 08 96 65 starck@starckdesign.com www.philippe-starck.com

»Das 21. Jahrhundert wird immateriell und menschlich sein.«

« Le 21ᵉ siècle sera immatériel et humain. »

1. **Low Cost Clock**/Wecker/réveil for Seven Eleven, 1998
2. ↓ **Gaoua** duffle bag on wheels/Reisetasche auf Rollen/
sac de voyage à roulettes for Samsonite, 2000

« Aujourd'hui, le problème est de ne pas produire plus afin de vendre plus. La question
fondamentale est celle du droit du produit
à exister. Le designer a le droit et le devoir
de s'interroger sur la légitimité du produit,
c'est là sa raison d'être. Selon la conclusion à
laquelle il parvient, l'une des choses les plus
positives qu'un designer puisse faire est de
refuser de faire quoi que ce soit. Ce n'est pas
toujours facile. Il devrait néanmoins refuser
quand l'objet existe déjà et fonctionne parfaitement bien. Le répéter simplement serait
un acte vénal, qui aurait de sérieuses conséquences, appauvrissant les richesses de la
terre, limitant et ternissant l'esprit des gens …
Nous devons remplacer la beauté, qui est un
concept culturel, par la bonté, un concept
humaniste. L'objet doit être de bonne qualité
et satisfaire un des paramètres modernes
essentiels, à savoir avoir la longévité … un
bon produit est un produit qui dure. »
PHILIPPE STARCK

3. ← **StarckNaked** seamless tubular garment with
integrated pantihose/nahtloses Schlauchkleid mit
integrierter Strumpfhose/collants intégrés à un tube,
sans coutures for Wolford, 1998
4. **Street Lamp**/Straßenlaterne/réverbère for JC Decaux,
1992

"Today, the problem is not to produce more so that you can sell
more. The fundamental question is
that of the product's right to exist.
And it is the designer's right and
duty, in the first place, to question
the legitimacy of the product, and
that is how he too comes to exist.
Depending on what answer he
comes up with, one of the most
positive things a designer can do
is to refuse to do anything. This
isn't always easy. He should refuse,
nevertheless, when the object already exists and functions perfectly
well. Simply to repeat it would be
a venal act, and one which has serious consequences, impoverishing
the wealth of the Earth, and impoverishing and dulling the minds
of people … We have to replace
beauty, which is a cultural concept,
with goodness, which is a humanist
concept. The object must be of good
quality, it must satisfy one of the
key modern parameters, which is
to be long-lived … A good product
is a product which lasts." PHILIPPE STARCK

»Heutzutage besteht die Aufgabe nicht darin, mehr zu produzieren, um mehr verkaufen
zu können. Die entscheidende Frage ist vielmehr die nach der Existenzberechtigung eines
Produkts. Die Designer haben das Recht und
die Pflicht, zunächst einmal die Legitimität
eines Produkts in Frage zu stellen, woraus
sich wiederum ihre eigene Daseinsberechti-
gung ergibt. Je nachdem, welche Antwort der
Designer darauf findet, ist eines der positiv-
sten Dinge, die er oder sie tun kann, sich zu
weigern, überhaupt etwas zu tun. Das ist allerdings nicht immer leicht. Trotzdem sollte ein
Designer einen Auftrag ablehnen, wenn das
Objekt bereits existiert und vollkommen zufriedenstellend funktioniert. Es einfach bloß
zu wiederholen, wäre ein korrupter Akt. Und
zudem einer, der ernsthafte Konsequenzen
hat, indem er die natürlichen Reichtümer der
Erde aussaugt und die Menschen geistig ver-
armen lässt und verdummt … Wir müssen das
kulturelle Konzept der Schönheit durch das
humanistische Konzept der Redlichkeit ersetzen. Ein Designobjekt muss von guter Qualität
sein, und es muss einem der wichtigsten modernen Parameter genügen, nämlich der Lang-
lebigkeit … Ein gutes Produkt ist ein Produkt,
das bestehen bleibt.« PHILIPPE STARCK

5. **TeddyBearBand** toy/Kuscheltier/nounours (Catalogue GOOD GOODS-La Redoute) for Moulin Roty, 1998
6. **Kayak Starck**/Kajak (Catalogue GOOD GOODS-La Redoute) for Rotomod, 1998

7. **Pedalcar**/Tretauto/voiture à pédales (limited edition)
for Vilac, 1998

		PHILIPPE STARCK	CLIENTS
BORN	1949	Neuilly, France	3 Suisses
STUDIED		self-taught	Alain Mikli
	1968	studied briefly at Ecole Nissim de Camondo, Paris	Alessi
PRACTICE	1968	established first company to produce inflatable objects	Aprilia
	1979	founded the Starck Product company	Baleri
	1993-96	worldwide artistic director for Thomson Consumer Electronics	Cassina
AWARDS	1982	VIA *Carte blanche* Award, Paris	Driade
	1986	Delta de Plaia à Barcelona	Fiam
	1988	Grand Prix National de la Création Industrielle, France	Flos
	1995	Primero Internacional de Diseno Barcelona	Fluocaril
	1997	Harvard Excellence in Design Award, USA	Hansgrohe
	1998	received a Commandeur dans l'Ordre des Arts et des Lettres from the French government	IDÉE
	1999	nominated Designer of the Year by the magazine *Architektur & Wohnen*, Hamburg	JCDecaux
	2000	Chevalier dans l'Ordre National de la Légion d'Honneur	Kartell
EXHIBITIONS	1988	*Avant Premiere*, Victoria & Albert Museum, London	Saba
	1989	*L'Art de Vivre*, Cooper-Hewitt National Design Museum, New York	Samsonite
	1990	*Les Années VIA*, Musée des Arts Décoratifs, Paris	Seven Eleven
	1994	*Philippe Starck*, Design Museum, London	Telefunken
	1995	*Mutant Materials in Contemporary Design*, Museum of Modern Art, New York	Thomson
			Vitra
			XO

8

9

10

11

12

13

8. **La Marie** chair/Stuhl/chaise for Kartell, 1998
9. **Magic Slab** light/Leuchte/luminaire for Flos, 2000
10. **Motó 6,5** motorcycle/Motorrad/motocyclette for Aprilia, 1995
11. **Low Cost Watch**/Armbanduhr/montre for Seven Eleven, 1998
12.-13. **Starck with Virgin theme CD** (Catalogue GOOD GOODS-La Redoute) for La Redoute, 1998

"Hands and machines are equal. Each works in its own way, each has its own beauty. The designer must find the right balance of human touch and mechanical structures."

Reiko Sudo

Reiko Sudo, c/o NUNO Corporation, B1F AXIS Bldg., 5-17-1 Roppongi, Minato-ku, Tokyo 106-0032, Japan
T +81 3 3582 7997 F +81 3 3589 3439 nuno@nuno.com www.nuno.com

»Hand und Maschine sind gleichwertig. Beide funktionieren auf ihre eigene Weise, beide haben ihre eigene Schönheit. Der Designer muss die richtige Balance zwischen menschlicher Note und mechanischer Konstruktion finden.«

« Les mains et les machines sont égales. Toutes deux fonctionnent à leur manière, toutes deux ont leur beauté. Le designer doit trouver le juste équilibre entre le doigté humain et les structures mécaniques. »

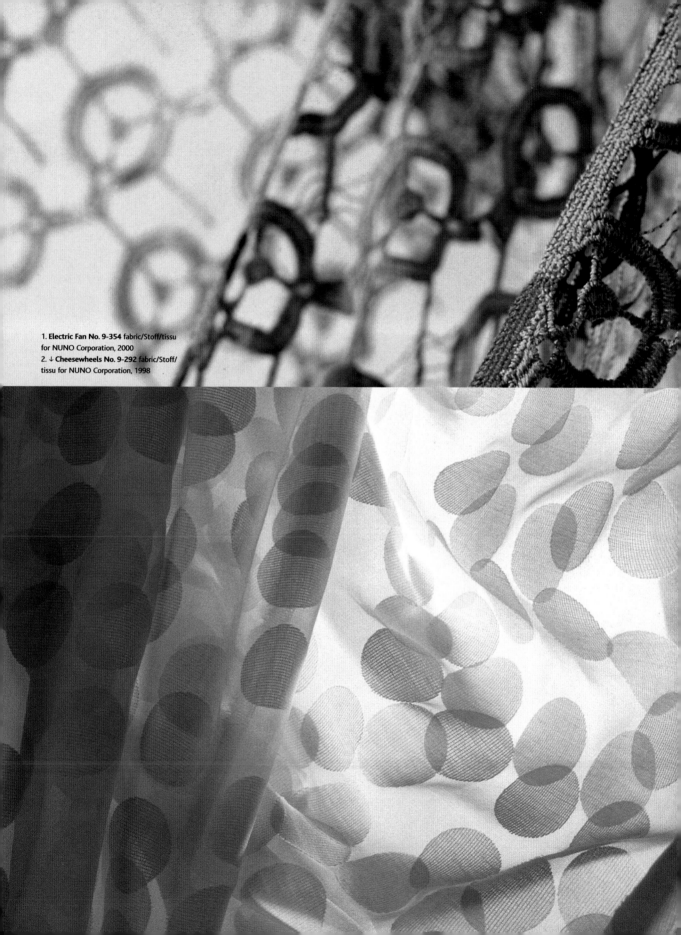

1. **Electric Fan No. 9-354** fabric/Stoff/tissu
for NUNO Corporation, 2000
2. ↓ **Cheesewheels No. 9-292** fabric/Stoff/
tissu for NUNO Corporation, 1998

»Design bringt Freude und Glanz ins Alltagsleben. Mein Ziel als Textildesigner ist es, Ge-
webe zu gestalten, die von unserer Epoche
(dem gegenwärtigen Moment) als schön angesehen werden. Wir bei Nuno glauben, dass
der ›Stoff‹ – eines der ältesten der Menschheit bekannten Materialien – den Menschen
der Gegenwart immer noch etwas zu sagen
hat, und deshalb ist unser Ziel die Produktion
›zeitgemäßer Stoffe‹. Während wir unsere
Inspiration aus der Jahrtausende alten Geschichte der Textil- und Webkultur beziehen,
lassen wir gleichzeitig neuen Ideen freien
Lauf und wenden die modernsten Technologien an in unserem Streben nach den aktuell-
sten kreativen Ausdrucksformen. In diesem
Sinne sind unsere Stoffe keineswegs typisch
für serienmäßig hergestellte Konsumartikel,
sondern in Qualität und Originalität näher
an traditionellen Webarbeiten oder Kunst-
werken. Da unsere Stoffe jedoch industriell
hergestellt werden – und keine handgefertig-
ten Einzelstücke sind – können wir gleichzeitig die Produktionskosten niedrig halten.
Diese Herangehensweise, mit der wir das
Beste aus beiden Welten herausholen, führt
zu einer Verflechtung von Schönheit und
Zweckmäßigkeit in unseren modernen Stof-
fen, welche ihnen die Vitalität verleiht, das
Leben von heute zu verschönern. Abschließend und als zukünftige Herausforderung
für Textildesigner möchte ich die Frage aufwerfen: Was wäre, wenn wir holographische
oder virtuelle ›meta-realistische‹ Bilder in
Textilien integrieren könnten?« REIKO SUDO

"Design brings pleasure and lustre
to everyday life. As a textile designer my aim is to create textiles
that our times (the present moment) will regard as beautiful. At
Nuno, we believe that 'fabric' –
one of the oldest materials known
to humankind – can still speak to
people in this day and age, and so
we set our sights on 'contemporary
fabric-making'. While deriving inspiration from the age-old history of
fabrics and weaving culture, we give
free rein to new ideas and employ
the latest technologies in the quest
for the most up-to-date creative expressions. In this sense, the fabrics
we make are not at all typical of
mass-produced commercial products; rather they are closer to
traditional weaving or artworks in
quality and originality. Yet at the
same time, since our fabrics are
industrially milled – not hand-
loomed one-off creations – we
can keep costs down. This best-of-
both-worlds approach makes for a
paradoxical weave of beauty and
utility that gives our contemporary
fabrics the vitality to grace today's
living. Finally, as a future challenge
for textile designers I raise the
question: what if we were able to
realise holographic or virtual 'meta-
realistic' imagery in textiles?"
REIKO SUDO

« Le design apporte du plaisir et de l'éclat à
la vie quotidienne. En tant que designer de
textiles, mon objectif est de créer des tissus
que notre époque (le moment présent) consi-
dérera beaux. Chez Nuno, nous pensons que
le tissu – l'un des matériaux les plus anciens
utilisés par l'homme – a encore des choses à
dire aujourd'hui et nous aspirons à être des
" tisserands contemporains ". Tout en puisant
notre inspiration dans l'histoire ancestrale du
tissu et de la culture du tissage, nous donnons
libre cours à de nouvelles idées et utilisons les
dernières technologies dans notre quête des
expressions créatives les plus actuelles. En
ce sens, nos tissus ne sont pas typiques de la
production de masse commerciale. Par leur
qualité et leur originalité, ils sont plus proches
des tissages traditionnels et artistiques. Toutefois, parce qu'ils sont réalisés industrielle-
ment – et ne sont pas des créations uniques
tissées à la main – nous pouvons réduire les
coûts. Cette démarche, qui consiste à prendre
le meilleur des deux mondes, débouche sur un
tissage beau et utile qui donne à nos tissus
modernes une vitalité parfaitement adaptée
à la vie actuelle. Enfin, en guise de défi aux
designers de textile, je soulève une question :
et si nous étions capables d'intégrer des
images " métaréalistes " virtuelles ou holo-
graphiques dans nos tissus ? » REIKO SUDO

3. **Kareha No. 9-304** fabric/Stoff/tissu for NUNO
Corporation, 1998 – co-designed with Yoko Ando
4. **Punchcard (Mongami) No. 9-303** fabric/Stoff/tissu
for NUNO Corporation, 1998 – co-designed with Zazu
Hiro Veno
5. **Sakuraso No. 9-288** fabric/Stoff/tissu for NUNO
Corporation, 1998 – co-design: Keiji Otani
6. **Hoshigaki No. 9-298** fabric/Stoff/tissu for NUNO
Corporation, 1998 – co-designed with RyoRo Sugiura

		REIKO SUDO	CLIENTS
BORN	1953	Niihari, Ibaragi, Japan	Nuno Corporation
STUDIED	1975-77	assistant to Prof. Hideho Tanaka at the Faculty of Textiles, Musashino Art University, Tokyo	
PRACTICE	1977-84	freelance textile designer working for (among others) Kanebo and Nishikawa	
	1984-89	textile designer, Nuno Corporation	
	1989-	director of Nuno Corporation; lecturer at the Faculty of Textiles, Musashino Art University	
AWARDS	1994	Roscoe Award, USA	
	2000	JID Award, Japan Interior Designer's Association	
EXHIBITIONS	1977	*Textile Exhibition*, Tokyo	
	1984	*Textiles Accessories*, Tokyo	
	1985	*Japan Creative*, Tokyo	
	1986	*Tokyo in Tokyo*, Minneapolis	
	1989	*Transfiguration*, Brussels	
	1990 & 91	*Color, Light, Surface*, Cooper-Hewitt National Design Museum, New York & Kyoto Industrial Center	
	1994	*2010 – Textiles and New Technology*, Crafts Council, London; *Japanese Design – A Survey Since 1950*, Philadelphia Museum of Art	
	1995	*Nuno – Japanese Textiles for the Body*, University of Oregon Museum of Art	
	1996	*Tokyo Creation Festival*, Tokyo; *Textile Magician*, Museum of Modern Art, Jerusalem; *Japanese Textile Design Exhibit*, Indira Ghandi National Centre for the Arts, India	
	1998	*Plastic Times – Plastic + Design*, Tel Aviv Museum of Art	
	1998-99	*Structure and Surface, Contemporary Japanese Textiles*, Museum of Modern Art, New York, The Saint Louis Art Museum of Art	
	2000	*Design World 2000*, Helsinki	

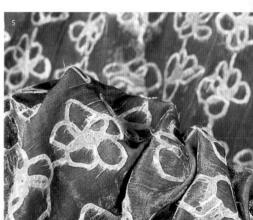

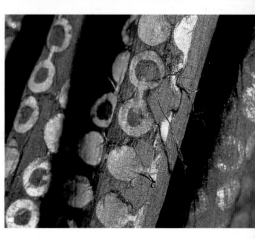

"I believe design is like poetry: absolute and precise with the minimal use of means employed to achieve the maximal result."

Ilkka Suppanen

Ilkka Suppanen, Studio Ilkka Suppanen, Punavuorenkatu 1A 7b, 00 120 Helsinki, Finland
T +358 9 622 78737 F +358 9 622 3093 info@suppanen.com www.suppanen.com

»Für mich ist Design wie Poesie: absolut und präzise mit einem minimalen Einsatz an Mitteln, um das maximale Resultat zu erzielen.«

« Pour moi, le design est comme la poésie : absolu et précis, utilisant le moins de moyens possible pour obtenir le meilleur effet. »

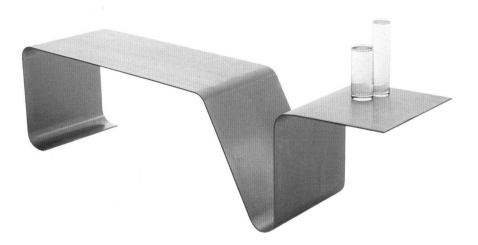

1. **Game-shelf**/Regal/étagère for Snowcrash, 1999
2. ↓ **Flying carpet** sofa/Sofa/canapé for Cappellini, 1998

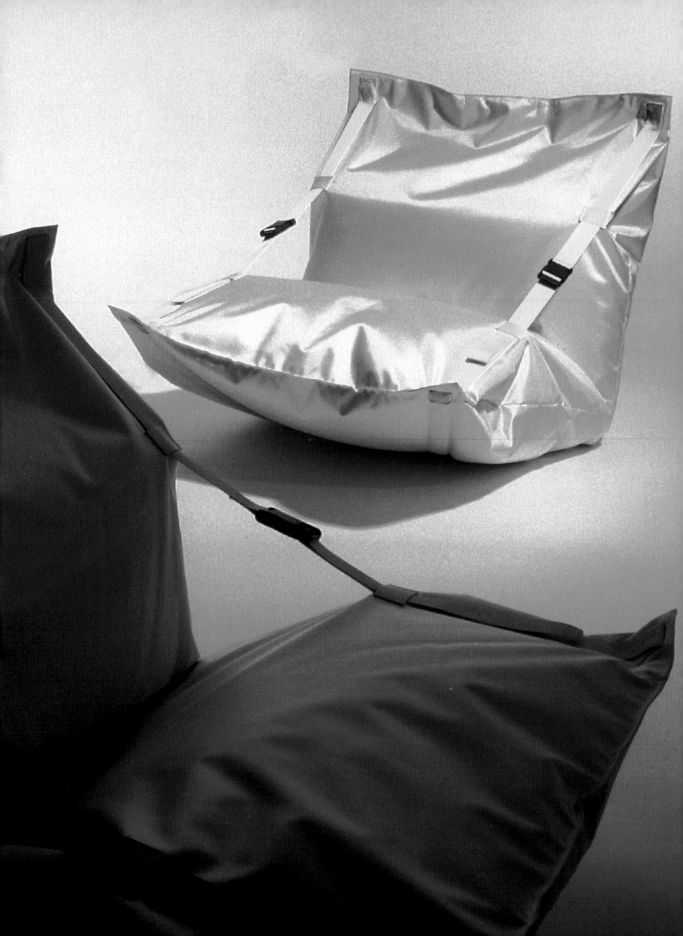

« La situation du design aujourd'hui est la même que celle de la psychologie au 19ème siècle : une pratique avec très peu de recul et de réputation. A l'époque, la psychologie n'était même pas considérée comme une science. Elle ne l'est devenue que grâce aux travaux d'avant-garde de " M. " Freud. Or, comme nous le savons, le 20e siècle tout entier a été celui de la psychologie. En tant que discipline, elle n'est devenue l'une des sciences les plus populaires et citées que grâce à la persévérance et la forte personnalité de Freud.

Comme la psychologie à ses débuts, le design est une pratique qui, contrairement à sa grande sœur l'architecture, n'est pas encore considérée comme scientifiquement importante. J'aimerais pouvoir prédire que le design connaîtra un avenir similaire à celui qu'a connu autrefois la psychologie et que lui aussi deviendra un jour une science respectée. Peut-être faut-il pour cela qu'un pionnier de la puissance et de la portée de Freud fasse l'unanimité. » ILKKA SUPPANEN

3. ← **Airbag** chair/Sessel/siège for Snowcrash, 1997 – co-designed with Pasi Kolhonen
4. **AV Rack** cabinet/Vitrinenschrank/armoire (self-production), 1998

"I believe the situation of design today is similar to that of psychology in the 19th century — a practice with very little history or reputation. Psychology was not even regarded as a science then. It only became such as a result of the pioneering work of 'Mr' Freud. And as we know, the whole of the 20th century was the century of psychology. As a discipline, it became one of the most popular and quoted sciences only because of the perseverance and strong personality of Freud.

Like psychology in its early days, design is a practice that is not yet seen as scientifically important. It is quite unlike its 'big brother', architecture. I wish I could predict that design will have a future similar to that which psychology once had and that it too will become a respected science. Perhaps this will only happen if something like the strength and vision of Freud is widely embraced." ILKKA SUPPANEN

»Ich glaube, das heutige Design befindet sich in einer ähnlichen Situation wie die Psychologie im 19. Jahrhundert — es ist eine Disziplin mit wenig Geschichte oder Ansehen. Damals wurde die Psychologie noch nicht einmal als Wissenschaft betrachtet. Das wurde sie erst dank der Pionierarbeit des ›Herrn Freud‹. Und wie wir wissen, war das gesamte 20. Jahrhundert das Jahrhundert der Psychologie. Die Psychologie wurde nur aufgrund der Beharrlichkeit und starken Persönlichkeit von Freud zu einer der populärsten und einflussreichsten Wissenschaftslehren.

Ebenso wie die Psychologie in ihren Anfangstagen ist Design eine Disziplin, die bislang nicht als wissenschaftlich relevant angesehen wird. Im Gegensatz zu seiner ›großen Schwester‹, der Architektur. Ich wünschte, ich könnte dem Design eine ähnliche Zukunft prophezeien, wie sie die Psychologie einst hatte, und dass es ebenfalls zu einer allgemein geachteten Wissenschaft werden wird. Vielleicht wird das nur eintreten, wenn so etwas wie die Stärke und Vision eines Freud allgemein Anerkennung erfährt.« ILKKA SUPPANEN

ILKKA SUPPANEN

BORN	1968	Kotka, Finland
STUDIED	1988	Faculty of Architecture, Helsinki University of Technology
	1989	University of Art and Design, Helsinki
	1992	Gerrit Rietveld Academy, Amsterdam
PRACTICE	1995	founded Studio Ilkka Suppanen
	1995-2000	taught design at the University of Art and Design, Helsinki
	1996	co-founded the Snowcrash design co-operative
	1998-99	research project in collaboration with Nokia Multimedia Terminals
	2000-	creative director of Snowcrash
AWARDS	1995	First Prize *Habitare* competition, Finland; winning entry, international *Textile for New Building* competition, Frankfurt/Main
	1998	nominated for Dedalus Prize, Bra, Italy; Young Designer of the Year, Germany
	2001	Young Designer of the Year, Finland
EXHIBITIONS	1992	the Fifth International Exhibition of Architecture, Venice
	1997	*Snowcrash*, Galleria Facsimile, Milan
	1998	*Modern Finnish Design*, Bart Center, New York
	1999	*New Scandinavian Design*, Stedelijk Museum, Amsterdam
	2001	*Work Spheres*, Museum of Modern Art, New York

CLIENTS

Artek
Cappellini
Castelli-Haworth
Kinnasand
Luhta
Nokia Multimedia Terminals
Proventus Design
Snowcrash
Saab
also self-production

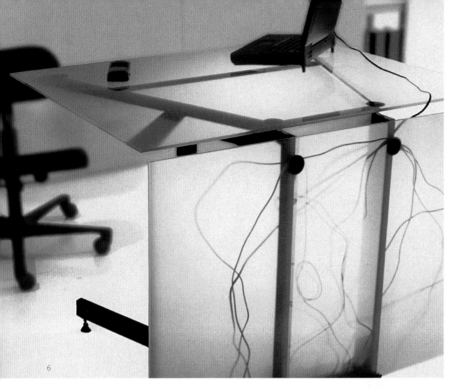

6

5. **Promotiva** office/Büro/bureau, Helsinki, 1997
6. **Luminet** office system/Büromöbel/système de bureau
for Luminet, 1996
7. **Nomad** chair/Sessel/siège (limited production –
self-production), 1997
8. **Roll-light** floor lamp/Stehlampe/lampadaire for
Snowcrash, 1997

7

8

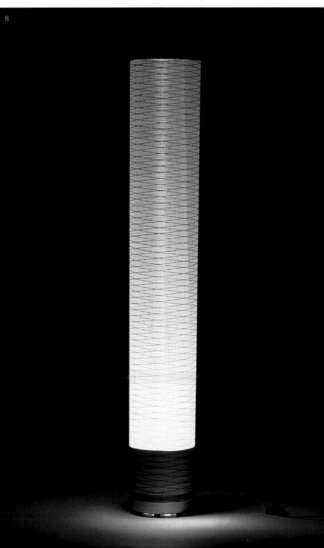

"Our work reflects society's need for individuality and expression in this age of uniform mass production."

Sydney 612

Sydney 612, 52, Regent Street, Paddington, Sydney, NSW 2021, Australia
T/F +61 2 933 17656 T/F +61 2 979 97195 ruth@ruthmcdermott.com a_tonka@hotmail.com

»Unsere Arbeit spiegelt das Bedürfnis der Gesellschaft nach Individualität und Ausdruck in diesem Zeitalter gleichförmiger Massenproduktion wider.«

« En ces temps de production de masse uniforme, notre travail reflète le besoin d'individualité et d'expression de la société. »

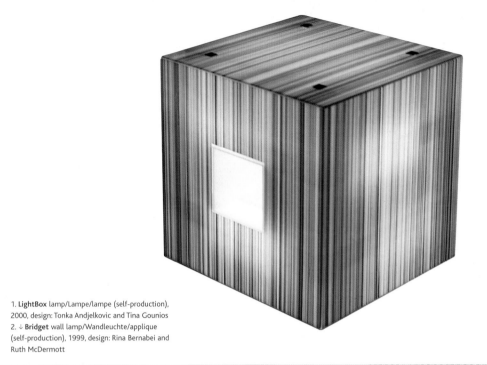

1. **LightBox** lamp/Lampe/lampe (self-production),
2000, design: Tonka Andjelkovic and Tina Gounios
2. ↓ **Bridget** wall lamp/Wandleuchte/applique
(self-production), 1999, design: Rina Bernabei and
Ruth McDermott

»Die vier unabhängigen Designgruppen, aus denen sich Sydney 612 zusammensetzt, haben das Anliegen, regionale Unterschiede anstelle der Einförmigkeit der Globalisierung zum Ausdruck zu bringen. Wir alle engagieren uns für ein Design der Zukunft, das unsere Umwelt bereichert anstatt sie zu verderben, und das einen Beitrag zum kulturellen Wohlergehen der Gesellschaft leistet. Unser Ziel ist es, schöne Objekte zu entwerfen, die Qualität und Integrität besitzen und andere Menschen dazu inspirieren, Design in ihr Alltagsleben zu integrieren. Als Designer beziehen wir unsere Inspiration aus Australiens kulturellem Schmelztiegel, Lebensstil und Umfeld. Wir haben die Vision, Australien einen festen Platz im internationalen Forum des Designs zu verschaffen, weil wir glauben, dass Design eine internationale Sprache ist, die unser Leben bereichert und von allen erlebt werden sollte. Unser Designkonzept besteht in einem langfristigen Ansatz, der die Menschen inspiriert, bildet und ihnen ein Gefühl von Glück vermittelt. Im Erforschen und Ausprobieren neuer Formen, Oberflächen und Materialien sind unsere Designlösungen durch die Fülle und Mannigfaltigkeit des urbanen Lebens am Rande des Pazifischen Ozeans beeinflusst. Unsere Arbeit zelebriert die kulturelle Interaktion zwischen Ost und West, die Grenzbereiche zwischen Kunsthandwerk und Massenproduktion und die Beziehung zwischen einer jungen Gesellschaft und einem uralten Land.« SYDNEY 612

"The four independent design groups that make up Sydney 612 are concerned with expressing regional difference rather than the sameness of globalization. We are all committed to a future design that enhances, rather than degrades, our environment and adds to the cultural well-being of society. Our aim is to create beautiful objects, which have quality and integrity and inspire others to incorporate design into their everyday lives. As designers, we draw on Australia's cultural melting pot, lifestyle and environment for inspiration. It is our vision to share and establish Australia in the international forum of design. We believe that design is an international language that enriches lives and should be experienced by all. The design direction that we follow is one of a long-term approach that inspires, educates and gives people a feeling of happiness. By investigating new forms, textures and uses of materials, our design solutions are influenced by the richness and diversity of urban life on the edge of the Pacific Ocean. Our work celebrates cultural interactions between east and west, the boundaries between craft and mass production and the relationship between a young society and an ancient land." SYDNEY 612

« Les quatre groupes de design indépendants qui constituent Sydney 612 cherchent à exprimer des différences régionales plutôt que l'uniformité de la mondialisation. Nous tenons tous à concevoir des créations qui respectent l'environnement au lieu de le dégrader et qui enrichissent le bien-être culturel de la société. Notre but est de créer de beaux objets, de qualité et intègres, qui incitent les gens à intégrer le design dans leur vie quotidienne. En tant que créateurs, nous puisons notre inspiration dans les modes de vie, la nature et le melting-pot australiens. Nous voulons partager notre vision et mettre l'Australie sur la carte mondiale du design. Nous considérons celui-ci comme un langage international qui enrichit les vies et devrait être vécu par tous. La voie que nous avons empruntée est une démarche à long terme qui inspire, éduque et donne aux gens une sensation de bonheur. Dans notre recherche de nouvelles formes, textures et matières nous nous laissons pénétrer par la richesse et la diversité de la vie urbaine de la côte du Pacifique. Notre travail célèbre les interactions culturelles entre l'est et l'ouest, les frontières entre l'artisanat et la production de masse, la relation entre une société jeune et une terre ancestrale. » SYDNEY 612

3. **Rei** wall lamp/Wandleuchte/applique (self-production), 1999, design: Rina Bernabei and Ruth McDermott
4. **Ariel** floor & table lamp/Steh- und Tischlampe/ lampadaire et lampe (self-production), 1999, design: Rina Bernabei and Ruth McDermott
5. **Odette** table lamp/Tischlampe/lampe (self-production), 1999, design: Rina Bernabei and Ruth McDermott

		SYDNEY 612	CLIENTS
FOUNDED	1999	Sydney, Australia – Sydney 612 is a liaison of four independent Australian design groups: Marc Schamburg (b. 1966) & Michael Alvisse (b. 1963); Michael Tyler (b. 1975); Rina Bernabei (b. 1968) & Ruth McDermott (b. 1957); Tonka Andjelkovic (b. 1968) & Tina Gounios (b. 1972)	NSW Department of Health Sydney Water Woodmark International also self-production
STUDIED		MARC SCHAMBURG	
	1987	BA Interior Design, Sydney College of Arts	
		MICHAEL ALVISSE	
	1985	BA Architecture, Western Australia Institute of Technology	
		MICHAEL TYLER	
	1999	diploma Interior Design, Sydney Institute of Technology	
		RINA BERNABEI	
	1989	BA Industrial Design, University of Technology, Sydney	
		RUTH MCDERMOTT	
	1979	diploma Industrial Design, Wellington Polytechnic	
		TONKA ANDJELKOVIC	
	1991	diploma Interior Design, Sydney Institute of Technology	
		TINA GOUNIOS	
	1993	BA Interior Design, University of Technology, Sydney	
AWARDS		R. MCDERMOTT & R. BERNABEI	
	1996	International Design Resource Award, Seattle	
	1998	Merit Award for Innovation, National Association for Women in Construction, Sydney	
EXHIBITIONS	1999	4 plus 1, Powerhouse Museum, Sydney	
	2000	Salone Satellite, Salone del Mobile, Milan; Designing Minds, Olympic Arts Festival, Sydney, Adelaide; Abitare Il Tempo – Beyond European Design, Verona	

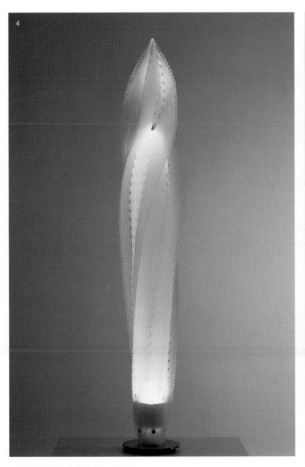

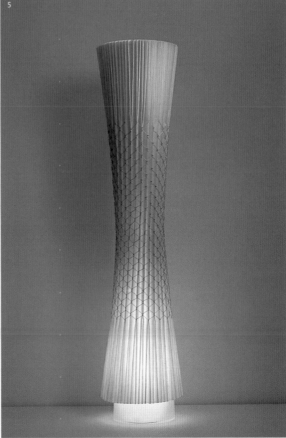

"I wonder if true inventions aren't always tied to an economy of the material and physical means used."

Martin Szekely

Martin Szekely, 39, Rue Hallé, 75 014 Paris, France
T +33 1 433 54132 F +33 1 453 85431 www.martinszekely.com

»Ich frage mich, ob echte Erfindungen nicht immer mit einer Ökonomie der Mittel bezüglich Material und Form verbunden sind.«

« Je me demande si toute invention authentique n'est pas toujours liée à une économie de moyens matériels et physiques. »

1. **La Brique à Fleurs Vallauris** flowerpot/Blumentopf/
pot de fleurs for Galerie Kreo, 1998
2. ↓ **Table 00 with bench**/Tisch mit Sitzbank/table avec
bancs for Galerie Kreo, 2000

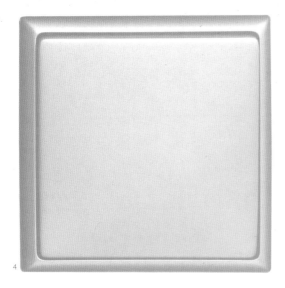

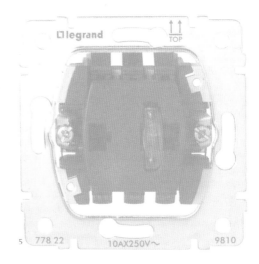

« Aujourd'hui mon travail m'apparaît comme une soustraction à l'expressionisme du dessin. C'est dans ma relation au design industriel et sa destination vers un public le plus large que cette notion s'est imposée. J'ai pour ambition un résultat économe qui ne soit même pas qualifiable de minimaliste. Un lieu commun. »
MARTIN SZEKELY

"Today, I see my work as detached from expressionism of the drawing. This idea grew out of my experience in industrial design which is directed at the broadest possible public. My aim is to achieve an economy in the result which can't even be defined as minimalist: a commonplace."
MARTIN SZEKELY

»Heute sehe ich meine Arbeit losgelöst von der Ausdruckskraft der Zeichnung. Diese Haltung entwickelte sich aus meiner Erfahrung mit Industriedesign, das sich an ein möglichst breites Publikum wendet. Mein Ziel ist es, schließlich einen Grad von Wirtschaftlichkeit zu erreichen, den man fast als minimalistisch bezeichnen könnte: ein Gemeingut.«
MARTIN SZEKELY

3. ← **Corolle** power pylons/Strommasten/pylônes électriques for Transel/EDF, 1994
4. **Tenara** light switch/Lichtschalter/interrupteur for Legrand, CMF design by Castelli, 1996-2000
5. **Creo** light switch (inside)/Lichtschalter (Innenansicht)/ interrupteur (intérieur) for Legrand, 1996-2000, co-designed with S. Thirouin
6. **Creo-Good Life** lamp switch/Lichtschalter/interrupteur for Legrand, CMF design by Castelli, 1996-2000
7. **Structura** light switch/Lichtschalter/interrupteur for Legrand, CMF design by Castelli, 1996-2000

MARTIN SZEKELY			CLIENTS
BORN	1956	Paris, France	Bernardaud
STUDIED	1972-74	Ecole Estienne, Paris	Christofle
	1977	Ecole Boulle, Paris	Delvaux
PRACTICE	1978	began working as a freelance industrial designer	Dom Pérignon
	1992	designed the podium for the XVI Winter Olympic Games, Albertville, France	European Neurological Society
	1996-	design consultant for Legrand Group	Hour Lavigne
AWARDS	1984	prize winner, Bourse Castelli	Hermès
	1987	Designer of the Year, Salon du Meuble, Paris; Grand Prix de la Critique de la Presse, France	JCDecaux
	1994	prize winner, International Design Competition, Frankfurt/Main	Kreo
EXHIBITIONS	1985	*PI Collection*, Neotu gallery, Paris	Legrand
	1988	*MDF*, Fondation Cartier, Paris; *Avant Premier – Contemporary French Furniture*, Victoria & Albert Museum, London	Neotu
			Perrier
	1990	*Les Anneés Via*, Musée des Arts Décoratifs, Paris	Saint Louis
	1991	*Initiales et Autres Meubles*, Neotu gallery, New York	SNCF
	1992	*Manifeste*, Centre Georges Pompidou, Paris	Swarovski
	1993	solo exhibition, CAPC Museum, Bordeaux	Terreal-Groupe Sainte-Gobain
	1995	travelling solo exhibition, originating in Barcelona	Transel-Groupe bouygues
	1996	solo exhibition, Centre Georges Pompidou, Paris	
	1998	*Premises*, Guggenheim Museum, New York; solo exhibition, Grand-Horun, Belgium	
	1999	*l'Armoire*, Purple Institute, Paris	
	2000	*Un Banquet*, Kreo Gallery, Paris	

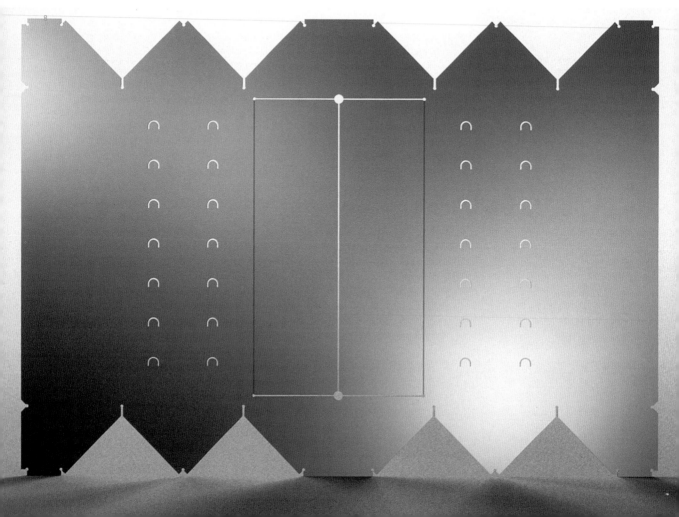

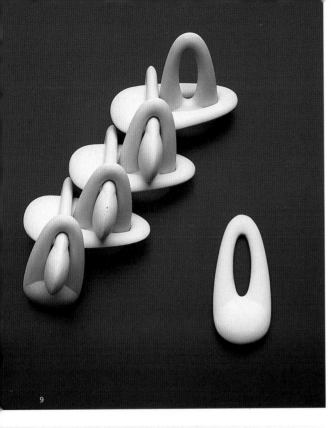

9

11

8. & 10. **L'Armoire** cabinet/Schrank/armoire for Galerie Kreo, 1999
9. **Reine de Saba** jewellery (chain and bracelet), resin model/Schmuck (Kette und Armreif), Harzmodell/ bijouterie (chaîne et bracelet), modèle en résine for Hermès, 1996
11. **Cork** chair/Korkstuhl/chaise en liège for Galerie Kreo, 2000

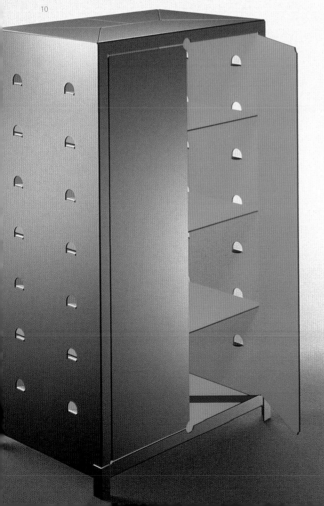

10

"The best products come from design thinking that is interwoven with your long-term business strategy."

Tangerine

Tangerine Product Direction and Design, 8, Baden Place, Crosby Row, London SE1 1YW, England
T +44 20 7357 0966 F +33 20 7357 0784 martin@tangerine.net www.tangerine.net

»Die besten Produkte entstehen aus einem gestalterischen Denken, das mit einer langfristigen Unternehmensstrategie verflochten ist.«

« Les meilleurs produits sont issus d'une pensée de design conjuguée à une stratégie commerciale à long terme. »

1. **Jasperware** experimental design/experimentelles Design/design expérimentel for Waterford Wedgwood, 1997
2. ↓ **Club World seat-bed**/Stuhl & Bett/fauteuil & lit for British Airways, 2000

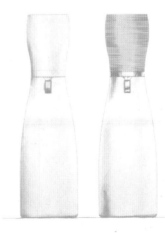

« En ce début de 21ème siècle, il se passe des choses vraiment positives dans le domaine des marques et du design multimédia. Les compagnies commencent à comprendre que leur marque a une valeur immense, exprimant bien plus que l'identité d'une entreprise ; dans de nombreux cas, elle caractérise même l'attitude et le comportement de la compagnie. La croissance du secteur du multimédia connectera les consommateurs aux compagnies de manières riches et variées, permettant des formes de dialogue plus diverses et étendues. J'ai bon espoir qu'à l'avenir les compagnies prendront conscience que les consommateurs ne sont jamais dupes très longtemps (j'en ai rencontré de nombreux exemples récemment). Les meilleurs produits ne viennent pas de plannings basés sur la production des concurrents ni de gadgets pondus par les départements de recherche et développement. On conçoit les meilleurs produits en observant les gens et en apprenant comment ils vivent, pensent, se comportent, etc ... Les designers peuvent ensuite conjuguer leur philosophie, les marques et les produits avec les valeurs de base de l'utilisateur afin de définir l'esprit et la substance d'articles nouveaux et meilleurs. » TANGERINE

3. ← **Activ** walking frame (prototype)/Gehhilfe (Prototyp)/ déambulateur (prototype), 1998 (co-designed with Benchmark modelmaking for Central St Martin's Design for Ability)

4.-6. **Oil candle** concepts/Entwürfe für Kerzenhalter/ concepts de bougie à l'huile for Waterford Wedgwood, 1998

"Really positive things are happening at the start of the 21st century in the areas of brand and multi-media design. Companies have begun to recognise that their brands are of tremendous value, expressing far more than just the identity of a company; in many cases even typifying the attitude and behaviour of the company. The surge of growth in the multi-media sector will connect customers to companies in rich and varied ways, enabling more diverse and extended forms of dialogue to take place.
The hope I have for the future (and we have encountered many examples of it recently) is that companies will wake up to the fact that the customer cannot be fooled for too long. The best products do not come from planning based on the benchmarking of competitors, or from widgets spun out of R&D departments. The best products come from observing people and learning about how they live, think, behave etc. Designers can then bring business ethos, brand values and product values together with core values from the life of the user, to define the spirit and substance of new and better products." TANGERINE

»Zu Beginn des 21. Jahrhunderts ereignen sich wirklich positive Dinge in den Bereichen Marken- und Multimedia-Design. Unternehmen erkennen, dass ihre Markenartikel von enormem Wert sind, da sie weit mehr als nur die Firmenidentität ausdrücken und in einigen Fällen sogar Einstellung und Verhalten des Unternehmens verkörpern. Der Wachstumsschub auf dem Multimedia-Sektor wird auf fruchtbare und vielfältige Weise Kunden mit Unternehmen in Verbindung bringen und damit mannigfaltigere und erweiterte Formen des Dialogs ermöglichen. Die Hoffnung, die ich für die Zukunft hege (und für die wir in letzter Zeit viele Beispiele erlebt haben), ist die, dass Firmen sich der Tatsache bewusst werden, dass man die Kunden nicht allzu lange für dumm verkaufen kann. Die besten Produkte entstehen nicht aus einer auf Wettbewerbsorientierung basierenden Planung oder aus irgendwelchen Spielereien, die sich die Forschungs- und Entwicklungsabteilungen ausgedacht haben. Die besten Produkte sind vielmehr darauf zurückzuführen, dass man die Menschen beobachtet und erfährt, wie sie leben, denken und handeln. Dann nämlich können die Designer Unternehmensethos, Marken- und Produktwerte mit den essentiellen Werten aus dem Leben des Benutzers kombinieren, um Geist und Gehalt neuer und besserer Produkte zu definieren.« TANGERINE

7. **Chaplet** e/web videophone/Internet-Videophone/
vidéophone électronique for Chaplet Information Systems,
1997

TANGERINE

FOUNDED	1989	London by Martin Darbyshire (b. 1961 Preston, Lancashire) and Clive Grinyer (who left Tangerine in 1993)
STUDIED		MARTIN DARBYSHIRE
	1983	BA (Hons) Product Design, Central St Martin's College of Art and Design, London
AWARDS	1987	Appliance Manufacturers USA Award
	1994	Shinanogawa Award, Technopolis, Japan
	1995 & 2001	Good Design Award, Chicago Athenaeum
	1995 & 2000	iF Design Award, Hanover
	1995	Presidents Award, Korea
	1997 & 2000	*I. D. Magazine Annual Design Review* Award, New York
	2000	D&AD Award Silver nomination, London; International CES Award
EXHIBITIONS		
	1990, 92, 94, 96, 97 & 98	The Design Museum, London
	1998	*High Definition*, British Council, Hong Kong
	1998	*Britain Online*, China
	1999	Glasgow Art Fair, Glasgow; *Creative Britain*, Stilwerk, Berlin
	2000	*Ideal Home* Exhibition, London; Expo 2000, Hanover

CLIENTS

Acco
Alcatel
Apple Computer
Bell Northern Research
British Airways
Cambridge Systems
DecaView
ElanVital
Fostex
GCS
Hitachi
Ideal Standard
LG Electronics
Maxon Cellular
Novamedix
Pace Micro Technology
Procter & Gamble
Samsung
Surgicraft
Unilever
Virgin Our Price
Waterford Wedgwood

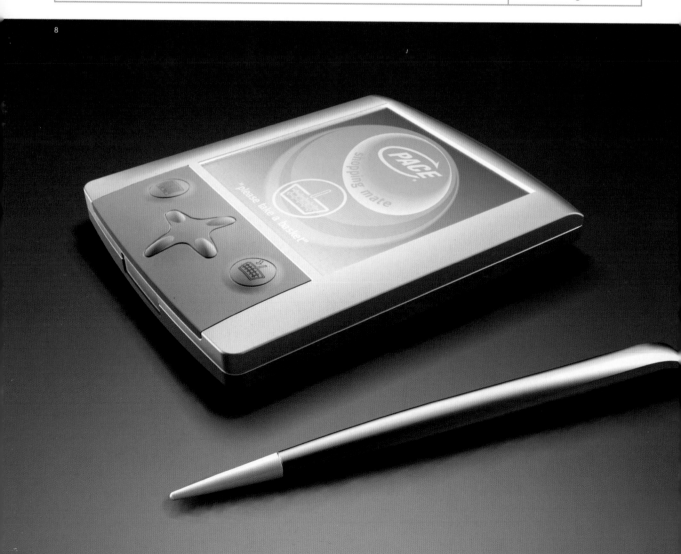

9

10

12

8. **Pace** home shopping tablet/Homeshopping-Schreib-tafel/terminal de commandes à domicile for Pace Micro Technology, 2000
9. **Blink** concept digital camera/Digitalkamera (Entwurf)/appareil photo numérique (concept) for Shinanogawa Technopolis, 1994
10. **Home facsimile** (concept)/Faxgerät (Entwurf)/télécopieur (concept), 1990
11. **Cutlery** (design concept)/Besteck (Entwurf)/couverts (concept) 1999
12. **GCS DECT** phone (concept)/Telefon (Entwurf)/téléphone (concept) for Global Cellular Systems, 1997

"The Milan system is our power:
involved in fashion currents, design
and architecture, we are ready
every day to renew our creativity."

Matteo Thun

Mattheo Thun, Studio Thun, Via Appiani 9, 20 121 Milan, Italy
T +39 02 655 691 202 F +39 02 657 0646 info@matteothun.com www.matteothun.com

»Das Mailand-System ist unsere Macht:
Aktiv beteiligt an Modeströmungen, Design und Architektur sind wir jeden Tag
bereit, unsere Kreativität zu erneuern.«

« Le système milanais fait notre force :
avec un pied dans les courants de la
mode, du design et de l'architecture,
nous sommes prêts chaque jour à
renouveler notre créativité. »

1. **A-Roma** bowls/Schalen/bols for Koziol, 1999
2. ↓ **Supersassi** sofa/Sofa/canapé for Rossi di Albizzate, 2000

»In meinem Zugang zu Design geht es um einfache Verfahren, einfache Materialien, schnelles Erkennen des Designobjekts, schnelle Fertigungstechnik und natürlich einen zügigen Gestaltungsprozess, der auf praktischen Erfahrungen in einer Vielzahl von Disziplinen beruht ... sowie, last but not least, eine ästhetische und materielle Dauerhaftigkeit. Als ein in Mailand lebender Architekt arbeite ich – im Einklang mit den Traditionen unserer Lehrer – gleichzeitig in kleinen und in großen Dimensionen: ›Vom Löffel zur Stadt‹ (Ernesto Rogers, Charta von 1952, Athen). Ohne Interaktion und wechselseitige Befruchtung mit dem großen Maßstab kann es im kleinen Maßstab keine Fortschritte geben und natürlich umgekehrt ... Ich ziehe die Heterogenität der Homogenität vor, weil es nicht nur die eine ›beste Methode‹ gibt, mit der das beste Ergebnis zu erzielen ist.« MATTEO THUN

"My approach to design involves simple processes, simple materials, fast recognition of the designed object, a fast manufacturing process and naturally a fast design process, drawing on a multiplicity of disciplinary experiences ... and last but not least, aesthetic and material durability. As an architect living in Milan, I am engaged simultaneously – in line with the traditions of our teachers – with the small and large scale: 'From the spoon to the city' (Ernesto Rogers, Charter of 1952, Athens). Without interaction and cross-fertilization with the large scale, there can be no advance in the small scale, and of course vice versa ... I prefer heterogeneity to homogeneity because there is not only one discernible 'best way' to obtain the best results." MATTEO THUN

« Ma démarche consiste à utiliser des procédés simples, des matériaux simples, une reconnaissance rapide de l'objet de design, des processus de fabrication rapides ainsi que, naturellement, un processus de design rapide, puisant dans une multiplicité d'expériences disciplinaires ... et enfin, le plus important, une longévité esthétique et physique. En tant qu'architecte vivant à Milan, je travaille simultanément – conformément à la tradition de nos maîtres – sur la grande et la petite échelle : " de la cuillère à la cité " (Ernesto Rogers, Charte de 1952, Athènes). Sans interaction et hybridation avec la grande échelle, il ne peut y avoir de progrès de la petite échelle, et, bien sûr, vice versa ... Je préfère l'hétérogénéité à l'homogénéité car il n'existe pas qu'un seul " meilleur moyen " discernable d'obtenir les meilleurs résultats. » MATTEO THUN

3. **Balance** cutlery/Besteck/couverts for WMF, 1993
4. **Calore** cups/Tassen/tasses for Stil Lavazza, 1999
5. **Sphera** table lamp/Tischlampe/lampe for Leucos, 2000

MATTEO THUN		CLIENTS
BORN	1952 Bolzano, Italy	AEG
STUDIED	1975 PhD Architecture, University of Florence, Italy	Alessi
PRACTICE	1981 co-founded Sottsass Associati and Memphis Design Group (with Ettore Sottsass)	Allia
	1983-96 Professor of Design, Hochschule für angewandte Kunst, Vienna	Bulgari
	1984 founded Studio Thun, Milan	Campari
AWARDS		Flos
	1987, 89 & 91 Compasso d'Oro, Milan	Franz Wittmann
	1987 *Design of the Year*, Austria	Illy
	1988 *Design of the Year*, Japan	Kartell
	1988, 89 & 96 iF Design Award, Hanover	Keramag
	1989, 90 (two) & 96 Roter Punkt Award, Design Zentrum Nordrhein-Westfalen, Essen	Koziol
EXHIBITIONS	1988 *Castelli in Fiore*, Milan	Lavazza
	1989 *Think Big*, Milan	Leucos
	1994 *Noname*, Salone del Mobile, Milan	MartinStoll
	1996 *Terre Cotte*, Milan	Memphis
	2000 *Essere Benessere*, Milan	Omega
		Pozzi Ginori
		Rosenthal
		Rossi di Albizzate
		Silhouette
		Tiffany
		United Office
		Vorwerk
		Wittmann
		WMF
		Zumtobel

"An open, well-informed mind is the best tool in the box."

TKO

TKO Design, 37, Stukeley Street, London WC2B 5LT, England
T +44 20 7404 2404 F +33 20 7404 2405 mail@tkodesign.co.uk www.tkodesign.co.uk

»Ein offener, wohl informierter Geist ist das beste Werkzeug.«

« Un esprit ouvert et bien informé est le meilleur des outils. »

1. **Millennium Diamond Oyster** diamond container/
Schmuckschatulle/écrin pour diamants for De Beers, 1999
2. ↓ **FM800** foetal & maternal monitor/Ultraschallgerät
zur Schwangerschaftskontrolle/moniteur fœtal et maternel
for Oxford Instruments Medical Systems Division, 1999

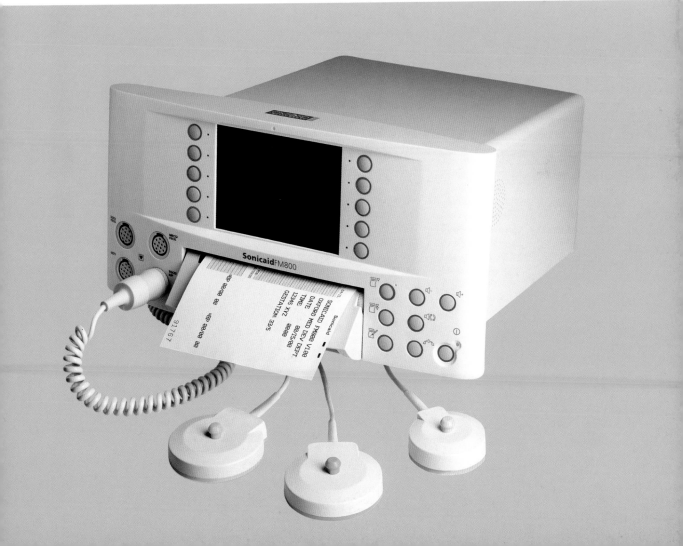

»Die aufregende Fragmentierung der Konsumgütermärkte und explosive Entwicklung in digitaler Technologie haben in beinahe gleichem Maße Chancen und Enttäuschungen mit sich gebracht – und dabei tiefe Schrammen in der industriellen Landschaft sowie viel Unsicherheit und Unschlüssigkeit in vorher erfolgsgewohnten Betrieben hinterlassen. Die spürbare Verlagerung vom Besitz von Produkten hin zum Erleben von Dienstleistungen bedeutet, dass die Kreativität der Designer als ein immer wertvolleres Gut Anerkennung finden wird. Der Kern guten gestalterischen Denkens ermutigt uns, neue Möglichkeiten für die Lösung realer Probleme und die Ausschöpfung echter Potentiale zu schaffen.« TKO

"The exciting fragmentation of consumer markets and radical explosion in digital technology has delivered opportunities and disappointment in almost equal measure – leaving deep scars on the manufacturing landscape and much uncertainty and hesitation within previously confident companies. The perceptible shift from owning products to experiencing services means designers' creativity will be recognised as an ever more valuable commodity – the core of good design thinking encourages us to create new opportunities, solve real problems and fulfil true potential." TKO

« L'excitante fragmentation des marchés de consommateurs et l'explosion radicale de la technologie numérique ont débouché sur autant de nouvelles possibilités que de déceptions, laissant de profondes cicatrices dans le paysage industriel et beaucoup d'incertitudes et d'hésitations au sein d'entreprises qui, auparavant, ne doutaient de rien. Ce mouvement perceptible entre le fait de posséder des produits et de recevoir un service signifie que la créativité des designers sera reconnue comme un bien encore plus précieux – l'essence de la philosophie du bon design nous encourage à créer de nouvelles opportunités, à résoudre de vrais problèmes et à réaliser son véritable potentiel. » TKO

3. **One Touch Easy DB** mobile phone/Handy/téléphone portable for Alcatel Telecom, 1999
4. **Titan** washing machine/Waschmaschine/machine à laver for Monotub Industries, 1999-2000
5. **Laptop computer** (prototype)/Laptop (Prototyp)/ordinateur portable (prototype) for NEC, 1997-98

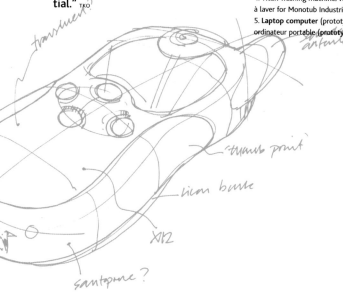

		TKO	**CLIENTS**
FOUNDED	1990	by Andy Davey (b. 1962 Eton, Berkshire) and Annie Gardener (b. 1961 Cuckfield, Sussex)	Alcatel
STUDIED		ANDY DAVEY	BayGen
	1984	BA Industrial Design, West Sussex College of Art and Design	Canon
	1986	MA Industrial Design, Royal College of Art, London	Daiko Electric
		ANNIE GARDENER	De Beers
	1983	BA Design History, Brighton Polytechnic	Expedo & Co.
	1985	MA Design History, Royal College of Art, London	Hasbro
AWARDS	1989	Award for *Most Outstanding British Product for the Working Environment*, D&AD, London	Honda
	1991	Award for *Most Outstanding Product for the Home*, D&AD, London; Grand Prize & Chairman's Prize, Ministry for International Trade & Industry (MITI), Japan	Jetta Company
			LEC
	1993	Award for *Most Outstanding Product for Health and Leisure*, D&AD, London	LMP
	1996	Best of Category, *I. D. Magazine Annual Design Review* Award, New York; Designer of the Year and Best Product, BBC Design Awards, London	Mars
			Monotub Industries
	1998	Design Distinction – Concepts, *I. D. Magazine Annual Design Review* Award, New York	NEC
	1999	Roter Punkt Award, Design Zentrum Nordrhein-Westfalen, Germany; G-Mark/Good Design Award, JIDPO, Tokyo	Oxford Instruments
			Procter & Gamble
EXHIBITIONS	1988	*Design It Again*, Design Council, London	Sanyo
	1989	*Leading Edge*, AXIS Gallery, Tokyo	Sekisui Corporation
	1991-92	*British by Design*, Design Council, London	Seiko
	1993	*British Design – Catalyst for Commercial Success*, British Council, Singapore	Sony
	1994	*Designed in One, Made in the Other – New Products of Collaboration Between Britain and Japan*, Design Museum, London	
	1995	*Thinktech!*, Design Museum, London	
	1996	*Design of the Times*, Royal College of Art, London	
	1997	*Shiny & New – Contemporary British Design in Metal*, British Council, San Francisco	
	1998	Powerhouse UK, London	
	2000	*Creative Britain*, Stilwerk, Berlin	

4

5

"Pensa globalmente, actua localmente –
Think globally, act locally."

Kazuhiko Tomita

Kazuhiko Tomita, 17-2 Uzumachi, Ishaya-ci, Nagasaki 8 540 061, Japan
T/F (Japan) +81 957 242 372 T (Italy) +39 333 590 462 F (Italy) +39 0429 2866 2.5-d.tomit@k.email.ne.jp

»Pensa globalmente, actua localmente –
global denken, lokal handeln.«

« Pensa globalmente, actua localmente –
Pense mondialement, agis localement. »

1. **Ciacapo** cast iron teapot/Teekanne aus Gusseisen/
théière en fonte for Covo, 2000
2. ↓ **Morode** cutlery/Besteck/couverts for Covo, 2000

3

»Ich versuche höchste Designqualität durch den Einsatz kunsthandwerklicher Fertigkeiten und lokaler Materialien zu erreichen. Dabei berücksichtige ich gleichzeitig die Anforderungen des globalen Markts und die ›Zeitlosigkeit der Zeit‹. Mein Interesse gilt röhrenartigen Formen – ein flaches Stück Papier lässt sich leicht zu einer Röhre rollen, die man umbiegen, schneiden, falten und gestalten kann. Die Japaner haben es immer schon verstanden, aus flachen Elementen kunstvolle Objekte zu arbeiten, indem sie sich die Flexibilität der ebenen Fläche zu Nutze machen. Das unterscheidet sich stark von der westlichen Welt, wo das Gestalten von Formen auf der Behandlung von Masse basiert. Einige Experten behaupten, die vierte Dimension liege zwischen der zweiten und der dritten, weshalb ich den Begriff ›2,5-dimensionales Design‹ auf mein Gestaltungskonzept anwende.
Gutes Design sollte eine Verbindung herstellen zwischen einfachen, innovativen Ideen und Technologie, handwerklichem Geschick, kulturellem Hintergrund, guter und angemessener Qualität, zufriedenstellender und adäquater Funktionalität sowie vernünftigem Preis. Obgleich ich immer darauf bedacht bin, etwas ›Zeitloses‹ zu schaffen, hört das gute moderne Design niemals auf, sich zu verändern. Unser Alltag lässt sich zwar durch gutes Design beeinflussen, aber Verbesserungen unseres täglichen Lebens können nur durch motivierte und positive Benutzer erreicht werden. Designer können unmöglich allen Leuten sagen, wie sie ihr Leben durch Design verbessern sollen – einige Benutzer müssen zuerst einmal lernen, den Wert von Design zu erkennen.«
KAZUHIKO TOMITA

"I try to achieve maximum design quality by applying fine hand-craft skills and local materials, while taking into consideration global market requirements and the 'timelessness of time'. I am interested in tubular forms – the flat plane of a piece of paper can be easily rolled into a tube that can be bent, cut, folded and transformed. The Japanese have always been good at elaborating objects from flat elements by utilizing the flexibility of the plane. This is quite different from the West, where the shaping of forms is based on the manipulation of mass. Some authorities maintain that the fourth dimension exists between the second and third, therefore, I apply the term '2.5-dimensional design' to describe my concept of design.
Good design should combine simple new ideas with technology, fine skills, cultural background, satisfying and appropriate quality, sufficient function and reasonable cost. I always intend to create something 'timeless', even though contemporary good design never stops changing. Everyday life can be influenced by good design but improvements in daily life can only be achieved by self-motivated and positive users. It is impossible for designers to tell everybody to make life even better with design – some users need first to be educated to appreciate design." KAZUHIKO TOMITA

« J'essaie d'obtenir la meilleure qualité possible en utilisant de hautes compétences artisanales et des matières locales tout en tenant compte des exigences du marché mondial et de " l'intemporalité du temps ". Je m'intéresse aux formes tubulaires. La surface plane d'une feuille de papier peut facilement se rouler en un tube qui peut être courbé, plié, coupé et transformé. Les Japonais ont toujours excellé dans l'art de façonner des objets à partir d'éléments plats en utilisant la flexibilité du plan. C'est différent en Occident, où le modelage des formes repose sur la manipulation de la masse. Certains affirment que la quatrième dimension se situe quelque part entre la deuxième et la troisième. Pour décrire ma conception du design, j'utilise donc le terme " design en 2,5 dimensions ".
Bon design est l'accomplissement créatif qui associe de nouvelles idées simples à la technologie, un grand savoir-faire, des références culturelles, une qualité satisfaisante et appropriée, une fonction suffisante et un prix raisonnable. Je cherche toujours à créer quelque chose " d'intemporel " mais le bon design contemporain n'arrête pas de changer. La vie quotidienne peut être influencée par le bon design mais elle ne peut être améliorée que par des utilisateurs motivés et positifs. Il est impossible aux designers de dire aux autres comment améliorer leur vie grâce aux design – les utilisateurs doivent vent d'abord avoir la mentalité nécessaire pour l'apprécier. »
KAZUHIKO TOMITA

3. **Tottotto** teapot/Teekanne/théière for Laboratorio Pesaro, 1996-97
4. **Atabow** stoneware dish/Steinzeug-Schale/plat en grès for Laboratorio Pesaro, 1996-98
5. **Morode** tableware/Geschirr/vaisselle for Covo, 1997-99

4

	KAZUHIKO TOMITA		**CLIENTS**
BORN	1965	Nagasaki, Japan	Covo
STUDIED	1989	B.Eng. Industrial Design, Chiba University, Japan	Laboratorio Pesaro
	1992	MA Furniture Design, Royal College of Art, London	Tottotto
PRACTICE	1993	established 2.5-Dimensional Design; produced stone bowls with Alessandro Mendini and Ettore Sottsass	Vittorio Bonacina
	2000-	Art Director for Covo, Rome	
AWARDS	1989	Judge's Prize, International *Design Eye '89*, competition, Nagoya	
	1990	Cassina Scholarship & British Council Grant to study at the Royal College of Art, London	
	1991	First Prize *Architectural Future of Stainless Steel* competition, London	
	1992	Marchette Award, Royal College of Art, London	
	1997	Roter Punkt Award, Design Zentrum Nordrhein-Westfalen, Essen; Asahi Modern Craft Award, Osaka; *Honourable Citizen Prize*, Verona	
	1998	Judge's Prize, International Ceramic Exhibition, Mino; G-Mark/Good Design Award, JIDPO, Tokyo	
	1999 & 2001	four Design Plus Awards, Frankfurt/Main	
EXHIBITIONS	1995	*Due Nagasakini*, Nagasaki	
	1996	*ViveRattan* group show, Milan	
	1997	*Broecke's Dozen*, Royal College of Art, London	
	1999	*2.5-dimensional design*, solo exhibition, Ozone Gallery, Tokyo	

5

"Never over-design a product. The form will be dictated by its function and the way it is made."

Arnout Visser

Arnout Visser, Alexanderstraat 31-33, 6812 BC Arnhem, The Netherlands
T +31 26 442 9046 F +31 26 351 4812 arnout.visser@planet.nl

»Man sollte ein Produkt niemals über-designen. Die Form eines Produkts wird von seiner Funktion und Produktions-methode diktiert.«

« Il ne faut jamais " sur-dessiner " un pro-duit. Sa forme doit être dictée par sa fonction et la façon dont il est conçu. »

1. **Archimedes** letterscale/Briefwaage/pèse-lettres
for DMD, 1990
2. ↓ **Glassdrop** floor tiles/Bodenfliesen/dalles pour le
sol for DMD, 1997 – co-designed with Erik Jan Kwakkel

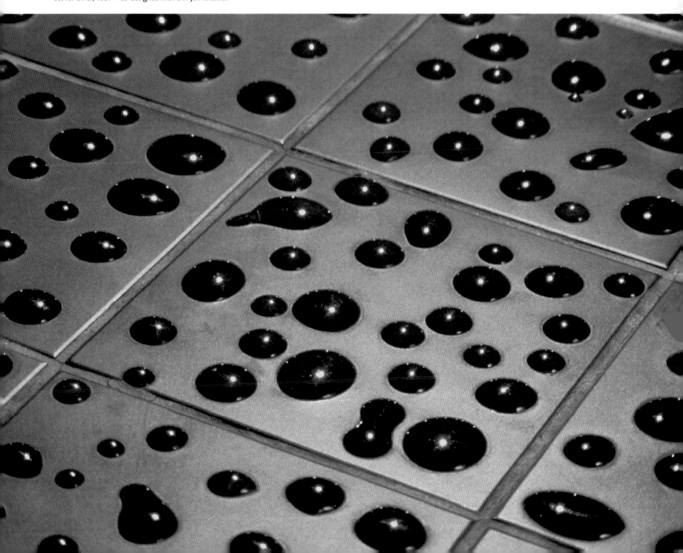

« A l'heure actuelle, la production de masse contrôle complètement le marché alors que nous (les consommateurs) cherchons des produits uniques. La beauté du produit à elle seule ne suffit pas, nous voulons connaître son histoire et voir les traces de sa fabrication manuelle plutôt que l'influence d'un " styliste ". L'idéal serait que le designer regarde le produit par-dessus l'épaule du consommateur et lui fasse partager son enthousiasme sur la manière dont il fonctionne. Ce produit deviendrait alors un ami pour la vie. » ARNOUT VISSER

3. ← **Milk & Sugar containers/**Milch- und Zuckergefäße/ récipients de lait et sucre for DMD, 1998
4. **Optic Glass** decanter/Karaffe/carafe for DMD, 1998

"At the moment, mass production is completely in control of the market, while we (the consumers) are looking for one-of-a-kind products. A beautiful product alone is not enough, we like to hear the story and see the marks of craftsmanship and not the influence of a 'styling' designer. The ideal situation would be the designer looking over the shoulder of the consumer at the product and sharing his or her enthusiastic wonder about how it works. The product should be a life-long friend." ARNOUT VISSER

»Zur Zeit wird der Markt vollkommen von der Massenproduktion beherrscht, während wir – die Konsumenten – nach individuell gefertigten Produkten suchen. Ein schönes Produkt allein genügt nicht. Wir wollen seine Geschichte kennen und ihm die Spuren von Künstlertum und nicht von ›Styling‹ durch einen Designer ansehen. Im Idealfall würde der Designer über die Schulter des Konsumenten hinweg sein Produkt betrachten und sein oder ihr begeistertes Staunen über die Art und Weise teilen, wie es funktioniert. Das Produkt sollte ein lebenslanger Freund sein.« ARNOUT VISSER

ARNOUT VISSER

BORN	1962	Middelburg, The Netherlands
STUDIED	1984-89	degree in Design, Arnhem School of Art
	1990	MA Industrial Design, Domus Academy, Milan
PRACTICE	1983-	working as independent designer and collaborating with Droog Design
AWARDS	1998	co-winner (with Erik Jan Kwakkel and Peter van de Jagt), Public Design Prize, Rotterdam
EXHIBITIONS	1997	*Mutant Materials in Contemporary Design*, Groningen
	late 1990s-	present Droog Design exhibitions, Milan, Paris, New York
	2000	*Droog and Dutch Design*, Park Tower Hall Living Design Center, Tokyo

CLIENTS

Droog Design
Habitat
Poll's Potten
Provincie Gelderland local
government
Silvania Lighting

5

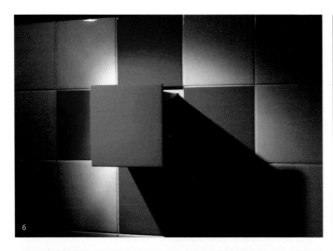

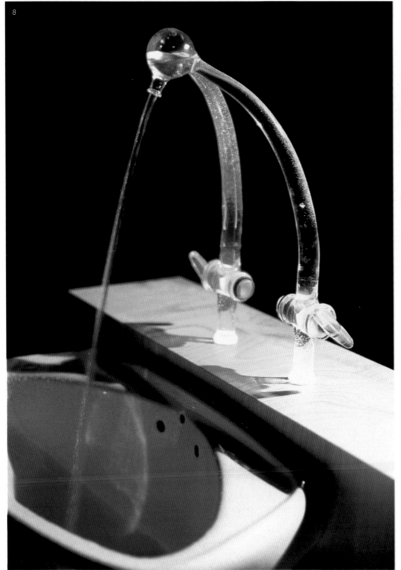

5. **Soft Toilet and bidet** project (prototype)/Toiletten- und Bidet-Projekt (Prototyp)/projet w.-c. et bidet (prototype), 2000 – co-designed with Erik Jan Kwakkel
6. **Red Cross** function tile (prototype)/Funktionsfliese (Prototyp)/carrelage (prototype) for DMD, 1997 – co-designed with Erik Jan Kwakkel and Peter van der Jagt
7. **Double walled tumblers**/zweiwandige Trinkbecher/ gobelet (self-production), 1997 – co-designed with Erik Jan Kwakkel
8. **Glass tap** (prototype)/Glashahn (Prototyp)/robinet en verre (prototype), 1997
9. **Microwave plates** (prototypes)/Teller für die Mikrowelle (Prototyp)/assiettes pour micro-ondes (prototypes) (self-production), 1997

"My role as a designer is to provoke change."

Jean-Pierre Vitrac

Jean-Pierre Vitrac, Vitrac (Pool) Design Consultance, 98, Rue de l'Ouest, 75014 Paris, France
T +33 1 40 44 09 50 F +33 1 40 44 7980 vitrac@design-pool.com www.design-pool.com

»Meine Rolle als Designer besteht darin, Veränderung zu provozieren.«

« Mon rôle de designer est de provoquer le changement. »

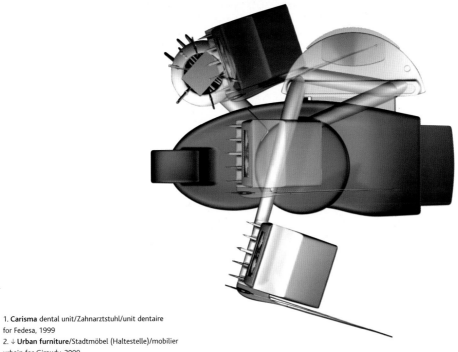

1. **Carisma** dental unit/Zahnarztstuhl/unit dentaire
for Fedesa, 1999
2. ↓ **Urban furniture**/Stadtmöbel (Haltestelle)/mobilier
urbain for Giraudy, 2000

« Le design a un avenir ! Oui, mais lequel ?
Ce qui est sûr, c'est que la création – la créativité – aura de plus en plus de place dans nos sociétés. La tendance la plus forte de ces dernières années, c'est l'éclatement des genres. La diversité des modes d'expression, la facilité et une plus grande liberté de communication favorisent l'accès, de la part des individus et des entreprises, à une conscience nouvelle : l'innovation, comme une composante normale de toute entreprise (dans le sens d'entreprendre).
Peu importe que les motivations soient la plupart du temps économiques. Peu importe que l'on agisse dans des contextes de plus en plus complexes – ce qui fait par ailleurs l'intérêt du métier de designer. La réalité est que les besoins d'évolution amènent plus de réflexion, plus de sens à nos productions. Beaucoup plus de gens se sentent concernés et s'impliquent dans des démarches créatives. Plutôt que d'être entraînés dans une sur-consommation de produits identiques, je pense que ce mouvement sera sélectif et génèrera, dans l'avenir, plus de diversité, plus de qualité. Et, en ce qui concerne le design, tout est ouvert. » JEAN-PIERRE VITRAC

3. ← **Information meeting point**/Informationsstelle und Treffpunkt/point d'information et de rencontre for Arcomat Mobilier Urbain, 1999
4. **Venet-Sea** lagoon boat (project)/Faltboot (Projekt)/ bateau (projet) for Venice, 2000

"Design has a future! Yes, but what kind? What is certain is that creativity is going to play an increasingly important role in our societies. The most obvious trend during the last few years has been an increasing break-up of the different genres or disciplines. Increasing diversity of expression as well as greater ease and freedom of communication allow both individuals and enterprises to attain a new kind of awareness: innovation as a normal component of any undertaking. It is not so important for the motivation to be an economic one. Nor is it so important to be moving towards an ever more complex context – which is what makes the design profession so interesting. The reality is that the necessities of evolution bring more reflection, more sense into our 'productions'. More and more people are beginning to feel concerned about design and are therefore entering into the creative process. Instead of continuing the process of simply consuming identical products, I think that there will be a movement towards greater selectivity which will result in greater diversity and better quality in the future. And so far as design is concerned, everything is open."
JEAN-PIERRE VITRAC

»Design hat eine Zukunft! Ja, aber was für eine? Sicher ist, dass die Kreativität in unseren Gesellschaften eine zunehmend wichtige Rolle spielen wird. Der eindeutigste Trend der letzten Jahre war ein beschleunigtes Aufbrechen der unterschiedlichen Genres oder Disziplinen. Wachsende Vielgestaltigkeit der Ausdrucksformen sowie größere Ungezwungenheit und Freiheit der Kommunikation erlauben sowohl Individuen als auch Unternehmen, zu einem neuen Bewusstsein zu gelangen: Innovation als normaler Bestandteil jeder Art von Unternehmung. Dabei muss die Motivation nicht unbedingt eine ökonomische sein. Und es ist auch nicht so wichtig, dass wir uns auf einen immer komplexer werdenden Kontext zu bewegen – was den Designberuf so interessant macht. In der Realität bringen die evolutionären Notwendigkeiten mehr Reflexion und mehr Sinn in unsere ›Produktionen‹ ein. Immer mehr Menschen fangen an, sich Gedanken über Design zu machen und treten folglich in den kreativen Prozess ein. Anstelle einer Entwicklung, in der der Konsum identischer Produkte einfach fortgesetzt wird, glaube ich, dass es eine Bewegung hin zu einer strengeren Auslese geben wird, die sich zukünftig in größerer Vielfalt und besserer Qualität auswirken wird. Und was das Design betrifft, so ist alles offen.« JEAN-PIERRE VITRAC

JEAN-PIERRE VITRAC

BORN	1944	Bergerac, France
STUDIED	1967	graduated sculpture, Ecole des Arts Appliqués, Paris
PRACTICE	1968	began designing packaging for Lancôme
	1970	established product design office
	1974	established Vitrac Design, Paris
	1978-84	operated Vitrac & C., Milan
	1983-93	operated Vitrac Japan-Pro Inter, Tokyo
	1991-95	partnership with Design Strategy and network with Minale Tattersfield (London) and Windy Winderlich (Hamburg)
	1998	established Vitrac (Pool); established professional design network Design (Pool) in collaboration with Jeremy Morgan
	2000	established Dézidés Production
AWARDS	1984	Clio Award, USA
	1987	G-Mark/Good Design Award, JIDPO, Tokyo
	1988	Prix du Nouvel Economiste, France
	1993	Grand Prix National du Design, Ministry of Culture, France
	1997	Janus De l'Industrie Award, France
	1998 & 2001	iF Design Award, Hanover
EXHIBITIONS	1989	*International Exposition of Universal Design*, Nagoya; solo exhibition, Seibu Yurakucho, Tokyo; solo exhibition, Galerie Binnen, Amsterdam
	1991	*Capitales Européennes du Nouveau Design*, Paris
	1992	solo exhibition, Institut d'Arts Visuels, Orléans
	1993	*Decorative Art and Design in France*, Cooper-Hewitt National Design Museum, New York; *Design, miroir du siècle*, Grand Palais, Paris
	2000	*Pavilion of the 21st Century*, Expo 2000, Hanover

CLIENTS

Alcatel
Allibert
Alpha Cubic
ATT & Barphone
Baby Relax
Bridgestone
Camping Gaz
Carrefour
Daewoo Electronic
Delsey
Descamps
Esselte Dymo
Honda
JCDecaux
Kansai Yamamoto
Kerastase
Kodak
Kyocera
Lancôme
Le Creuset
Louis Vuitton
Mobilier International
National Panasonic
Philips
Sabatier au Lion
Shell Butagaz
Sony
Subaru

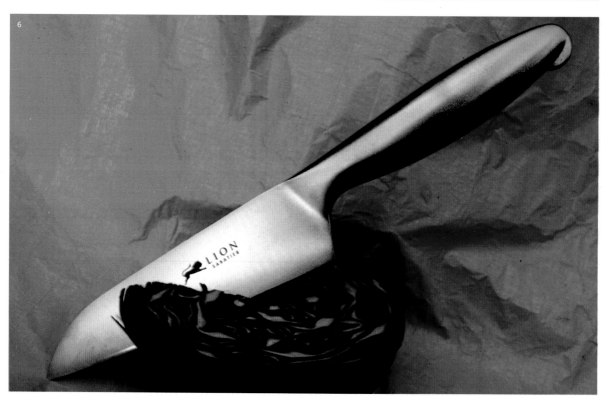

6. **Fuso** knife/Messer/couteau for 32 Dumas Sabatier au Lion, 1998
7. **Baby Move** child traveller/Kinderwagen/poussette de voyage for Marco Skates, 1999
8. **U.Bik** exterior lighting/Außenbeleuchtung/luminaire d'extérieur for Noral, 1999
9. **Flash Vote** everday democracy/tägliche Demokratie/ démocratie permanente for Expo 2000
10. **Crossing Radio**/Radio/poste de radio for Arco Impex, 2001

7

8

9

10

"Continuity between tradition and
the present is important."

Pia Wallén

Pia Wallén AB, Nybrogatan 25, 11 439 Stockholm, Sweden
T +46 8 665 3329 F +46 8 663 3801 info@piawallen.com

»Die Kontinuität zwischen Tradition und
Gegenwart ist wichtig.«

« La continuité entre la tradition et le
présent est importante. »

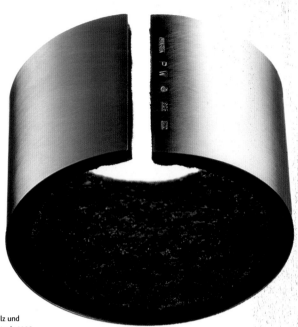

1. **Felt & silver sterling bracelet**/Armreif aus Filz und
Silber/bracelet en argent et feutre (self-production), 1998
2. ↓ **Crux blanket**/Decke/couverture for Element Design,
1991

»Ich arbeite im Hier und Jetzt. Materialien – deren Merkmale, Oberflächen, skulpturalen Eigenschaften sowie die Methoden ihrer Bearbeitung – wecken mein Interesse und dienen als Ansatzpunkt für meine Arbeit. Meine früheren Produkte spielen eine wichtige Rolle bei der Entwicklung neuer Designs. Ich bin bestrebt, das Maximum aus einzelnen Techniken herauszuholen und interessiere mich sehr für die konstruktionsspezifischen Aspekte von Design. Häufig braucht meine Arbeit Zeit, um zu ›reifen‹, und gelegentlich dauert es lange, bis ein neues Design ausgearbeitet ist. Das wechselseitige Spiel von Ideen ist sehr wichtig, damit ich sie zu einem fertigen Produkt ausbauen und dabei gleichzeitig für alle Möglichkeiten offen bleiben kann. Was die Werkstoffe betrifft, so mag ich besonders den Filz und habe mich seit 1983 intensiv mit den Techniken seiner Verarbeitung beschäftigt. Filz stellt die älteste Form textiler Materialien dar und hat eine faszinierende Geschichte. Jahrhunderte lang war Filz ein Überlebensmittel. In meiner Arbeit lasse ich diese alte Tradition wieder aufleben, um daraus etwas Neues zu schaffen. Aus globaler Perspektive gesehen ist es interessant, Design wieder mit nationalen Traditionen, Verwendungsarten, Klimaverhältnissen und Bedürfnissen zu verknüpfen. Es ist wichtig, dass wir auch weiterhin Materialien und Techniken aus unseren natürlichen Ressourcen entwickeln.« PIA WALLÉN

"I work in the here and now. Materials – their properties, texture, sculptural qualities and the methods of working them – awaken my interest and serve as a point of departure for my work. My earlier products play an important role in the development of new ones. I aim to get the most out of techniques and have a real interest in the constructional aspects of design. My work often needs time to 'ripen' and occasionally it takes a long time for a new design to be developed. The interplay of ideas is very important in order to develop them into a finished product, while at the same time remaining open to all possibilities. As far as materials are concerned, I am especially fond of felt and, since 1983, I have delved deeply into the techniques of working with it. It has a fascinating history and represents the oldest form of textile material. For centuries felt has been a material of survival. In my work I revive this old tradition so as to create something new. From a global perspective, it is interesting to link design once again to a national tradition, usage, climate and need. It is important to continue to develop materials and techniques from our natural sources." PIA WALLÉN

« Je travaille dans le " ici et maintenant ". Les matières – leurs propriétés, textures, qualités sculpturales et les techniques pour les travailler – éveillent mon intérêt et servent de point de départ à mon travail. Mes premiers produits jouent un rôle important dans le développement des nouveaux. Je cherche à tirer le meilleur profit des techniques et suis très intéressée par les aspects architecturaux du design. Mon travail a souvent besoin de " mûrir " et il faut parfois attendre longtemps avant qu'un nouveau design soit au point. L'interaction entre les idées est très importante afin de les faire déboucher sur un produit fini tout en restant ouvert à toutes les possibilités. Pour ce qui est des matériaux, j'affectionne particulièrement le feutre et, depuis 1983, me suis plongée dans différentes techniques pour le travailler. Il a une histoire fascinante et représente la plus ancienne forme de textile. Pendant des siècles, il a été une matière de survie. Dans mon travail, je ranime cette tradition ancienne de sorte à en faire quelque chose de nouveau. D'un point de vue mondial, il est intéressant de relier le design à une tradition, un usage, un climat et des besoins nationaux. Il est important de continuer à développer des matières et des techniques à partir de nos ressources naturelles. »
PIA WALLÉN

3. **Felt bowl**/Filzschale/coupe en feutre (self-production), 1992
4. **Felt bag**/Filztasche/sac en feutre (self-production), 2000
5. **Hooded sweater**/Kapuzen-Pullover/pull-over à capuche (self-production), 1997
6. **Felt slippers**/Filzpantoffel/pantoufle en feutre for Cappellini Progetto/Ogetto, 1992

PIA WALLÉN

BORN	1957	Umeå, Sweden
STUDIED	1980-83	fashion, Beckman's School of Design, Stockholm
PRACTICE	1979	established Pia Wallén Form
	1992	Felt Programme for Progetto Oggetti Cappellini
	1999	established Pia Wallén AB
AWARDS	1984 & 92	honorary mention at Excellent Swedish Design Award, Stockholm
	1989	received *Designer of the 90s* Award from *Sköna Hem* magazine, Sweden; designer prize, *Dagens Nyheter* newspaper, Sweden
	1993	awarded 10-year work grant, The Swedish Artists' Board
EXHIBITIONS	1988	*French and Scandinavian Design*, Berlin and Copenhagen
	1989	*Carpets*, Upplands Lans Museum of Art, Sandviken, Sweden
	1991	*Axplock*, Swedish Embassy, Tokyo
	1995	*O Mode*, The House of Culture, Stockholm
	1997	*Carl & Karin Larsson*, Victoria & Albert Museum, London
	1999	*New Scandinavia*, Museum für Angewandte Kunst, Cologne; *Swedish Style in Tokyo*, Swedish Embassy, Tokyo; *Ideé Design House*, Tokyo
	2000	*Design World 2000*, Helsinki

CLIENTS

Asplund
Cappellini Progetto/Ogetto
Element Design
IKEA
Pia Wallén AB

"We are here to create an environment of love, live with passion and make our most exciting dreams come true."

Marcel Wanders

Marcel Wanders, Jacob Catskade 35, 1052 BT Amsterdam, The Netherlands
T +31 20 422 1339 F +31 20 422 7519 marcel@marcelwanders.nl www.marcelwanders.com

»Wir sind hier, um eine Umgebung der Liebe zu schaffen, mit Leidenschaft zu leben und unsere aufregendsten Träume wahr werden zu lassen.«

« Nous sommes ici pour créer un environnement d'amour, vivre avec passion et concrétiser nos rêves les plus excitants. »

1. **VIP** chair/Sessel/fauteuil for Moooi, 2000
2. ↓ **Textile wall for a Lunch Lounge**/textile
Wandinstallation für eine Kantine/mur en tissu
pour salle de restaurant for Co van der Horst,
1999

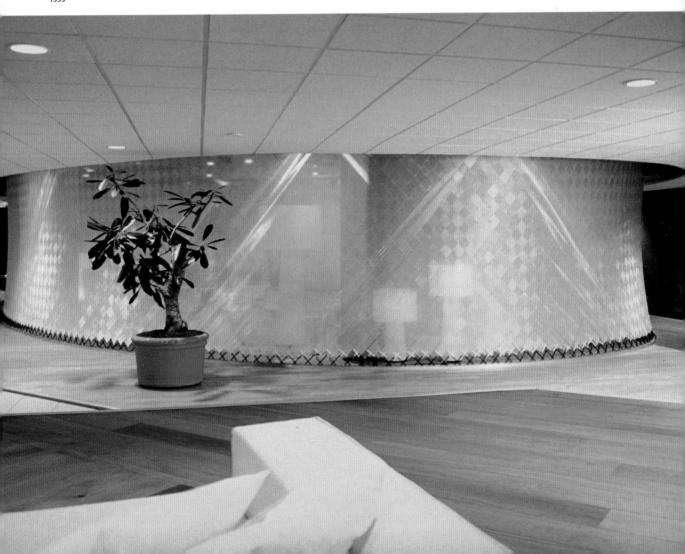

« Notre culture manque de respect pour le passé. Nous préférons le nouveau à l'ancien. Tout ce qui est récent est considéré comme meilleur. Les nouvelles d'hier n'ont plus rien de nouveau. Les produits doivent être lisses, tendus et sans défauts. Hélas, il semblerait que cette obsession du neuf et de la jeunesse soit encore plus répandue chez les designers (moi y compris). Je les soupçonne d'avoir encore moins de respect pour le vieux que les autres, car créer du nouveau est leur métier. Nous souffrons de ce que j'ai appelé " la fixation sur la peau de bébé ".

L'espérance de vie des designs à peau de bébé est très brève. Cela en fait des amis provisoires sur lesquels les utilisateurs ne peuvent vraiment compter et qui ne feront jamais vraiment partie de leur vie. La fixation sur la peau de bébé est un problème dans un monde où l'on attache de l'importance à la durabilité d'un produit et à son lien unique avec l'utilisateur.

Comme j'aimerais que beaucoup de mes produits aient une relation à long terme avec leur utilisateur, j'utilise un mélange de métaphores nouvelles et anciennes dans les matières et les expressions matérielles que j'applique. En utilisant de vieilles métaphores dans mes produits, je communique un respect pour la vieillesse en général. Cela entraîne un vieillissement plus respectueux, plus acceptable et plus naturel de mes produits (ils vieillissent dignement). Ils ont la possibilité de gagner en qualité au cours de leur existence, ils sont plus durables et il est possible d'avoir avec eux une relation à long terme.

La longévité dans le domaine des idées, des relations, des objets, etc. permet non seulement de créer un monde où l'on gaspille moins, mais également des relations plus profondes et constructives avec notre environnement. » MARCEL WANDERS

3. ← **Shadows Series** table and floor lamps/Tisch- und Stehlampen/lampes et lampadaires for Cappellini, 1998
4. **Lucy** candlestick/Kerzenständer/chandelier for Goods, 1999

"Our culture lacks respect for the old. We prefer the new to the old. New things are considered better, old news is no news. Products have to be smooth, taut and flawless. Sadly, it appears that this fixation on the new and the young is even stronger among designers than other people. I suspect that they (including myself) have even less respect than others for the old, as it is their profession to create new things. We suffer from what I call 'baby-face fixation'.

The life expectancy of baby-face designs is very short. This makes them temporary friends on which users cannot truly rely and which will never become a real part of their lives. Baby-face fixation is a problem in a world in which lasting quality and a unique bond between product and user is important.

Since I would like many of my products to enter into a long-term relationship with the user, I use both old and new metaphors in the materials and material expressions that I apply. By using old metaphors in my products, I communicate a respect for old age in general. This leads to a more respectful, more acceptable and more natural ageing of my products (age with dignity). These products have the possibility of gaining quality during their life, they are more durable and it is possible to have a long-lasting relationship with them.

Durability in the field of ideas, relationships, objects, and so on, not only to create a world that is less wasteful but also to create deeper and more meaningful relationships with our environment." MARCEL WANDERS

»Unserer Kultur mangelt es an Respekt für das Alte. Wir ziehen das Neue dem Alten vor. Neue Dinge werden als höherwertig betrachtet, die Neuigkeiten von gestern sind keine Neuigkeiten. Produkte müssen glatt, sauber und fehlerfrei sein. Leider scheint diese Fixierung auf das Neue und Junge unter Designern noch stärker ausgeprägt zu sein als unter anderen Leuten. Ich habe den Verdacht, dass Designer – mich selbst eingeschlossen – das Alte so wenig achten, weil es ihr Beruf ist, neue Dinge hervorzubringen. Damit leiden wir unter etwas, was ich ›Babyface-Fixierung‹ nenne.

Die Lebenserwartung von ›Babyface-Design‹ ist sehr kurz. Das macht solche Objekte zu flüchtigen Bekannten, auf die sich die Benutzer nicht wirklich verlassen können, und die niemals zu einem realen Teil ihres Lebens werden. Die Babyface-Fixierung stellt ein Problem dar in einer Welt, in der dauerhafte Qualität und eine individuelle Bindung zwischen Produkt und Benutzer wichtig sind.

Da ich möchte, dass möglichst viele meiner Produkte eine langfristige Beziehung mit ihren Benutzern eingehen, verwende ich sowohl alte als auch neue Metaphern in meinen Materialien und Ausdrucksformen. Indem ich alte Metaphern in meine Produkte einbeziehe, vermittle ich meinen Respekt für das Alter im Allgemeinen. Das führt zu einer würdevolleren, angenehmeren und natürlicheren Alterung meiner Produkte – sie altern also in Würde. Diese Produkte haben die Möglichkeit, im Laufe ihres Lebens an Qualität zu gewinnen, sie sind dauerhafter, und man kann eine langfristige Beziehung mit ihnen haben. Dauerhaftigkeit auf dem Gebiet der Ideen, Beziehungen und Objekte ermöglicht nicht nur, eine weniger verschwenderische Welt zu schaffen, sondern auch eine tiefere und sinnvollere Beziehung zu unserer Umwelt.«
MARCEL WANDERS

MARCEL WANDERS			CLIENTS
BORN	1963	Boxtel, The Netherlands	acme
STUDIED	1981-82	Academie voor Industriële Vormgeving, Eindhoven	Air UK
	1982-85	Academie voor Toegepaste kunsten, Maastricht	Boffi
	1983-85	Academie voor Schone kunsten, Hasselt, Belgium	British Airways
	1985-88	Hogeschool voor de Kunsten, Arnhem (1988 Cum Laude Certificate)	Cacharel
PRACTICE	1986	trained at Artifort	Cappellini
	1987	trained at BRS Premsela Vonk, Gijs Bakker, Amsterdam	Conran Shop
	1988-90	independent product designer	Droog Design
	1990-92	designer for Landmark Design & Consult b.v., Rotterdam	Floriade
	1992-95	partner of WAAC's Design & Consults, Rotterdam	Flos
	1995-2001	director of Wanders Wonders, Amsterdam	Habitat
	2001-	director of Marcel Wanders Studio	KLM
AWARDS	1986	First Prize *Café Modern (Nescafé)*	Mandarina Duck
	1986	First Prize *Olympic Design 1992*	Magis
	1989	First Prize *Verzamelband*, Rotterdam	Randstad
	1996	Kho Liang Lee consolation prize	Rosenthal
	1997	winner of Rotterdam Design Award	Royal Leerdam
	1998	winner of *Woonbeurspin* Award; honorable mention for Compasso d'Oro, Milan	Salviati
	2000	Alterpoint Design Award, Milan	Swatch
EXHIBITIONS	1993	*Made in Holland*, Museum für Angewandte Kunst, Cologne	Virgin Atlantic Airlines
	1995	*Mentalitäten*, Securitas Gallery, Bremen & Design Center Stuttgart; *Droog Design*, Taideteolisuusmuseo, Helsinki; Centraal Museum, Utrecht; Stilwerk Design Center, Hamburg	WMF
	1995 & 97	*Mutant Materials in Contemporary Design*, Museum of Modern Art, New York and Groninger Museum, Groningen	also self-production
	1999	*Wanders Wonders – Design for a New Age*, Museum het Kruithuis, Den Bosch	
	2000	*Wanders Wanted*, Gallery Material Connection, New York; *Droog Design*, touring exhibition, USA	

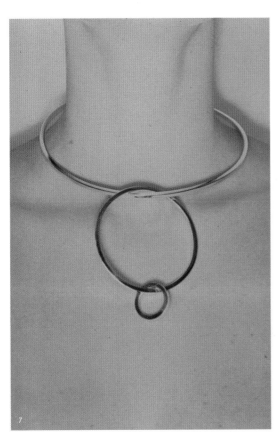

5. **Willow chair**/Korbsessel/fauteuil en osier for Oranien-baum, 1999
6. **Sponge vase**/Vase for Moooi, 1997
7. **Trinity necklace**/Kette/collier for Chi ha paura, 1998
8. **Henna table**/Tisch for Cappellini, 2000
9. **Nomad carpet**/Teppich/tapis for Cappellini, 1999

"My pieces are the essence of the time,
of abilities and of dreams."

Robert Wettstein

Robert Wettstein, Structure Design, Josefstrasse 188, 8005 Zurich, Switzerland
T +41 1 272 9725 F +41 1 272 0717 robert.wettstein@gmx.ch www.wettstein.ws

»Meine Arbeiten sind die Essenz von Zeit,
Fähigkeiten und Träumen.«

« Mes pièces sont l'essence du temps,
des facultés et des rêves. »

1. **Art. 003S** chair/Sessel/fauteuil for ctc, 2000
2. ↓ **Cement lamp** with mirrored bulb (prototype)/
Zementlampe mit verspiegelter Glühbirne/lampe en
ciment avec ampoule miroir (prototype), 1998

»Für mich liegt die Zukunft des Designs in einer Analyse der Konzepte zeitgenössischer Kunst. Die verblüffendste Kombination von Materialien ist möglich, wodurch sich ständig verändernde Wahrnehmungen und neue Arten des Begreifens von Materialien ergeben. Die Zukunft des Designs liegt in der Fähigkeit, die Zeiten widerzuspiegeln und die Grenzen des Vertrauten zu überschreiten. Design stellt die älteste Form der Abbildung gesellschaftlicher Konzepte und Einstellungen dar. Die Produkte der Zukunft werden die Bedeutung immaterieller Werte wie Ethik, Dienstleistung und geistige Haltung anerkennen. Das Design der Zukunft wird durch die Miniaturisierung der Technologie, den Verkaufspreis, die Interpretation von Kulturen und durch die Vergangenheit geprägt sein, denn die Zeit verleiht dem existierenden Design seine Wertschätzung. Design wird die Worte bilden, um ein Produkt zu beschreiben. Markenzeichen des Designs werden die Technologie und die Natur sein.« ROBERT WETTSTEIN

"For me, the future of design lies in an analysis of concepts from contemporary art. The most surprising combination of materials is possible, providing ever-changing perceptions and new ways of understanding materials. The future of design lies in reflecting the times and in crossing the boundaries of the familiar. Design presents the earliest recognition of society's concepts and attitudes. The products of the future will acknowledge the importance of such non-material values as ethics, service and attitudes. The future of design lies in the miniaturization of technology, in the selling price, in the interpretation of cultures and in the past, for time gives esteem to existing designs. Design will become the words to describe a product. Technology and nature will be the hallmarks of design." ROBERT WETTSTEIN

« Pour moi, l'avenir du design repose sur une analyse des concepts de l'art contemporain. Les combinaisons de matériaux les plus surprenantes sont possibles, à condition que les perceptions changent constamment et qu'apparaissent de nouvelles manières de comprendre les matières. L'avenir du design réside dans notre capacité à refléter le temps et à franchir les frontières du connu. Le design représente la plus ancienne reconnaissance des concepts et des attitudes de la société. Les produits du futur reconnaîtront l'importance de valeurs non matérielles telles que l'éthique, le service et les attitudes. L'avenir du design dépend de la miniaturisation de la technologie, des prix de vente, de l'interprétation des cultures et du passé car, avec le temps, on accorde de l'estime aux designs existants. Le design deviendra les mots pour décrire un produit. La technologie et la nature seront les caractéristiques du design. » ROBERT WETTSTEIN

3.-4. **Art. 002T.** club table/Tisch mit zweiseitig verwendbarer Platte/table de jeux for ctc, 1999
5. **Art. 001G** wardrobe/Garderobe/garde-robe for ctc, 1999
6. **Europalette** tray/Serviertablett/plateau for ctc, 2000
7. **Putzer** broom/Handfeger/balai for Die Imaginäre Manufaktur (DIM), 1998

ROBERT WETTSTEIN

BORN	1960	Zurich, Switzerland
STUDIED		self-taught (trained in orthopaedic technology)
PRACTICE	1985	established own office and workshop
	1986	established Structure Design
AWARDS	1992	Design Plus Award, Frankfurt/Main
	1993	honourable mention, Design-Preis Schweiz, Switzerland
	2000	honourable mention, Design for Europe Award, Interieur Biennial, Kortrijk
EXHIBITIONS	1986	*Wohnen von Sinnen*, Kunstmuseum, Düsseldorf
	1990	*Geordnete Arbeiten*, Galerie Hiltrud Jordan, Cologne; *Oggetti Inattesi*, Studio Scalise, Naples
	1991	*Mehrwerte Schweiz und Design der 80iger*, Museum für Gestaltung, Zurich
	1992	*Kreaturen*, Galerie Papenheim, Zurich
	1993	*The Minimal Animal Interior*, Galerie Dilmos, Milan; *Design-Preis Schweiz*, Kunstmuseum, Solothurn
	1994	*Polstermöbel und Schaukelleuchten*, Preussisch Oldendorf, Germany
	1996	*Design im Wandel*, Übersee-Museum, Bremen
	1997	*Dea Design Europeo Anteprima*, Milan
	1999	*Black Schwarz*, Musée des Arts Decoratifs, Lausanne
	2000	*Europalette*, Swiss Center, Milan

CLIENTS

Anthologie Quartett
Authentics
ctc (change.to/comfort)
Die Imaginäre Manufaktur (DIM)
Noto/Zeus
also self-production

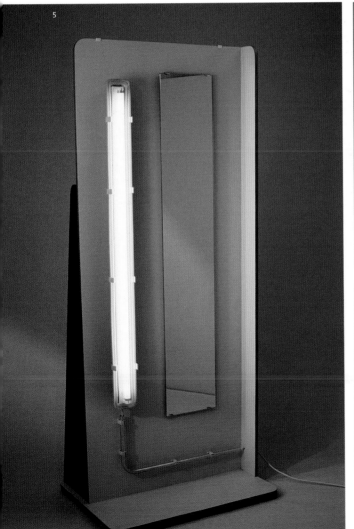

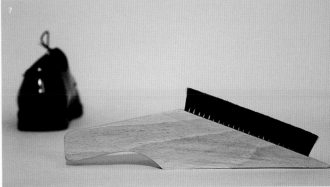

"Focus on achieving the maximum impact with the minimum use of materials."

Kazuhiro Yamanaka

Kazuhiro Yamanaka, 25, Woodvale Way, London NW11 8SF, England
T/F +44 20 8452 3018 kaz@ma.kew.net

»Konzentration darauf, die maximale Wirkung mit dem minimalen Einsatz an Mitteln zu erzielen.«

« Chercher à avoir un impact maximal avec un minimum de matériaux. »

1-2. **How slow the wind** swivel chair/Drehstuhl/chaise tournante (self-production), 1999

3. **Can we be friends?** bench with chairs/Bank und Stühle/ banc avec chaises (self-production), 2000

»In Zukunft wird Design als ein bedeutsamer Faktor in dem uns umgebenden Raum definiert werden. Designer sollten über die Leere reflektieren, die ihre Objekte umgibt, über den Raum zwischen den Objekten und die Beziehung zwischen diesen Objekten. Ich glaube, dass Möbelstücke – Stühle, Tische, Lampen – wie eine Konstellation von Sternen aufgefasst werden können, und dass wir diese mittels Linien im dreidimensionalen Raum verbinden und dadurch eine besondere Geschichte konstruieren können. Und ich glaube, dass es meine Aufgabe als Designer ist, solche Geschichten zu ersinnen.« KAZUHIRO YAMANAKA

"In the future, design will be defined as being a significant factor in the space around us. Designers should contemplate the void that surrounds objects, the space between objects, and the relation between those objects. I believe furniture – chairs, tables, lights etc. – could be like a constellation of stars, and we could make lines to connect them three-dimensionally and thereby construct a specific story. As a designer, I believe it is my task to create those stories." KAZUHIRO YAMANAKA

« A l'avenir, le design se définira comme un facteur significatif de l'espace autour de nous. Les designers devraient réfléchir au vide qui entoure les objets, à l'espace et à la relation entre les objets. Les meubles – chaises, tables, luminaires, etc. – pourraient être comme une constellation d'étoiles et nous pourrions tracer des lignes pour les relier en trois dimensions et construire ainsi une histoire spécifique. En tant que designer, je crois que ma tâche est de créer ces histoires. » KAZUHIRO YAMANAKA

4. **What a little moonlight can do** wall lamp/ Wandleuchte/applique (self-production), 1999
5. **Beyond the moon** floor light/Bodenlampe/ luminaire (self-production), 2000
6. **What a little moonlight can do** table lamp/ Tischlampe/lampe (self-production), 1999

KAZUHIRO YAMANAKA			CLIENTS
BORN	1971	Tokyo, Japan	Boffi
STUDIED	1992-95	BA (Hons) Interior Design, Musashino Art University, Tokyo	self-production
	1995-97	MA Furniture Design, Royal College of Art, London	
PRACTICE	1997-	independent furniture/interior designer	
AWARDS	1994-95	Musashino Art University Scholarship	
	1994 & 95	winner Interoffice Office Furniture Competition	
	1999	100% Design/Crafts Council Bursary Award, London	
	2000	finalist *Blueprint*/100% Design Award, London; finalist *design report* Award, Milan	
EXHIBITIONS			
	1994-95	*Future Office Design*, Tokyo Design Center	
	1995	*Interior Design*, Ozone Gallery, Tokyo	
	1996	*Getyerhandsdirty*, Royal College of Art, London	
	1997	*Summer Show*, Royal College of Art, London; *New Designers*, Business Design Centre, London	
	1998	*Bare*, O-porto Gallery, London	
	1999 & 2000	100% Design, London	
	2000	Ambiente, Frankfurt/Main; Salone Satellite, Milan	

5

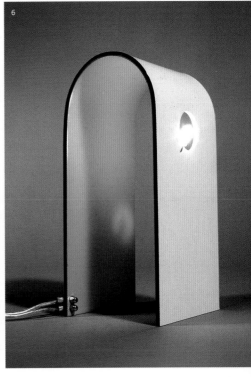

6

"All my designs are essentially paintings about colour, shape and space."

Helen Yardley

Helen Yardley, A-Z Studios, 3-5, Hardwidge Street, London SE1 3SY, England
T +44 20 7403 7114 F +44 20 7403 8906

»Alle meine Designs sind im Wesentlichen Gemälde über das Thema Farbe,
Form und Raum.«

« Toutes mes créations sont essentiellement des peintures sur la couleur, la
forme et l'espace. »

1. **Arc Nero** rug/Teppich/tapis for
Toulemond Bochart, 1998

»Alle meine Designs sind im Wesentlichen Gemälde über das Thema Farbe, Form und Raum. Es kommt vor, dass sich ein bestimmter Malstil leichter in eine Stickerei oder einen Druck übertragen lässt, aber immer kommt die ›Malerei‹ zuerst. Mit meinen Bildern, Teppichen und Wandbehängen strebe ich an, ein Objekt mit einer visuellen Wirkung zu schaffen, das aber gleichzeitig auch eine vielschichtige Bedeutung enthält. Für mich muss es im Design etwas Dauerhafteres geben als reine Dekoration.

Teppiche sind zweidimensional. In vielerlei Hinsicht kann man sie als Zeichnungen für den Boden sehen. Man muss sie jedoch von jedem Blickwinkel aus betrachten, um ein Unten und ein Oben zu vermeiden. Das macht die Gestaltung von Dynamik innerhalb der vorgegebenen Parameter zu einer größeren Herausforderung, als wenn man etwas für die Wand entwirft.

Wenn ich meine Arbeit in ihrer Gesamtheit analysiere, dann lässt sie sich in drei Kategorien aufgliedern: Die erste Gruppe von Entwürfen ist das Resultat einer direkten visuellen Stimulation – ich sehe etwas, das mir eine zündende Idee eingibt. Der zweite Zugang ist weniger unmittelbar, und ich würde ihn als sensualistisch beschreiben. Dieser Prozess beginnt mit einer Idee, die ausschließlich auf Farbe und der Wahrnehmung eines ›Gefühls‹ basiert. Die dritte Gruppe von Entwürfen entsteht aus meiner Reaktion auf die äußere, räumliche Umgebung des Objekts, wie es häufig bei Auftragsarbeiten der Fall ist. Diese Kategorisierung ist jedoch rein theoretisch. Wirklich wichtig ist für mich, etwas herzustellen, das gut aussieht, gleichzeitig aber auch eine Funktion erfüllt.« HELEN YARDLEY

"All my designs are essentially paintings about colour, shape and space. A certain style of painting may more readily be translated into a needlepoint or a printed piece but the 'painting' always comes first. What I aim for with these paintings/rugs/wall-hangings is to make something that works visually but also carries layers of meaning. There must be something rather more lasting than pure decoration.

Rugs are two-dimensional. In many ways they are like drawings for floors but one does need to consider them from every angle, so as to avoid an up and a down. This makes creating a dynamic within the parameters rather more of a challenge than when one is designing for the wall.

When I analyse the work as a whole it seems to break down into three categories. The first group of designs are the result of direct visual stimulation – I literally see something that sparks me off. The second route is less direct and is what I would describe as sensational. This process starts with an idea based purely in colour and the notion of a 'feeling'. The third group of designs come about as a response to the physical space, as is often the case with commissioned work. These delineations are purely theoretical. What is really important to me is to make something that looks good but also performs a function."
HELEN YARDLEY

« Toutes mes créations sont essentiellement des peintures sur la couleur, la forme et l'espace. Il arrive qu'un certain style de peinture soit plus facilement transposable au point de croix ou sur un imprimé, mais la " peinture " vient toujours en premier. Mon objectif, par ces tableaux / tapis / tapisseries, est d'aboutir à une création qui fonctionne visuellement tout en portant différents niveaux de sens. Elle doit offrir quelque chose de plus durable que le simplement décoratif. Les tapis sont bidimensionnels. A de nombreux égards, ils sont comme des dessins pour le sol sauf qu'on doit pouvoir les regarder sous tous les angles, ce qui évite d'avoir un haut et un bas. En ce sens, créer une dynamique au sein de paramètres établis est plus excitant que de dessiner simplement pour les murs.

Lorsque j'analyse mon travail dans son ensemble, il semble se diviser en trois catégories. La première est le résultat d'une stimulation visuelle directe, je vois littéralement quelque chose qui m'inspire. La seconde est moins directe et repose davantage sur les sens. Ce processus démarre sur une idée basée uniquement sur la couleur et la notion d'une " émotion ". La troisième catégorie est le fruit d'une réaction à un espace physique, comme c'est souvent le cas avec les commandes. Ces classifications sont purement théoriques. Ce qui compte réellement pour moi, c'est de créer un objet qui soit beau tout en servant à quelque chose. » HELEN YARDLEY

2. **Spice No. 2** rug (drawing)/Teppich (Zeichnung)/ tapis (dessin) (one-off), 1999
3. **Roma** rug/Teppich/tapis for Toulemond Bochart, 1998
4. **Pampas** rug/Teppich/tapis (one-off), 1999
5. **Cafe** rug/Teppich/tapis (one-off), 1999

HELEN YARDLEY

BORN	1954	Plymouth, England
STUDIED	1972-73	Plymouth College of Art (Foundation Studies)
	1973-76	BA Hons (1st Class) Printed & Woven Textiles, Manchester Polytechnic
	1976-78	MA Textiles, Royal College of Art, London
EXHIBITIONS	1985	*Wall Hung Textiles*, British Crafts Centre, London
	1987	*New Spirit in Craft and Design*, Crafts Council, London
	1990	*Great British Design*, Tokyo
	1993	*Visions of Craft*, Crafts Council, London
	1995	*Out of This World*, Crafts Council, London
	1998	Cambridge Contemporary Art, Cambridge

CLIENTS

Arthur Andersen
British Airways
British Rail
British Telecom
Cathay Pacific
Coca-Cola
Harrods
Lewis Moberley
Sony
Thames Television
Toulemond Borchart
Walt Disney

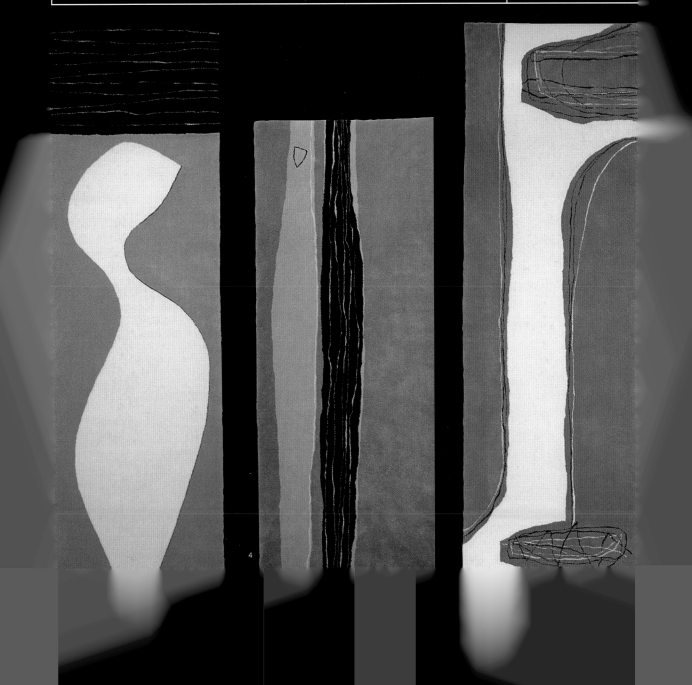

"Our work is an investigation into wrapped form and human reference."

Yellow Diva

Yellow Diva, 326, Kensal Road, London W10 5BZ, England
T +44 20 7565 0012 F +44 20 7565 0013

»Unsere Arbeit ist eine Untersuchung der verhüllten Form und der menschlichen Bezüge.«

« Notre travail est une enquête sur les formes emballées et les références humaines. »

1. **W2** chair/Sessel/fauteuil (self-production), 2000
2. ↓ **SS1** sofa/Sofa/canapé (self-production), 2000

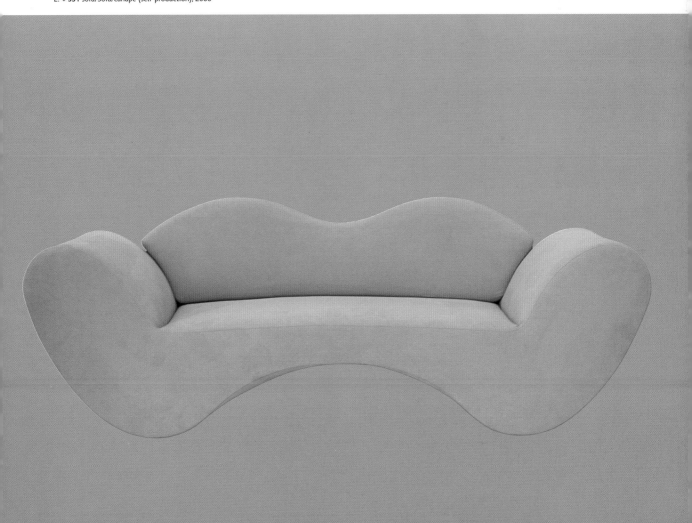

»Die Zukunft wird von der Vergangenheit geschaffen. Große kulturelle Bewegungen oder in deren Rahmen stattgefundene individuelle zukunftsträchtige Ereignisse sind bedeutsam für uns, weil sie sich auf die menschliche Leistung und Natur beziehen und sie absorbieren. Ohne die Anhäufung von Wissen kommt es zu Rückschritt statt Fortschritt. Deshalb betrachten wir das Design des 21. Jahrhunderts als Fortsetzung der unglaublichen Odyssee der Menschen von der Antike über die Renaissance bis hin zur Moderne. Die Moderne wird die treibende Kraft für den Fortschritt im Design des 21. Jahrhunderts bleiben. Politik und Gesellschaft waren noch nicht ganz bereit für die Moderne, als sie entstand. Wir hoffen, dass die Welt heute im Allgemeinen fairer ist als in der Zeit um 1900; eine auf Freiheit, Gleichheit und Ehrlichkeit beruhende kulturelle Bewegung sowie eine Suche nach Sinn kann nun von neuem anfangen, sich zu etablieren. Viele Menschen behaupten, die Zukunft liege in der virtuellen und nicht in der wirklichen Welt. Da reale Konsumgüter (sowie deren Verpackung und Vertrieb) naturgemäß belastend für die Umwelt sind, hat das Virtuelle in einer konsumorientierten Gesellschaft offensichtliche Vorteile. Wir glauben jedoch, dass die reale Welt ein für unseren Organismus lebenswichtiges Maß an emotionaler und physischer Nahrung zur Verfügung stellt. Deshalb prophezeien wir, dass reales Design auch im Jahr 2100 noch lebendig sein wird – möglicherweise in einer beweglichen, sinnlichen, taktilen Form, um eine nüchterne binäre Existenz kompensieren zu können.« YELLOW DIVA

"The future is created by the past. Great cultural movements or individual seminal events within them gain meaning for us through their referencing to and absorption of human achievement and the human condition. Without cumulative wisdom we have regression instead of progression. We see, therefore, 21st-century design as a continuation of the incredible human journey from the Classical world, through the Renaissance and on to Modernism. Modernism will continue to be the driving force of progress in 21st-century design. Politics and society were not fully ready for Modernism as it emerged. Hopefully the world is now a generally fairer place than it was in 1900 and a cultural movement based on freedom, equality and honesty and the search for meaning can now begin to re-establish itself. There are many who maintain that the future lies in the virtual world and not in the actual one. Actual consumer products (and their packaging and distribution) are inherently demanding on the environment, so there are obvious benefits to the virtual in a consumer-oriented society. We feel, however, that the actual world provides an essential level of emotional and physical nourishment needed by our physiology, so we predict that actual design will still be alive by 2100 – perhaps as a fluid, sensual, tactile thing to compensate for what might become a rather dry binary existence."
YELLOW DIVA

« Le futur est créé par le passé. Les grands mouvements culturels ou les événements déterminants individuels qu'ils contiennent prennent un sens par les références que nous y faisons, ainsi que par leur absorption des conditions et des accomplissements humains. Sans sagesse cumulative, nous régressons au lieu de progresser. Nous voyons donc le design du 21e siècle comme la continuation de cet incroyable odyssée humaine qui va de l'Antiquité à la Modernité en passant par la Renaissance. La Modernité continuera d'être la locomotive du progrès. Quand elle est apparue, la politique et la société n'étaient pas encore prêts pour elle. Espérons que le monde soit aujourd'hui plus juste qu'en 1900 et qu'un mouvement basé sur la liberté, l'égalité, l'honnêteté et la quête de sens puisse enfin se rétablir.
Nombreux sont ceux qui soutiennent que l'avenir réside dans le monde virtuel et non dans le vrai. Les produits de consommation actuels (y compris leur emballage et leur distribution) font payer un lourd tribut à l'environnement et on comprend les avantages du virtuel dans une société basée sur la consommation. Toutefois, le monde réel nous offre un niveau essentiel de nourriture physique et émotionnelle dont notre physiologie a besoin, aussi nous prévoyons que le design actuel existera encore en 2100, peut-être sous une forme fluide, sensuelle et tactile qui compensera la sèche existence binaire. » YELLOW DIVA

3. **Unzip** wine cooler/Weinkühler/étui à bouteille rafraîchissant (self-production), 1998-2000
4. **CS1** sofa/Sofa/canapé (self-production), 1998
5. **Table/Chair** project (prototype)/Projekt (Prototyp)/ projet (prototype), 1998
6. **WS1** sofa/Sofa/canapé (self-production), 1998

		YELLOW DIVA	CLIENTS
FOUNDED	1994	London by James Davis (b. 1965 Banbury, Oxfordshire) and David Wallery (b. 1960 Wodonga, Australia)	Microsoft
STUDIED		JAMES DAVIS	The Foreign & Commonwealth Office
	1990	BA Architecture, Polytechnic of Central London	Virgin Group
	1994	Diploma Architecture, University of Westminster	also self-production
		DAVID WALLEY	
	1982	Diploma Industrial Design, Royal Melbourne Institute of Technology	
AWARDS	1998	shortlisted for *Blueprint*/100 % Design Award, London	
EXHIBITIONS	1995	*Sit '95*, Business Design Centre, London; International Furniture Fair, Tokyo	
	1996	Salone del Mobile, Milan; 100 % Design, London	
	1997	International Furniture Fair, Cologne; *British Design*, Museum für Angewandte Kunst, Cologne; *UK Now*, Melbourne; Galerie Langenberg, Amsterdam	
	1998	*Zoltan*, Milan	
	1999	*Create Britain*, Taipei	
	2001	*At Home with Plastics*, Geffreye Museum, London	

"I'm just looking at new yet rational
ways of realizing objects."

Michael Young

Michael Young, MY Studio, PO Box 498, 121 Reykjavik, Iceland
T +354 561 2327 F +354 561 2315 michaelyoung@simnet.is www.michael-young.com

*»Ich halte einfach nur Ausschau nach
neuen und dennoch rationalen Möglichkeiten, Objekte zu realisieren.«*

« Je cherche simplement des manières
nouvelles mais néanmoins rationnelles
de réaliser des objets. »

1. **MY 083** table/Tisch for Magis, 2001
2. ↓ **Armed chair**/Sessel/fauteuil for Cappellini, 1999

"Currently, 'designed' objects challenge only a tiny percentage of the world market. The majority of products are in real terms engineered copies. Present-day technology means that a designed product may be copied by mass-market competitors in less than one year. Protecting an innovation in either manufacturing technique or idea would seem to be of utmost importance to design in the future. Especially so when computer programmes will soon be able to morph surprisingly beautiful objects at random without designers and provide all the necessary production data as well. On a positive note, this would leave design in a position where innovation will become the human aspect rather than style." MICHAEL YOUNG

« A l'heure actuelle, les objets de designers ne constituent qu'un infime pourcentage du marché mondial. La majorité des produits sont des copies fabriquées en termes réels. La technologie d'aujourd'hui signifie qu'un objet conçu par un designer peut être copié par les concurrents travaillant sur le marché de masse en moins d'un an. A l'avenir, protéger une idée ou une innovation dans les techniques de fabrication devrait être de première importance, surtout dans la mesure où les programmes informatiques pourront bientôt " morpher" de manière aléatoire des objets d'une beauté surprenante sans l'aide de designers, tout en fournissant toutes les indications nécessaires à leur production. Sur le plan positif, le design se retrouvera ainsi dans une situation où l'aspect humain se situera dans l'innovation plutôt que dans le style. »
MICHAEL YOUNG

3. ← **Sticklight**/Stableuchte/luminaire for Eurolounge, 1999
4. **MY 082** table/Tisch for Magis, 2001
5. **MY 080** bedtray/Tablett für das Bett/plateau petit-déjeuner for Magis, 2001
6. **Magis Pens**/Stifte/crayons for Magis, 2001

»Gegenwärtig beanspruchen ›designte‹ Objekte nur einen winzigen Prozentsatz des Weltmarkts. Bei der Mehrzahl der Produkte handelt es sich genau genommen um maschinell gefertigte Kopien. Die moderne Technologie bedeutet, dass ein Designprodukt von der Konkurrenz des Massenmarkts in weniger als einem Jahr kopiert werden kann. Für das Design der Zukunft scheint der Schutz einer Innovation, entweder im fertigungstechnischen oder im ideellen Bereich, von äußerster Wichtigkeit zu sein. Besonders dann, wenn Computerprogramme bald imstande sein werden, verblüffend schöne Objekte aufs Geratewohl und ohne Beteiligung von Designern ›morphogenetisch‹ herzustellen und außerdem alle erforderlichen Produktionsdaten zu liefern. Das Positive an dieser Entwicklung könnte sein, dass sie dem Design eine Position überlässt, in der Innovation mehr den menschlichen Aspekt als den Stil betrifft.«
MICHAEL YOUNG

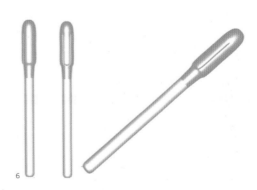

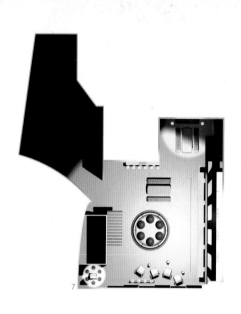

7.-14. **Astro Bar** nightclub (interiors), Reykjavik/Nachtclub (Innenansichten)/night-club (intérieurs), Reykjavik, 2000

MICHAEL YOUNG

BORN	1966	Sunderland, England
STUDIED	1988-89	Art Foundation Course, Sunderland Polytechnic
	1989-92	BA (Hons) Furniture and Product Design, Kingston University, London
PRACTICE	1990-94	worked in Tom Dixon's studio, Space
	1994	established MY 022 design studio in London (also in Reykjavik)
AWARDS	1995	Winner of Talente '95 design competition, Munich
EXHIBITIONS	1994	solo exhibition, Galerie Gladys Mougin, Paris; group shows in Paris, London, Tokyo and Hong Kong
	1995	*E&Y co.*, solo exhibition, Tokyo
	1996	Salon du Meuble, Paris; *E&Y/MY 022* presentation, Paris, Kyoto
	1997	Salon du Meuble, Paris; *Internos*, Milan; *Synapse*, Fukuoka
	1998	*Oikos*, Athens; *Totem*, New York, group shows in London, Cologne, Milan
	1999	*Jasper Morrison, Marc Newson, Michael Young*, Reykjavik Art Museum
	2000	designed and co-curated *Design in Iceland*, Reykjavik Art Museum

CLIENTS

Cappellini
E&Y
Eurolounge
Idée
Laurent Perrier
Magis
Sawaya & Moroni
MY O22
Rosenthal
S. M. A. K. Iceland

15

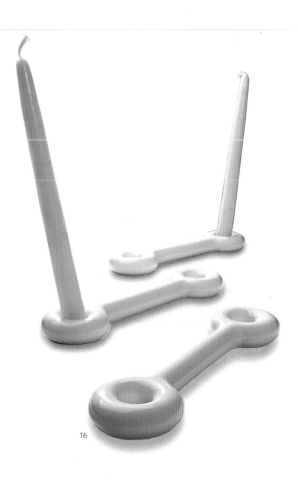

16

15. **Champagne glass**/Sektglas/flûte à champagne for Laurent Perrier, 1999
16. **Candlestick**/Kerzenhalter/bougeoir for Sawaya & Moroni, 1999
17. **Slit** chairs/Sessel/sièges for Sawaya & Moroni, 1999
18. **Wood table**/Holztisch/table en bois for Sawaya & Moroni, 1999
19. **MY 086** light/Leuchte/luminaire for Idée, 2000
20. **MY 068** chairs/Stühle/chaises for Sawaya & Moroni, 1998

We are immensely grateful to those designers, design groups, photographers and manufacturers who have allowed us to reproduce images from their archives. The publisher has endeavoured to respect the rights of third parties and if any rights have been overlooked in individual cases, the mistake will be correspondingly amended where possible.

L = left/links/à gauche
R = right/rechts/à droite
T = top/oben/ci-dessus
C = centre/Mitte
B = bottom/unten/ci-dessous

3 Azumi, photo: Kumi Saito
14 Dumoffice, photo: Matthíjs van Roon
16 T Emmanuel Dietrich
16 B Sam Hecht
17 Philippe Starck, photo: Studio Bleu – Michel Lelièvre for GOOD GOODS/La Redoute
19 Japan Airlines, photo: Lee Funnell for *Domus* magazine
21 Alberto Meda, photo: Vitra
23 Ford Motor Company
24 Sydney 612, photo: Jamie Gray
25 Dahlström Design
26/27 Büro für Form, photo: David Steets
28 Studio Aisslinger, photo: Steffen Jänicke
29 T Studio Aisslinger
29 B Studio Aisslinger, photo: Steffen Jänicke
30-31 Studio Aisslinger, photos: Steffen Jänicke
32 T L & T R Zanotta, photos: Adriano Brusaferri
32 B Studio Aisslinger, photo: Philip Radowitz
33 T R Studio Aisslinger
33 C & B Studio Aisslinger, photos: Steffen Jänicke
34-35 Studio Aisslinger, photos: Steffen Jänicke
36 Ron Arad Associates, photo: Perry Hagopian
37 T Ron Arad Associates, photo: Guido Pedron
37 B Ron Arad Associates, photo: Wilhelm Moser
38 Ron Arad Associates, photo: Wilhelm Moser
39-41 Ron Arad Associates
42-43 Moroso, photos: A. Paderni
44-45 Jane Atfield
46 Fiell International Ltd., photo: Paul Chave
47-49 Jane Atfield
49 B R Oreka Kids
50 Azumi, photo: Julian Hawkins
51 T Azumi, photo: Michael Tesmann
51 B Azumi, photo: Julian Hawkins
52 Azumi, photo: Brühl&Sippold
53 Azumi, photos: Julian Hawkins
54 T L Azumi, photo: Hiroyuki Hirai
54 T R Azumi, photo: Thomas Dobbie
54 B L Azumi, photo: Shin Azumi
54 B R Azumi
55 T Azumi, photo: Thomas Dobbie
55 B L Azumi, photo: Julian Hawkins
55 B R Azumi
56 Azumi, photo: Julian Hawkins
57 T L & T R Azumi, photos: Studio Synthesis
57 B L Azumi, photo: Julian Hawkins

57 B R Azumi, photo: Lapalma
58 Babylon Design
59 T Babylon Design, photo: Hans Hansen
59 B Babylon Design, photo: Mainstream Photography – Ray Main
60 Babylon Design, photo: Hans Hansen
61 L Babylon Design, photo: Hans Hansen
61 T R & B R Babylon Design
62 Bartoli Design
63 T Bartoli Design – Di Palma
63 B Bartoli Design, photo: Segis
64-65 Bartoli Design, photos: Snr. Mascheroni/Obiettivo F
66 B L Bartoli Design, photo: Deltacolor
67 B R Bartoli Design, photo: Studio Uno
67 B Bartoli Design – Di Palma
68 Sebastian Bergne
69 T Sebastian Bergne, photo: WMF
69-70 Sebastian Bergne, photos: Authentics, Artipresent GmbH
71 Sebastian Bergne
72 T L Sebastian Bergne
72 R Sebastian Bergne
72 B L Sebastian Bergne, photo: O-Luce
73 T Sebastian Bergne, photo: Vitra – Hans Hansen
73 B Sebastian Bergne, photo: Wireworks UK
74 Sebastian Bergne, photo: Talis Milano
75 T L, T R & B L Sebastian Bergne, photos: Authentics, Artipresent GmbH
75 B R Oreka Kids
76 Bibi Gutjahr
77 T Bibi Gutjahr, photo: Edra
77 B Bibi Gutjahr, photo: Hidden SDB
78-79 Bibi Gutjahr, photos: Hidden SDB
80 Riccardo Blumer
81 Alias
82 Artemide
83 Alias
84-87 Jonas Bohlin Design
88-93 Ronan & Erwan Bouroullec, photos: M. Legall
94-99 Studio Brown
100-103 Debbie Buchan
104 Büro für Form
105 T Büro für Form, photo: Bjarne Geiges
105 B Büro für Form, photo: David Steets
106 Büro für Form, photo: David Steets
107 L Büro für Form, photo: Daniel Mayer
107 T R Büro für Form, photo: Bjarne Geiges
107 B R Büro für Form, photo: David Steets
108 Studio Campana, photo: J. R. Duran
109-115 Studio Campana, photos: Andrés Otero
116 Antonio Citterio, photo: Gitty Darugar
117 T Antonio Citterio, photo: Hackman
117 B Antonio Citterio, photo: B&B Italia – Fabrizio Bergamo
118 Antonio Citterio, photos: B&B Italia
119 Antonio Citterio, photo: Flos
120 Antonio Citterio, photos: B&B Italia
121 L Antonio Citterio, photo: Flos
121 R Antonio Citterio, photo: Hackman
122-127 Dahlström Design

128-133 Emmanuel Dietrich
134 Dumoffice
135 T Dumoffice
135 B Dumoffice, photo: Oof Verschuren
136-137 Dumoffice, photos: Matthíjs van Roon
138 Dumoffice, photo: Thomas Rabsch
139 T L & T R Dumoffice, photos: Oof Verschuren
139 B L Dumoffice
139 B R Dumoffice, photo: Matthíjs van Roon
140-145 Dyson
146-149 Ecco Design
150-153 El Ultimo Grito
154-159 Elephant Design
160 Naoto Fukasawa, photo: IDEO-Japan
161-165 IDEO-Japan
166 photo: © Mario Pignata Monti
167 T photo: © Mario Pignata Monti
167 B Jean Marc Gady, photo: Jeoffrey Bello
168 Jean Marc Gady, photo: © Vincent Muracciole
169-171 photos: © Mario Pignata Monti
172 Giovannoni Design
173 T Giovannoni Design, photo: Alessi
173 B Giovannoni Design, photo: Segno
174 Giovannoni Design, photo: Alessi
175 B L Alessi
175 C Giovannoni Design, photo: Magis
175 T R Giovannoni Design, photo: Alessi
176 Giovannoni Design, photo: Magis
177 Giovannoni Design, photo: Alba-Seiko
178 L Giovannoni Design, photo: Alba-Seiko
178 R Giovannoni Design, photo: Alessi
179 Giovannoni Design, photos: Alessi
180 Konstantin Grcic, photo: © Daniel Mayer
181 T Konstantin Grcic
181 B Konstantin Grcic, photo: © Eva Jünger
182 Konstantin Grcic, photo: ClassiCon
183 Konstantin Grcic
184 L Authentics, photo: Christian Stoll
184 T R Konstantin Grcic, photo: Authentics
184 B R Konstantin Grcic, photo: Iittala
185 T & C Konstantin Grcic
185 B Konstantin Grcic, photo: Iittala
186-191 IDEO-Europe
192 Helfet Design
193-194 Jaguar
195 T L & T R Helfet Design
195 B L & B R Jaguar
196 Matthew Hilton, photo: Corinna Dean
197 T SCP Ltd.
197 B Oreka Kids
198 Authentics GmbH
199-200 SCP Ltd.
201 T & C L Driade
201 C R & B SCP Ltd.
202 Hollington Associates
203 T Hollington Associates, photo: © Hollington
203 B Hollington Associates, photo: © Eastman Kodak Co, Rochester, NY, USA
204-205 Hollington Associates, photos: © Hollington
206 Isao Hosoe Design

207 т Isao Hosoe, photo: Studio 33
207 в Isao Hosoe, photo: Segis – Miro Zagnoli
208 Isao Hosoe, photo: Facchinetti Forlani
209 L & т R Isao Hosoe, photos: Facchinetti Forlani
209 в R Isao Hosoe, photo: Luxo Italiana
210-212 Inflate, photos: Jason Tozer
213 Inflate
214 Inflate, photo: Jason Tozer
215 т L Inflate, photo: Jason Tozer
215 т R & в Inflate
216 Iosa Ghini Srl
217 т Iosa Ghini Srl, photo: Bonaldo
217 в Iosa Ghini Srl, photo: Roche Bobois
218 Iosa Ghini Srl, photo: Bonaldo
219 т L Iosa Ghini Srl, photo: Dornbracht
219 т R Iosa Ghini Srl, photo: Bonaldo
219 в L Iosa Ghini Srl, photo: Massin Tuttoespresso
219 в C & в R Iosa Ghini Srl, photos: Bonaldo
220-222 James Irvine
223 James Irvine, photo: Magis
224-225 Arabia
226 т L James Irvine, photo: BRF
226 в L James Irvine, photo: Cappellini
226 R James Irvine, photo: BRF
227 т James Irvine, photo: CBI
227 в James Irvine, photo: B&B Italia
228 Apple Computer, photo: Catherine Ledman
229-233 Apple Computer
234-237 IXI
238-241 Jam, photos: Jason Tozer
239 Jam, photo: Paul Musso
242-243 Jam
244-245 Jam, photos: Jason Tozer
246-249 Hella Jongerius
250-253 Ouzak Design Formation
254 King-Miranda
255 т King-Miranda, photo: © Tommaso Pellegrini
255 в King-Miranda, photo: © Andrea Zani
256 King-Miranda, photo: Baleri Italia
257 L King-Miranda
257 R King-Miranda, photo: Belux – Thomas Egloff
258-261 Tom Kirk
262 Ubald Klug
263 т Ubald Klug, photo: © Alfred Hablützel
263 в Studio Petraschke/Hablützel,
photo: © Alfred Hablützel
264 Ubald Klug
265 Ubald Klug, photo: © Alfred Hablützel
266 Iittala
267 т Hackman
267 в Iittala, photo: Marco Melander
268 Harri Koskinen, photo: Teret Tolvanen Oy
269 Harri Koskinen, photo: Marva Helander
270 т Arabia
270 в L & в R Iittala
272-273 Iittala
274 Kristiina Lassus, photo: Anne Saarenoja
275 т Zanotta, photo: Marino Ramazzotti
275 в Kristiina Lassus, photo: Markku Alatalo
276 Kristiina Lassus, photo: Alessi

277 Kristiina Lassus, photo: Poltronova
278 Studio Lazzeroni, photo: Stefano Baroni
279 т Studio Lazzeroni, photo: Luminara
279 в Studio Lazzeroni, photo: Frighetto
280 Studio Lazzeroni, photo: Luminara
281 т L & в L Studio Lazzeroni, photos: Ceccotti
281 т R & в R Studio Lazzeroni, photos: Luminara
282-285 Isabelle Leijn
286 L Design
287 т L Design
287 в Snowcrash
288-289 L Design
290 Lissoni Associati
291 Lissoni Associati, photos: Living Divani
292-293 Lissoni Associati, photos: Porro
294-295 Ross Lovegrove/Studio X, photos: John Ross
296 Ross Lovegrove/Studio X
297-299 Ross Lovegrove/Studio X, photos: John Ross
300 т Ross Lovegrove, photo: John Ross
300 в Japan Airlines, photo: Lee Funnell for *Domus*
magazine
301-303 Ross Lovegrove/Studio X, photo: John Ross
304-309 Lunar Design
310 Enzo Mari
311 т Zani e Zani, photo: Marirosa Ballo
311 в Magis Srl
312 Glaskoch Leonardo
313 Arnolfo di Cambio
314 L Arnolfo di Cambio
314 R Robots SpA
315 т Arte e Cuoio
315 в L Zani e Zani, photo: Marirosa Ballo
315 в R Arte e Cuoio
316 Michael Marriot
317 т Oreka Kids
317 в Michael Marriot
318-319 Michael Marriot
320-323 Sharon Marston
324-327 Ingo Maurer GmbH
328-333 Ford Motor Company
334 Alberto Meda
335 т Alberto Meda, photo: Alias
335 в Alberto Meda, photo: Luceplan
336 Alberto Meda, photo: Vitra
337 Alberto Meda
338 Alberto Meda, photo: Alias
339 L Alberto Meda, photo: Kartell
339 R Alberto Meda, photo: Ramak Fazel
340 Office for Design, photo: Emily Anderson
341-347 Office for Design
348 Pascal Mourgue
349 Pascal Mourgue, photos: Cinna-Ligne Roset
350 Pascal Mourgue, photo: Artelano
351 L Pascal Mourgue, photo: Fermob
351 т R & в R Pascal Mourgue, photos: Cinna-Ligne Roset
352-355 N2
356 Marc Newson, photo: Karin Catt
357-361 Marc Newson
362-363 Ford Motor Company
364-365 Marc Newson

366 PearsonLloyd, photo: Sandra Lousada
367-371 PearsonLloyd
372 Vent Design, photo: Rick English Pictures
373-375 Vent Design
376 Jorge Pensi
377 т Jorge Pensi
377 в IDPA, Perobell
378-379 Jorge Pensi, photos: IDPA
380 Jorge Pensi, photo: Mobles 114
381 Jorge Pensi, photos: IDPA
382-385 Electrolux Zanussi SpA
386 Christophe Pillet
387 т Christophe Pillet, photo: Cappellini
387 в Christophe Pillet, photo: E&Y
388-389 Christophe Pillet
390 L Christophe Pillet, photo: AV Mazzega
390 т R Christophe Pillet, photo: Domeau & Perès
390 в R Christophe Pillet, photo: Marie Claire
391 т Christophe Pillet, photo: Domeau & Perès
391 C & в Christophe Pillet, photos: Fiam
392-397 Radi Designers
398 Orrefors, photo: Hans Gedda
399 Orrefors, photo: Rolf Lind
400-401 Orrefors, photos: Roland Persson
402 Orrefors, photos: Bengt Wanselius
403 т Orrefors, photo: Bengt Wanselius
403 в Orrefors, photo: Rolf Lind
404-405 Karim Rashid
406 Karim Rashid, photo: Ilan Rubin
408 т L & в Karim Rashid, photos: Ilan Rubin
408 т R Karim Rashid
410-411 Karim Rashid
412 Prospero Rasulo
413 т BRF
413 в Zanotta
414 BRF
415 L BRF
415 R Foscarini
416 Riveran Design, photo: Nicho Södling
417-419 Riveran Design, photos: Johan Wiklund
420 Muotoilutoimisto Salli Ltd., photo: Marja Helander
421 Muotoilutoimisto Salli Ltd., photos: Marco Melander
422 Muotoilutoimisto Salli Ltd., photo: Ulla Hassinen
423 Muotoilutoimisto Salli Ltd., photo: Kaj Ewart
424 Muotoilutoimisto Salli Ltd., photos: Marco Melander
425 т Muotoilutoimisto Salli Ltd., photo: Timo Salli
425 в L & в R Muotoilutoimisto Salli Ltd.,
photos: Marco Melander
426-427 Sandell Sandberg
428 Sandell Sandberg, photo: IKEA
429 т L & т R B&B Italia
429 в Sandell Sandberg, photo: Von Wedel/Mobileffe
430 Marta Sansoni
431 Alessi
432-433 Marta Sansoni
434-439 Santos & Adolfsdóttir
440 Schamberg + Alvisse
441 т Schamburg + Alvisse, photo: John Webber
441 в Schamburg + Alvisse – Michael Tyler
442 Schamburg + Alvisse, photo: John Webber